For
motivating inspiration
and
creative vision
we
dedicate this work
to
O. G. L.

EPIGRAPH: THE MYTHIC VISION

It was by no means easy for minds attached to occidental logic to penetrate systems of thought such as these in which analogies and the power of symbols have the value of facts. . . . The Africans with whom we [i.e., Marcel Griaule and Dieterlin] have worked in the region of the Upper Niger have systems of signs which run into the thousands, their own systems of astronomy and calendrical measurements, methods of calculation and extensive anatomical and physiological knowledge, as well as a systematic pharmacopoeia. . . . In African societies which have preserved their traditional organization the number of persons who are trained in this knowledge is quite considerable. This they call "deep knowledge" in contrast with "simple knowledge" which is regarded as "only a beginning in the understanding of beliefs and customs" that people who are not fully instructed in the cosmogony possess.

Germaine Dieterlin

As Miguel León-Portilla has made clear in his great work on Aztec thought, although all the people were deeply religious, there was a group in Aztec society that specialized in deeply philosophical questions, such as the meaning of life and death and the destiny of humankind after death. This class of thinkers probably existed among the elite of all Mesoamerican state societies, and perhaps at even a simpler level of social development. For instance, among the Navajo of southwestern United States, some curing specialists are persons of deep esoteric and even scientific knowledge, and such "men of high degree" are known around the world from supposedly simple, tribal societies. With a people like the Classic Maya, such specialists must have been formidable indeed.

Michael Coe

Whether the myth was originally an illustration of the philosophical formula, or the latter a distillation out of the myth, it is today impossible to say. Certainly the myth goes back to remote ages, but so too does philosophy. Who is to know what thoughts lay in the minds of the old sages who developed and treasured the myth and handed it on? Very often, during the analysis and penetration of the secrets of archaic symbol, one can only feel that our generally accepted notion of the history of philosophy is founded on a completely false assumption, namely that abstract and metaphysical thought begins where it first appears in our extant records.

Joseph Campbell

In spite of our modern romantic tendency to think otherwise, there is an objective and intellectually cogent aspect to the life of the spirit.

Herbert Fingarette

The imagery of myth is . . . by no means allegory. It is nothing less than a carefully chosen cloak for abstract thought. The imagery is inseparable from the thought. It represents the form in which the experience has become conscious.

Henri and H. A. Frankfort

Concepts and words are symbols, just as visions, rituals, and images are; so too are the manners and customs of daily life. Through all of these a transcendent reality is mirrored. They are so many metaphors reflecting and implying something which, though variously expressed, is ineffable, though thus rendered multiform, remains inscrutable. Symbols hold the mind to truth but are not themselves the truth.

Heinrich Zimmer

Emphatically, . . . the accent in Indian art is not upon the welter of images before one's eyes, but on the background of an unseen power (*brahman*) or void (*sunyam*), over which they dance. For they are of the delusive veil of *maya*, magical apparitions, bursting as foam from the breaking waves of a cosmic sea, which in its depth is still.

Joseph Campbell

THE FLAYED GOD

THE FLAYED GOD

THE MESOAMERICAN MYTHOLOGICAL TRADITION

SACRED TEXTS
AND
IMAGES
FROM PRE-COLUMBIAN MEXICO
AND
CENTRAL AMERICA

ROBERTA H. MARKMAN
AND
PETER T. MARKMAN

HarperSanFrancisco
A Division of HarperCollins*Publishers*

LIBRARY OF CONGRESS CATALOGING-IN-PUBLICATION DATA

Markman, Roberta H.
    The flayed God: the mesoamerican mythological tradition: sacred texts and images from pre-Columbian Mexico and Central America/ Roberta H. Markman, Peter T. Markman. — 1st ed.
        p. cm.
    Includes bibliographical references and index.
    ISBN 0–06–250528–9 (acid-free paper)
       1. Indians of Mexico—Religion and mythology.   2. Aztecs—Religion and mythology.   3. Mayas—Religion and mythology.
4. Indians of Central America—Religion and mythology.
I. Markman, Peter T.   II. Title
F1219.3.R38M24   1992   91–58158
299'0792—dc20   CIP

92 93 94 95 96 ❖ RRD(H) 10 9 8 7 6 5 4 3 2 1

This edition is printed on acid-free paper that meets the American National Standards Institute Z39.48 Standard.

CONTENTS

MYTHS AND MYTHIC IMAGES

ACKNOWLEDGMENTS

Many influences from as many different sources have helped to make this book a reality. The earliest ideas for the book were the result of our stimulating discussions over the years with our beloved friend and mentor Joseph Campbell. Then another friend, our former editor at the University of California Press, Scott Mahler, helped us rethink that original plan, allowing the book to take its present form.

The strongest encouragement, invaluable help, and a number of brilliant suggestions came from our resourceful friend, the writer and scholar Jamake Highwater, a man without whom this book, like the one before it, would probably never have been written. Marija Gimbutas and Ron Smith took an active interest in the project from the beginning and with Jamake Highwater wrote wonderfully effective letters of support to the National Endowment for the Humanities, letters that were instrumental in gaining us the joint NEH Fellowship for the academic year 1989–90 that allowed us an uninterrupted year to pursue our research and writing.

Our wonderful friends in Mexico City, Armando Colina and Victor Acuña of Galeria Arvil, not only were constantly encouraging but also put us in touch with a number of helpful people, aided us in finding books and illustrations that would otherwise never have been available to us, and in a multitude of other ways helped to make this book much better than it could have been without them. In addition, they have made Mexico "home" for us now. And Victor Fosado and his daughter Pilar Fosado with Irene Ortega continued to entice us into more and more of Mexico's past. The helpful staff at the Museo Nacional de Antropología in Mexico City, including especially José Luis Cruz, who made it possible for us to take photographs at the museum; Carolyn Baus de Czitrom, an archaeologist who spent hours tracking down information for us; and Felipé Solis and the rest of his staff at the Departamento de Arqueología went out of their way to help us in innumerable ways. In addition, the enthusiastic Enrique Fuentes Castilla of Libreria Madero assisted us in obtaining a number of difficult-to-find books.

We would also like to thank Munro Edmonson, Willard Gingerich, Doris Heyden, H. B. Nicholson, and Linda Schele for their generous help via telephone conversations, and Merle Greene Robertson for her notes of encouragement. Our appreciation also goes to Glenn B. Hoffman for his personal interest in and professional advice concerning the development of our photographs and to Michael Mertz of MPS, who took the time to oversee the printing of the final photographs for the book.

Without the strong interest, encouragement, confidence, suggestions, and patience of our editor, Thomas Grady of Harper San Francisco, this publication would surely not have been possible. Thanks also to his able assistant, Kevin Bentley, and to our associate editor, Caroline Pincus, production editor, Jeff Campbell, designer, Jamie Brooks, and Robin Seaman, marketing manager, whose work will make it possible for others to have the opportunity to share our excitement about the magnificent mythological system of Mesoamerica.

Special accolades and thanks must go to the three translators who have done outstanding translations specifically for this book. Willard Gingerich (Professor, St. John's University, Jamaica, New York) first took on the tremendous task of translating the *Leyenda de los Soles* from the Nahuatl, making it possible to publish that valuable document in its entirety for the first time in English and then prepared a brilliant translation of a portion of the *Anales de Cuauhtitlan.* Scott Mahler (Editor, Harvard University) translated portions of the *Historia de los Mexicanos por sus Pinturas,* a work that has not been translated into English for almost a century, and the Mixtec myth of creation. And Frederick M. Swensen (Professor Emeritus, California State University, Long Beach), a wonderful friend and colleague, translated portions of the *Histoyre du Mechique* from the French into English, portions never before published in English.

Without the generous assistance with funds and released time from the administration at California State University, Long Beach, particularly the support from President Curtis L. McCray; Vice-President and Provost Karl W. E. Anatol; Dean of Humanities Virginia Warren and her administrative services manager, Linda McConnell; and James R. Brett, Director of University Research and his Faculty Research Committee, this book could not have been written. And to Roberta Markman's assistant, Toshie Sweeney—the jewel of a lifetime—there is no possible way to enumerate or to say thanks for all the big and little things she did to keep the work going and to brighten the days when it seemed impossible to manage all the details of everything that had to be done.

We are particularly appreciative of the special personal interest and continued encouragement of Barry Munitz, Chancellor of the California State University.

Finally, we are very much in debt to the National Endowment for the Humanities for their granting us joint Fellowship Awards for College Teachers for 1989–90 and for two NEH Travel-to-Collection Grants awarded to Roberta in 1984 and 1987 that made it possible to take photographs throughout various areas and in a number of museums of Mexico for both this book and our 1989 publication *Masks of the Spirit: Image and Metaphor in Mesoamerica* (University of California Press).

GUIDE TO PRONUNCIATION

The names one encounters in Mesoamerican myths can be daunting. It has even been suggested that were the names of the gods of Mesoamerica, names such as Tlahuizcalpantecuhtli and Xiuhtecuhtli, for example, as easy to pronounce as those of Zeus or Thor, this marvelous mythology would be far better known than it is. Whether or not that is true, it is obvious that most readers have some difficulty with the pronunciation of the names of the gods and places found in the myths.

Those readers should be heartened to know that the problem of pronunciation is not as great as it might at first appear. As in Spanish, but unlike English, letters are always pronounced in the same way. The vowels are simple:

a is pronounced "ah," as in park (Chac is *chahk*)

e is pronounced "eh," as in pet (Ix Chel is *eesh chehl*)

i is pronounced "ee," as in peek (ixtle is *eesh tleh*)

o is pronounced "oh," as in old (Tlaloc is *tlah lohk*)

u is pronounced "oo," as in poor (Uxmal is *oosh mahl*), except when it comes before another vowel; then it is pronounced as an English *w* (Huehueteotl is *weh weh teh ohtl*)

With the exception of *ll* and *x,* the consonants are pronounced as they are in modern Spanish, and therefore only a few of them are sufficiently different from English to cause a problem:

ll is pronounced as a prolonged English *l*

x is pronounced "sh" (Xipe is *shee peh;* the only major exception to this is Oaxaca, which is pronounced *wah hah kah*)

c is pronounced as English *k* except when it comes before *e* or *i;* then it is pronounced as English *s*

hu is pronounced as the *w* in *w*ant

qu is pronounced as the English *k* when it comes before *e* or *i* (therefore Quetzalcoatl is *keh tsahl coh ahtl,* not *kwe tsahl coh atl*)

tl is pronounced as a unit as in bat*tle*

Accents in all but Maya words tend to fall on the next-to-last syllable, while Maya words tend to be stressed on the last syllable. The Maya site Chichen Itza is thus pronounced *chee CHEHN ee TSAH,* while the Toltec capital, Tula, is pronounced *TOO lah.*

Following these rules, then, Tlahuizcalpantecuhtli would be pronounced *tlah wees cahl pahn teh COOH tlee.* Perhaps the key to pronouncing such formidable names as that one (the name of Quetzalcoatl in his manifestation as the Morning Star) is to take them one syllable at a time. That way even the longest word can be broken down into manageable parts.

THE FLAYED GOD

I

INTRODUCTION

THE HISTORICAL FRAMEWORK

Pre-Columbian Mesoamerica 1500 B.C.–A.D. 1500

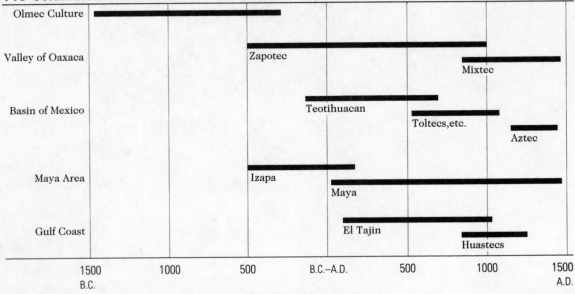

	1500 B.C.	1000	500	B.C.–A.D.	500	1000	1500 A.D.

- **Olmec Culture**
- **Valley of Oaxaca** — Zapotec · Mixtec
- **Basin of Mexico** — Teotihuacan · Toltecs, etc. · Aztec
- **Maya Area** — Izapa · Maya
- **Gulf Coast** — El Tajin · Huastecs

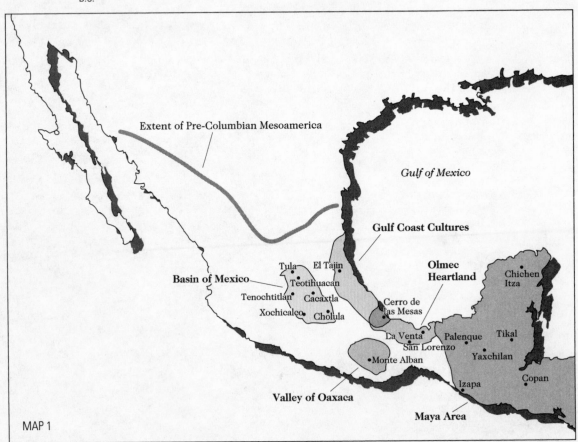

Extent of Pre-Columbian Mesoamerica

Gulf of Mexico

Gulf Coast Cultures

Olmec Heartland

Basin of Mexico

Tula · El Tajin · Chichen Itza

Teotihuacan

Tenochtitlan · Cacaxtla

Xochicalco · Cholula

Cerro de las Mesas

La Venta · Palenque · Tikal

San Lorenzo · Yaxchilan

Monte Alban · Copan

Izapa

Valley of Oaxaca

Maya Area

MAP 1

THE FLAYED GOD

When the Spanish adventurers we have come to know as the Conquistadores confronted the mythological tradition of the culture they had conquered—that of the Aztecs in the Basin of Mexico in the early 1500s as we reckon time—they were astounded by the welter of strange supernatural creatures the natives worshiped as gods and the bizarre, often macabre, rituals enacted in their honor. The Conquistadores and the missionary friars who accompanied them in order to extend the Conquest into the souls of the "heathens" tried mightily to comprehend these alien gods by comparing them to those of the pagan tradition of Greece and Rome with which they were already familiar. But what little understanding they did manage could be only superficial because they had no real conception of the totality of the mythological environment in which these flayed gods and feathered serpents flourished. And without an understanding of the structure of the mythological tradition that spawned these multitudinous, strangely interconnected creatures of myth, the Spanish conquerors could not possibly grasp their significance or the role each played in the grand mythological structure on which was based the culture of the peoples of Mesoamerica.

The conquerors' failure to understand the native gods, however, paled before their bewildered amazement at the sacrifices of blood and hearts these gods required. Although they were certainly not themselves the gentlest of men with the most delicate sensibilities, even they found the blood-drenched shrines appalling:

> A little way apart from the great Cue [pyramid] there was another small tower which was also an Idol house, or a true hell, for it had at the opening of one gate a most terrible mouth such as they depict, saying that such there are in hell. The mouth was open with great fangs to devour souls, and here too were some groups of devils and bodies of serpents close to the door, and a little way off was a place of sacrifice all blood-stained and black with smoke, and encrusted with blood, and there were many great ollas and cantaras and tinajas [pottery vessels] of water inside the house, for it was here that they cooked the flesh of the unfortunate Indians who were sacrificed, which was eaten by the priests. There were also near the place of sacrifice many large knives and chopping blocks, such as those on which they cut up meat in the slaughter houses. . . . I always called that house "the Infernal Regions."[1]

And even today, in an age of Buchenwalds and Hiroshimas, we are still appalled. But if we are to understand those sacrifices—which surely does not mean condoning them—it is imperative that we see them in the context of the mythological tradition that gave them the most sacred character to those who performed them, so sacred, in fact, that even the gods, as the myths will show us, were sacrificed to enable life to exist. Thus, the humans who were sacrificed were reenacting the original sacrifice of the gods. They were playing their parts in the continuing creation of life, demonstrating once more that death must precede life in the grand cycle of the cosmos.

There is no better single example of this fundamental idea that life comes from death, that sacrifice releases the life force, than the flayed god of our title—Xipe Totec, Our Lord, the Flayed One. By donning the skin of a sacrificial victim who had been flayed, the priest became the god. He was Xipe Totec, the inner essence, life itself, that is hidden always beneath the outer covering. The sacrificial death and flaying thus reveal that essence as the inner graphically and literally becomes outer. We will discuss Xipe and his ritual in detail later, but the principle for which his flayed body stands must be comprehended if the mythological tradition of which he is an integral part is to be understood.

Unfortunately, today's understanding of that mythological tradition—one of the handful of great mythological traditions created by humanity—by all but a few scholars is still as confusing and superficial as it was at the time of the Conquistadores. And today we must consider an additional problem as well. The Aztec culture confronted by the Spanish was a very late-flowering and relatively short-lived development of the tradition of which it was an integral part; the Aztec myths and gods are but the very tip of the iceberg that is the mythological tradition of Mesoamerica, the high-culture area comprising the southern two-thirds of today's Mexico, all of Belize and Guatemala, and portions of Honduras and El Salvador, a culture reaching back at least to 1400 B.C. in its history of urban civilizations, with the earlier village-culture roots of those civilizations going back at least another thousand years.

Thus the problem is an obvious one: the Aztec gods and rites cannot be understood without a grasp of the mythological structure from which they emanate, and that structure cannot be understood without a grasp of the whole tradition as it developed in time and space. Although that tradition must obviously be understood in terms of its historical development, a starting place for that development is hard to find. While on the one hand we must necessarily begin somewhere, designate some point as the beginning of the particular tradition with which we deal; on the other hand we know that there is no discernible beginning, for beyond each potential date we might choose there lies still another episode to take us farther back. For one who would study the Mesoamerican tradition, the usual starting point is provided by the original human inhabitants of the Americas crossing from their Siberian homeland over the narrow land bridge then existing in the frigid waters that we know as the Bering Straits, perhaps as long as forty thousand years ago, and thus unwittingly beginning the population of what was even then the New World. But that was not really the new beginning it might seem to be because, of course, they brought their old world with them in their eons-old accumulation of the lore of the animals and plants that provided their sustenance, in their learned ability to make the tools they required in their nomadic life of hunting and slaughtering those animals and gathering those plants, and, most important from our point of view as mythologists, their shamanic view of the fundamental reality of the world they lived in, a view that provided the basis for the way of life they led.

As Mircea Eliade, the renowned historian of religions, puts it, "a certain form of shamanism spread through the two American continents with the first wave of immigrants."[2] That shamanism bequeathed to later Mesoamerican religion the fundamental assumption that all phenomena of the world of nature are animated by a spiritual essence, the common possession of which renders insignificant our usual distinctions between human and animal and even the organic and inorganic. In the shamanic world everything is alive, and all life is part of one mysterious unity by virtue of its derivation from the spiritual source of life—the life force. Because matter and spirit are separate yet joined, and material realities are the results of spiritual causes, to change material reality, the spiritual causes had to be found and addressed through ritual and the visionary activity that enabled the shaman as mediator to move between the visible and the unseen worlds, thus linking the natural with the supernatural and life with death.

This shamanistically conceived world was, therefore, not a world of animals and plants, of killing and harvesting so that they might survive, but a world of the spirit made manifest in these material things that surrounded their material bodies. When those bodies were injured or fell ill, or when the herds of animals were not to be found at the appointed place and time, or when the plants withered and died instead of ripening, the shaman would leave this everyday world and enter, through trance, the *real* world, the world of the spirit, to discover the cause of the problem in this contingent world that we have lately come to accept as reality. But what were their myths, the tales and images that embodied this cosmology? What stories did they tell around their fires in the evening before they went to their beds to encounter the world of the spirit more directly in their dreams? What mythic images did they create on the wood and skins that have long since crumbled and disappeared? These we will never know, for the pitifully few artifacts that remain of Paleolithic humanity tempt us mightily to imagine that earlier reality, but they can never satisfy our desire to know it fully. Ultimately, we must do what the mythic artists themselves have done, for only art can reconstruct the mythic past. We must also go deeply into ourselves to supply those things that are hidden deep in the well of the past. For the men and women who initially populated our continents, those first Americans, were, after all, human beings like ourselves, and their myths, like ours, served to image forth the essential relationship between the human psyche and the world it inhabits.

If one were to use the information we do have to try to reconstruct the stages in the progression of humanity in the Americas from that nomadic life of hunting and gathering to the urban life of the high civilizations of Mesoamerica, one would no doubt see the first stage as a gradual movement from the original nomadic life to horticulture, a movement complemented by the equally gradual transition to settled life in small villages. Along with those changes would come a fundamental shift in mythology from what the great mythologist Joseph Campbell has called "the way of the animal powers" to "the way of the seeded earth," a movement away from a mythology related fundamentally to the hunter's

> ceremonial life [that] was addressed largely to the ends of a covenant with the animals, of reconciliation, veneration, and assurance that in return for the beasts' unremitting offering of themselves as willing victims, their life-blood should be given back in a sacred way to the earth, the mother of all, for rebirth.[3]

The emergent mythology of the planting cultures would be more a change of emphasis than a new vision, for now the maternal earth was to be seen as "the dual goddess, the great mothering power of the two worlds, of the dead and the living, the planted and the sprouting seed"[4] (see Figure 6; Color Plates 1, 2, and 3; and Images 1, 2, and 3). She was thus the ultimate reality, both the apparent world of nature and the sustaining world of spirit. Under this new dispensation, one engaged in reconstructing the past would no doubt imagine a gradual growth in those planters' villages and the beginning of stratification and specialization among the inhabitants. Those developments would ultimately lead to the acquisition of power by chiefs and priests, who would direct the increasingly complex economic and social affairs of the group. Ultimately, an urban society with a mythology based on what Campbell has called "the way of the celestial lights" would emerge as the arts of writing and mathematical computation were developed in conjunction with the astronomical observations that would lead to an understanding of the absolute, unearthly order of time as it was to be read in the majestic, orderly movements of those celestial lights.

THE VILLAGE CULTURES

With a single exception, that imagined course of events, nicely ordered, neat and tidy, would fit quite well what we know of the sequence of the cultural development of Mesoamerica. What little evidence we have of very early times indicates that until about 8000–7000 B.C. all of the peoples of Mesoamerica lived in small groups or microbands moving from one location to another in their quest for the food provided either by migrating animals or by seasonally ripening plants. From time to time, often seasonally, these microbands coalesced into larger groups or macrobands, settling momentarily in a particularly fruitful spot and engaging in ritual activities no doubt related to that fecundity of the earth.[5] Although we have no direct evidence of the mythology underlying this ritual, it is reasonable to assume, on the basis of Old World models and later evidence from North America and Mesoamerica, that it followed the development Campbell has suggested. Gradually, archaeologists tell us, that way of life began to change as settled communities took root in ecologically favorable locations and began a rudimentary seed-plant horticulture, more an extension of their earlier food-plant use than a dramatic change to agriculture. Over the next five or six thousand years, as we would expect, the peoples of Mesoamerica gradually evolved the relatively simple village cultures within which their lives could be led in harmony with the seasonal cycles through which their sustenance was provided. In those simple villages a new mythology was born. Centered on the female figure (see Figure 6; Color Plates 1, 2, and 3; and Images 1, 2, and 3) and lacking any evidence of what we would call gods, this mythology, still essentially shamanistic in its most fundamental assumptions, saw the earth as the repository of spirit and saw that spirit, or life force, as the source and sustainer of all life, an abiding maternal presence to which the omnipresent female figurines gave mythic form.

What the noted archaeologist Marija Gimbutas has said in *The Language of the Goddess* about the mythological thought of the Old World at the comparable stage of development fits these New World assumptions and figurines perfectly:

> The main theme of Goddess symbolism is the mystery of birth and death and the renewal of life, not only human, but all life on earth and indeed in the whole cosmos. Symbols and images cluster around the parthenogenetic (self-generating) Goddess and her basic functions as Giver of Life, Wielder of Death, and, not less importantly, as Regeneratrix, and around the Earth Mother, the Fertility Goddess young and old, rising and dying with plant life. She was the single source of all life who took her energy from the springs and wells, from the sun, moon, and moist earth. This symbolic system represents cyclical, not linear, mythical time.[6]

That period reached its highest point of development in what is known to Mesoamerican scholars as the Preclassic or Formative period (ca. 2000 B.C.–A.D. 200), in the latter part of which a decisive movement throughout Mesoamerica gave initial form to the emerging high civilizations in the valleys of Oaxaca and Teotihuacan, on the Veracruz coast, and in the highlands and lowlands of the Maya. These cultures were to derive their mythological assumptions from the heavens rather than the earth as the regular cyclical movements of the sun and moon, planets, and distant stars revealed to them a quadripartite order through which they could understand and guide their lives. They came to believe that both time and space—two aspects of a unitary whole—were four-part divisions of an essential unity, a unity of the spirit (see Image 15). But, for them, this unity manifested itself primarily in masculine gods and in the social and physical divisions of complex urban societies rather than in the feminine, maternal forms conceived by the earlier household-based cultures.

THE PRECOCIOUS OLMEC

While that brief description of the gradual movement toward complex urban cultures by the peoples of Mesoamerica fits perfectly the imaginary scenario we suggested above, it leaves out one monumental development that changes the picture entirely. All of the Mesoamerican high cultures *but one* arose as we suggested at the end of the Preclassic. That one, the precocious Olmec culture of the Gulf coast (Map 2), arose much earlier, by 1400 B.C. at the latest, at San Lorenzo in what is today the state of Veracruz, and thus had the effect of placing a culture that seems, certainly by the time of the development of the urban center of La Venta (ca. 900 B.C.), to have had most, if not all, of the characteristics of the highly stratified, highly complex, later-developing cultures of the Classic period squarely in the temporal midst of the simpler village cultures of the Preclassic. The problems related to understanding the reasons for the Olmec culture's early development, and the nature and effect of its impact on its simpler neighbors, are compounded by the scarcity of available data, since archaeological research in this time period is still in its infancy, and the ravages of nature and later human cultures have obliterated most traces of those early peoples.

The fascination engendered by the spectacular remains of the Olmec civilization, which seems to have disappeared by 400 B.C., has led all who view them to speculate upon their origins, since archaeology has not yet discovered solid evidence of an earlier, simpler culture in the Olmec heartland on the Gulf coast[7] that seems capable of having given rise to that stone sculpture (see Figure 1; Color Plate 4; and Images 27, 45, and 47) and ceremonial center construction, which so clearly indicates a well-developed state and an extremely complex mythology. Yet common sense tells us that such an earlier culture must have existed; these remaining works of mythic art were not created by gods who arrived in chariots, after all. One can hope that archaeology will soon discover the Olmec forebears, perhaps in the earliest levels at the site of San Lorenzo or in the area of the nearby Tuxtla mountains, but until that happens there is sufficient evidence throughout Mesoamerica of the gradual increase in sophistication of the mythic art of the village cultures from roughly 6500 to 2000 B.C.

Our understanding of this period is complicated by the fact that the Olmec civilization, the first of the high cultures to rise out of those

The Spread of Olmec Culture   1400–400 B.C.

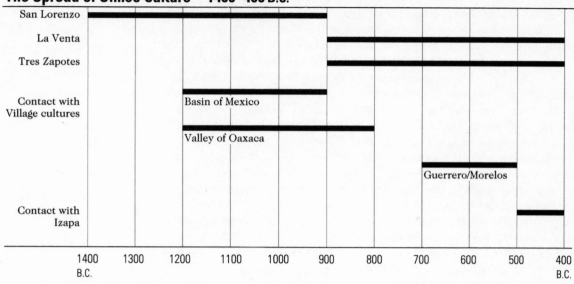

| | 1400 B.C. | 1300 | 1200 | 1100 | 1000 | 900 | 800 | 700 | 600 | 500 | 400 B.C. |

San Lorenzo
La Venta
Tres Zapotes

Contact with Village cultures — Basin of Mexico — Valley of Oaxaca

Guerrero/Morelos

Contact with Izapa

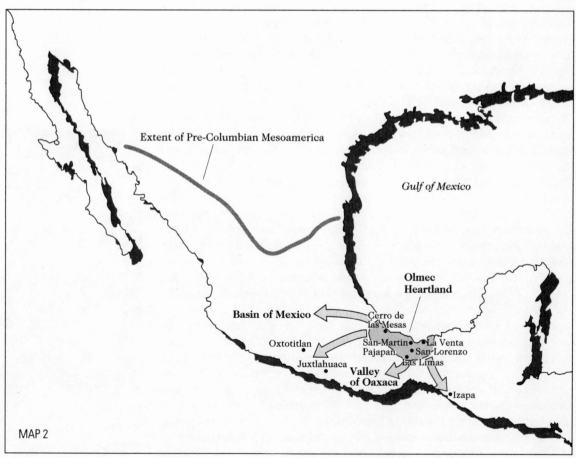

Extent of Pre-Columbian Mesoamerica

Gulf of Mexico

Olmec Heartland

Basin of Mexico

Cerro de las Mesas

Oxtotitlan

San-Martin Pajapan

La Venta
San Lorenzo
Las Limas

Juxtlahuaca

Valley of Oaxaca

Izapa

MAP 2

simpler village cultures, coexisted for a time with these simpler cultures in several areas outside the Olmec heartland on the Gulf coast. Archaeology has revealed to us the evidence of an Olmec presence of some kind in the villages of the highland areas of Oaxaca, Morelos, Guerrero, and the Basin of Mexico as well as on the Pacific slope, and that evidence has been interpreted to suggest that it was through that contact that the Olmec civilization—often called the "mother culture" of Mesoamerica—was somehow instrumental in creating the later civilizations of Monte Alban, Teotihuacan, the Maya, and El Tajin (Map 3). The Olmecs, it was first thought, brought the blessings and burdens of civilization to these innocent peoples, who were, like their art, "simple and unassuming, but gay and sensitive, free of religious themes."[8] Mesoamerican religion and the mythology on which it was based were, in this view, an Olmec creation.

There is no doubt that that creation found its most important focus in the composite creature known today as the Olmec werejaguar. Nothing makes the vast difference between the existing mythology of the village cultures and the emerging mythology of the urban cultures clearer than the visual contrast between the simple, beautiful, maternal figurines (see Figure 6; Color Plates 1, 2, and 3; and Images 1, 2, and 3) of the earlier time—images drawn from nature—and this often fearful, fantastic creature (Figure 1). While it was once thought that all Olmec mythic art was dominated by the were-jaguar, it has now become clear that the Olmecs, like all of the cultures that would follow them, had a variety of images of the supernatural, all of them fantastic creatures of myth with faces and bodies made up of varying combinations of features drawn from the creatures of nature. This insight was developed most forcefully by the Mesoamerican scholars Michael Coe and Peter David Joralemon on the basis of a striking Olmec figure, called the "Lord of Las Limas" (Color Plate 4), that displays a compendium of images of these mythic creatures. While we do not know the names the Olmecs gave these denizens of the realm of the spirit and have not even a hint of the narrative myths that must have detailed their metaphoric exploits, we do know that these enigmatic masked images provided the framework upon which all subsequent mythologies in Mesoamerica would be constructed. They are the prototypes of all of the composite creatures to come—the gods of the peoples of Mesoamerica.

That the Olmecs were significantly involved in the creation of the later civilizations and their mythologies is undoubtedly true. However, it is now becoming clear that each of the seemingly simple village cultures was, in fact, not so "simple and unassuming" but well along the path toward the complexity of a stratified society when contact with Olmec civilization occurred, and each contributed a great deal of its own to the high culture that succeeded it. To put it more precisely, Olmec influence on the existing village cultures in various parts of Mesoamerica acted as a catalyst, sparking the local cultures to make

FIGURE 1

The Olmec were-jaguar, a jade ritual celt known as the "Kunz axe"

Classic Period Cultures   A.D. 150–900

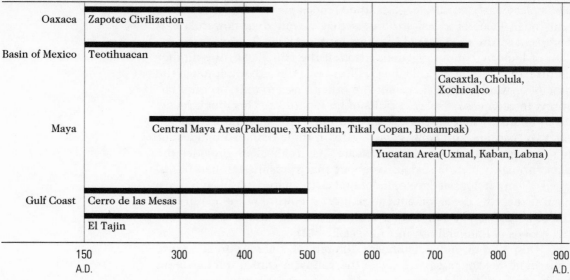

Oaxaca	Zapotec Civilization
Basin of Mexico	Teotihuacan
	Cacaxtla, Cholula, Xochicalco
Maya	Central Maya Area(Palenque, Yaxchilan, Tikal, Copan, Bonampak)
	Yucatan Area(Uxmal, Kaban, Labna)
Gulf Coast	Cerro de las Mesas
	El Tajin

150   300   400   500   600   700   800   900
A.D.   A.D.

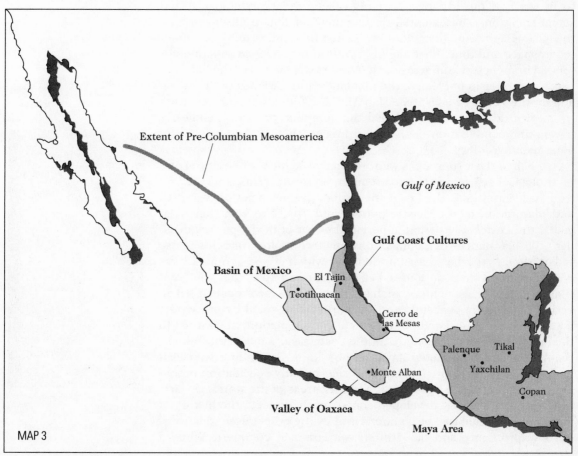

Extent of Pre-Columbian Mesoamerica

Gulf of Mexico

Gulf Coast Cultures

Basin of Mexico

El Tajin

Teotihuacan

Cerro de las Mesas

Palenque   Tikal

Yaxchilan

Copan

•Monte Alban

Valley of Oaxaca

Maya Area

MAP 3

the leap to urban civilization. As the well-known French Mesoameri-canist Jacques Soustelle suggests, the Olmecs planted "religious ideas and rough ideas of social structures that germinated, flowered, and bore fruit in the classic era."9 But what was carried forward was a fu-sion of imported and indigenous ideas. If the Olmec was the mother culture, the particular local village culture was the father (although the metaphor would be far more apt the other way around), and the off-spring in each case displayed traits of both parents. This much seems clear, and the exact means of transmission of the cultural heritage of the two "parents," probably based more on trade than on conquest or missionary activity, is becoming clearer as archaeology provides the data through which earlier ideas about that transmission can be re-fined. No mythological development makes the nature of this influence clearer than the development by each great culture of the features of the god of rain and storm from the Olmec original into its own god (see "The Gods of Rain and Storm," Images 27–42).

Despite their quite significant differences, the four great culture areas that developed as a result of the catalytic Olmec influence are to be seen as quadripartite variants of one great mythological and social tradition. The essential development of that tradition is rela-tively simple, but to understand it we must first understand its unfold-ing in space and time. Spatially, that tradition developed separate but related branches in four areas of Mesoamerica. Located in the Valley of Oaxaca, the Basin of Mexico, the highlands and lowlands of the Maya, and on the Veracruz coast (see Map 3), these four great cultures, each in its own distinct way, developed the complex, profound, endlessly fascinating combination of tales and images that we know as Meso-american mythology.

Each of these four areas went through a sequence of cultural and mythological stages; in the most commonly used terms, each moved from its beginnings in the Preclassic period, through a period of growth and maturation in the Classic period, and finally to what has been called the Postclassic period, a period thought of in the past as deca-dent. With a number of modifications this terminology remains in use today, though the basic assumptions on which it was founded have been discarded. It is no longer believed, for example, that the great Classic period urban centers, such as Monte Alban, Teotihuacan, Tikal, and El Tajin, were peaceful ceremonial precincts ruled by priests de-voted to astronomical and philosophical contemplation, in contrast to the harshly militaristic societies of the Postclassic, such as the Toltecs, the Aztecs, and the Yucatec Maya. We now know that militarism began early, no doubt with the Olmecs, and that priestly speculation proba-bly began at the same time. As in all other areas of the world, the arts of war and philosophy developed concurrently; indeed, the history of Mesoamerica could well be characterized by the ever-present duality of devout spirituality and bloodthirsty warfare and conquest. While a well-documented period of upheaval did occur at the end of the Classic period, a time of transition out of which new societies emerged throughout Mesoamerica, these new Postclassic societies were not as different from their predecessors as had once been thought.

THE VALLEY OF OAXACA

The first of the four Classic period civilizations to develop, the Zapotec, was located in the Valley of Oaxaca (Map 4). The Olmec influence in Oaxaca can be seen as early as 1150 B.C. in mythic symbols connected with the ritual activity that accompanied the growth of urban civilization. The period of Olmec contact seems to have ended by 850 B.C., but the Olmec influence left its mark. As John Paddock, a an archaeologist who has devoted his professional life to the study of the Valley of Oaxaca, puts it in discussing three ceramic pieces from about 300 B.C., "Somebody in the Valley of Oaxaca had a total understanding of Olmec style in a cultural setting that was no longer Olmec."[10] The transition from the alien culture to an indigenous one had been made. That indigenous culture, the Zapotec, constructed the mountaintop urban center of Monte Alban at about 550 B.C. and from that remarkable site dominated the Valley of Oaxaca for more than a thousand years. Archaeologists have divided that lengthy period into four stages, each associated with developments in the style of the decorated urns the Zapotecs placed with their honored dead (Figures 2 and 3; Images 28, 29, and 30). It is through these urns that we know most of what we know about Zapotec mythology, and what we know is both very little and very confusing. After the Conquest a few "god lists" were compiled by friars in the area, who, unfortunately, seem to have confused deified ancestors with gods. To add to the confusion, the definitive work on the funerary urns, the 1952 *Urnas de Oaxaca* by the celebrated Mexican scholars Alfonso Caso and Ignacio Bernal, was based on the premise that all of the urns depicted gods. It now seems clear, however, that most of them depict human beings, no doubt important ones, some of them in ritual dress and therefore impersonating gods, while only a few actually portray gods, notably those depicting the rain god, Cocijo (Images 28, 29, and 30).

During the Postclassic period, the Mixtec culture of the mountainous areas of northern and western Oaxaca gradually rose to prominence throughout the Valley of Oaxaca as the Zapotec culture gradually waned in power and influence. The Mixtecs created their own distinctive art style and architecture, as at Mitla, and eventually occupied the mountaintop site of Monte Alban, placing their own dead in the tombs constructed by the Zapotecs. While we have no remaining Zapotec codices, as the screenfold, painted "books" or narrative myths of pre-Columbian Mesoamerica have come to be known, we do have a few myths of the Mixtecs, both in the codices and as recorded by Spanish

The Zapotec and Mixtec Civilizations of Oaxaca   500 B.C.–A.D. 1500

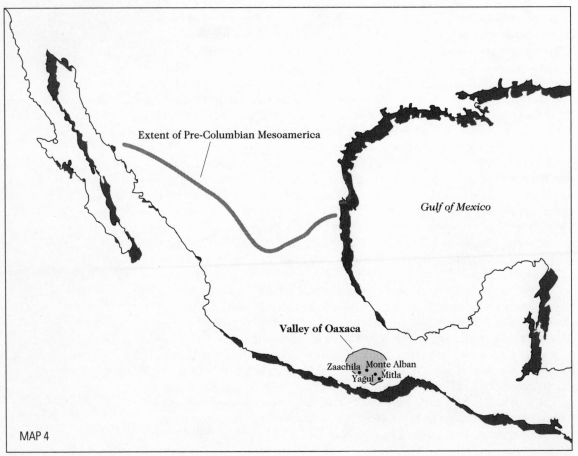

	Period 1	Period 2		Period 3					
Zapotec	Monte Alban								
Zapotec and Mixtec							Zaachila, Mitla, Yagul		
Mixtec									Mixtec Kingdoms

500 B.C. 250 B.C.–A.D. 250 500 750 1000 1250 1500 A.D.

Extent of Pre-Columbian Mesoamerica

Gulf of Mexico

Valley of Oaxaca

Zaachila Monte Alban
Yagul Mitla

MAP 4

FIGURE 2
A Zapotec ceramic
funerary urn, perhaps
an image of the de-
ceased, from Monte
Alban Tomb 77

FIGURE 3

A Zapotec ceramic
funerary urn, from a
tomb at Monte Alban,
showing a person wear-
ing a serpent mouth
mask

priests after the Conquest. The most notable of these is the creation myth recorded both by Fray Gregorio García and in the *Codex Vindobonensis* (Color Plate 5, Image 6), a rare case of a single myth recorded in both pre-Conquest and post-Conquest documents. It is believed as well that the Mixtecs were responsible for the codices in the Mixteca-Puebla style, such as the *Codex Borgia* (Color Plates 7 and 23, Images 11 and 16), but the authorship of these documents is far from fully understood.

THE BASIN OF MEXICO

While these developments transpired in the Valley of Oaxaca, somewhat to the north, in what is known as either the Valley or the Basin of Mexico, an even clearer and, one might argue, more significant process of development was taking place (Map 5). That great Basin that now houses Mexico City, soon to be the largest city in the world, has been for a very long time the seat of cultures that dominated, or at least tried to dominate, the rest of Mesoamerica. The first of these great cultures was Classic period Teotihuacan. At about the time of Christ and the inauguration of the Old World mythological tradition that bears his name, the people of the area of Teotihuacan began the building of the monumental Pyramid of the Sun directly above what must have been the holiest of sanctuaries, a cavern deep within a long, sinuous cave formed when the lava of the area cooled millions of years before. The pyramid was designed so that that cavern was directly under the temple atop the pyramid and the entrance to the cave coincided with the base of the staircase leading up to the temple. From the outset Teotihuacan must have been seen as a sacred place, and that aura remained long after its decline and fall, since even the much later Aztecs believed it was the place where the gods had been born. In fact, the Aztec myth of the creation of the sun through the sacrifice of the gods, which we present in "The Myths of Creation," was set at Teotihuacan.

The city gradually grew in size, complexity, and grandeur until, "at the height of its power, around A.D. 500, Teotihuacan was larger than Imperial Rome. For more than half a millennium it was to Middle America what Rome, Benares or Mecca have been to the Old World: at once a religious and cultural capital and a major economic and political center."[11] From the mythologist's point of view, of course, its religious function was paramount, and of that function, René Millon, the preeminent archaeologist working at that site, says that the great city

> was above all a religious center without equal in its time. We see this manifested in its great pyramids, in the multiplicity of its temples, in the monumentality of its principal avenue that overwhelms viewers today and that anciently must have induced religious awe in believers. Teotihuacan has the unmistakable aura of a sacred city. . . . Like sacred cities elsewhere it was likely regarded as the center of the cosmos and, it can be argued, the place where time began. If the latter were the case,

The Basin of Mexico 100 B.C.–A.D. 1500

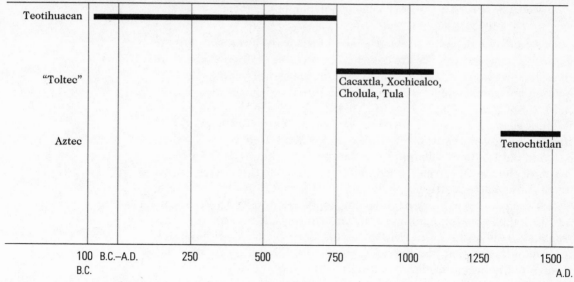

Teotihuacan					
"Toltec"			Cacaxtla, Xochicalco, Cholula, Tula		
Aztec					Tenochtitlan

| 100 B.C.–A.D. | 250 | 500 | 750 | 1000 | 1250 | 1500 |
| B.C. | | | | | | A.D. |

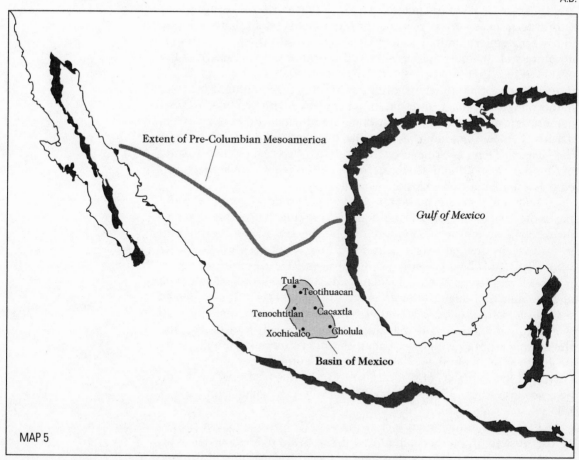

Extent of Pre-Columbian Mesoamerica

Gulf of Mexico

Tula
Teotihuacan
Tenochtitlan
Cacaxtla
Xochicalco
Cholula

Basin of Mexico

MAP 5

whether or not celebrated in ritual, the very existence of Teotihuacan would have been a perpetual commemoration of the coming into existence of the present cycle of time.[12]

As scholars have recognized, many of the gods of the later Toltec and Aztec cultures are already clearly recognizable at Teotihuacan, although a great deal of the obviously mythic imagery contained in the painted murals that decorated most of the inner and outer walls of that sacred city (Color Plates 19 and 20) still puzzles today's scholars.[13] What is clear to everyone, however, is that this city was the center of the mythological tradition of the Basin of Mexico, a tradition that reached out to Monte Alban, to the Veracruz coast, and deep into the realm of the Maya, as references to Teotihuacan mythic forms in the art of those cultures attest.

When that great city declined in importance, falling to ruins in A.D. 750 after a widespread fire of unknown origin, the economic and social systems of the Basin fell into chaos as rival cities competed for the preeminence that had been Teotihuacan's. What happened to the Basin's mythological tradition during the decline and after the fall of Teotihuacan? While our understanding of that period is as murky as our understanding of the reasons for the fall of such a mighty society, in the rather more limited area of our concern with myth, one thing is absolutely clear: the tradition survived essentially unchanged the fall of the culture that had conceived it. Whether that survival was due to the survival of the priestly tradition of Teotihuacan among those who found refuge elsewhere or to the use of Teotihuacan's symbols by newcomers on the scene eager to legitimize their own power by associating it with the fallen grandeur of Teotihuacan is uncertain. But whatever the historical process that brought it about, the development of the mythological tradition of the Basin of Mexico remained essentially unchanged in its most basic forms.

That stability is remarkable in view of the developments in the Basin of Mexico that brought influences from all over Mesoamerica to bear on the area. The vacuum created by the fall of Teotihuacan was soon filled by several urban centers in and on the periphery of the Basin. Tula and Cholula were most involved, with Tula ultimately gaining the ascendancy, but Xochicalco and El Tajin as well as Cacaxtla also reached their highest development during this period and played a role in the politics of the region that is not yet clearly understood. That it was a time of ferment is indicated archaeologically by the fact that the mythic art of each of these urban centers combines symbolic artistic forms from a number of Mesoamerican cultures. As our pictorial survey of the rain gods of these cultures indicates (see Images 34 and 35), however, the mythological tradition evolved in what seems to be a relatively normal fashion.

Out of the ferment of this time in the early Postclassic the Toltecs of Tula rose to prominence, dominating the Basin of Mexico. Their influence was felt throughout Mesoamerica as well, most notably among

THE FLAYED GOD

the Yucatec Maya, where the ceremonial center of Chichen Itza bears remarkable similarities to that of Tula.[14] Significantly, it is at about this time that Kukulcan, the Maya Feathered Serpent, makes his entrance into Maya mythology, a striking fact since Quetzalcoatl, the Toltec Feathered Serpent, seemingly both god and man, was both ruler and patron god of Tula. But as the hero journey myths we present in "The Mythic Structure of Rulership" demonstrate, Tula, like its predecessor, fell, inaugurating another period of chaos in the Basin beginning at about 1150 or 1200.

From that chaos emerged the Aztec state, but it was a slow emergence with a humble beginning. That beginning was recounted in Aztec myth and legend (Images 52 and 53), most notably the migration myths also presented in "The Mythic Structure of Rulership," but it has been difficult for modern scholars to agree on the historical, as opposed to the mythic, realities. The myth is clear: the Aztecs, led by their god Huitzilopochtli, came to Tenochtitlan, an island in the middle of a lake, after a period of wandering from their original home in Aztlan, an island in the middle of a lagoon. In Tenochtitlan they founded their city, which gradually, under the protection of Huitzilopochtli, the young god who led them there, and Tlaloc, the ancient god of the Basin, grew in power and came to the position of dominance it held when Cortés and his men first surveyed its grandeur:

> We saw so many cities and villages built in the water and other great towns on dry land and that straight and level Causeway [the Causeway of Cuitlahuac separating the lake of Chalco from the lake of Xochimilco] going towards Mexico, [that] we were amazed and said that it was like the enchantments they tell of in the legend of Amadis, on account of the great towers and cues and buildings rising from the water, and all built of masonry. And some of our soldiers even asked whether the things that we saw were not a dream. . . . I stood looking at it and thought that never in the world would there be discovered other lands such as these, for at that time there was no Peru, nor any thought of it. Of all these wonders that I then beheld to-day all is overthrown and lost, nothing left standing.[15]

What was lost, of course, in addition to the material world of the Aztecs and the wondrous culture they had developed, was the mythological tradition that had been developing in the Basin for thousands of years. But "lost" is not precisely the right word, since even in today's Indian villages one can see evidence of the fusion of that dynamic and still vital tradition with the mythological tradition brought from the Old World by the friars.

This is the Aztec story told by the myths, but the historical tale is more prosaic. The Mexica, a subgroup of the Aztecs, probably did make their humble arrival at their island place of settlement at about 1325. Whether they came from the north, either from an island (the Aztlan of the myth) or from the deserts bounding Mesoamerica, or from the Basin itself is still hotly debated by scholars, but archaeology has provided a record of their efforts once they arrived. The recent excavation in Mexico City of the Templo Mayor, the principal pyramid-temple complex of the ceremonial center of their capital at Tenochtitlan, testifies to the humble beginnings of the Mexica. Like many Mesoamerican pyramids the Templo Mayor underwent successive rebuildings in which a new "shell," a new pyramid, was constructed over the existing one, and the recent excavations have revealed seven such "stages" and unearthed the temple atop the second stage almost intact. Compared to the later splendor described by the eyewitness Díaz del Castillo, this early temple is a rather modest affair. But the Mexica Aztecs prospered, and the fact that we know them today as the Aztecs, their compatriot groups having faded from memory, indicates that prosperity as well as anything else. By about 1425 they had come to dominate the Basin through alliances and military dominance, and by the time of the Conquest in 1519 their soldiers and merchants effectively controlled a substantial portion of Mesoamerica.

THE MAYA

While the Basin of Mexico was the home of a series of expansionist cultures that spread their dominion—and their mythology—throughout Mesoamerica, the realm of the Maya, comprising all of Mesoamerica lying east of the narrow Isthmus of Tehuantepec (Map 6), developed its own distinct culture. Often compared in the past to the Greeks, in contrast to the "Romans" of the Basin of Mexico, the Maya civilization grew as a series of powerful city-states, generally at war with each other but often linked through marriages and alliances. No single city became dominant even within the area, much less throughout Mesoamerica. While the mythology of the Maya is clearly related to that of the other areas of Mesoamerica, the images in which it is expressed are quite distinct, as are its emphasis on the cult of the ruling dynasty and its fascination with the calendrical science through which the multitudinous cycles of time could be charted.

Scholars generally believe that the mythology of the Maya, like that of all of the other cultures of Mesoamerica, developed from Olmec sources. But the case of the Maya is more complex than that of the others, for it is difficult to demonstrate much direct contact between the Olmec and the earliest Maya. Rather, the Olmecs seem to have influenced the Izapan culture of Pacific slope Guatemala and Chiapas (ca. 1200 B.C.–A.D. 200), which in turn influenced the Maya. Scholars have traced the depictions of gods and ritual impersonators of the gods on Izapan stelae, the upright stone slabs carved in relief (Images 7, 22, and 39), to Olmec roots and have demonstrated similarities between the images on the stelae and later Maya mythic images. While both of these types of similarities are evident, it is also abundantly clear that the mythology of Izapa was neither Olmec nor Maya. The images on the stelae[16] are clearly revelatory of a series of now-lost narrative myths that in their details are distinct from those of any of the cultures

The Maya To A.D. 1500

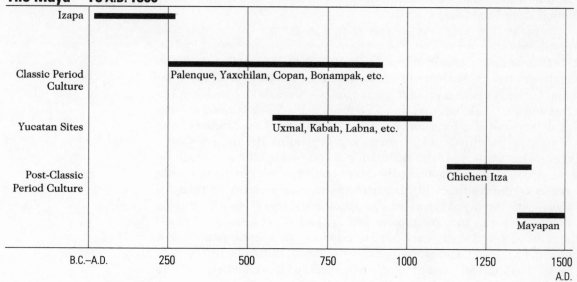

	B.C.–A.D.	250	500	750	1000	1250	1500 A.D.

Izapa

Classic Period Culture — Palenque, Yaxchilan, Copan, Bonampak, etc.

Yucatan Sites — Uxmal, Kabah, Labna, etc.

Post-Classic Period Culture — Chichen Itza

Mayapan

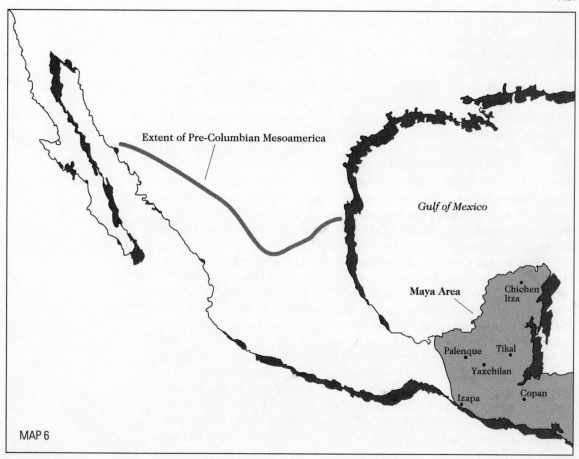

Extent of Pre-Columbian Mesoamerica

Gulf of Mexico

Maya Area

Chichen Itza

Palenque · Tikal

Yaxchilan

Copan

Izapa

MAP 6

we know and that seem also to differ in detail from anything to be found among the Olmec.

From that catalytic contact with the Izapan civilization and mythology, the mythological tradition of the Classic period, urban Maya civilization presumably arose in the proto-Maya village cultures of the contiguous lowlands in and surrounding the great jungle swampland of the Peten that bridges Mexico and Guatemala and includes Belize and parts of Honduras and El Salvador. By 500 B.C. monumental sculpture and the forerunners of the ubiquitous Maya stelae of the Classic period (Image 48) begin to appear, and by the time of Christ this region witnessed "the emergence of the rank called ahau and the rise of kingdoms throughout the Maya country. . . . From the Pacific slopes of the southern highlands to the northern plains of Yucatan, these lords displayed themselves and their royal regalia on monuments carved with narrative pictures recording their ritual actions."[17] These monuments and their successors throughout the Classic period were generally the stelae to which we have referred, and collectively they image forth the Maya myth of divine rulership, as we suggest in "The Mythic Structure of Rulership."

By A.D. 250 the Classic period had begun, characterized throughout the course of its development by monumental architecture, the stela cult, and by far the most elaborate glyphic writing developed in the New World. That cultural development was exceedingly complex and is only now beginning to be understood in detail, and the same can be said of the accompanying development of the Maya mythological tradition. While the glyphic system and the art style of the Maya differ radically from those of the Basin of Mexico (compare, for example, Images 16 and 40 or Images 23 and 48), it is becoming increasingly clear that most of the Maya gods had analogues in the myths of the Basin of Mexico and that the fundamental mythic structures of the two cultures were essentially similar. The complex developments of the Classic period in the lowlands, which saw such magnificent achievements as those at Tikal, Copan, Yaxchilan, and Palenque, came to an end by A.D. 900, the usual date given for the Maya "collapse."

The reasons for and the extent of that collapse are still not entirely clear, but we do know that the focus of Maya civilization and of the Maya mythological tradition shifted from the lowlands of the Peten and the surrounding area to the Yucatan peninsula. In the Yucatan the stela cult, with its mythic emphasis on the divine ruler (Image 48), seems to have given way to a focus on the god of rain, who seems also to have been the mythic patron of rulership. Wherever today's explorer of the archaeological sites of the Postclassic Yucatec Maya turns, he or she is confronted by masks of Chac. They look down from the walls and corners of temples and palaces (Image 42), their mouths form the doorways of these buildings, their faces decorate urns, and their human likeness is to be found in the codices probably painted in this time and place (Image 40). The early development of the period can be seen at sites such as Uxmal, Kabah, and Labna, while Chichen Itza, with its blending of Maya imagery with that reminiscent of the Basin of Mexico, dominates the later developments. At Chichen one senses a reunification of the mythological tradition originally separated at the outset of the Classic period.

Despite the dominance of first the lowlands and then the Yucatan in the development of the civilization and mythological tradition of the Maya, the only sustained narrative myth that remains, the *Popol Vuh,* comes from the Pacific highlands area of Guatemala dominated by the Quiché Maya. It is perhaps the most important single Mesoamerican mythological work because it contains many of the elements of a complete mythology. We present its creation myth in "The Myths of Creation" and its paradigmatic hero journey undertaken by the Hero Twins in "The Mythic Structure of Rulership," and it also contains a long migration myth. As it exists today, it is a post-Conquest document probably preserved from a Postclassic culture. But there is a great deal of evidence, notably on the painted pottery found in Classic period graves (Image 41), that the myths it contains date at least to the Classic period and that those myths were part of an even larger mythic cycle.[18]

THE GULF COAST

The development of a Classic period civilization on the Gulf coast (Map 7) is associated with the site of El Tajin (Image 17), but that development is by far the least understood of the four Classic period civilizations because there has been relatively little archaeological work done at the site of El Tajin or in the area it dominated. It is thought that Olmec influence, operating through such intermediary early urban centers as Tres Zapotes and Cerro de las Mesas, gradually metamorphosed into the culture of El Tajin. Although the art style of El Tajin is distinctive in its grace and beauty (Images 17 and 20), we know relatively little about the meaning of such narrative scenes as those carved in relief on El Tajin's ballcourts or on panels meant to grace the Pyramid of the Niches or other sacred structures beyond the fact that the ritual ball game and its attendant mythology were of tremendous importance. In the Postclassic a body of mythic stone sculpture (Image 51), probably relating rulers to Quetzalcoatl, who is often thought to have had a Gulf coast origin, in the context of life and death was created by the people of the Huasteca, an area lying north of El Tajin, but Postclassic developments on the Gulf coast seem to have been dominated by the imperial might and the mythology of the Basin of Mexico. Sites such as the one at Castillo de Teayo (Images 36 and 37) are indistinguishable architecturally and mythologically from those in the Basin.

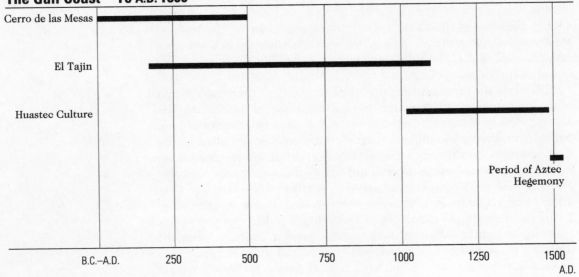

The Gulf Coast   To A.D. 1500

Cerro de las Mesas

El Tajin

Huastec Culture

Period of Aztec
Hegemony

B.C.–A.D.   250   500   750   1000   1250   1500   A.D.

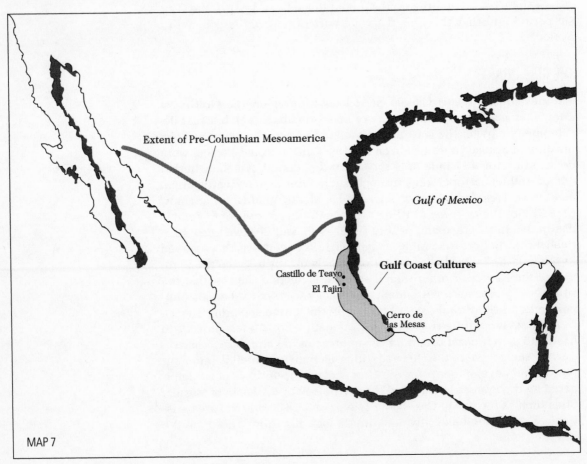

Extent of Pre-Columbian Mesoamerica

Gulf of Mexico

Gulf Coast Cultures

Castillo de Teayo

El Tajin

Cerro de
las Mesas

MAP 7

THE SOURCES

While the quadripartite social and political development of Mesoamerican civilization can thus be summarized fairly simply, however complex and puzzling it becomes when examined in detail, our knowledge of the development of the mythological tradition is not as clear. The difficulties arise from the fact that there are virtually no undeniably pre-Conquest narrative myths extant. What we do have in great abundance are mythic images carved in stone, formed in ceramic, and painted on ceramics, walls, and in the screenfold "books" made of bark paper or skin called codices. We have a large body of such images from each of the cultures of Mesoamerica, but these fantastic composite creatures of myth, seemingly infinitely varied in their strange and wondrous combinations of features drawn from the denizens of the natural world but reordered metaphorically to suggest the lineaments of the realm of the spirit—are very difficult to understand apart from the context supplied by the mythology that embraced them and told their metaphoric stories.

Unfortunately, very few of the narrative myths that recounted the exploits of these flayed gods, feathered serpents, were-jaguars, obsidian butterflies, and snake women have survived, and those that do remain are almost all from one area—the Basin of Mexico—and in the form in which they were recorded after the Conquest. While undoubtedly, before the Conquest, there existed a great number of codices that "told" the myths in picture form, as does the *Codex Vindobonensis,* for example (See Figures 9 and 10, Color Plate 5, and Image 6), virtually all of the few remaining codices that survived the Christian priests' burning of the "books of the devil" and the ravages of time are essentially ritual calendars. These served as "prompt books" designed for native priests conducting rituals or determining the auguries of particular days in the complex calendrical system (Figure 4). As "prompt books," they did not tell the underlying story, even when they had occasion to refer to the myths; rather, they depended on their user's knowing the story already. However, in too many cases these are stories *we* do not know. One has only to page through one of the more complex codices, such as the *Codex Borgia,* to be struck by the mythic complexity of the scenes (Figure 5), a complexity that was obviously designed to communicate very precise meanings. But if one reads the few twentieth-century interpretations of such scenes, one will be equally struck by the almost incredible variety of interpretations proposed by modern scholars. In order to understand these images from the codices, and all of the myriad other mythic images of pre-Columbian Mesoamerica, we should have many more of the myths themselves than are actually available to us now.

But we must make use of what we have, and our primary purpose in this volume is to present in modern English translations virtually all of the important myths that remain. These are the key texts with

FIGURE 4

A pictorial representa-
tion of a calendar from
the *Codex Borgia*

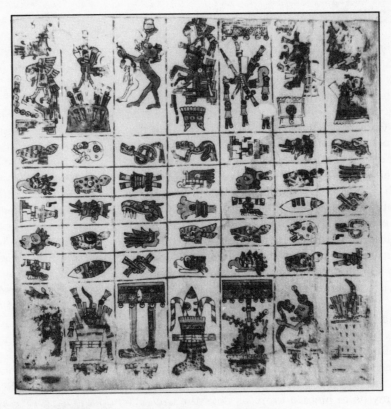

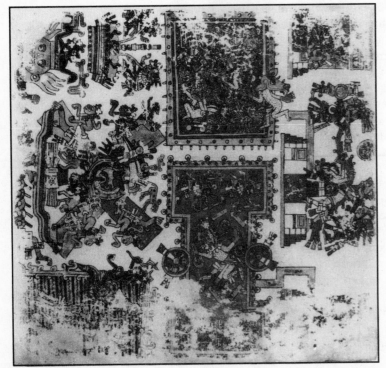

FIGURE 5

An enigmatic mythic
scene from the *Codex
Borgia*

which any understanding of the unbelievably complex and beautiful Mesoamerican mythological tradition must begin. However, with the primary, and notable, exception of the highland Maya *Popol Vuh,* which surfaced long after the Conquest,[19] our knowledge of the narrative myths of the peoples of pre-Columbian Mesoamerica comes almost entirely from the Basin of Mexico and is made up of material collected and preserved by the missionary friars who accompanied the conquerors to the New World and of the works of native historians after the Conquest, historians who worked, as the *Popol Vuh* puts it, "amid the preaching of God, in Christendom now." Furthermore, these are works whose focus is rarely on myth; the myths that remain were inserted here and there in historical or what we would call ethnographic accounts, but are rarely central. What we need, and what we will never have, is a way of peering into the mind of the indigenous seer, for that is where the mythological tradition—in all its metaphoric fullness and grandeur—existed. The myths that we present here allow us a glimpse of that beauty and profundity, but that glimpse is seen "through a glass darkly"—a glass provided by the Christian conquerors.

The most prolific of the friars who accompanied those conquerors was, without a doubt, Bernardino de Sahagún, a Franciscan priest who arrived in Mexico in 1529, only ten years after the Conquest, and died there in 1590. He devoted a great portion of this time to the systematic recording of the knowledge of surviving Aztec elders, and to his great credit he preserved his informants' Nahuatl accounts as well as composing his own Spanish transcriptions of them. His culminating work is the twelve-book *Historia General de las Cosas de Nueva España,* the collection of diverse information known more simply as the *Florentine Codex.* A number of the myths we present in this volume are modern translations of the Nahuatl accounts in this work, but unfortunately the great bulk of Sahagún's work is made up of accounts of ritual and descriptions of Aztec life; he presents relatively few myths.

The works of other friars in the Basin of Mexico, such as Diego Durán and Gerónimo de Mendieta, as well as friars in other areas such as Gregorio García in Oaxaca, are similar to that of Sahagún, but they are less voluminous, probably based on reports from fewer informants, and were recorded only in Spanish. These works are complemented by a group of works, presumably also by friars, whose authorship is no longer known. Outstanding within this group of writings, from the point of view of the mythologist, is the *Historia de los Mexicanos por sus Pinturas,* a manuscript that was undoubtedly written to accompany a painted codex, probably one drawn after the Conquest at the request of a friar. There are a number of such codices that were designed to familiarize the friars with the native religion, and two of them, the *Codex Vaticanus A* and the *Codex Magliabechiano,* along with their several cognates, are particularly valuable since they contain explanations by these unknown commentators on the pictures, explanations that provide identifications of a number of the Aztec gods.

In addition to these religious chroniclers, a number of native historians attempted to preserve a record of the history and beliefs of their forebears. The authors of two of the most important works, the *Leyenda de los Soles,* which we present in its entirety for the first time in English, and the *Anales de Cuauhtitlan,* are no longer known, but in both cases it is clear that they were Indians who were not working under the guidance of priests. In addition to these two works, the writings of Hernando Alvarado Tezozómoc and Fernando de Alva Ixtlilxóchitl are of fundamental importance, especially Tezozómoc's *Crónica Mexicayotl.* While we are fortunate to have these works, which contain, among many other things, portions of the mythology of the Aztecs, none of them, nor all of them put together, even begins to present that entire mythology, and of course they are mute regarding the other mythologies of Mesoamerica.

Their presentation here in the translations of a variety of the most respected scholars, rather than in our own summaries of their contents, is important. Were we to present our own summaries of the myths, our own retellings, we would inevitably "filter" the myths through our understanding of what they mean. In our essays we have given our own interpretations, but obviously other interpretations are possible. The texts and images themselves—*not* the summaries or interpretations—are what are important. They are what remains of the Mesoamerican mythological tradition. One must realize, however, that most of the myths we present here have already passed through the mental "filter" of a Christian missionary or a native writer influenced to some degree by such a missionary and the tradition he brought with him from Europe.

Still, we are fortunate to be able to present what remains of one of the world's great mythological traditions, and even in these "fragments shored against the ruins" we can still sense the magnificence of that tradition. We feel its greatness first in the earliest images—the simple but profound female figurines created in the village cultures—and then in the more complex creations of the urban tradition: in the majestic, fourfold unfolding of the gods, the cosmos, and man from the unity of the creative principle; in the brilliant conception of the feathered serpent who unites the earth and the heavens; in the macabre and intensely metaphoric flayed god who dramatically separates and unites inner and outer; in the fierce were-jaguar, god of storm and rain; in the great goddess, whose essence takes on myriad names and forms but always signifies fertility and the maternal earth from which we come and to which we shall return; in the breathtaking hero journeys of the hero twins and Topiltzin Quetzalcoatl, the paradigmatic rulers; and in all of the strange and exalted creatures that populate the profoundly metaphoric tales and images of this incredibly rich tradition.

THE FLAYED GOD

THE FIGURE OF THE GODDESS:

THE MYTHOLOGICAL IMAGES OF THE VILLAGE CULTURES

INTRODUCTION

FERTILITY AND THE GODDESS

Wherever traces are discovered of the village cultures from the period preceeding the development of the great urban civilizations of Mesoamerica, the mythology of those groups is consistently imaged forth in simple ceramic figurines, which are so common as to be diagnostic of those settlements. Almost always female and either nude or wearing ritual attire of some sort, their physical characteristics relate them clearly to fertility and suggest the development of a conceptualization of that force, which took place during the gradual evolution of a sedentary, agricultural way of life. That way of life, despite its having finally been subordinated to the demands of the great urban civilizations, never has changed for the peasants of Mesoamerica, despite the sweeping changes brought about by the rise and fall of the successive high cultures of Mesoamerica. Significantly, similar figurines are found in a rural context throughout all of the stages of Mesoamerican development and are still to be found in a variety of forms in today's Indian villages. That they are metaphoric is clear, and equally clear is their essential import. They represent the fertility of the bountiful earth as it gives and supports life. In that sense they *are* life—they embody the fundamentally spiritual force that has its origin in the shamanistically conceived spirit world that underlies and supports the world of nature. They are the remaining evidence that, for these peoples, "all that lived was bound into a sacred fabric, 'the larger web of the life force,' part of a whole."[1]

The mythology of these cultures evolved directly from that conceptualization of fertility. All of the mythic images illustrate one aspect or another of that movement of spirit into the world of nature and the return, at death, to the world of the spirit. They focus on the materialization of spirit and the spiritualization of matter in a cyclical movement, and that concern with emergence and return provided the foundation for all of the intricate mythic thought of the high cultures of pre-Columbian Mesoamerica. For all of these peoples, then, human life existed in harmony with the seasonal cycles through which their sustenance was provided. And the figure of the goddess—the embodiment of the essentially feminine force of regeneration—as we might aptly call these simple figurines of the period known as the Preclassic (see Figure 6; Color Plates 1, 2, and 3; and Images 1, 2, and 3), is at the center of that mythic conception.

The recent excavations carried out by the French archaeologist Christine Niederberger at the site of Zohapilco have unearthed the data through which we can tentatively mark the beginning of the development of the fertility-related mythology in villages of the Basin of Mexico at about 6000 B.C. Those excavations took place on the eastern shore of the shallow freshwater lake that until Aztec times filled the southern part of the Basin, the remains of which today house the "floating gardens" of Xochimilco, a persistent reminder of the relationship of that fertile margin between lake and land and the intensive agriculture that had its beginnings there thousands of years earlier. The stratigraphy of Zohapilco reveals that settled communities occupied that lakefront site from as early as 6000 B.C., finding there an optimal ecological zone characterized by lush vegetation and abundant game and fish. Among the archaeological evidence of that natural bounty, Niederberger found the hunter's stone cutting tools fashioned by the earliest inhabitants. In the course of time, however, grinding tools related to food-plant preparation begin to appear, testifying to the growing diversity of the diet of these early settlers.

The archaeological evidence thus suggests that the environment encouraged a sedentary way of life based on the rhythmical change of the seasons well before the development of agriculture. Zohapilco may thus be seen as the beginning of the long history of settled life in the Basin of Mexico, a history that would include the great civilizations of Teotihuacan, the Toltecs, and the Aztecs as well as that of colonial and modern Mexico City. Because we know that both the Olmec and the Maya civilizations also developed in such estuarian zones, we may well regard the evidence of mythic thought at Zohapilco as typical of that which must have existed throughout Mesoamerica at this time of the dawning of the planting cultures. At Zohapilco, as in other areas of Mesoamerica, then, the foundation of the corn-based economies of all the subsequent periods of Mesoamerican development was being laid down.

Along with that gradual evolution of a sedentary way of life, ultimately to be related to agriculture, came the mythic structures consistent with such a way of life, structures remarkably similar to those developed elsewhere in the world under similar circumstances but retaining throughout their development a strong local inflection. The most significant later development at Zohapilco in this connection comes in the period from 3000 to 2200 B.C. During that time what Niederberger calls "a remarkable advance" occurred in the manufacture of stone grinding tools. And, of utmost importance to us, while no trace of ceramic vessels is yet to be seen, "One of the notable events of work in the large hearth area was the discovery in situ of a small baked-clay anthropomorphic figurine [Image 1], indicative of the existence of new conventions in plastic expression and of practices related to a set of beliefs."[2]

That figurine, the earliest so far discovered in Mesoamerica, was fashioned about 2300 B.C. to express the beliefs that linked its maker to the source both of human life and of the living food that sustained that life. That simple figurine marks for us the beginning of the long parade of mythological images—many of the later ones almost unbelievably elaborate—that would be created by the peoples of Mesoamerica until the time of the Conquest. While Niederberger points out that "it is difficult to find stylistic equivalents for it since it belongs to a cultural level which, until now, has scarcely been studied,"[3] even a cursory glance reveals instantaneously both the meaning carried by that highly symbolic little figure, with its rudimentary breasts and its bulging hips, and the line of development it would initiate. For that glance reveals that we are in the presence of the earliest image portraying the Mesoamerican vision of the great goddess mother of us all—a mythic image seemingly inevitably associated by planting cultures throughout the world with the fertility of the earth—and the ancestress of the bewildering array of earth goddesses that would be elaborated in the mythologies of the Mesoamerican high cultures.

Like the earliest female figurines from Old Europe, this image is, in Joseph Campbell's terms, "a conceived abstraction delivering a symbolic statement,"[4] and that statement equates the fertility of the female with the fertility of the earth and thus ultimately sees humanity as the child being nurtured by the earth in its role as the great mother. Marija Gimbutas points out in this connection that in Old Europe "caves and tombs [i.e., the entrances into the earth] are interchangeable with womb, egg, and uterus symbolism."[5] Both the human female and the female earth are thus seen as "the mystery vessel of life,"[6] the birth from which enables spirit to enter the world of nature.

It is surely no coincidence that such a figure would appear precisely in the midst of the evolution from one way of life based on gathering the existing bounty of nature to another based on human actions designed to bring that bounty from the earth. As we know from every shred of evidence left to us by archaic peoples, it was necessary that those actions be accompanied by ritual in order to be efficacious. This was required since, in archaic terms, agriculture was a spiritual enterprise whereby the sacred maternal earth provided sustenance for her children. Modern scholars, in their study of the development of our species, focus on the development of agriculture from a technical and scientific perspective, asking where corn, for example, was first hybridized, what its ancestors were, how that hybridization was accomplished, and how a way of life centered on agriculture came into existence. But archaic humanity, it is abundantly clear, focused rather on the miracle of rebirth through which the dead seed, invigorated by spiritual energy, sprouted anew. When that sprouting took place under human aegis, it was seen as an action that must be accompanied by the ritual that would recognize and reciprocate the spiritual energy that drove the cycle of regeneration. As the renowned historian of religions Mircea Eliade puts it, "Generation, death, and regeneration were understood as the three moments of one and the same mystery, and the entire spiritual effort of archaic man went to show that there must be no caesuras between these moments."[7] Thus life could be counted on not to end, for the life force was eternal.

Through the transformative process of regeneration manifested in the annual renewal of plant life, most notably in the growth of corn, the world of the spirit sustained mankind. Corn was mankind's proper sustenance, the very substance from which he was formed in the creation myths of Mesoamerica's high cultures. As Robert Bruce, an anthropologist who lived and worked among the Lacandones in the southernmost part of Mexico, reports, even today, much as it must have been in these earlier times, the basic cycle of time is not related as much to the sun or to human life,

> but [to] the corn, so inseparably linked with the life of the Mayas. The dry, apparently dead grains are buried in the spring. . . . The plants grow from tender, green youth to maturity and are then called to descend to their destiny in the shadows. The plants wither, they are "decapitated" or harvested, shelled, cooked, ground, and eaten—though a few grains are saved. . . . Then the cycle begins anew.[8]

Applied metaphorically to human life, the cyclical pattern of the growth of the corn, like the phases of the moon in its rising, dying, and self-renewing, promises the immortality of regeneration, a promise especially clear to the agricultural communities of pre-Columbian Mesoamerica, where "the milpa cycle runs many times during the lifetime of a man, which has the same characteristics." The cycle of the corn teaches the same lesson as all the cycles of nature: all that is to come has already been; "more correctly, 'it simply is' "[9] in the vast cyclic drama of the cosmos. For, as Marija Gimbutas points out, "immortality is secured through the innate forces of regeneration within nature itself."[10] Though this belief was later to be expressed in the almost incredibly elaborate mythic images of the high civilizations of Mesoamerica, it can be seen to have had its first expression in such simple forms as that female figurine of baked clay fashioned at Zohapilco. While we can have no idea, of course, of the precise nature of what Niederberger calls the "practices" related "to the set of beliefs" held by those who lived out their lives at Zohapilco, we surely know their general tenor.

As the sedentary way of life in the Basin became more directly tied to horticulture, and as the villages in which these horticulturists lived grew in size, the figurines that they created to express their fundamental mythology became finer, more complex, more varied, and much more abundant. Their ubiquity, in fact, has made the system into which they are classified the framework for our understanding of the archaeological history of the Basin. Before the remarkable discovery by Niederberger at Zohapilco, it had been thought that the earliest figurines were those known as the Cañitas type, simple, gingerbread-style female figures more detailed than the figurine of Zohapilco but with the eyes indicated by indentations in the same way, though here surrounded by a circle of small punctations, and the nose indicated, as at Zohapilco, by a vertical ridge dividing the face. The prominent feminine characteristics of these figurines, however, are their full breasts rather than the ample hips of the Zohapilco figure. Found at both Cuicuilco and Tlatilco, these are perhaps as old as 1600 B.C.

These Cañitas figurines gave way to what archaeologists term C-type figurines (see Figure 6) found at El Arbolillo, Zacatenco, and Tlatilco, which in turn led to an even more highly developed form, the D-type figurines (Color Plates 1 and 3, Image 2). To study these figurines we must now turn to the villages on or near the northwest shore of the lake in the Basin. Chief among these villages in size, wealth, complexity, and importance, as well as in the number of artifacts it has yielded, is Tlatilco. But it was as a cemetery rather than as a village that it was first discovered. In the 1930s workers digging clay in a brickyard near Mexico City began unearthing and selling to collectors fascinating objects buried with the dead of that very early village.

The people of Tlatilco who placed these objects in the graves of their loved ones were farmers who, following the way of life developed by their ancestors thousands of years earlier at the site of Zohapilco— perhaps half an hour from Tlatilco on today's roads—grew corn, squash, and chile and ate domesticated dogs as well as the deer, rabbits, ducks, and other waterfowl they hunted. Their dwellings and tools were simple, as was their way of life in an essentially household-based culture. But their art shows us the richness and beauty of their ritual life and the mythology it reflected as well as the simplicity of their daily lives. It is particularly intriguing that in the graves of Tlatilco women appear to have been the central figures, and they are accompanied by men and children who were sacrificed, apparently when the women died. These burial practices, coupled with the wealth of female figurines, point to the high status of women in the early village cultures.

But such an economic or political interpretation of the remains of the people of Tlatilco should not obscure the central mythological importance of the female principle, an importance evidenced by the mythic images accompanying the dead. We know that these people of Tlatilco were in contact with the Olmec because pottery and figurines of Olmec design are found in their graves side by side with forms indigenous to the Basin. However, the continuing existence of those indigenous forms testifies to the vitality of the mythological tradition they embody and express, a tradition dating at least from that simple figurine fashioned at Zohapilco. Thus, the high status of the female at Tlatilco suggests a relationship between fertility and social rank that continued even after contact with the male-dominated, aggressive Olmec culture, a complex urban culture that, as we shall see, related fertility and rulership in quite a different, more male-centered way.

Chief among the mythic images modeled by hand by the artists and artisans of Tlatilco, Zacatenco, and El Arbolillo—all villages on the northwestern shore of the lake in the Basin—were the C-type and D-type solid clay figurines. The earlier C-type figurines are always nude or nearly so, with features formed by punching holes in the clay or adding small strips and formed pieces to it. The figurines were often painted with red, black, and white designs to reproduce the designs of the body painting worn by the women of the villages. More elaborate than the Cañitas figurines and much more realistic than the Zohapilco figurine (Image 1), these female figures retain the exaggerated hips and the full breasts of the earlier prototypes and add to that preoccupation with fertility an occasional figurine holding a baby in her arms (Figure 6). It is in the D-type figurines (Image 2), however, that the art of the village cultures generally, and Tlatilco specifically, reaches the height of its development. These figures

FIGURE 6
A C-type female figurine

> are among the most beautiful objects of their size in all of the New World. . . . The small arms, wasp waists, inflated thighs, and tiny vestigial feet of these figures give them a charm which is matched by the sophistication of facial features. A curious feature of D1 and D4 faces is that the eyes are identical with the mouth—extremely narrow lenticular slashes in the clay, with a tiny central punctation carried out with the end of a thorn. . . . D4 figurines, the rarest and most valuable, have imaginatively treated bodies with greatly swollen thighs, wider and narrower eyes and mouth, and more use of post-fire polychroming.[11]

The majority are female with "young, shapely bodies" emphasizing full breasts, and many of them are clothed in ritual regalia of one sort or another, while others hold infants either straddled on the hip or in a cradle board, all of these features making clear the continuing emphasis on fertility.

Earlier, the Mexican artist and scholar Miguel Covarrubias, like most scholars who would follow him in studying the figurines of the Preclassic, had been fascinated by those figurines that had seemingly unnatural features, those with two heads or two noses, two mouths, and three eyes on a single head (Color Plate 1). He found these "reminiscent of certain paintings of Picasso,"[12] while Hasso von Winning later indicated that they might suggest twins or perhaps "represent a freak of nature which, because of its rarity, was endowed with magical properties."[13] Joseph Campbell, taking a more mythic view, suggests that the double-headed forms "may refer (as they do in Old Europe and the Ancient Near East) to the dual domination of the goddess in the worlds of the living and the dead (as Demeter and Persephone, Inanna and Ereshkigal)."[14] Each of these explanations, the artistic, the ethnographic, and the mythic, approaches the unnatural figurines on a different level, and each may well contain a germ of truth. Since our concern is that of the mythologist and since the graves of Tlatilco provide ample evidence, which we will discuss in the following section, to indicate that the people of that village were concerned with the complementarity of life and death, Campbell's interpretation is significant.

The Basin of Mexico, in its mythology and in its development, seems to have been typical of the Mesoamerican Preclassic. The village cultures here had their counterparts throughout the area, and those counterparts created similar figurines no doubt expressive of similar mythologies growing out of fundamentally similar mythological bases and essentially similar experiences. Speaking of similar female figurines from the westernmost portion of what came to be the area of the Maya, figurines created at La Victoria between 1500 and 1000 B.C. (Image 3), Coe says:

> Such objects were made by the thousands in many later Preclassic villages of both Mexico and the Maya area, and while nobody is exactly sure of their meaning, it is generally thought that they had something to do with the fertility of crops, in much the same way as did the Mother Goddess figurines of Neolithic and Bronze Age Europe. For the New World, the earliest appear by 3000 B.C. in Ecuador and it may be that those of Mesoamerica were ultimately derived from that direction.[15]

In this he echoes the earlier, often visionary, documentary historian Wigberto Jiménez Moreno, who wrote in 1958 that the nude figurines were probably related to fertility, leading to the conclusion that

> we could say of the Valley of Mexico, "In the beginning was the woman, the mother: the Mother Earth and the fruitful earth." In fact in the post-Toltec period ethnic groups of low cultural level, such as the Chichimecs of Xolotl, limited their religion to the worship of the "Sun Father" and the "Earth Mother." I suggest that in doing so, they were retaining forms of primitive stages of religious development. In other words, the Earth Goddess was of ancient origin, and her importance seems to have lasted until the Spanish conquest, when the Virgin of Guadalupe took her place. Thus, already at this time it appears that Mexico was incubating in the valley of its name under the symbol of the mother.[16]

Between them, Coe and Jiménez Moreno suggest both the antiquity and the universality of this figurine tradition representative of the great mother goddess on which was founded the magnificently profound mythological tradition to come in Mesoamerica. Although the narrative myths from this early time have not survived, the figurines of the goddess remain to "tell" the myth of transformation: of birth, death, and regeneration.

LIFE IN DEATH AND DEATH IN LIFE

In what seems a paradox, the graves of Tlatilco contained countless female figurines whose physical features emphasized the giving of birth and the nourishment of the newborn child, and in that emphasis they provided the perfect metaphor for the creation and sustenance of life within a shamanic mythic system that understands the cosmos as essentially spirit. Life, in that view, is but a transformation of spirit into matter, and the most obvious example of that transformation is the

⌇

birth of the human child, who emerges into the world of nature to be fed from the body of the woman who gave the child life. In human experience life comes into being, the spirit enters nature, only through the female. Thus it is particularly noteworthy that these female figurines at Tlatilco, although not always elsewhere, are found in great numbers in burials, placed there as a part of the ritual that marked the movement of the life force within the individual back to a union with the essence of that force in the world of the spirit. This placing of the body of a deceased family member or friend in a grave furnished with simple offerings and buried in an extended position with figurines that were "killed," or ritually broken, during the entombment is in itself telling evidence of the conception of an enchanted world of the spirit from which all life comes and to which it will return, of a life force separable from the body and the world of nature. Paradoxically, this life force is approached through death, which alone can "cause" rebirth.

Almost as if to make this symbolic statement about the nature of life as clear as possible, Tlatilco's graves contained both masks and figures revealing faces and bodies half-fleshed, half-skeletal (Image 4). These depict death within life as the correlative of the maternal figure's revelation in these graves of life within death. These seemingly contradictory references, to the moment of life's entrance into the world and the moment of its departure, give form to the mythological idea of the movement, in a variety of ways and for a variety of purposes, between the hidden, inner world of the spirit—the world imaged forth in the dreams of the night—and the visible, experiential world of nature perceived by the senses in the day. Significantly, this division into spirit and matter is characteristic of the shamanism brought over the Siberian land bridge tens of thousands of years earlier by the remote ancestors of these peoples of the village cultures. It is a division that focuses the attention of the believer on the movement of energy across the interface between those two forms of reality. The movement from spirit to nature is apparent in the birth and growth of animal and man, the growth of crops, the coming of the rains—that is, in all of the ways that the creation and maintenance of life can be seen in the world. And the movement in the other direction takes place through death, the harvest, and the dry fallow season. These countervailing movements, arranged as they are in cyclical progression, provided the basic rhythm of life for the agriculturists of the village cultures, and that rhythm can be felt in the objects they placed so carefully with their dead as one further assurance that through the familiar regenerative process death would necessarily be followed by life. That familiar process provided as well the most fundamental mythic structure of Mesoamerica, both in these early village cultures and in the high civilizations to come.

It is therefore both interesting and significant that at Tlatilco ritual masks appear often in burials, perhaps suggesting a conceptual relationship between ritual and funerary masks, a relationship that might well have been derived from the idea that the deceased was involved in the ritual movement from one state to another in a way very similar to the comparable movement of the shaman, whose "death" enabled him to travel to the world of the spirit. The type of mask found there that depicts a face half-fleshed and half-skeletal (Image 4) is a conception that can only represent this liminal state of the deceased in his movement from life to absorption in the spirit, "the land of the fleshless," as a much later Aztec poet called it, from which rebirth must come. This striking manifestation of the dualism at the heart of Mesoamerican thought can also be seen in a centuries-later, Classic period funerary figure from Soyaltepec, Oaxaca, which exhibits the identical motif (Color Plate 8) and thus indicates the persistence of this mythic view.

The Tlatilco mask and the Mixtec figure from Oaxaca, taken together, suggest a profound truth: the relatively simple mythological themes apparent in the art of the village cultures developed into the complex mythologies of the Classic period cultures that were to follow. Both embodied the fundamental conception of a world of the spirit—mysterious, inaccessible, and synonymous with the life force—which provided the counterpart to a world of nature that was inextricably involved with death. Permanence was to be found in that other world. This world offered only change culminating in death, which permitted entrance to the other, an entrance characterized in the high cultures as deification in the case of great leaders and culture heroes. In the last phase of autonomous indigenous thought before the cataclysm of the Conquest, that distinction was at the heart of a religious and philosophical genre of Aztec poetry. One Aztec poet addressing this theme wrote,

> Let us consider things as lent to us, O friends;
> only in passing are we here on earth;
> tomorrow or the day after,
> as your heart desires, Giver of Life,
> we shall go, my friends, to His home.[17]

The conclusion was inescapable that "somewhere else is the place of life."[18] Permanence was to be found in the world of the spirit; this world could offer only flux ending in death.

Thus, as the contents of the graves of Tlatilco make amazingly clear, at that crucial point of movement toward the development of the high cultures that were to exist in the Basin of Mexico, the peoples of Mesoamerica converted death into a passage to the essence of life. In this sense all of the imagery associated with death in both Mesoamerican myth and art—all the skulls, bones, and skeletal figures that were to follow those buried in the graves of Tlatilco—are emblematic not so much of death as of the essence and regeneration of life.[19] "The place of the fleshless, the region of mystery" is, after all, the home of the eternal life force. And in that realm, "in one way or another," according to the poet, life mysteriously continues.[20] But the awareness of this underlying unity of life and death never negated the awe with which the peoples of Mesoamerica viewed the mystery of death. That mystery suggested the sacred nature of the cycle which transcended earthly matters and made human beings aware of their contingent nature. "Life is but a mask worn on the face of death. And is death, then, but another mask? 'How many can say,' asks the Aztec poet, 'that there is, or is not, a truth beyond?'"

> *We merely dream, we only rise from a dream*
> *It is all as a dream.*[21]

Another poem from the same body of late Aztec poetry, however, using the metaphoric identification of flower and song with poetry itself, was able to lift the mask and find beneath it the assurance of "a truth beyond."

> *O friends, let us rejoice,*
> *let us embrace one another.*
> *We walk the flowering earth.*
> *Nothing can bring an end here*
> *to flowers and songs,*
> *they are perpetuated in the house*
> *of the Giver of Life.*[22]

The "story" buried in the graves of Tlatilco provides the same profound assurance.

But that assurance of life's renewal from the grave carried with it a sacred responsibility for the living. This responsibility arose from the mythic equation by which the giving of life by the world of the spirit required the reciprocal return of life from the world of nature. The symbol of that life to be returned was blood, and sacrificial blood flowed freely and abundantly throughout the history of Mesoamerica in the ceaseless struggle to keep the cycle of life in motion. Burials from as early as early as 6000 B.C. in the Tehuacan Valley suggest both ritual sacrifice and the ritual consumption of human flesh, which was to accompany that sacrifice until the moment of the Conquest. As the research data on this early period of Mesoamerican development accumulates, it is becoming more and more clear that the human sacrifice, as well as the ritual cannibalism that often accompanied it, so characteristic of the historic period of pre-Columbian Mesoamerica, was not a late innovation: evidence from the earliest times suggests that the later rituals had a very long tradition behind them, as might be expected among a planting people who saw death as a "cause" of life since it must precede regeneration in the cyclical process through which the body of the earth produced the food that nourished humanity. Through the sacrifice of blood and life that regeneration could be assured.

Human sacrifice also existed among the village cultures of the basin of Mexico, as the very early evidence from the Tehuacan Valley suggests it would. Several collective graves uncovered at Tlatilco hold a central skeleton and the remains of others presumably sacrificed in order to accompany that central personage. At another village-culture site near present-day Mexico City, Tlatelcomila, the Mexican archaeologist Rosa María Reyna Robles has excavated a large number of bones—both human and animal—that had been discarded with other refuse. Marks on the human bones provide evidence of ritual cannibalism, and one of the skulls shows relatively certain evidence of sacrifice in that two of the cervical vertebra remain attached to it, indicating ritual decapitation. This study also cites evidence for ritual cannibalism, presumably following sacrifice, at the Preclassic sites of Tlapacoya, a later site in the same locale as Zohapilco, and Tlatilco as well as at the even earlier site of Texcal, Puebla.[23]

Very late in the period of the village cultures in the nearby Valley of Teotihuacan, at about the same time that the first evidence of the construction of the monumental architecture characteristic of the later high civilization is apparent, there begin to appear curious figurines with absolutely smooth, featureless faces containing three indentations, one defining a mouth and the others two eyes (Figure 7). These faces are often ringed with a band and at times have another band stretched across the forehead, giving the impression of a mask, and in this case a very particular mask. Anyone familiar with the later art of the high cultures of central Mexico will see immediately in these figurines the portrayal of a ritual performer wearing what was known among the Aztecs as the mask of Xipe Totec, Our Lord the Flayed One, a "mask" that was the skin flayed from a sacrificial victim, then donned and pulled taut by the living performer, whose eyes and lips, in later representations, can be seen through the slits in the skin that had earlier revealed the eyes and mouth of the still-living victim (see Image 19). While there is a substantial distance in time and sophistication between the late Preclassic beginnings of Teotihuacan (ca. 100 B.C.) and the late Postclassic Aztec ritual celebrating Xipe Totec (ca. A.D. 1450), which we will consider below, the mythic images that have survived from the earlier times tell us that in this instance, as in many others, the mythology and the ritual life of the Aztecs grew out of the myths and rituals of the Preclassic.

FIGURE 7
Two tiny heads from ceramic figurines of Xipe Totec from early in the development of Teotihuacan

THE MASK AS METAPHOR

That late Preclassic mask of Xipe Totec found on the early figurines of the Valley of Teotihuacan is but one of many masks to be found among the remains of the village cultures. A number of actual ceramic masks were placed in the graves of Tlatilco alongside the figurines, and among these masks, the half-fleshed, half-skeletal type we have discussed above is but one variant. There are relatively realistic human faces, distorted faces, old men, animals, and grotesque masks combining features of man and animal. Though found in graves, where they were placed as part of the final ritual returning life to its source, these masks were first used in ritual dance, as the holes pierced on their sides to accommodate the twine that once held them in place over the dancer's face attest. Accompanying these masks into the graves are masked figurines (Figure 8), demonstrating that these small masks were worn covering the lower portion of the face of the ritualist and showing the other elements of ritual costume.

Partially on the basis of the early figurines, Kent Flannery, a scholar specializing in the earliest Mesoamerican cultures, has characterized very early Mesoamerican religious practice this way:

> It often seems that, for Early Formative Mesoamerica, there was only one religion. . . . It was a religion in which dancers, summoned by conch shell trumpets and accompanied by turtle shell drums, dressed in macaw plumes and equipped with gourd and armadillo shell rattles, performed in the disguises of mythical half-human, half-animal creatures. All this is suggested archaeologically; what eludes us is the underlying structure.[24]

But that elusive mythic structure can also be detected archaeologically, if only partially, for the practice of ritual masking carries with it certain fundamental mythic assumptions. Wherever and whenever the ritual mask is worn, it symbolizes not only particular gods, demons, animal companions, or spiritual states but also a particular relationship between matter and spirit, the natural and the supernatural, the visible and the invisible. The mask, a lifeless, material thing, is animated by the wearer, and this is, of course, precisely the relationship between men and the gods—human beings are created from lifeless matter by the animating force of the divine, and their life can continue only as long as it is supported by that divine force. Thus, in a striking reversal of inner and outer, the wearer of the ritual mask almost literally becomes the god—he is, for the ritual moment, the animating force within the otherwise lifeless mask, exactly the case, as we shall see below, with the wearer of the macabre "mask" of Xipe Totec.[25]

Those now-lifeless masks in the graves of Tlatilco, as well as the countless other masks of that early period and those that were to come in the later stages of the development of the mythological tradition of Mesoamerica, thus stand as a metaphor for a mythic view of reality that saw the world of nature as animated by a spiritual force manifesting itself in every instance of life in the world. That life force, which seems only to have begun to harden conceptually into "gods" at the moment of transition from the village culture to the civilizations of the urban cultures, provided the true reality for the peoples of Mesoamerica, since it alone was eternal, putting on "mask" after "mask" to show itself in the world of appearances.

FIGURE 8
A Tlatilco figurine representing a masked ritual figure

Those who wore the masks in ritual thus entered a liminal realm in which the reality of the temporal, mundane world was simultaneously juxtaposed to and fused with the timeless world of the spirit. In Mesoamerica that liminal realm was delimited by the mask, and in that realm the masked ritualist could conjure the reality of the world of the spirit. That masked ritual provides a marvelous example of symbolic anthropologist Victor Turner's definition of metaphor "as a means of effecting instantaneous fusion of two separated realms of experience into one illuminating, iconic, encapsulating image."[26] At the same time, it makes clear that these ritualists not only illustrated the meaning of the metaphor but themselves underwent the very experience of metaphor in the unification of spirit and matter. For them, the spiritual vision rather than that of day-to-day living was true, because only that vision could capture the full nature of reality in both its material and spiritual aspects. Throughout Mesoamerica it was through the agency of the mask that man entered the liminal zone of "no-time and no-place" where the essence of the world of the spirit could become manifest. In that liminal masquerade he played his part in the transformational drama through which the material world was infused with spirit, and life was enabled to continue. The ritual mask, then, was simultaneously the instrument of the liminal and the metaphor for the liminal fusion of spirit and matter. A mythological "story" dwelt within its metaphoric features, and the mask itself stood as a metaphor for the idea of the inner spiritual reality of human beings and the cosmos becoming "outer" as spirit manifested itself in the world.

This profound mythic truth underlies those simple ceramic masks placed reverently in the graves of Tlatilco by the new generation of dancers as they buried the older in recognition of the fact that man and mask, dancer and dance had become one. One is inevitably reminded of William Butler Yeats's equation of matter and spirit through art in "Among School Children":

> O body swayed to music, O brightening glance,
> How can we know the dancer from the dance?

FIRE AND ETERNITY

One important mythic image originating in the village cultures of the Basin of Mexico remains to be explored, and fittingly, it ties together all of the mythic themes we have so far enumerated. By the late Preclassic at Cuicuilco and at Ticoman, and perhaps slightly earlier in the graves of Tlatilco, curious ceramic figures representing seated, hunched-over old men with wrinkled, toothless faces bearing large braziers on their backs had begun to appear (Image 5). As the urban culture of nearby Teotihuacan developed, these early figures were replicated again and again in carved stone (see Figure 12). This seated figure was later known by the Aztecs as Huehueteotl, if his aged character was to be emphasized, or as Xiuhtecuhtli, if his connection with fire was paramount. He is the oldest god recognizable in the artifacts remaining from the early cultures of the Basin of Mexico. It seems fitting that a god of fire would be born in an area and time of great volcanic activity.

In fact, Cuicuilco, the provenance of most of the early images of the god, was soon to be intimately associated with volcanic activity, as it was destroyed some time around A.D. 100 by the eruption of a young volcano, Xitle, which first spewed dust and ashes and then poured great quantities of molten lava over Cuicuilco and the surrounding area. Such an eruption would obviously have overwhelming mythic implications for a people with a shamanic worldview. As we have seen, that worldview understands nature as enveloped by spirit with the earthly plane existing between planes of spirit above and below. Thus the volcanic fire would have been seen as a spiritual emanation in the same way that the seed sprouting from the earth or water flowing from a spring was understood as spirit entering nature from the "heart" of the earth. We in the twentieth century think with horror of the material destruction of volcanic activity, as did the fleeing inhabitants of Cuicuilco, no doubt, but how much greater must have been their horror when they saw the cataclysmic death and destruction as emanating from the world of the spirit, the source of all life.

The painful lesson must clearly have been that the spirit that gives life also destroys it, and that man must somehow fit his life to that terrible rhythm so spectacularly illustrated by fire belching from the unstable earth. From this simple insight the high cultures would eventually elaborate complex calendrical orderings of that rhythm, thereby seeing earthly life as involved in a sequence of creations and destructions. All reality was perceived as cyclical: the days, the "months," the years, the fifty-two-year "centuries," and the eons. And at the center of that intricate calendrical thought was to be seen Xiuhtecuhtli in his manifestation as the Lord of Time, the driving force behind the cyclical movement, the still center of the turning universe (Color Plate 6, Image 15).

To understand the Preclassic village culture basis of that later mythic conception, we must think briefly about fire as those villagers would have experienced it. The fire of volcanic activity was clearly a highly unusual occurrence, one most villagers would never themselves experience. But another fire, the fire of the hearth, was not only a daily experience but also one around which their lives were necessarily built. With our central heating, electric lighting, and modern ranges, we may find it difficult to appreciate immediately the centrality of the hearth and its fire to people who lacked those modern conveniences. To such a people fire must have meant life. It warmed their bodies, cooked their meals, and provided the only light when the sun, the "fire" of the daytime sky, departed on its underworld course. Their lives revolved around the hearth. For that reason, no doubt, even among the Aztecs in the last phase of autonomous Mesoamerican culture, the fire in the hearth was the center of household ritual, which was particularly concerned with offerings of food and drink to the deity manifested by that fire, and one of the most sacred duties of the priest was to keep the eternal flame burning in the temple consecrated to the god. But one suspects that for the earliest of the village cultures, there was no named and conceptualized deity; the fire itself was a manifestation of the spirit—beneficial in its domestic form, striking terror in its volcanic form, perhaps evoking a greater terror than did the thunderbolts of Zeus half a world away.

It is not surprising, then, that the deity associated with that fire was the first to appear in the conceptual development of named deities. These deities represented the fluid and omnipresent aspects of the world of the spirit that, until then, had not hardened into the fixed concepts that would be known by the conquerors and modern scholars as "gods." And the appearance of that male god signals the fundamental change in the mythology of Mesoamerica that would accompany the development of urban culture. It is therefore particularly fitting that the bearer of the brazier of the village cultures was the god of fire conceived as the god of age, of the last phase of the cycle of life. The dual reference to matter's becoming spirit links that metamorphosis to the underlying concern we have seen with fertility, whereby the life force enters nature through birth, and death, whereby that force leaves nature only to return again through birth in the cyclical rhythm of all life. Thus the old god bearing the brazier has the features of the last stage of life, with their implications of mortality, and those symbolic lines and wrinkles point beyond the grave to the permanence of the cycle within which human beings live their lives.

Two things are clear. First, fire was seen as central to an understanding and rendering of the mystery of the spiritual plane of reality, which was constantly creating and upholding the contingent reality of nature, perhaps because fire so obviously "dematerialized" natural things, perhaps because life is characterized by warmth, perhaps because the fiery sun ruled the heavens, or perhaps for all these reasons. Second, that conception was ancient, as its manifestation in the village cultures attests. On that ancient base the high cultures built an imposing edifice of shape-shifting masked gods, but the essential conception never changed. As the geometric figures decorating the sides of those braziers indicate, this conception was an integral part of the identity of Huehueteotl/Xiuhtecuhtli, and it was, we would argue, a conception rooted in the cyclical perceptions of the seers and artists of the village cultures, whose mythology is wonderfully expressed in the works of art they have left us. The fire of Xiuhtecuhtli lit the darkness, both literally and figuratively, for them, and through the offerings they placed in their graves that fire can shine again, illuminating the vast darkness of the past as well as the darkness within each of us.

THE MYTHIC IMAGES

IMAGE 1

THE FLAYED GOD

The First Figurine: The Goddess of Zohapilco

Christine Niederberger, the archaeologist who discovered this small, baked-clay, anthropomorphic figurine in the large hearth area of Zohapilco, describes the magnificently abstract piece in this way: "The head and body form a single armless shaft. The incipient contour that defines the forehead forms a T with the line of the prominent arched nose. Four depressions, which presumably represent the eyes, make up most of the mouthless face."[27] The rudimentary breasts and slightly bulging hips identify the figurine clearly with the fertility of the earth and with the countless number of figurines to follow her in the development of Mesoamerican mythic thought and art.

On the basis of the radiocarbon analysis of charcoal fragments found in close proximity to the figurine, Niederberger concludes that it was probably fashioned about 2300 B.C., making it the earliest figurine yet found in an archaeological context in Mesoamerica. Scientific analyses of the paste that was used to form the figurine reveal that it was made at the site itself, and according to Niederberger, the quality of the paste is indicative of developed techniques for "the selection, preparation, and firing of the clay."

Niederberger concludes from her research at this and other Preceramic and Preclassic sites that this figurine was "indicative of the existence of new conventions in plastic expression and of practices related to a set of beliefs." Thus it is extremely significant to this study of myths in Mesoamerica, for this tiny figurine marks the inception of a long line of mythic images associated with fertility. She is the first of the multitudinous earth-mother goddesses to come, and "the practices related to a set of beliefs" are the forerunners of all the complex and profound rituals that would be devoted to these mythic figures. The "set of beliefs" is, in short, the Mesoamerican mythic vision to which this study is dedicated.

The Goddess as Mother: A D-1 Figurine from Tlatilco

Speaking of the Upper Paleolithic period of Europe, Alexander Marshack makes the fascinating point that the repertoire of images found there "suggests a storied, mythological, time-factored, seasonal, ceremonial and ritual use . . . of images." He goes on to say that "while the art was sometimes 'realistic,' it was always storied and, while it was sometimes abstract and symbolic, it had even then references to a core of observation and cognition."[28] Although the Tlatilco figure that we see here is from a time very much later than that of those images Marshack is discussing and from a place half a world away, we can see that his observation that "every process recognized and used in human culture becomes a story, and every story is an event which includes characters,"[29] provides as valuable an angle of vision for our appreciation of this charming terracotta figurine as it did for the earlier pieces he discussed.

This "pretty lady," as these figurines are called by archaeologists, is from the Preclassic village of Tlatilco, located on the northwest outskirts of what is now Mexico City, a village whose name fittingly means "where things are hidden." But she is much more than just another "pretty lady." In Marshack's terminology, she is "storied," and her story is the elemental tale of fertility and motherhood told in feminine images. That story is articulated by her nude body, with its exposed vulva and exaggerated thighs, and by the child she carries on her back. Like thousands of others, this beautifully wrought figurine was found in a burial uncovered and looted at Tlatilco by workers digging clay for the making of bricks. Although we cannot be sure of the original function of these figurines, it seems likely that they were buried with the dead in order to extend the fundamental conception of fertility and rebirth into human life.

This particular figurine is an example of what is known as a D-1 type figurine, which Michael Coe, who has studied their development in detail, claims "are among the most beautiful objects of their size in all of the New World."[30] This one, like all of the other Tlatilco figurines, was fashioned by hand, with small fillets or strips formed with the fingers added to the body and head; maguey thorns were used to imprint additional details. After the firing, color pigments were added in the fashion of body painting.

We must realize, however, that this is not merely another pretty piece of ceramic unearthed by a looter and catalogued by an archaeologist; surely what we see here is the miracle of the feminine in all of its glorious generative and regenerative potential. Is it any wonder that the people of Tlatilco found it essential to bury such pieces with the dead in order to assure their rebirth? The "story" they told gave the promise that the life force was eternal.

The Pregnant Goddess: A Figurine from Copalche, Guatemala

This figurine from the Las Charcas Phase of the Preclassic period in Guatemala (ca. 800–500 B.C.), probably from Copalche, is another magnificent illustration of Alexander Marshack's comment that "every process recognized and used in human culture becomes a story."[31] This one tells the story of the mystery of the womb, of the renewal of life. The creator of this piece told that story by focusing on the woman's pregnancy through the placement of her hands on her swollen abdomen and by exposing her breasts under the short garment she wears over her shoulders. Each pierced in the center to specify the nipples, the breasts are clearly the source of sustenance for the child who is to come. But as that artist would surely have known and as we must remember, this is the mother goddess, and the child she carries within her represents all of the life in the world of nature that the goddess creates and nurtures.

The figurine presented here is typical of those from Las Charcas Phase sites, with its well-defined grooves marking the eyes and in each eye a single central punctation to indicate the pupil. The nose is broad and wedge shaped, with the hair emphasized by an ornament at the center of the head. Albert Kidder, an archaeologist working at these sites, tells us that he never recovered "the whole or even most parts of any one figurine. . . . Pieces of broken ones seem simply to have been thrown on the rubbish that accumulated from day to day. . . . It is generally and probably correctly believed that they played a part in some cult, presumably of fertility, as they so often depict females, generally pregnant."[32] But through these common features and despite the fact that only half of this figure remains, nobility and pride are expressed here, a feeling of strength and endurance that is communicated even to us, far removed in time and culture as we are from those to whom this goddess brought the blessings of the fertility she symbolized.

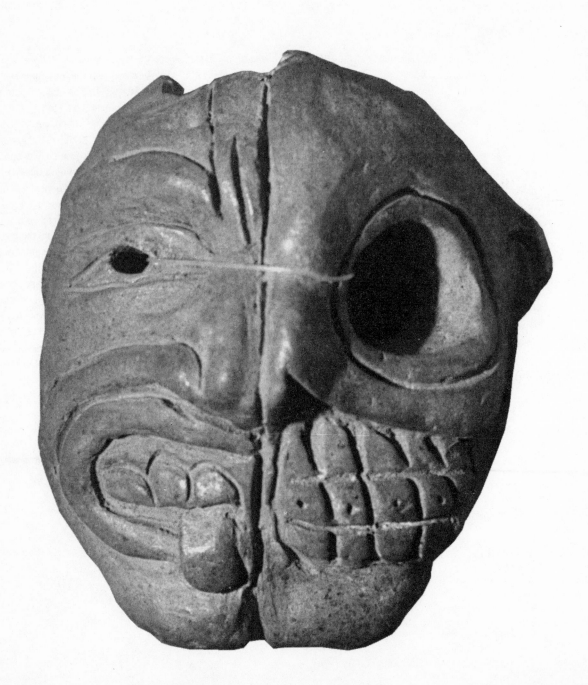

The Mask of Life and Death: A Ceramic Mask from Tlatilco

This is one of many masks found interred with the dead at Tlatilco. Although its striking features are not typical of all of the clay masks found at that site, it does have the circular, convex shape of the others, and the "life side," with its staring eye, manifests the often-seen tongue protruding from the lower part of the mouth. These were ritual masks, as can be seen by the holes pierced in them that allowed them to be attached to the lower part of a ritual dancer's face in the manner shown on the masked figurines also found in Tlatilco graves (see Figure 8).

In the much later creation myths of the Aztecs, in the "beginning" was the creative principle or supreme celestial being known as "the Lord of Duality," Ometeotl, who was at the source of all creation. He/she was the lord of all beings, the one who embodied and dominated the contrary forces of the cosmos. He/she encompassed all dualities, including those of masculine and feminine, life and death, and spirit and matter. When we realize that his/her abode was in the place of duality, the thirteenth heaven that rose above all the other heavens (Image 8), we can begin to understand the absolutely seminal role that the concept of duality played in the philosophic underpinnings of Mesoamerican cosmogonic thought. But this duality did not simply involve two aspects of a basic view of reality; instead, it usually involved two contradictory values juxtaposed to each other and existing simultaneously in a symbiotic relationship. It is the essence of this sophisticated and complex view of reality that we find already epitomized in this clay mask from the early village of Tlatilco.

With this portrayal of the juxtaposition of life and death worn over a man's face in ritual, the viewer of the ritual would *experience* the realization that death is an essential part of life and that life comes from death; that same realization would be expressed throughout the centuries of the development of the mythic art of pre-Conquest Mesoamerica. This pottery mask interred in a Tlatilco grave is a marvelously simple statement of that idea, which culminated centuries later in such pieces as the magnificently complex statue of Coatlicue and the more famous "mask" of life and death found at Soyaltepec, near Monte Alban (Color Plate 8). Skulls juxtaposed to the symbols of life are ubiquitous reminders in Mesoamerican art of this basic duality and of the need for death to exist, not alone, but in the presence of life.

Cuicuilco's Old God of Fire

Cuicuilco, the site of a small Preclassic urban center and the first pyramid in the Basin of Mexico, was built on the southern outskirts of what is now Mexico City. The small city and its people flourished there until about 100 A.D., when the eruption of the volcano Xitle ended its prosperity. The inhabitants who survived fled to new homes, leaving the area abandoned and the structures, until our time, concealed by lava. The pyramid is one of the most ancient and interesting in Mesoamerica since it is constructed of a stair-shaped series of circular earthen platforms, later covered by similar platforms of uncut stone, and built on a large circular base with a ramp leading up to the temple at its top. Using heavy stone to face the clay made it possible to build wider circular-stepped bases to support temples at the top—an important innovation and an architectural concept that became basic to all Mesoamerican ceremonial architecture. It is from this area of innovative architecture and volcanic devastation that this simple but superb incense burner in the form of the old god of fire comes.

As we explain in the Introduction to Part II, and further in "The Myths of Creation," this fire god embodied the most essential features of Mesoamerican myth and spirituality. One of the oldest gods, he was the god known as Xiuhtecuhtli when related to fire and as Huehueteotl when his aged characteristics were being emphasized. His great significance is suggested by the fact that he originally raised the four trees to hold up the sky and by the fact that he presides over the birth of the sun.

In this very early depiction of the god found at Cuicuilco, he lacks the symbol of the quincunx that at times accompanies him (see Image 13), identifying him with the four directions and suggesting his role at the center of the life force. Bent over, with the wrinkles that mark his advanced age, he is presented here with his characteristic brazier on his back, the vessel that holds the transformative fire that he represents. It is fascinating to realize that for fifteen hundred years his images continued to manifest precisely the same attributes depicted here, up to the moment of the Conquest, as can be seen from the Teotihuacan and Aztec representations of the god sculpted in stone (see Figures 12 and 18), images iconographically identical to this early ceramic figure.

III

OF TIME, SPACE, AND EARTH

THE MYTHOLOGY OF THE URBAN TRADITION

As we have seen, the fragmentary remains from which we can reconstruct the basic mythic structures of the relatively simple village cultures of the Mesoamerican tradition suggest a comparably simple mythology concentrating on fertility and the cycle of life and death as it manifested itself in the lives of human beings and of the plants and animals that sustained them. From that simple beginning, however, grew a complex, profound, endlessly fascinating mythology, a mythology on which was constructed one of the world's great systems of spiritual thought—the mythology of the urban cultures of Mesoamerica: that of the Olmecs and of those cultures that developed from the Olmec catalyst in the Valley of Oaxaca, in the Basin of Mexico, in the Maya area, and along the Veracruz coast (see Maps 2–7). The complexity of that mythic tradition is most apparent in the pictographic and written sources that date from the final periods of its development, but the evidence we have from the mythic art of earlier times—going as far back as the Olmec—suggests, when viewed in the light of these later sources, that the basic mythological structures came into being very early in the development of the urban tradition in Mesoamerican civilization.

In the Mesoamerican tradition, as in the mythological tradition of every civilization, cosmogonical and cosmological myths embody the sacred history of the people. They reveal the essence of the way this particular people understood the meaning of human life and its relationship to the universe, to time and space, and most importantly to absolute reality, the mystery dimension of life that is ultimately unknowable because it lies beyond the range of conscious human conception. In an attempt to answer the primary philosophical questions regarding the nature of that absolute reality, myths furnish the culture with a "logical" model by means of which the human mind can comprehend and even celebrate the ambiguities and paradoxes of human experience. The cosmogonical myths—those that delineate the creation of things and therefore suggest their basic nature—tell of the transformation accomplished by the primordial source, the creator, the life force. And because the way to understanding the spiritual or invisible can only be through the material or visible, the cosmological myths—those that set forth the sacred order of things—link the transcendent, that which is universally, eternally true, with the immanent, that which is specifically, factually true in a particular time and place.

This joining, of course, is the function of metaphor, the vehicle through which the inexpressible can find expression and the means by which man can achieve an instantaneous fusion of the realms of nature and spirit in a single illuminating image. If we are to understand the meaning of a culture's myths, we must see them in this light. They are a metaphoric, sacred history that cannot be understood literally. As metaphors they will be seen to involve multiple layers of meaning existing simultaneously; they will manifest a multivocality suggesting finally that the structure, the hidden system itself, is the "meaning" of the myth, the final locus of the sacred. Thus it is only through that mythic structure, expressed in metaphor, that such varied aspects of observable reality as stars, the sun and the moon, and the cycles of time can be seen in their spiritual aspect as gods or aspects of the life force, that is, as manifestations of the realm of the spirit. The concrete, objective terms of the myths are simply a means—the only means—to an understanding of the true sacred reality, and it is in their metaphorical quality that they are universal.

They are universal in another sense as well, because the time of myth is *always;* it is past, present, and future. David Carrasco, for example, points out that in the codices of Mesoamerica one discovers a very clear relationship "between ancient and mythic events and future or prophetic events. . . . We see the focus on sequences of events, loaded with sacred meanings, that were set in motion in a remembered past, are enacted in the present, and will lead toward an expected repetition in the future."[1] When seen in a sacred manner and thus truly understood, time devolves into eternity. Thomas Mann, in his prelude to *Joseph and His Brothers,* takes us into the world of the myth, articulating this implication of timeless universality: "Very deep is the well of the past. Should we not call it bottomless?" Thus he begins, adding finally: "For it *is,* always *is,* however much we may say It was. Thus speaks the myth, which is only the garment of the mystery."[2]

For this reason, more than any other, myths are valuable not only to the people whose stories they are but also to all of us, because they allow us to ask those same ultimate questions that our predecessors asked and that those who come after us will of necessity also ask: Who are we? What is our relationship to the cosmos? to the life force? to the flow of time? Only questions of that order can take us, finally, beyond the pairs of opposites to the ultimate singularity of the mystery of life and thus link human existence to the order of the cosmos. Jamake Highwater, in an allusion to Plato's cave, articulates this ability: "Through the sensual and metaphoric transformation of a reality composed of shadows they are able, at least momentarily, to allude to the fire."[3]

Although the Mesoamerican myths of the spirit share a number of features with other mythologies, in one very important characteristic they are virtually unique, comparable only in some respects to the mythological tradition of India. At the foundation of the mythology of the urban cultures of Mesoamerica there is not, in the way of Greek mythology, for example, a formal pantheon of gods who control the forces of nature and of human destiny and who were thought to be agents of a higher divine being. Nor was there any notion of a god who could have any "real" relationship with mortal flesh. While they are often imaged forth anthropomorphically as ritual performers, sometimes "disguised" in animal form with animal features, Mesoamerican gods were imagined as invisible forces of the realm of the spirit.

Even though there is a fundamental connection between natural forces and the gods in Mesoamerica, it is important to realize that the relationship was far closer than has often been thought. Though frequently characterized as gods, that is to say, intermediaries between the essence of the life force and the countless living things in the world of nature, in Mesoamerica they seem to be more precisely the spiritual components of the natural forces themselves. The names of the gods are often no more than the names of those forces. There is often no intermediate stage. And the same holds true for such more abstract conceptions as the creative spirit and the patrons of rulership. The "god" in each case is an aspect of the realm of the spirit, and "the closer one searches for a personal identity so vividly displayed by the anthropomorphic deities of the Mediterranean world, the more evanescent and immaterial they become, dissolved in mists of allusion and allegory with which . . . poets and sculptors expressed their sense of the miraculous in the world about them." For such artists of the spirit "the world was perceived as being magically charged, inherently alive" with the essence of spirit, and all "transitory phenomena had the capacity to manifest some aspect of the sacred."[4] As Gerard Manley Hopkins wrote in "God's Grandeur," a masterpiece of the mythic art of his own tradition,

> The world is charged with the grandeur of God.
> It will flame out, like shining from shook foil.

Adding to the complexity of the Mesoamerican conception of the gods, most of the major gods were conceived within a structure that placed them simultaneously in oppositional and complementary positions in respect to each other, each defining their particular "reality" in terms of the others. In addition, they often manifested opposing characteristics within themselves, being both masculine and feminine, having both benevolent and malevolent aspects, manifesting both youth and age, or having apparently opposed functions.

As Joseph Campbell put it, "In all mythology, the several aspects of the divinity may separate into independent personages."[5] In Mesoamerica that separation of the several aspects of the divinity into separate manifestations has been characterized as an unfolding of the divine essence into the created world, where it is apprehended by humanity as a spectrum of life forces. Eva Hunt suggests that for the peoples of Mesoamerica, "reality, nature, and experience were nothing but multiple manifestations of a single unity of being. God was *both* the one and the many. Thus the deities were but his multiple personifications, his partial unfoldings into perceptible experience."[6] This conception is particularly clear in the creation myths that we will present below, but it is implicit and fundamental in all the myths. We can see, for example, that the Aztec Ometeotl, called "our mother, our father," a god who is simultaneously the one, the two, the four, and the many, represents the unity of the divine essence from which the "opposed" forces of male and female mysteriously unfold to create a world in their image, a world that is, in a sense, a manifestation of Ometeotl on the level of human reality. It is a creation metaphorically likened to birth through its use of the human process of reproduction, but now manifesting the self-transformation of an originally undifferentiated, all-generating divine substance. Thus the "natural" fact of procreation through the uniting of the opposed sexes reveals, when read "spiritually," the essence of creativity in the sacred realm of the spirit.

The various aspects of the prime source separate into independent personages, each representing various abstractions and natural phenomena as well as various aspects of the same phenomenon, such as Tezcatlipoca, who mysteriously "unfolds" from Ometeotl, the ultimate ground of being, and is at once unitary, dual, and quadripartite.[7] Ometeotl, then, is the imaging forth of the godhead in a curiously abstract sense. No idols were made of this figure, nor was he/she the focus of ritual activity. Tezcatlipoca, on the other hand, while having many of the same functions as Ometeotl and even being designated by many of the same names, existed on a less abstract level and was thus more accessible. His image appears often in religious art, and he was impersonated in ritual and addressed in prayer. In the same way, the black Tezcatlipoca is a manifestation of the Tezcatlipoca essence on still another level. Each unfolding of the divine essence thereby creates another level of spiritual being, and each succeeding level is somewhat more accessible to humanity through ritual. Thus, all of these so-called gods are ultimately manifestations of a single divine essence, "personifications," in a sense, of the impersonal forces of the universe rather than having the wholly independent existence that the idea of a "god" often suggests.

In this way the process of unfolding generates an enormously complex system, one that is often difficult for us to comprehend. We are puzzled when one god seems to have become another right before our eyes or when a single god suddenly becomes four. But an understanding of this process of "unfolding" allows us to understand the continuum of divine beings, linked together in a pattern of transfigurations, that makes up the system of Mesoamerican gods. Ultimately, this state of kaleidoscopic change is not as bewildering as it at first appears, because it is governed by the constancy of the divine essence or spirit that manifests itself through each of the transformations of the unfolding process. Once we understand that this wondrous display of seemingly separate gods is really a depiction of the *process* through which the world of the spirit continuously manifests itself, we can begin to understand and appreciate the beauty and profundity of the Mesoamerican mythic vision. The vast complexity becomes profound simplicity when we realize that for the seers of Mesoamerica who elaborated this marvelous system, all observed reality, all the gods and spiritual forces, are finally manifestations on various planes of "reality" of the unitary essence of all being that is complete in and of itself.

But while the profound depth of the Mesoamerican system of mythic thought can be seen in its final supposition of an overarching spiritual unity, the seemingly endless fascinating enchantment of the manifestations of this unity are to be seen in the myths themselves, filled as they are with the multiplicity of the world in which we live. Turning from fundamental assumptions to the myths themselves, we will present, in turn, the myths of creation, the myths of fertility, and the myths of rulership. These are not merely arbitrary categories or handy themes. Rather, they present the movement from the original and constant unity of the spirit into the multiplicity of this temporal world in three stages. First, the "original" transformation of the one into the many can be seen in the myths of creation. Second, the "eternal" processes of the world of nature through which the cycle of life must move, the cyclical processes of the rebirth of life on all levels, is depicted in the myths of fertility. Finally, the movement of the spirit into history, into the world of the state, is characterized in the myths of rulership.

IV

THE FOURFOLD UNFOLDING

THE MYTHS OF CREATION

INTRODUCTION

The creation myths of the Classic period cultures of Mesoamerica, like the origin myths of other peoples, delineate metaphorically the process by which the One becomes the Many, by which the original unity existing *in illo tempore* becomes the present multiplicity. They account for the world's coming to be what it is and explain why mankind is mortal and forced to procreate, till the soil, and sacrifice in order to survive. In the myths telling of the procession of the eras or "suns" preceding this one, we are given not only an account of a mythical past time but also an explanation of the nature of the present world in which humanity exists. By realizing the basic patterns embodied in the creation myths of a people, as Mircea Eliade points out, we can understand their view of the principles "which govern the cosmic process and human existence. . . . [The myth] unveils the structures of reality and of their own proper mode of being. What happened in the beginning describes at once both the original perfection and the destiny of each individual"[1] within the culture.

And there is no structure more fundamental to the Mesoamerican worldview than the basic duality at the core of the created world, a duality that separates that world into such pairs of opposites as light and darkness, male and female, inner and outer, above and below. As perceived in Mesoamerica, however, this is a duality in which the pairs of opposites are ironically considered simultaneously contrary and complementary. And, perhaps even more ironically, it is a duality "doubled," as all of reality finally resolves itself into a quadriplicity that is often, if not always, a duality constructed of pairs of paired opposites unfolding from, and revolving around, a central unity.

The Mesoamerican tales of the creation of the world, of humanity, and of the world's various natural phenomena are preserved for us primarily in the mythologies of the Maya and the Aztecs, since what must have been an extensive mythology of the peoples of the Valley of Oaxaca and of coastal Veracruz has been, for the most part, irretrievably lost. The remaining Aztec material is the most detailed and extensive, perhaps because there was more interest in recording the Aztec myths by the Spanish immediately after the Conquest than there was in recording those of the Maya. It is also true that the older, more sophisticated Maya civilization of the Classic period had almost completely disappeared by then, whereas the Aztecs preserved more fully the legacy of their Classic period predecessors in the Basin of Mexico.

Although the remaining creation myths from the land of the Maya and the Basin of Mexico as well as the fragments from the Valley of

Oaxaca are clearly parts of a single mythological tradition, their essential unity may not always be immediately clear to a reader. Their apparent diversity has at least two causes: first, there are many variations in specific details and in the sequence in which the specific details of any given myth are presented as that myth appears in different sources. Names of gods and humans, places, and even specific actions change while the underlying pattern remains the same. Second, the various creation myths allude to different stages of creation, for creation in the mythology of Mesoamerica is a lengthy, often convoluted process rather than an event, and the relationship among the stages as they appear in variant myths is not always easily perceived beneath the superficial differences.

Resolving this surface confusion is possible through an understanding of the complex, repetitive patterns and philosophical assumptions, the "deep structure," that underlies all of the variants. Through that understanding we may come to comprehend the essence of Mesoamerican mythological thought. Then, and only then, can we put into perspective the myriad superficial details that were the inevitable result of each group's modifications of the basic metaphors of the tradition.

THE ORIGINAL UNITY

Among the Aztecs of the Basin of Mexico at the time of the Conquest, "perhaps evolving out of the sun and earth cults, the belief in an all-begetting Father and a universal Mother, as a supreme dual deity, came into being. Without losing his unity in that the ancient hymns always invoke him in the singular, this deity was known as Ometeotl, 'The Dual God,' He and She of our Flesh, Tonacatecuhtli and Tonacacihuatl, who in a mysterious cosmic coition originated all that exists."[2] The simultaneous unity and duality of Ometeotl are of the same order of mystery as the Christian Trinity; the obvious difference between the two can be seen in the Mesoamerican use of the natural sexual metaphor of the union of the two sexes in one creative being. Such a union suggests the basic nature of the duality at the heart of Mesoamerican thought; it is always the duality of the cyclical, regenerative forces of the natural world. Male and female are "opposed" forces merging to create life.

That this metaphor implied a continuous and therefore cyclic "act" of creation is perhaps most clearly seen in the words addressed by Aztec midwives to newborn children: "Thy beloved father, the master, the lord of the near, of the nigh, the creator of men, the maker of men, hath sent thee; thou hast come to reach the earth."[3] Known as "Our Mother, Our Father," "Giver of Life," "Lord of Everywhere," and "He and She of Our Flesh," Ometeotl was the self-created life force, eternally creating, ordering, and sustaining the world. There could be no visual image of this supreme dual deity, because it was in actuality the undifferentiated numinous, generative force diffused throughout the universe rather than a "god" whose existence could be separated from his creation. Fittingly, its place was Omeyocan, the place of duality, the thirteenth heaven, which rose majestically above all the other heavens (Image 8).

In a mysterious way Ometeotl also existed as Tezcatlipoca, "Smoking Mirror," the all-powerful god of the Aztecs who, unlike Ometeotl, could be depicted in mythic images and addressed in ritual. But just as Ometeotl, the ultimate ground of being, is at once unitary and dual, similarly Tezcatlipoca is mysteriously unitary, dual, and quadripartite. As half of a duality, Tezcatlipoca, "Smoking Mirror," finds his opposite in Tezcatlanextia, "Mirror Which Illumines." Tezcatlipoca is thus associated with the night, with its obscured vision, while Tezcatlanextia is linked to the day, illumined by the sun. The fact that "Tezcatlipoca and Tezcatlanextia . . . constituted a double title for Ometeotl in the remotest times of Nahuatl culture"[4] makes clear the nature of the process we have characterized earlier as unfolding. Tezcatlipoca is both created by and identical to Ometeotl. He is a manifestation of the divine essence characterized as Ometeotl on another plane. Significantly, perhaps, the Ometeotl duality uses the union of the male and female as its metaphor for creativity, while the Tezcatlipoca duality uses the union of day and night. These are, of course, the two clearest manifestations of cyclical rebirth in human life.

The unfolding continues. According to the *Historia de los Mexicanos por sus Pinturas,* Ometeotl and Omecihuatl (the female aspect of Ometeotl), known in that account as Tonacatecuhtli and Tonacacihuatl, begot four sons, each an aspect of Tezcatlipoca. Thus each of the four deities who unfold from him share with him the creativity characteristic of Ometeotl; together they constitute the cosmic powers necessary for the world to exist. These four gods, each of whom exalted himself over the others by assuming, in sequence, the role of the sun, another manifestation of the creative essence of the cosmos, are the red Tezcatlipoca, who is Xipe Totec (see Figure 7, Color Plates 9 and 12, and Image 19), or Camaxtli-Mixcoatl, a god associated with the east and sunrise who embodies the creative power that provided the corn as man's sustenance; the black Tezcatlipoca (Image 11), a god commonly known simply as Tezcatlipoca, the warrior of the north and of the nadir, or midnight, position of the sun, who was in many ways the most powerful and the most dangerous to man, or, as the *Historia* puts it, "the biggest and the worst"; the blue Tezcatlipoca, who was Huitzilopochtli ("Hummingbird on the Left"), the warrior of the south (see Figure 20) and the zenith, or high-noon, position of the sun, who was responsible for the creation and maintenance of the Aztec state; and Quetzalcoatl (see Figures 9 and 10 and Color Plates 22 and 23), probably a white Tezcatlipoca, a god also known as Yohualli Ehecatl ("Night and Wind," by extension "Invisible and Intangible," an appellation given also to Ometeotl), who was associated with the west and sunset and was widely considered to be the creator of human life.[5]

Because Ometeotl, from whom these four gods unfolded, was the creative principle, it is not surprising that these four were given credit in various myths for having created fire, the calendar, twelve of the thirteen heavens, and the land of the dead. They were also the creators of the first man and woman—Cipactonal and Oxomoco—and thus the parents of mankind. Each was characterized by unique facial painting and a distinct costume, which together served as a "mask," giving a specific identity to a particular aspect of the underlying creative force that was known as Ometeotl, the supreme dual deity. Tezcatlipoca thus exists simultaneously as the unitary being who unfolds into four and is a manifestation of Ometeotl, as one unit of a duality (Tezcatlipoca/ Tezcatlanextia or night/day), and as one of the four divisions of the quadripartite Tezcatlipoca, each associated with one of the four directions (the four basic divisions of space) and with one of the four "cardinal" points on the sun's daily course (the four basic divisions of time). In his range of transformations, then, Tezcatlipoca is both the unitary divine essence and the created world of time and space. These fundamental concepts of unity, duality, and quadriplicity that are manifest in Ometeotl and Tezcatlipoca form the basis of Mesoamerican spiritual thought and of the cosmological vision, expressed metaphorically in myth, that arises from and expresses that thought.

The creation myths of the Maya present the same fundamental structure, but in very different form. The Maya counterpart of Ometeotl, Hunab Ku, "the unified god," is a shadowy figure for us, because he is mentioned only in very late sources, and no myths detailing his activities remain. Like Ometeotl, he apparently "had no image because [according to the Motul dictionary of 1590] . . . being incorporeal, he could not be pictured,"[6] and, again like Ometeotl, he unfolded into ritually accessible deities but was not himself the focus of ritual. Directly paralleling the conceptions of central Mexico, Hunab Ku gave rise to Itzam Na, a quadripartite deity. The unfolding of Hunab Ku into Itzam Na was sometimes seen as a birth, Itzam Na being seen as the son of the supreme god, Hunab Ku. Like Tezcatlipoca, Itzam Na was associated with colors and directions: the red Itzam Na with the east, the white with the north, the black with the west, and the yellow with the south.

In addition, Itzam Na was at times imagined as four iguanas standing upright at the cardinal points, each forming one of the walls of the "house" of the universe, with their heads together composing the roof. In this context his earth aspect was known as Itzam Cab Ain, the soil that receives the rain, as is indicated by the mask he wears on the carved panel in the Temple of the Foliated Cross at Palenque, where his head is decorated with vegetation. In that connection the name Itzam Na referred to his celestial aspect, the sender of the rain, and his iguana body is often decorated with symbols representing the sun, the moon, and various planets. Thus Itzam Na, "Iguana House," is the spatial and temporal universe in the same way that Tezcatlipoca was the world of time and space.

Although there is a great deal of controversy among Maya scholars about Itzam Na, many see him as a creator god, often referred to in
this sense as Hunab Itzam Na (Hunab meaning here unique or single
one). But in his creative role he may well have been seen as dual as
well. The concept of the supreme dual deity unfolding into a divine
primeval pair who were creators of the world is expressed in Maya
mythic thought through the sun god manifestation of Itzam Na, Kinich-
Ahau Itzam Na, whose female aspect, or "wife," was probably called Ix
Chebel Yax, or, more simply, Ix Chel (see Figure 17), who was most
fundamentally associated with the moon, although she had numerous
other manifestations. Thus the dual creator aspects of Itzam Na can be
seen in this way to be associated not only with male and female but
also, as with Tezcatlipoca, with night and day.

Itzam Na is also known to scholars as God D and as God K,[7] and
to add to the confusion, mythic images of this god take both the reptil-
ian form we have described and human form as well. In his human
form he is pictured in the codices as an old man with a Roman nose
and alluded to as the inventor of writing and the patron of learning. He
has a tube in his forehead, thought to represent a cigar from which
emerge scrolls probably representing coils of smoke, marking him in
still another way as the clear counterpart to the Aztec Tezcatlipoca,
"Smoking Mirror." Like that powerful god of the Basin of Mexico, Itzam
Na is both the unitary divine essence *and* the created world and seems
to encompass most of the other major gods as different forms of his
various aspects.

An alternative Maya creation myth has been reconstructed by
Martin Pickands, who delineates a pan-Maya belief in a dualistic creator god, or first father, named Acantun, who was miraculously born
from a celestial tree and who was himself symbolized as a heavenly
tree. This, according to Pickands, is indicative of his dual nature, because Acantun means literally a tree of dual aspect, thus containing
such pairs of opposites as male and female and good and evil. Acantun
represents the original pair of ancestors, and his offspring include a
pair of twins, probably represented in mythic images as either God L
and God D or as two Gods M. This creator deity, as we find him in the
Popol Vuh, is called Huracan in Quiché, meaning, according to Pickands, "one, his tree," and Acantun in Yucatec refers "to the fact that
the two aspects share a single identity, represented by the unity of
their *acan.*"[8] In the *Popol Vuh,* where we also find tree symbolism associated with the first father, these two aspects of the creator principle
are most often called Xpiacoc and Xmucane, "Begetter of Children"
and "Conceiver of Children."

The few fragments that remain of the mythological tradition of the
Valley of Oaxaca and surrounding regions populated by the Zapotecs
and Mixtecs bear clear witness to the fact that these traditions were an
integral part of the larger Mesoamerican tradition. Though the name
each of these peoples use for themselves means "The Cloud People" in

their own language, and thus suggests their common origin, there is no hint of clouds in what remains of their creation myths, and of the Zapotec creation myths, what remains is very little. It seems clear from what there is, however, that in those lost myths there was a Zapotec counterpart of the Aztec Ometeotl and the Maya Hunab Ku, for Father Juan de Córdova's Zapotec dictionary of 1578, one of the primary sources of our mythological information for that culture, contains a list of Zapotec gods, and on that list we find both Pijetao, described as a "God without end and without beginning, so they called him, without knowing whom," and Coquixee, "the uncreated lord, who has no beginning and no end."[9] According to de Córdova, creation was the task of Cozaana, creator and maker of all beasts, and of Huichaana, the female aspect of the creator and maker of men and of fishes; these two would seem clearly to be the unfolding of the creative force into male and female generative deities. Aside from these tantalizing hints, the sources are mute concerning the creation myths of the Zapotecs.

Our knowledge of the Mixtec creation myths is somewhat fuller, because two important versions remain of what was presumably the basic creation myth. They differ somewhat from each other in at least two important respects. In the first place, the version contained in the *Codex Vindobonensis* is pre-Hispanic and completely pictorial, while the other, a narrative, was recorded by Fray Gregorio García about ninety years after the Conquest, although scholars believe that it reflects the pre-Hispanic tradition. In addition, although it has been difficult for scholars to interpret, the codex version gives a much fuller account of the lengthy creative process than does García's narrative, since a series of the images of the codex seems to relate to creation. The first of these images occurs on the second portion of the opening page[10] and depicts two pairs of aged gods, who probably correspond to the Aztec Ometeotl pair, Ometeotl and Omecihuatl, the dual aspects of the creative force. Following these aged gods, the codex depicts another, younger pair of male and female gods, who both have the calendric name 1 Deer, a pair who seem to be the "unfolding" of the initial aged gods. This younger pair then produces numerous progeny, two of whom, 7 Rain and 7 Eagle, take an active part in the "tree birth" episode, which occurs later. Since 1 Deer is also the name of the male/female pair in García's narrative, it seems clear that the codex at this point is giving the pictorial version of that tale.

The next stage of the process of creation shows 9 Wind, the Mixtec cognate of Quetzalcoatl, descending to earth after having been given his symbolic attributes by the male creative gods in the heaven of the creative pairs depicted on the opening page (Figure 9). In him the gods provide a ritually accessible manifestation of themselves with particular "earthly" functions, functions symbolized by the attributes given him. After his descent to earth, 9 Wind is shown separating the heavens and the waters from the earth,[11] thus making life on earth possible (Figure 10), and this image is followed by a lengthy section

FIGURE 9

The birth of Quetzalcoatl from
the *Codex Vindobonensis*

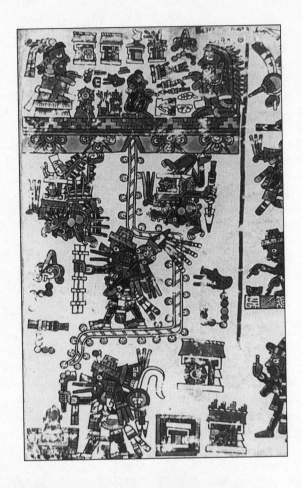

FIGURE 10

Quetzalcoatl separating
the heaven from the
earth, an image from the
Codex Vindobonensis

THE FLAYED GOD

depicting in great detail the appearance of the ancestors of the Mixtecs. The key image in this section (Color Plate 5, Image 6), and one of the most important creation images in Mesoamerican art, depicts the birth of one of these ancestors from a stylized tree, which is shown with two quincunx-like sets of branches flanking a cleft in its trunk. Emerging from this cleft is an unnamed, nude male who wears symbolic red face painting and whose body is painted completely red. On either side of the tree's trunk stand 7 Rain and 7 Eagle engaged in some activity presumably connected with this emergence.

But a closer look reveals the fact that this is not merely a tree. At its base is a female human head whose body is the tree, and from the vaginal cleft in her body the unnamed male emerges. Following that emergent pair, the codex depicts forty-nine more figures representing the lineage of the Mixtec people. Thus the woman/tree is to be seen as the divine source of humanity. It is significant in this regard that while the tree is predominantly female, having a woman's head, a swollen body, a vaginal cleft, and other feminine characteristics, one side of it is marked with masculine symbols, thereby suggesting its dual nature. And that dual, male/female nature, of course, is the key to the process of creation as it will continue on earth through the efforts of the just-created male/female pair, whose forty-nine descendants follow them in the pictures of the codex.

While the images of the codex describe the process of creation from its beginnings with the cosmic creative force to its eventual culmination in the existence of the Mixtec people, García's narrative myth deals in detail with only a portion of that process. In his version the primordial 1 Deer couple, also called Lion Serpent and Jaguar Serpent, are described as the father and mother of all the gods. Their first offspring are two sons, "Wind of Nine Serpents" and "Wind of Nine Caves,"[12] who manifest their own creative powers by transforming themselves into birds and animals, suggesting the origin of the concept of the nagual, the spirit animal who is the "soul" of a living being. These two brothers live in a paradiselike garden in which they initiate sacrifice and through that sacrifice petition their parents to bring the sky and light into being, to found the earth, and to separate the land from the waters. Significantly, the garden of García's myth has no counterpart in the *Codex Vindobonensis* version, but that version, as we have seen, does focus on a central tree in one of its crucial episodes. García's garden may well derive from the influence of Christianity, which might then account for the transformation of the birth tree of the pre-Hispanic codex into the trees of the later post-Conquest garden. Interestingly, this episode in the narrative is followed by a universal flood, a feature common to Mesoamerican and Christian creation myths, after which the sky, and presumably the waters of the flood, are separated from the earth, the human race is restored, and the Mixtec lineage is established, exactly the sequence of events in the codex.

Thus the basic pattern is clear: in the mythologies of the Aztec, the Maya, the Zapotec, and the Mixtec the fundamental creative principle—Ometeotl and Hunab Ku in the first two cases—not only becomes the creative pair and the manifest world but also unfolds into a staggering number of other gods. As we will see in the following sections dealing with myths of fertility and rulership, there are parallels between the gods of the various cultures at these levels as well. We shall see that many of them are fundamentally associated with the directions and colors of the quadripartite universe and are thus fourfold. In addition, there are various assortments of dual gods: gods who have consorts of the opposite sex, gods who in themselves manifest a union of opposites, or twinned gods who sometimes represented both opposing and complementary elements, such as male and female, as in the case of the 1 Deer couple of the Mixtecs, or day and night, or paired astronomical bodies such as the twin heroes of the *Popol Vuh.* All of these are mythic representations of the multiplicity of the created world, a multiplicity that is but a manifestation, however dazzling and wondrous in its complexity, of the original and enduring unity.

THE FOUR SUNS

It is clear from both the archaeological record and the written accounts that the various cycles of the sun, not simply the gods, were seen throughout Mesoamerica as embodying the spiritual order of the universe. In and through them the spiritual force emanating from the mystical unity of Ometeotl operated in the world of nature. The sun, as a symbol of the mystical life force, was seen at times as itself the source of all life, a cyclic source whose act of creation was an ongoing process rather than a unique event. Thus life itself was linked metaphorically to the solar cycles. In the *Popol Vuh,* for example, that cycle precedes "the gods themselves and constitutes the 'Prime Element' of Maya cosmogony, and approximates our unimaginable concept of Infinity."[13] An Aztec narrative suggests a similar view: once the essential elements of the world had been created, each of the four basic gods was challenged to establish his power over each of the others, and there followed a series of four separate ages, or suns, each a manifestation of one of the four and each a single stage in a solar cycle and in the ongoing process of creation. Each was therefore a "sun," the length of which varies considerably according to which version of the myth one reads.[14]

THE VERSIONS OF THE BASIN OF MEXICO: THE FIRST FOUR SUNS

The myth of the four suns is uniquely Mesoamerican. It provides a structural paradigm imaging forth the relationship of space and time to each other and to the realm of the spirit of which they are but manifestations, a fundamental relationship underlying the tradition's cosmology, which in turn provided a foundation for the pre-Columbian belief system. Although the variant extant versions of the myth do not coincide in every detail, it is possible to identify the basic ingredients that serve as common denominators and thus to construct a composite representing the basic story of the myth. In most of the Aztec versions there were four suns, or eras in the past, followed by the present age, that of humanity and historical time, which is known as the Fifth Sun. Each sun was ruled by a separate deity, peopled by different types of humans, and destroyed by a universal cataclysm, in which the people of the age were either completely destroyed or transformed into some other form of life. Thus the attempts of each of the gods to create humanity in each of the four different periods resulted in failure.

Each age was named according to the day of the tonalpohualli, or ritual calendar, on which the age ended, a name that indicated the type of destruction involved in its demise. In one important version the First Sun, presided over by Tezcatlipoca and identified by the calendric name 4 Ocelotl or Four Jaguar, was populated by acorn-eating giants who were ultimately devoured by ferocious jaguars, often a symbol of the night sky and thus the dark forces of the universe; the Second Sun, 4 Ehecatl or Four Wind, presided over by Quetzalcoatl, was peopled by humans subsisting on piñon nuts and ended with a devastating hurricane that transformed those who survived it into monkeys; the Third Sun, 4 Quiahuitl or Four Rain, was associated with Tlaloc, the god of rain, and with humans who subsisted on an aquatic seed and who were victims of a fiery rain, the survivors of which were transformed into dogs, turkeys, and butterflies; and the Fourth Sun, 4 Atl or Four Water, presided over by Chalchiuhtlicue, was populated by humans whose food was another kind of wild seed called cencocopi or teocentli, possibly an antecedent of corn, who were victims of a great flood, the survivors of which were transformed into fish. Following these initial suns, the skies collapsed on the earth, leaving all in darkness.

The relationship between these first four world ages, or suns, is more complex than it might at first seem. It is apparent that each is unique and complete in itself; one age does not appear to build on another. Thus everything had to be created anew in each succeeding age. Even the gods disappeared until the next period began, indicating perhaps that not even they were exempt from the destruction of the end of an era. Moreover, because there is so much variation in the different accounts, there may never have been an "original" order. It would seem to follow, then, that the four suns "do not simply succeed each other. Rather they overlap and co-exist each in its own order and dimension of time."[15] In addition, there is considerable disagreement among scholars as to whether or not one age was an improvement over the previous ones,[16] or if anything at all in one age might have led to a more advanced stage in its successor.

Significantly, however, their progression can be seen in both linear and cyclical terms. If one takes a "historical" view and sees the Fifth Sun as the last stage in a progression, the final age of the world, the movement is conceptually linear. But if, in contrast, one takes a "mythic" view, seeing the repetition of the ages as a metaphor for the fundamental reality of death and rebirth, the movement is cyclical. Thus both the idea of movement through time and space and the notion of cyclicity are implied in the creation stories. In addition, it is important to realize, in the light of what we know about the essence of Mesoamerican spiritual thought, that the ages existed in a complex pattern of juxtaposition to each other, an essentially quadripartite pattern in which the Fifth Sun served as the center or hub of the cosmos. According to Mircea Eliade, such a center is the ultimately sacred place where the planes of spiritual and material reality intersect, the place where the sacred manifests itself in its totality.[17]

THE WORLD OF THE FIFTH SUN

Whatever the relationship of the first four suns, they are all, in one sense at least, a collective prelude to the Fifth Sun, the age of the present reality. In one version of the basic myth, all was motionless and dark after the destruction of the Fourth Sun; there could be no life without a sun and its movement. In order for the present era to begin, the gods, realizing that they could begin anew only if they settled their differences and ruled in harmony, came together at Teotihuacan and built a sacrificial fire. Two of the assembled gods volunteered to sacrifice themselves by leaping into the fire so that they could be transformed into a new sun. Tecuciztecatl, a wealthy, cowardly, but proud god, who did his penance with costly objects, was the first to attempt the jump, but he retreated in terror from the heat of the fire, whereas Nanahuatzin, a poor, sickly god, who as penance could offer only grass and maguey branches, bravely threw himself into the flames, thereby conquering death, purifying himself, and becoming the sun. In shame, Tecuciztecatl leapt into the dying ashes, transforming himself into the more dimly lighted moon. In Sahagún's account the sun and the moon shone equally brightly at first, until one of the gods threw a rabbit at the moon and its brightness was lessened, and in Mendieta's version Tecuciztecatl went into a cave and was there transformed into the moon. In all the accounts, however, the metaphoric message is clear: the sun, the essence and source of the physical reality of the Fifth Sun, is created through a transformation of spirit—the gods themselves—into matter.

And this transformation continues in the myth with a renewed emphasis on sacrifice; following the self-sacrifice of Nanahuatzin and Tecuciztecatl, the other gods offer themselves in sacrifice in order to set the new sun in motion, nourish it with their blood, and maintain their own newly established harmony, a harmony signifying the harmony of the aspects of nature that each of them represented. In the Fifth Sun was thus established the kind of cosmic order missing from its predecessors, the lack of which brought about their destruction. By performing this self-sacrifice, the gods created for all time a model for humans to follow, and they initiated the process by which the sun would forever move through the four points, which would be identified with the four manifestations of Tezcatlipoca. Thereafter the sun would rise on the eastern horizon each day carried by the fire serpent, Xiuhcoatl (Figure 15), an aspect of the male/female creator pair and escorted by warriors killed in battle. At high noon the souls of five females who died in childbirth (Color Plate 17) would rise up from the west to pull it down into the underworld, where it would disappear on the western horizon until it was sufficiently nourished by further sacrifice to rise renewed from its temporary death. Thus began the present world age, with its complex cycles of birth and death and its quadripartite reality. This was the age of the Fifth Sun, 4 Ollin or Four Motion, the age populated by humans destined to provide sacrifices to keep the sun, and thus life, in motion.

The various myths delineating the creation of this world of the Fifth Sun are consistent in their emphasis on duality and quadriplicity and in their depiction of the creation of matter from spirit. At a time when the earth was still covered with the waters that remained after the demise of the Fourth Sun, according to the account in the *Historia de los Mexicanos por sus Pinturas,* the fifth creation was begun by creating four roads through to the center of the earth so that the four sons of Ometeotl, along with four others who were created for this task, could penetrate to the center in order to "raise the sky" from that central point. Thereafter Tezcatlipoca and Quetzalcoatl transformed themselves into huge world trees in order to support the firmament. As a reward their father made them lords of the sky and the stars, that is, rulers of the world of the spirit, and they went to dwell in the Milky Way, which serves as their road through the heavens, where they continue to live. The account given in the *Histoyre du Mechique* attributes the creation of the earth to that same basic pair of opposites, Tezcatlipoca and Quetzalcoatl, who bring those elements of duality into the world they create. These two gods entered the body of the Earth Monster, Tlaltecuhtli (here rendered as Tlalteutl), Tezcatlipoca through the mouth and Quetzalcoatl through the navel. Upon meeting at the heart, that is, the cosmic center, they then raised and supported the sky from that central point. In both of these cases the emphasis on quadriplicity and duality is coupled with an emphasis on the cosmic center as the point from which the final creation, which is described as a separation of spirit and matter, must take place.

A drawing in the *Codex Fejérváry-Mayer* shows Tezcatlipoca using his enormous foot as bait to tempt the Earth Monster to come to the surface of the water (Figure 11), thus allowing a separation of the land from the waters. She swallowed his foot but in the struggle lost her lower jaw, and as a result of her injury she was unable to return to the depths, thus allowing the earth to be created from her body. In a fourth version (presented later with the myths of fertility) also in the *Histoyre du Mechique,* Tezcatlipoca and Quetzalcoatl looked down from the heavens on the Earth Monster, seeing her as a "wild beast" swimming in the waters of the unformed void. Transforming themselves into huge serpents, one of them grasped the monster by the right hand and left foot and the other by the left hand and right foot. Pulling hard, they split her down the center into two pieces, forming the earth from one half and taking the other half to the heavens. The other gods, angered by the destruction of the Earth Monster, descended to console her, making amends by decreeing that all the things of the earth necessary to sustain life for mankind would issue from her. Trees, flowers, and herbs would issue from her hair; grass and smaller flowers from her skin; wells, springs, and small caverns from her eyes; large caves and rivers from her mouth; mountains from her shoulders; and the valleys of the mountains from her nose. But the Earth Monster cried out that she could not provide these necessities if she were not fed with human hearts and soaked with blood, thus establishing for all time the need for humanity to perform sacrifice. In all of these versions the world of the Fifth Sun is created from the body of the god, a metaphor comparable in structural effect to its being created out of the cosmic center. In both cases matter is formed from spirit.

But who was to populate this newly formed world of the Fifth Sun? In the account given in *Leyenda de los Soles* the task of creating humanity was given to Quetzalcoatl, who was to descend to the underworld to find the bones and ashes of those who had died in the past suns. From these he would "recreate" humanity. After using his

FIGURE 11

Tezcatlipoca losing his foot to the Earth Monster, Tlaltecuhtli, an image from the *Codex Fejérváry-Mayer*

shrewdness to overcome many obstacles along his journey, Quetzal-coatl was finally given the impossible task, by Mictlantecuhtli, the lord of the underworld, of sounding a trumpet shell that had no holes in it and therefore could not be blown. With the help of worms who made the holes for him and bees that flew inside to make the shell sing, Quetzalcoatl passed this test. Then Mictlantecuhtli reluctantly gave him one long bone, only to change his mind and pursue Quetzalcoatl with his demons to get it back. Running in flight, Quetzalcoatl dropped the bone, causing it to break into many pieces, thus accounting for the small stature of humans. But he gathered the pieces, made his way back from Mictlan, and gave the bones to the woman called Cihua-coatl, perhaps Quetzalcoatl's consort, in Tamoanchan, who ground them into a kind of flour. Making a dough from this, she put it into a womblike earthen receptacle into which first Quetzalcoatl and then the other gods bled their penises in a ritual of autosacrifice. In four days a male child, Oxomoco, appeared, and four days later, a female, Cipactonal; together they became the parents of a new humanity. This myth, with its complex set of allusions to life and death and to procre-ation, makes clear that man must sacrifice his own blood in reciproca-tion for the sacrifice of the gods, to which he owes his existence. He is thus central to the continuing process of the creation of life.

Taken together, these myths suggest metaphorically that in the world of the Fifth Sun "man was conceived to be the center of the cos-mos, born at a time when the five points of the terrestrial plane met in equilibrium, a being in whom it was believed the qualities of all the components of the universe converged."[18] Humanity, living at the cos-mic center, between the regions of above and below and between the periods of birth and death, at the center of the four quadrants and in the center of the vertical universe, was responsible for maintaining the continuing motion of the cosmos and was thus perceived, in this mythic view, as a balanced synthesis of the universe.

According to the myths, however, humankind, the population of the Fifth Sun, is destined to meet its end by being devoured by celestial monsters, the survivors to be destroyed by earthquakes. The logic of the myth suggests that there could never be a sixth sun because the Fifth Sun is the synthesis of the quadrants of reality and their qualities as well as a synthesis of the other four suns and would therefore not be subject to the great law of continuous change through destructive catastrophe. The world must end "forever when the structures which confer sense, meaning and order on reality no longer apply."[19] Accept-ing the prediction literally, the Aztecs were prepared for horrendous events to take place at the end of every fifty-two-year cycle, when the calendar systems had run their full course and the new cycle had not yet begun.[20] This was a liminal interval, a dangerous interlude betwixt and between the old life and the creation of new life, a perilous mo-ment of nonexistence. Either the new cycle would begin, or it would not. In this "no time," this period of limbo, all fires were extinguished, pregnant women covered their faces with maguey leaves and were locked up or carefully guarded lest they change into beasts that could devour mankind, sacrifices were made, and the priests anxiously watched the heavens for a sign—the movement of the star we call Aldebaran past the "middle" of the night sky—that the new cycle had begun and the danger had passed. This was the most critical of moments, the point in time at which it would be determined whether the Fifth Sun, the center of all reality, was to be the end of time itself or whether it would continue as "the navel of the earth," the continuing source of all creation.

THE MAYA VERSIONS

The myth of the four suns has its counterpart in myths of multiple creations among the Maya. The most complete and best known of these Maya variants is to be found in the *Popol Vuh* of the Quiché Maya of Guatemala, which in its initial section narrates the story of the origin of life. In the beginning, "whatever might be is simply not there: only murmurs, ripples, in the dark, in the night. Only the Maker, Modeler alone, Sovereign Plumed Serpent [Gucumatz, the Quiché translation of Quetzalcoatl, the Aztec god responsible for the creation of man], the Bearers, Begetters" existed in the middle of the dark waters of the void. Then followed the creation of life, "the emergence of all the skyearth":

> *the fourfold siding, fourfold cornering,*
> *measuring, fourfold staking,*
> *halving the cord, stretching the cord*
> *in the sky, on the earth,*
> *the four sides, the four corners,*

In other words, a quadripartite creation

> *by the Maker, Modeler,*
> *mother-father of life, of humankind,*
> *giver of breath, giver of heart,*
> *bearer, upbringer in the light that lasts*
> *of those born in the light, begotten in the light;*
> *worrier, knower of everything, whatever there is:*
> *sky-earth, lake-sea.*

After much deliberation Heart of Sky (who is a tripartite being also called Hurricane—"Thunderbolt Hurricane comes first, the second is Newborn Thunderbolt, and the third is Raw Thunderbolt") and Sovereign Plumed Serpent resolved to create the world; they cried "Earth," and the earth came into being. With the word as the mechanism of creation, everything that did not yet exist was named and all appeared.

Attempting to create humanity, the gods three times formed creatures incapable of proper worship;[21] only on the fourth try were they successful. First, birds and animals were created, but they could not speak to worship their creators "and so their flesh was brought low"; they were condemned thereafter to be killed for food. The second attempt resulted in men made from "earth and mud" but was equally unsuccessful since they had misshapen, crumbling bodies, and their speech was senseless; they, too, were incapable of the worship required by their creators. After destroying these men, the gods next fashioned "manikins, woodcarvings," but their speech was equally useless because "there was nothing in their hearts and nothing in their minds, no memory of their mason and builder." These manikin people were destroyed by a flood as well and by their animals, plants, utensils, and the natural objects they had ungratefully abused in their stay on earth. They tried to escape to the roofs, but the houses collapsed, and the caves and trees refused them shelter. Thus they were destroyed, and those few surviving the destruction became the present-day monkeys.

After describing these first three attempts to create a proper population for the earth, the myth leaves the story of the creation to narrate the adventures of the hero twins, and it is not until that lengthy interlude is concluded that it tells of the creation of present-day humanity, specifically, the Quiché. The gods, learning of a mountain filled with yellow corn and white corn that was discovered by the fox, coyote, parrot, and crow, directed Xmucane, the divine midwife who existed prior to all birth, to grind the corn that, mixed with water, provided the material with which they created the first men: Jaguar Quitze, Jaguar Night, Mahucutah, and True Jaguar, the men who would be called the "mother-fathers" of the Quiché people. "They were good people, handsome," and they gave thanks for having been made and for the good things they were given.

But this time the gods had succeeded too well; these men were godlike. They could see and understand everything, and there was a real danger that they might equal the gods in wisdom. In order to put them into their proper relationship to their makers, "They were blinded as the face of a mirror is breathed upon. . . . And such was the loss of the means of understanding, along with the means of knowing everything, by the four humans. The root was implanted." Having been created from the life-giving corn, they were thereby linked to the annual seasonal cycle, and then the gods, making a wife for each of them, linked them in yet another way, this time through the necessity of procreation, to the cycle of death and rebirth. This was the beginning of history, for the leading Quiché lineages descended from these pairs.

But all was still in darkness; all mankind waited for the sun. Finally, after much sacrifice and prayer, they saw the morning star and gave thanks, waiting patiently through a long series of events until at last the sun appeared, the first time "like a person when he revealed himself," with heat so strong that several gods and animals were turned to stone. Thereafter, however, the sun, which was to appear daily, would not be that "real" sun but "only his reflection," providing heat moderated sufficiently to nurture rather than to destroy life. Interestingly, the *Popol Vuh* contains another story of the creation of the sun, one that is reminiscent of the Aztec myth of the creation of the sun at Teotihuacan. At the end of the tale of the hero twins in the *Popol Vuh*, the twins, who have descended into the underworld to defeat the lords of death, who killed their father and uncle, themselves undergo a sacrificial death before being reborn, manifesting their triumph over death and the underworld by returning finally as the sun and the moon.

Thus it is clear from the *Popol Vuh* as well as from all the other cosmogonical myths that have been preserved from the world of pre-Columbian Mesoamerica that those peoples viewed creation as the complex process by which spirit manifested itself as the visible reality of the world of time and space. Creation was for them not a one-time event but an ongoing process through which the essence of divinity—the life force—continually creates and maintains life. While the myths, as metaphors, speak of specific events occurring at specific times and places, as myths always must, it is clear that they are attempting, as myths always do, to characterize reality everywhere and everywhen.

THE COSMOLOGICAL VISION

When we turn from a consideration of that mythic conception of creation, the cosmogony, to an examination of the cosmological vision of the peoples of pre-Columbian Mesoamerica, their view of the essential structure of reality, we find a comparable complexity, equally fascinating in its wealth of metaphoric detail and, finally, in its profundity. But it is important to remember that the complexity of the detail expressing that cosmological view is a surface complexity. Under it lies the simplicity of a central unity that is finally the only true reality, a unitary reality that displays itself in the kaleidoscopic show of changing forms and colors we experience. Whether in the quadripartite surface of the earth, the tiered levels of the heavens and underworld, the various cycles through which time was seen to move, or the stages of the development from the creation to the present era, all the details of the structure find their point of unification, their "justification," in that center.

It is thus remarkably fitting that among the peoples of the Basin of Mexico, as we have seen, the first god to emerge from the rather different spiritual vision of the preceding village cultures was the god who came to be identified by the Aztecs with exactly that concept of the center, a god described by Sahagún as "the mother of the gods, the father of the gods, Huehueteotl, who is set in the center of the hearth, in the turquoise enclosure, Xiuhtecuhtli, who batheth the people, washeth the people, and who determineth, who concedeth the destruction, the exaltation of the vassals, of the common folk." He was known as Huehueteotl when seen in his identity as the old god, the primordial god—the source—(Figure 12; see also Figure 18 and Images 5 and 13) and as Xiuhtecuhtli when he was seen in his role as the lord of time—the center of the dynamic display that is the temporal world (See Color Plate 6, Image 15). He was lord of the sun, the fire of the central hearth, and thus the creative, sacred fire of life, and, significantly, he was also addressed as Tlalxictentican, "He who is at the Edge of the Navel of the Earth." As Xiuhtecuhtli he is generally depicted as a young, standing, dynamic figure, and his nagual, the fire serpent known as Xiuhcoatl (see Figure 15), suggests his active role in the world since the Xiuhcoatls carry the sun through the heavens, and it was with a Xiuhcoatl that Huitzilopochtli struck off the head of Coyolxauhqui in the myth (Image 24). It is this god who is portrayed at the center of the space-time paradigm found on the first page of the *Codex Fejérváry-Mayer* (Image 15). From him the four world directional trees grow, and around him move the segments of the sacred calendar. He is the center of a dynamic world.

This paradigmatic drawing is actually a quincunx, a cross with arms of equal length, a cross in which the central point, the meeting place of the arms, is as important as the arms. While the drawing in the

FIGURE 12
The old god of fire, Huehueteotl, a stone brazier from Teotihuacan

codex places Xiuhtecuhtli in that central position, the symbol of the quincunx is sometimes found decorating the brazier, which his alter ego, Huehueteotl, bears on his back or head (Image 13). Both the quincunx and the brazier that the seated god bears suggest that the old god of fire was seen as the driving force behind all cosmic movement, the center around which all cosmic space revolves. But as Huehueteotl, the aged figure always seen seated in repose, bearing his burden of the central fire, he is "the still point of the turning world," the unmoved mover of the continual motion of the world, the fire of life eternally burning at the center of the cosmos. Huehueteotl and Xiuhtecuhtli are thus two ways of "saying" the same thing; both are the center from which the integrity of the system derives. So fundamental, from the Mesoamerican point of view, is the dual perspective through which humanity must apprehend reality that even that notion of the fundamental unity into which all dualities resolve themselves must, once again, be apprehended as dual: Huehueteotl and Xiuhtecuhtli.

This essential structure is symbolized in the quincunx imaging forth the space-time continuum in its most abstract form. Ubiquitous throughout Mesoamerica, nowhere is this symbolic form more clear in its import than on the face of the Aztec "calendar stone" (Image 14), on which the sequence of the ages of the world and the calendrical cycles of time are organized spatially. This quincunx, like all the others, unites the earth and the cosmos, life and motion, within the endless cyclic whirling of time; it symbolizes a fundamental cosmic order that underlies all reality, an order that is expressed in space and time but is itself beyond space and time. In the quincunx the peoples of Mesoamerica could see the world, the world of the earth's surface, which changes, dies, and is reborn in each year and in each age or "sun" and relate that to the span of man's life from birth to his disappearance at death, which was the necessary prelude to his rebirth. Wherever the quincunx is found in Mesoamerica—in hieroglyphic writing, on sculpture, on the walls of temples, or pecked into stucco floors and rocks— it always refers to the unification of the basic spatial order and the equally basic temporal order. Through their unification human life was made one with the spiritual life of the cosmos. The quincunx thus testifies, wherever it is found, to the ultimate unity underlying every area of Mesoamerican mythology.[22]

This quadripartite symbol of ultimate reality calls powerfully to mind another Aztec god—Tezcatlipoca, the manifestation of the generative force, Ometeotl. Tezcatlipoca, as we have seen, is himself both one and four, both the center and the extensions of reality. The image of the quincunx represents exactly the image of Tezcatlipoca's characteristic quadriplicity[23] as he unfolds into four different aspects, each representing one of the four cardinal directions and one of the four segments of daily time marked out by the sun's diurnal course. These aspects are linked to the periods of duration of each of the ages of the four suns, with the Fifth Sun at the center providing a point of synthesis, an *axis mundi,* metaphorically comparable to the unitary Tezcatlipoca, a place that is sacred above all. This is the point at which the vertical (sky, earth, underworld) and the horizontal (the four quadrants of space, the world of the Fifth Sun) worlds intersect, just as the unitary Tezcatlipoca is the "meeting place" of the four gods who are his unfoldings.

Omnipresent and omniscient in human affairs, Tezcatlipoca was the master of human destiny precisely because he represented the center of the cosmos and ruled the four directions. The black Tezcatlipoca, his most powerful unfolding, a capricious, nocturnal god whose foot was replaced by a mirror, was the god of darkness. Protector of magicians and sorcerers, he was himself a trickster whose nature it was to tempt and tease mankind. Capable of evil, he was not what one would consider a devil; rather, he was more clearly revealed as the alter ego of Quetzalcoatl, the white Tezcatlipoca. He was the darker, rather than the evil, side of a single nature (Color Plate 22). Their cosmic conflict, expressed on various levels in various myths, symbolizes the struggle between the creative and destructive forces of nature: opposing light to dark, good to evil, priest to ruler, spirit to matter, and life to death.

But to understand this duality in Mesoamerican terms, we must try to think in a Mesoamerican way. We must understand two fundamental facts about this opposition. First, the balance was certainly not as rigid as these oppositions might suggest. Second, neither side of any of these pairs of opposites is a consistent characteristic of either god. The dual relationship was a complementary one. In fact, it is very unlikely that the Aztecs even thought of Tezcatlipoca and Quetzalcoatl in terms of opposing forces since at times they even wore each other's adornments and shared the same appellations. They must be understood as complex manifestations of a single source in much the same way that we understand the multiple facets of a person's singular personality. In both cases it is the unity that is the overriding factor, and the manifestations of it must be understood in terms of their source. Thus we must "see through" the pairs of opposites—Tezcatlipoca and Quetzalcoatl in this case—to discern the otherwise invisible central unity.

Capable of transforming himself into a bewildering variety of forms, this protean god, Tezcatlipoca, is one of the most difficult gods to recognize, another suggestion of his complete unpredictability. However, his appearance as Tepeyollotl, his jaguar nagual, is probably the most common of his alternative guises and indicates his basic identification both with Tlaloc and the earth and therefore with fertility. But since the jaguar was also associated with fire, Tezcatlipoca was closely related to that essential element as well. His closeness to fire can also be seen in another way, since in his own guise he can be identified by the mirror that replaced his foot and was responsible for his name "Smoking Mirror." A mirror that does not shine, it is a blackened dark spot reflecting the night sky, an instrument of divination through which sorcerers could look into the future and by which Tezcatlipoca could see all that took place in the world. And it was Tezcatlipoca who provided fire for humanity, even before the first man and woman were created, when, according to the account in the *Historia de los Mexicanos por sus Pinturas,* he transformed himself into Mixcoatl-Camaxtli and produced fire by twirling two fire sticks.[24]

All of these connections with fire point obviously to a link, perhaps historical, between Tezcatlipoca and the old god of fire, Huehue-teotl/Xiuhtecuhtli, a connection that would seem to be implicit in their similar relationships to the cosmic center. That Tezcatlipoca does, in fact, have a long history in the development of the Mesoamerican mythological tradition is suggested in a curious way. In archaeological excavations of sites dating from Olmec times, dark concave mirrors have been found that were fashioned by the laborious polishing of iron ore or obsidian. Generally associated with the burials of people of high rank, it is thought that they might have been used, perhaps in ritual, as burning mirrors. The name "Smoking Mirror" comes immediately to mind, of course, and we have yet another possible link, this one very early, between Tezcatlipoca and the old god of fire.

Nothing makes the complexity of Mesoamerican cosmological thought more apparent than the fact that Tezcatlipoca, the enigmatic trickster, was seen by the Aztecs as the apparent center of all reality, the "visual" manifestation of Ometeotl. They seem to have felt that as one approaches the center, reality becomes progressively harder to understand and more difficult to control. At the center is a unity that is beyond man's power even to comprehend. But it is that unity that holds every detail of the cosmos together, and it is through that unity that the transformative movement by which death passes again into life is accomplished. For this reason, perhaps, one of Tezcatlipoca's many names was Titlacahuan, "We Are His Slaves."

In the context of that complex Mesoamerican cosmological vision that unifies time and space in the abstract figure of the quincunx and in Tezcatlipoca and his counterparts in the other cultures, it is fascinating to hear the words, describing another mythic vision, in Richard Wagner's *Parsifal,* which Lévi-Strauss sees as "probably the most profound definition that anyone has ever offered for myth."[25] Sung by Gurnemanz as the scene shifts from a wooded spring to the hall of the Holy Grail, where the knowledge of the transformation of spirit into matter will be presented to the still-innocent Parsifal, the words might as well have been used to denote the central mystery enshrouded in Mesoamerican mythology:

> *You see my son,*
> *Here, time turns into space.*

THE TEMPORAL ORDER

One of the most fascinating and challenging of Maya myths, the tale in
The Book of Chilam Balam of Chumayel recounting the birth of the
twenty-day "monthly" cycle of time, the uinal, portrays exactly that
transformation of time into space. Munro Edmonson, the translator of
the version we present here, calls it a "delicate allegory" that "likens
the birth of time to the origin of man, a man traveling like the heavenly
bodies on the road of days, time, sun, and fate." But this travel, of
course, is paradoxical since it is ultimately cyclical, coming inevitably
to a "self-regenerative end."[26] Similarly, and more basically, the cycle
of the sun provides another mythic image of "time turning into space."
As we have seen, this image is the quincunx, in which the "arms" of
the cross may be seen either as spatial or as temporal: the north-south
arm also represents the nadir and zenith points of the sun's course,
while the east-west arm may also be seen as the "path" of the sun. The
conception that we find metaphorically reflected in the image of the
quincunx and the birth of the uinal provides a key to understanding
the sophisticated and complex calendrical systems developed by Mesoamerican seers as a way of comprehending the temporal order lying
just behind the world of appearances.

It must have become clear to those seers very early in the development of the mythological tradition of Mesoamerica that the temporal dimension of this world moved always in cycles, cycles in which
their very lives were enmeshed: the cycles of life, death, and regeneration of the plants and animals that sustained them; the cycle of humanity's own life, death, and regeneration; the similar cycles of the sun
and moon and the corresponding cycles of our own bodies; and the cycles of the various heavenly bodies that traversed the night skies. Of all
of these, the cycles of the sun seem to have been most basic to their
understanding of the mystic regularity of time. Its rise at daybreak and
setting at dusk provided the perfect metaphor for life and echoed the
cycle of sleep and waking built into their own bodies. That its movement was cyclical no doubt provided assurance that there was an order
beneath the chaotic surface of life, an order that ensured that death
was not an end but the prelude to rebirth.

Time itself came to be considered "the primordial reality, the
deity of multiple countenances, periods, cycles." It was the very framework within which life existed. Miguel León-Portilla explains that for
the Maya "*kin,* sun-day-time, is a primary reality, divine and limitless.
Kin embraces all cycles and all the cosmic ages. . . . Because of this,
texts such as the *Popol Vuh* speak of the 'suns' or ages, past and present."[27] Robert Bruce makes that idea even clearer. The *Popol Vuh,* he
says, consists of "the same cycle running over and over," and that
cycle is "the basic cycle, the solar cycle [which] pervades all Maya
thought."[28] In contrast, "*kin,*" meaning both "sun and time," indicates

that time is the sun's cycle itself and not just a schedule that the sun follows; time is thus a reality, not an abstract concept. What was true for the Maya was equally true for all of the other peoples who shared the Mesoamerican mythological tradition. For all of them the essential order of reality, an order derived from the world of the spirit, was revealed by the cycles of the sun.

While the daily cycle of the sun provided one view of this order, the annual cycle of the sun—observed through the movement on the horizon of its rising and setting points—led them to an understanding of a different sort of order, the order embodied in the cycle of the solar year, with its repeating pattern of the seasons, an order mysteriously involved with the provision of their sustenance. From this cycle they derived one of the two fundamental calendars in use throughout Mesoamerica from the times of the earliest civilizations. That was the solar calendar of 360 days divided into eighteen "months" of twenty days, with five "unlucky" days added to complete a 365-day cycle, a calendar called the *xihuitl* in central Mexico and the *haab* by the Maya. Evidence from Oaxaca suggests it was already in use in the early Preclassic. Obviously the systematic solar observations upon which the original solar calendar and its elaborate variations—which we will discuss briefly below—were founded must have begun in remote antiquity, probably by the Olmecs, and been dutifully continued until the Conquest, with the numerous dates and calculations of early times no doubt written on perishable materials, such as wood, skin, and bark paper.

Were these to have survived, they would have testified to the ancient and enduring Mesoamerican fascination with the connection between the regular movement of the sun and the orderly progression of time. The mythic nature of this calendrical thought suggested so clearly in the tale of the birth of the uinal and in the quincunx is also apparent in the primary use to which the solar calendar was put—the ordering of the ritual life of the culture, a ritual life designed to harmonize man's existence with the life force symbolized by the sun. In central Mexico at the time of the Conquest, for example, the Aztecs followed the annual cycle of the sun in the observance of the *veintena* festivals, the great feasts with their stunning rituals and elaborate sacrifices that ordered the movement of time by celebrating the end of each of the eighteen twenty-day periods of the solar year.

But the mystic and mythic nature of time is revealed even more clearly by the other calendrical cycle developed and elaborated by the peoples of Mesoamerica throughout their long history. This one, unique in the history of the civilizations of the world, was a sacred calendar tied directly to no single cycle observable in the world of nature (see Image 14). Like the quincunx, it embodied and celebrated the essence of cyclicity abstracted from its occurrence in natural phenomena. This was the calendar used for prophecy and divination since in its workings it allowed man his closest approach to, his clearest view of, the essential workings of the world of the spirit. In the Mesoamerican mind, it complemented the solar calendar in the same way, perhaps, that the realm of the spirit complemented the natural world. This sacred calendar was essentially mathematical in its permutation of two different time sequences against each other, one consisting of twenty named days, each symbolized by a day sign, and the other of thirteen numbered days. The two sequences ran simultaneously, so that any given day was designated by one of the twenty names and one of the thirteen numbers, making possible 260 different combinations within the sacred cycle. It thus took 260 days before the same combination of day sign and number reappeared.

Each of the thirteen numbered days was associated with a god and revealed the attributes of that god and the mysteries of his multiple identities. In one of the calendar's variants, for example, Ometecuhtli is the patron of the first day of the 260, *cipactli,* while Omecihuatl is the patron of the last, *xochitl,* so that all time existed between these two representations of the creative essence of the cosmos. In addition, each of the twenty days was associated with both a god and a sacred volatile or winged creature, and each of the volatiles also had a patron god. It is interesting that although nineteen of the twenty day signs represent various concrete beings or things such as rain or jaguar, the seventeenth day sign was *ollin,* movement, which according to Paul Westheim suggests that the movement of time and the universe was considered a concrete entity like the rain or jaguar.[29]

Each of the days of the sacred calendar, with its name and number and all of the associations that went with them, was prophetic. Understanding calendrical lore allowed a special group of priests to understand the implications of the signs of the calendar and to divine the future, since each of the multiple signs had its own import. These priests could determine the augury of each of the days, since the essence of the day (*kin* among the Maya) was in itself the prophecy (also *kin*). And if "all the influences and interrelationships were fathomed . . . the key to the whole ordered scheme of existence" would become clear.[30] The cyclical nature of reality guaranteed that the repetition of the combination of symbols associated with any given day would coincide with the same phenomena the next time that combination appeared. Furthermore, each person knew that by virtue of having been born on a particular day of the calendar, he was linked to the supreme order of the cosmos; "as the *Popol Vuh* economically expresses it: 'one's day, one's birth' was identical with his destiny."[31]

Why the 260-day period was selected is not known and will probably never be known for certain. That there is no obvious correspondence to any important observable cycle of time is suggested by the fact that no other civilization in the world used a 260-day cycle as the basis for a calendar. However, a variety of natural cycles coincide fairly well with the calendar's 260-day period. Some of these are astronomical cycles. The interval between the appearance of Venus as morning and evening star is close to 260 days, Mars's synodic period is exactly three cycles of 260 days, and 260 is close to numbers used in predicting possible eclipses. Biologically, the number is also close to the gestation period for humans, and Barbara Tedlock's research among the contemporary highland Maya suggests that possible base.[32]

None of these cycles, however, has gained universal acceptance among scholars as the foundation of the calendar. The most widely held view is that the 260-day period may simply be the result of the permutation of its two subcycles; thirteen and twenty are numbers of considerable ritual and symbolic importance throughout Mesoamerica. There is no compelling reason to suppose that 260 is significant in its own right. Thus the calendar may well have been essentially mathematical; given the astronomical, numerological, and biological coincidences, regardless of its origin, the number probably grew to be significant precisely because it reflected so many of nature's cycles. These coincidences no doubt suggested to the Mesoamerican mind that a mathematical key to the various cycles that embodied the fundamental order underlying the world in which they lived had been discovered, a key revealing the order of time itself and one that enabled man to give appropriate form to the essence of time that was beyond visual reality. The elimination of the connection with visible phenomena characteristic of the solar calendar must have made this system seem a purer, more direct conceptualization of the sacred knowledge of ultimate reality, a means of lifting the mask covering the world of the spirit.

Modern scholarship has not discovered the original sacred calendar; we have only a series of variants presumably derived from an ancient, perhaps Olmec, prototype. These variants include the Aztec version known as the *tonalpohualli,* literally meaning "the count of day signs" (see Figure 4), the Yucatec Maya version, which scholars often refer to as the *tzolkin,* although we do not know what the Maya called it, and the most ancient of them, the Zapotec variant known as the *piye.* In all of its local embodiments, however, it was a sacred calendar used for divination and prophecy and thus complemented the solar calendar, which was used to regulate the more mundane affairs of life as well as the grand ritual cycle, which allowed earthly life to be led in harmony with the cosmic order.

However, not only did it complement the solar calendar, but it also ran simultaneously with the 365-day solar year to create a fifty-two-solar-year cycle, at the completion of which the beginning date of each calendar again fell on the same date. That mathematically derived fifty-two-year cycle was of great importance throughout Mesoamerica. Called the Calendar Round by Maya scholars, it was of such significance to the Maya that they never indicated dates in hieroglyphic texts or historical documents by the solar year designation alone. Most often the date was specified by its designation in the Calendar Round. The Aztecs, following the traditions of their predecessors in the Basin of Mexico, referred to the fifty-two-year cycle as a bundle of years or a Perfect Circle of years. The perfection referred to, of course, is the perfection of the completed cycle, and this moment of completion was, as we have seen, both a moment of renewal—the beginning of a new cycle—and a potential moment of disaster—the end of the old cycle—since the Aztecs believed that the continuance of the present world age was at that moment in jeopardy. Interestingly, the length of the cycle of the Calendar Round is of human scale, so that most people had a chance of living through a complete cycle.

Mesoamerican observers were aware of other cycles mathematically congruent with the 260-day cycle of the sacred calendar. Venus completed sixty-five of its cycles every 104 solar years, a doubling of the fifty-two-year cycle called *huehueliztli,* an old age, by the Aztecs, who regarded it as significant since it merged again the 260-day cycle with the cycles observable in the heavens. In the Maya codices the same tendency can be seen: "In the lunar tables a count of 46 Tzolkins is necessary to create a re-entering moon-phase cycle which fits the possible occurrence of eclipses. The 1,820-day count in the Paris zodiacal table and the 780-day count of the Mars table were probably both chosen because they are exact multiples of the 260-day count."[33]

In addition to all of these cycles, the Maya created an even grander one by merging the solar year with the cycles of creation. Called the Long Count by Maya scholars, this cycle calculated time from a base point in the past that was the beginning of the present world age. According to the Goodman-Martínez-Thompson correlation, this date, in our calendar, was August 12, 3113 B.C., from which point in time the present age would last a little over five thousand years. The Long Count used a number of units of increasing size based on the solar day and the solar year to make these calculations. The smallest unit was the day, and twenty days combined to form a *uinal.* Eighteen of these monthlike units formed a *tun* or year. Twenty *tuns* made up a *katun,* and twenty *katuns* a *baktun.* There is some disagreement as to the existence of larger named units, but large periods of time were measured; periods of millions of years into the past and future were recorded on Classic period monuments.

For us, however, the important point is that the Long Count was used to record the number of days elapsed since the beginning of the current Long Count cycle and was, therefore, another indication of the penchant of Mesoamerican seers to build larger and more complex cycles by combining cycles with which they were already familiar. Although the great length of the Long Count might lead us to see it as manifesting a linear rather than a cyclical concept of time, we know that the Maya did not see it in that way: "In their inscriptions they made a concerted effort to underscore the essential symmetry of time by emphasizing cyclic repetition of time and event. The actions of contemporary kings were declared to be the same as those of their near and remote ancestors and the same as those of the gods tens of thousands—even millions of years—in the past."[34]

Through their calendars the seers of Mesoamerica were able to chart and integrate the regular cycles of time in which their very existence was embedded and thus gain fundamental insight into the most sacred processes of the cosmos. What Giorgio de Santillana and Hertha von Dechend say of the ancient peoples of Europe and the Middle East seems even more true of their counterparts in Mesoamerica. Our forebears, they say, not only built

> time into a structure, *cyclic time:* along with it came their creative idea of Number as the secret of things. . . . Cosmological Time, the "dance of stars" as Plato called it, was not a mere angular measure, an empty container, as it has now become, the container of so-called history; that is, of frightful and meaningless surprises that people have resigned themselves to calling the *fait accompli.* It was felt to be potent enough to control events inflexibly, as it molded them to its sequences in a cosmic manifold in which past and future called to each other, deep calling to deep. The awesome Measure repeated and echoed the structure in many ways, gave Time the scansion, the inexorable decisions through which an instant "fell due." Those interlocking Measures were endowed with such a transcendent dignity as to give a foundation to reality that all of modern Physics cannot achieve; for, unlike physics, they conveyed the first idea of "what it is to be," and what they focused on became by contrast almost a blend of past and future, so that Time tended to be essentially oracular.[35]

It seems abundantly clear, then, that the peoples of Mesoamerica, in a manner similar to those of the archaic civilizations of Old Europe and the Middle East, perceived an inner, spiritual reality as metaphorically underlying and supporting the perceptible reality of the everyday world in which they found themselves. This underlying reality was most apparent to them in the regularity of the cycles to which everything in the natural, temporal world seemed to conform. The calendars that they constructed to reveal this reality were thus, at their highest level, myths—metaphoric constructs that revealed the underlying reality of the spirit—rather than merely tools for measuring the passage of time in an essentially mechanical way. As each cycle was recorded and added to those already known, they must have felt they were coming closer and closer to a revelation of the essence of divinity, the very principle of spiritual order underlying the universe.

Through the creation of the profound and complex metaphor that was their calendrical system, the seers of pre-Columbian Mesoamerica were able to look behind the mask of nature to see the face of divinity itself; and through modern scholarship's study of the system they constructed from what they saw there, "if we look carefully, we can gain a tantalizing glimpse of the supreme mental genius of these people."[36] In *Magister Ludi* Hermann Hesse describes the Glass Bead Game, his own metaphor for the supreme intellectual construct, or myth, capable of revealing the spiritual unity of all experience:

> In the language, or at any rate in the spirit of the Glass Bead Game, everything actually was all-meaningful, . . . every symbol and combination of symbols led not hither and yon, not to single examples, experiments, and proofs, but into the center, the mystery and innermost heart of the world, into primal knowledge. . . . [Each] was, if seen with a truly meditative mind, nothing but a direct route into the interior of the cosmic mystery, where in the alternation between inhaling and exhaling, between heaven and earth, between Yin and Yang, holiness is forever being created.[37]

One cannot help but believe that the shapers of the calendrical system of Mesoamerica would have seen in Hesse's myth the perfect metaphor for their own profound mythic work.

THE SPATIAL ORDER: THE HORIZONTAL WORLD

As we know, the divine essence unfolded into a spatial dimension as well as a temporal one, and for the Aztecs that spatial dimension, the earth, was *cem-anahuac,* "the place surrounded by water." It was envisioned as a body of land or a disk floating in an ocean of water, which extended up at the horizons to merge with the sky, forming in that way an "envelope" within which the life of the Fifth Sun existed. The land mass, which was conceived as the transformation of a deity, sometimes male, sometimes female, took the form of a quincunx; it consisted of four quadrants of space extending out from the cosmic center, or navel of the earth, each quadrant representing one of the four directions as they related to the passage of the sun. Each quadrant was named according to its direction and was associated with its own sacred tree, which was envisioned as one of four sky bearers. Each quadrant housed a sacred bird and was associated with a color, a god, specific year and day signs, and a particular atmosphere.[38] The various Aztec sources portray this horizontal universe using somewhat different images. In the *Historia de los Mexicanos por sus Pinturas,* for example, the earth is symbolized as a spiny monster, *cipactli,* similar to a large crocodile, from which all vegetation grew, whereas in Mendieta's account it is described as a great toad, Tlaltecuhtli (Image 25), that swallowed the sun in the evening and spewed it forth at dawn. In each case the Earth Monster was conceived as floating on the primeval waters arising from the paradise of the rain god, Tlalocan (Color Plate 19).

The cosmology of the Maya envisioned a "horizontal" reality similar to that of the Aztecs. For them the earth was a flat rectangle, each of whose corners represented a cardinal direction and was associated with a particular tree, a color, and a god, who was one of the quadripartite manifestations of Chac in one version. The sun rose in the east, the red direction at the apex of the cosmological round, whose god was

Chac-Xib-Chac; the sun disappeared in the west at the bottom of the round, a direction whose god was Ek-Xib-Chac and whose color was black. North, the direction from which the rain came, was associated with white, and its god was Zac-Xib-Chac, and south was yellow because of its association with the sun and with its god, Kan-Xib-Chac. The center was green, the color of life, and had its own bird, god, and tree. The world of mankind that was demarcated by these directions was imagined as the back of a turtle, a crocodile, or another amphibious being floating in the primordial sea, and these creatures often symbolize the earth in the mythic art of the Maya.

Alternatively, as we have seen, the earth was metaphorically conceived as an "iguana house," thus giving it the name Itzam (iguana) Na (house), of the most important of the Maya creator gods. In this conception, each of the four Itzam formed a "side" of reality and was associated with a particular color and one of the four world directions. Each had both a celestial and terrestrial aspect, on the one hand sending rain from the heavens, and on the other forming the soil that accepted the rain and used it in the generational process that provided the plant life that sustained humanity. At the points where the four Itzam touched the horizon and the place where the "sides" met the heavens, they bent, forming the roof, walls, and floor of the world, thus completing the rectangle-become-a-cube that is the iguana house. It is important to note that this vision of the world brings together the two major aspects of Itzam Na: both his celestial aspect as the creator god and his terrestrial aspect, called Itzam Cab, which forms the surface of the earth. That "conception of Itzam Na is, indeed," as the great Mayanist Eric Thompson says, "a majestic one."[39]

In still another variation on the basic theme, the Maya saw the sky, considered male in this context, as multitiered and supported at its corners by four Bacabs, gigantic Atlantean gods known as "water sprinklers," each with the color association appropriate to the direction he represented and each presiding over one-quarter of the 260-day period, thus uniting, again, time and space. The sky was also imagined as being supported by four different species of trees, each a different color, with the sacred green ceiba tree positioned as a world tree at the center.

Metaphorically, then, as all of these images suggest, the world is both a transformation of spirit and enclosed within an "envelope" of spirit. Its surface is replete with sacred places, which provide openings to that omnipresent underlying (and overlying) world of the spirit. Mountains and caves that reach into and thus allow access to the upper and lower realms are the clearest examples of such sacred places, and caves were considered particularly sacred by both the Aztecs and the Maya: the creation of the gods and man was thought to have taken place in a cave, the womb of the earth mother who gave birth to all life, and in some sources the sun and the moon came forth from a cave. These beliefs seem to have a long history in Mesoamerica, as some evidence suggests that caves were central to the Olmec myth of origin, a centrality that may well have given birth to the tradition, which we will examine in more detail in our presentation of the mythic structure of rulership, of the origins of various peoples in caves. The Aztecs, for example, saw Chicomoztoc, "Seven Caves" (Color Plate 24, Image 53), as the mythical place of their origin.

Mankind, at the direction of the gods, according to the myths, furnished the created world with sacred structures and communal areas: pyramids that were artificial mountains, temples that were artificial caves, and cities that replicated the quadripartite pattern of time and space in their layout and siting. These human creations repeated the work performed by the gods when the natural world was created and thus became the sacred places where the world of the spirit could "break through" into this world of time and space, the sacred places where the all-important rituals could be performed at the sacred times determined by the seers capable of understanding and interpreting both the complexity of the sacred lore and of the astronomical phenomena that gave shape to time and therefore made evident the underlying order of the cosmos.

THE SPATIAL ORDER: THE VERTICAL DIMENSION

As this description of the sacrality of certain places in the "horizontal" universe suggests, there was also a "vertical" dimension to reality. If the horizontal world was the extension of the world of nature, this vertical world was the extension, of necessity metaphoric, of that world into the world of spirit. As one would expect of the Mesoamerican mythological tradition, the conception of the vertical universe is much more complex than that of the horizontal. The Aztec priests described a tiered cosmos, each stratum representing one category of a heavenly body or spiritual phenomenon and a particular deity, although it seems to have been possible for the various celestial bodies to move from one level to another. This heavenly realm generally had thirteen layers but was conceived in various ways. According to some sources the thirteenth level, Omeyocan, the place of duality, was the highest, but others suggest that they were arranged pyramidally, with six levels going up and six coming down, the seventh layer being the highest and the one where the gods resided. The first of these versions is given visual form in the *Codex Vaticanus A* (Image 8), a post-Conquest codex of the Basin of Mexico reflecting pre-Conquest belief. Above the earth, in tiered succession, rise the heavens. Closest to the earth is the paradise of the rain god, known as Tlalocan, followed by the heavens associated with various gods, goddesses, and heavenly bodies, culminating in the thirteenth heaven, Omeyocan. The Maya also envisioned the sky as a living place teeming with the activities of innumerable supernaturals and dead ancestors. As in the Aztec view, they imagined a thirteen-layered heaven, each layer with its own god, with the moan bird as the symbolic denizen of the highest heaven.

Both Maya and Aztecs conceived of a nine-layered underworld below the earth, a land of the dead called Mictlan by the Aztecs. As with the heavens, these subterranean levels were either imagined as extending in layered progression down to the ninth level, the domain of the lord of the underworld, Mictlantecuhtli (Color Plate 23), the counterpart of the heavenly Ometeotl, or as descending as an inverted pyramid, the fifth level then being the lowest. The underworld thus depicted was the place through which the spirits of most of the dead would journey. It was thought that that journey lasted for four years after death and involved a number of painful obstacles and a series of difficult trials. Led by a yellow dog across rivers and deserts, the spirits of the dead would finally arrive at Mictlan, the lowest level, to rest there for eternity, a metaphor, perhaps, for the return of the spirit to the anonymity of the life force represented by the gods of the dead (Figure 13 and Color Plate 23). Not all the dead went to Mictlan, however; one's place after death depended on the way one died. The most coveted fate was bestowed upon warriors who died in battle or were sacrificed and women who died bearing children (Color Plate 17). The former traveled with the sun on its morning journey for four years and then returned to earth as hummingbirds or butterflies that flew back and forth from heaven to earth, while the latter accompanied the sun in its afternoon journey, eventually becoming goddesses who might unexpectedly appear on earth and frighten the living.

FIGURE 13
The god of death, a stucco relief from Tomb 1, Zaachila, Oaxaca

There were, however, neither rewards nor punishments in the afterlife for one's behavior in this world. Miguel León-Portilla suggests that the idea that one survived for four years after death implies that there was a belief in the existence of something beyond the material body, and he suggests that this is indicated by the name Ximoayan, "the place of the fleshless," where the dead were separated from their bodies, leaving only the bones.[40] As we have seen, in one of the myths of man's creation, Quetzalcoatl "resurrected" humanity by sprinkling blood drawn from his penis on the bones of the previous generation, a complex metaphor for death and regeneration suggesting again that the dead return to the life force, which in turn creates new life in an endless creative cycle. A drawing on page 52 of the *Codex Borgia,* in fact, suggests the copulation of the god and goddess of death, indicating in still another way that the land of the dead is to be seen as the prelude to life, the "cause" of life.

The Maya underworld, Xibalba (the place of fright) was also nine-layered, with each level associated with one of the nine lords of the night. Alternatively, it seems to have been imagined as existing beneath the waters in which the earth floated. Like the earth, however, it had a landscape, plants, animals, and other inhabitants, and at sunset it may have been conceived as rotating from beneath the earth. Xibalba was populated with a range of gods. God L (Figure 14), who wears an owl headdress and smokes a cigar, was the underworld counterpart of Itzam Na in the same way that Mictlantecuhtli was the counterpart of Ometeotl among the Aztecs. Among the innumerable other deities were two other aged divinities: God N and God D, also related to Itzam Na.

The Maya idea of death is beautifully exemplified on the lid of Pacal's sarcophagus in the Temple of Inscriptions at Palenque (Image 49), as that ruler falls into the maw of the Earth Monster, leaving the realm of the living to continue his existence in another form. Much of the remaining Maya funerary art as well as the relevant episodes of the *Popol Vuh* describe in great metaphoric detail the form that existence after life would take. As with the Aztecs, the Maya dead are seen as embarking on a journey, replete with adventures and trials, through which a union with the life force will ultimately be achieved and death will, in that sense, be defeated. This is the journey of the hero twins of the *Popol Vuh,* which we will discuss in connection with the mythic structure of rulership. Those who were defeated by the competitions with the lords of death faced eternal extinction and burial in the underworld, that is, the anonymity of a union with the life force, but the experiences of the hero twins, who survived the trials and outwitted the lords of Xibalba, exemplify the alternative possibility. In their ascension to the sky as the sun and moon, they parallel the fate of Aztec warriors and indicate a similar cosmological structure.

The Mesoamerican worldview as expressed in all of the varied cosmogonical and cosmological myths seems almost infinitely varied

FIGURE 14

The Maya God L, a relief carving in the style of the codices from the Temple of the Cross at Palenque

in its detail. All of these myths of the spirit served to explain the origins and functioning of the cosmos to which were inextricably linked the daily lives of human beings, lives formed of their actions and the beliefs that motivated those actions. Chief among them was the view that this world was but the visual manifestation of the world of the spirit and that true reality was not here but there. That view led to the ubiquity of sacrifice because through sacrifice humanity played its role in keeping the cosmic flux in motion. Sacrifice was necessary to maintain the ongoing process of creation, since in this world life, like the corn that comes from the "dead" seed, can be born only from death. The myths crystalized this "fact" by showing the sacrifices of the gods, through which this world was created and maintained. But there is another, more subtle level of sacrifice: on this level it became a means, perhaps the most effective means, by which the gap between the world of nature and the mysterious world of the spirit could be bridged. Without such a bridge, such a link, life itself would be inconceivable since neither nature without spirit nor spirit without nature can truly be called life.

MAYA CREATION MYTHS

The Birth of the Uinal, from *The Book of Chilam Balam of Chumayel*

The Book of Chilam Balam of Chumayel is a collection of documents
written in the colonial period, consisting mostly of chronicles and histories. Involved with various aspects of life in the Yucatan, it is supposedly the work of a Chilam Balam, or Jaguar Priest, one of the
scholar-sages after whom these Yucatec community books, written in
the Maya language, but in European script learned from the missionaries, are named. While the narration throughout manifests some Spanish influence, Edmonson, the translator of this book, feels that the
Christian influence on this particular myth exists only "to a highly limited degree."[41] Under the Christian veneer a perceptive reader can still
find the essence of the ancient religious and mythological tradition.

Only two real myths appear in the collection, the most important
of which is told in Chapter 20 of the Edmonson translation[42] and is
entitled "The Birth of the Uinal." Composed in 1559 (9 Ahau), its interpretation depends on an understanding of the complex Maya calendrical system, on the culturally specific symbolic meaning of its
multileveled language, and on an understanding of the extent to which
the syncretic fusion of the Christian and indigenous religions had penetrated below the surface. However, the basic metaphoric concept is so
remarkably a reflection of the importance of time in the life of the
Maya, its profound relationship to space, and its essence as the origin
of all things that it clearly reflects the pre-Conquest mythological tradition.

In the Maya calendar the uinal is the sacred cycle of twenty
named days. Comparable in function to our month, thirteen of these
basic units make up the 260-day ritual calendar known to us as the
tzolkin. It is the basic unit in the sense that all other cycles are
formed from it. Here the uinal begins on 13 Oc and ends on 6 Muluc,
having passed through a total of twenty day events. In this progression each of the day names is a pun, and the multiple meanings
thereby suggested make an exact translation extremely difficult. In
addition, further depth and complexity come from the fact that each
of the days of the uinal is associated with one of the basic set of
twenty Maya gods.

Since the Maya word for "twenty" has the same root as the word
for "man" (uinic), there is a natural and immediate linguistic association of time and man. The basic metaphor underlying this myth thus

brings together the image of the birth of time and the origin of man in the same encapsulating moment. Nothing exists until movement, the essential sign of life, makes its appearance. The uinal moves: "And it began to run/By itself, Alone." That movement is also the man on the road, whose footprints can be measured in space as he comes from the east, the place where the cosmos begins: the sky, earth, water, land, stone, and tree. The birth of the uinal is thus "the occurrence of the awakening of the world." Upon its birth, time becomes part of space.[43] The women who precede him, anticipating his existence, seem to represent the feminine principle, providing, as Edmonson suggests, "an exquisite recognition that women counted time more precisely by the moon,"[44] linking humanity to time in still another way. And so the great mystery of the creation of the first uinal, that is, the beginning of time, which in turn is the beginning of everything else, is fittingly the subject of Chapter 20 of this Book of the Jaguar Priest of the town of Chumayel.

THE BIRTH OF THE UINAL

Translated from the Yucatecan Maya by Munro S. Edmonson. Originally published in *Heaven Born Merida and Its Destiny: The Book of Chilam Balam of Chumayel.* Translated and annotated by Munro S. Edmonson (Austin: Univ. of Texas Press, 1986), 120–26. Reprinted by permission of the publisher.

> *Thus it was read by the first sage,*
> *Melchisedek,*
> *And the first prophet,*
> *Puc Tun,*
> *The priest,*
> *And the first sun priest.*
> *This is the sermon of the occurrence*
> *Of the birth of the uinal,*
> *Which was before the awakening of the world occurred,*
> *And it began to run*
> *By itself,*
> *Alone.*
> *Then said his mother's mother,*
> *Then said his mother's sister,*
> *Then said his father's mother,*
> *Then said his sister-in-law,*
> *"What is to be said*
> *When a man is seen on the road?"*

So they said
Whilst they were going along,
But no man occurred.
And then they arrived
There
At the east.
And they began to say,
"Who is it that passed
By here,
Now?
Here are his tracks,
Right here.
Measure them with your foot
According to the word of the planter of the world."
Then they were to measure the footprint of our Father
Who is the holy God.
This was the beginning of saying
The count of the world by footsteps.
This was
12 Oc.
This is the account of his birth.
For 13 Oc occurred,
And they matched each other's paces
And arrived
There
At the east.
They said his name,
Since the days had no name then,
And he traveled on with his mother's mother,
And his mother's sister,
And his father's mother,
And his sister-in-law.
The month was born
And the day name was born,
And the sky was born
And the earth,
The pyramid of water
And land,
Stone

And tree.
There were born the things of sea
And land.
On 1 Monkey (Chuen) he manifested himself
In his divinity
And created heaven
And earth.
On 2 Peak (Eb)
He made the first pyramid.
He descended,
Coming from
There in the heart of heaven,
There in the heart of the water.
For there was nothing
Of earth,
Or stone,
Or tree.
On 3 Ben
He made all things,
Each and every thing,
The things of the heavens
And the things of the sea
And the things of the land.
On 4 Ix
There occurred the separation
Of heaven
And earth.
On 5 Men
Occurred the working of everything.
On 6 Cib
Occurred the making of the first candle:
There occurred the illumination,
For there was no sun or moon.
On 7 Caban
There was first born
The earth,
Which we didn't have before.
On 8 Etz'nab
He planted

His hands
And feet
And made birds
Upon the earth.
On 9 Cauac
Hell was first tasted.
On 10 Ahau
Occurred the going
Of evil men
To hell,
Because the holy God
Had not yet appeared.
On 11 Imix
Occurred the shaping
Of stones
And trees.
This was what was done
On this day.
On 12 Wind (Ik)
Occurred the birth of breath.
This was the beginning of what is called breath,
Because there is no death on it.
On 13 Akbal occurred the taking of water.
Then he moistened earth
And shaped it
And made man.
On 1 Kan
He was first
Disturbed at heart
By the evil that had been created.
On 2 Chicchan
Occurred the appearance of everything evil,
And he saw it
Even within the towns.
On 3 Death (Cimi)
He invented death.
It happened that then was invented
The first death
By our Father

Who is God.
On 4 Manik
. . . . . [45]
On 5 Lamat there was the invention
Of the seven floods of rain,
Water,
And sea.
On 6 Muluc
Occurred the burial
Of all caves
And this was before the awakening of the world.
This occurred
By the commandment
Of our Father
Who is God.
Everything that there was not
Was then spoken in heaven,
For there had been no stones
And trees.
And then they went and tested each other,
Then he spoke as follows.
"Thirteen heaps
And seven heaps make one."
He said for speech to emerge,
For they had no speech.
Its origin was requested
By the first lord day,
For their organs of speech were not yet opened
So that they could speak to each other.
They went there to the heart of the sky
And took each other by the hand.
And then they stood there
In the middle of the country
And divided it up,
And they divided
The Burners,
The four of them.
4 Chicchan the Burner,
4 Oc the Burner,
4 Men the Burner,

And 4 Ahau the Burner.
These are the lords:
The four of them.

8 Muluc
9 Oc
10 Chuen
11 Eb
12 Ben
13 Ix
1 Men
2 Cib
3 Caban
4 Etz'nab
5 Cauac
6 Ahau
7 Imix
8 Ik
9 Akbal
10 Kan
11 Chicchan
12 Cimi
13 Manik
1 Lamat

This was the birth of the uinal
And the occurrence of the awakening of the world.
There was finished heaven
And earth
And trees
And stones.
Everything was born
Through our Father
Who is God, then;
Who is holy.
For there was no heaven
Or earth,
So there he was in his divinity,
In his nebulousness,
By himself,
Alone.

And he caused to be born
Everything that was invented.
And he moved to heaven
In his divinity,
Which was thus a great event,
And he was the ruler.
The account of all the days
Through which the beginning is counted
Was in the east,
As has been told.

The Birth of All of Heaven and Earth, from the *Popol Vuh*

There is little question that the original form of the *Popol Vuh*—the richest, most valuable, and without doubt the best authority for highland Maya mythology—was a pre-Columbian hieroglyphic manuscript that continued to be used as the basis for oral performances after the Conquest by the Quiché Maya of Guatemala. Around 1550–55 a text, probably the account of such a performance, was written in Quiché in the European alphabet in Santa Cruz Quiché by an unknown writer. That manuscript, which has been lost since 1855, was copied by a young Dominican parish priest, Francisco Ximénez, who came upon it in Chichicastenango in the early eighteenth century. Noting that the text reflects some influence of Christianity, Munro Edmonson, himself a noted translator of the *Popol Vuh,* insists that "it remains fundamentally an aboriginal work, expressing and documenting the historical experience of the largest and most powerful of the Mayan peoples of Guatemala in the centuries before the Spanish came."[46]

Reflecting the unity of the Mesoamerican mythological tradition, the *Popol Vuh* reveals a cyclical conception of creation remarkably similar to the Aztec vision, but perhaps somewhat more mystical. In the *Popol Vuh* the initial creation is accomplished through the word: "For the forming of the earth they said 'Earth.' It arose suddenly, just like a cloud, like a mist, now forming, unfolding." But as is always the case in the Mesoamerican tradition, multiple creations follow this beginning. There are four creations of life, the last of which, comprising almost half of the entire text, brings into being the world of the Quiché people, whose first fathers were made by the creator from corn.

Through the series of creations, the text moves from a time when "only the sky alone is there; the face of the earth is not clear" to its culmination with the creation of men who "were blinded as the face of a mirror is breathed upon." Thus the world came to be populated by humans who not only praised and worshiped the gods but also, even more important, understood their relationship to them and the necessity to make sacrifices to sustain the gods. Like the Greek hero Oedipus, man would live with only limited vision and "could only see [what was] nearby." Thus the *Popol Vuh*, and all the other myths, used the materials of the "nearby" world metaphorically to provide a glimpse of the hidden world of the spirit.

 ## THE BIRTH OF ALL OF HEAVEN AND EARTH

Translated from the Quiché Maya by Dennis Tedlock. Originally published in Dennis Tedlock, trans., *Popul Vuh: The Mayan Book of the Dawn of Life*, 71–86, 163–67, 181–82. Copyright © 1985 by Dennis Tedlock. Reprinted by permission of Simon & Schuster. The division into sections is that of the editors.

Part I: The Initial Creation

This is the beginning of the ancient word, here in this place called Quiché. Here we shall inscribe, we shall implant the Ancient Word, the potential and source for everything done in the citadel of Quiché, in the nation of Quiché people.

And here we shall take up the demonstration, revelation, and account of how things were put in shadow and brought to light

> *by the Maker, Modeler, named Bearer, Begetter,*
> *Hunahpu Possum, Hunahpu Coyote,*
> *Great White Peccary, Tapir,*
> *Sovereign Plumed Serpent,*
> *Heart of the Lake, Heart of the Sea,*
> *Maker of the Blue-Green Plate,*
> *Maker of the Blue-Green Bowl,*

as they are called, also named, also described as

> *the midwife, matchmaker*
> *named Xpiyacoc, Xmucane,*
> *defender, protector,*
> *twice a midwife, twice a matchmaker,*

as is said in the words of Quiché. They accounted for everything— and did it, too—as enlightened beings, in enlightened words. We shall write about this now amid the preaching of God, in Christendom now.

We shall bring it out because there is no longer a place to see it, a
Council Book,

> a place to see "The Light That Came from
>   Across the Sea,"
> the account of "Our Place in the Shadows,"
> a place to see "The Dawn of Life,"

as it is called. There is the original book and ancient writing, but he
who reads and ponders it hides his face. It takes a long performance
and account to complete the emergence of all the skyearth:

> the fourfold siding, fourfold cornering,
> measuring, fourfold staking,
> halving the cord, stretching the cord
> in the sky, on the earth,
> the four sides, the four corners,

as it is said,

> by the Maker, Modeler,
> mother-father of life, of humankind,
> giver of breath, giver of heart,
> bearer, upbringer in the light that lasts
> of those born in the light, begotten in the light;
> worrier, knower of everything, whatever there is:
> sky-earth, lake-sea.

This is the account, here it is:
Now it still ripples, now it still murmurs, ripples, it still sighs, still
hums, and it is empty under the sky.
Here follow the first words, the first eloquence:
There is not yet one person, one animal, bird, fish, crab, tree,
rock, hollow, canyon, meadow, forest. Only the sky alone is there; the
face of the earth is not clear. Only the sea alone is pooled under all
the sky; there is nothing whatever gathered together. It is at rest; not
a single thing stirs. It is held back, kept at rest under the sky.
Whatever there is that might be is simply not there: only the
pooled water, only the calm sea, only it alone is pooled.

Whatever might be is simply not there: only murmurs, ripples, in the dark, in the night. Only the Maker, Modeler alone, Sovereign Plumed Serpent, the Bearers, Begetters are in the water, a glittering light. They are there, they are enclosed in quetzal feathers, in blue-green.

Thus the name, "Plumed Serpent." They are great knowers, great thinkers in their very being.

And of course there is the sky, and there is also the Heart of Sky. This is the name of the god, as it is spoken.

And then came his word, he came here to the Sovereign Plumed Serpent, here in the blackness, in the early dawn. He spoke with the Sovereign Plumed Serpent, and they talked, then they thought, then they worried. They agreed with each other, they joined their words, their thoughts. Then it was clear, then they reached accord in the light, and then humanity was clear, when they conceived the growth, the generation of trees, of bushes, and the growth of life, of human-kind, in the blackness, in the early dawn, all because of the Heart of Sky, named Hurricane. Thunderbolt Hurricane comes first, the second is Newborn Thunderbolt, and the third is Raw Thunderbolt.

So there were three of them, as Heart of Sky, who came to the Sovereign Plumed Serpent, when the dawn of life was conceived:

"How should it be sown, how should it dawn? Who is to be the provider, nurturer?"

"Let it be this way, think about it: this water should be removed, emptied out for the formation of the earth's own plate and platform, then comes the sowing, the dawning of the skyearth. But there will be no high days and no bright praise for our work, our design, until the rise of the human work, the human design," they said.

And then the earth arose because of them, it was simply their word that brought it forth. For the forming of the earth they said "Earth." It arose suddenly, just like a cloud, like a mist, now forming, unfolding. Then the mountains were separated from the water, all at once the great mountains came forth. By their genius alone, by their cutting edge alone they carried out the conception of the mountain-plain, whose face grew instant groves of cypress and pine.

And the Plumed Serpent was pleased with this:

"It was good that you came, Heart of Sky, Hurricane, and Newborn Thunderbolt, Raw Thunderbolt. Our work, our design will turn out well," they said.

And the earth was formed first, the mountain-plain. The channels of water were separated; their branches wound their ways among the mountains. The waters were divided when the great mountains appeared.

Such was the formation of the earth when it was brought forth by the Heart of Sky, Heart of Earth, as they are called, since they were the first to think of it. The sky was set apart, and the earth was set apart in the midst of the waters.

Such was their plan when they thought, when they worried about the completion of their work.

Part II: The Creation of the Animals

Now they planned the animals of the mountains, all the guardians of the forests, creatures of the mountains: the deer, birds, pumas, jaguars, serpents, rattlesnakes, yellowbites, guardians of the bushes.

A Bearer, Begetter speaks:

"Why this pointless humming? Why should there merely be rustling beneath the trees and bushes?"

"Indeed—they had better have guardians," the others replied. As soon as they thought it and said it, deer and birds came forth.

And then they gave out homes to the deer and birds:

"You, the deer: sleep along the rivers, in the canyons. Be here in the meadows, in the thickets, in the forests, multiply yourselves. You will stand and walk on all fours," they were told.

So then they established the nests of the birds, small and great:

"You, precious birds: your nests, your houses are in the trees, in the bushes. Multiply there, scatter there, in the branches of trees, the branches of bushes," the deer and birds were told.

When this deed had been done, all of them had received a place to sleep and a place to stay. So it is that the nests of the animals are on the earth, given by the Bearer, Begetter. Now the arrangement of the deer and birds was complete.

And then the deer and birds were told by the Maker, Modeler, Bearer, Begetter:

"Talk, speak out. Don't moan, don't cry out. Please talk, each to each, within each kind, within each group," they were told—the deer, birds, puma, jaguar, serpent.

"Name now our names, praise us. We are your mother, we are your father. Speak now:

'Hurricane,
Newborn Thunderbolt, Raw Thunderbolt,
Heart of Sky, Heart of Earth,
Maker, Modeler,
Bearer, Begetter,'

speak, pray to us, keep our days," they were told. But it didn't turn out that they spoke like people: they just squawked, they just chattered, they just howled. It wasn't apparent what language they spoke; each one gave a different cry. When the Maker, Modeler heard this:

"It hasn't turned out well, they haven't spoken," they said among themselves. "It hasn't turned out that our names have been named. Since we are their mason and sculptor, this will not do," the Bearers and Begetters said among themselves. So they told them:

"You will simply have to be transformed. Since it hasn't turned out well and you haven't spoken, we have changed our word:

"What you feed on, what you eat, the places where you sleep, the places where you stay, whatever is yours will remain in the canyons, the forests. Although it turned out that our days were not kept, nor did you pray to us, there may yet be strength in the keeper of days, the giver of praise whom we have yet to make. Just accept your service, just let your flesh be eaten.

"So be it, this must be your service," they were told when they were instructed—the animals, small and great, on the face of the earth.

And then they wanted to test their timing again, they wanted to experiment again, and they wanted to prepare for the keeping of days again. They had not heard their speech among the animals; it did not come to fruition and it was not complete.

And so their flesh was brought low: they served, they were eaten, they were killed—the animals on the face of the earth.

Part III: The Human Made of Earth and Mud

Again there comes an experiment with the human work, the human design, by the Maker, Modeler, Bearer, Begetter:

"It must simply be tried again. The time for the planting and dawning is nearing. For this we must make a provider and nurturer. How else can we be invoked and remembered on the face of the earth? We have already made our first try at our work and design, but it turned out that they didn't keep our days, nor did they glorify us.

"So now let's try to make a giver of praise, giver of respect, provider, nurturer," they said.

So then comes the building and working with earth and mud. They made a body, but it didn't look good to them. It was just separating, just crumbling, just loosening, just softening, just disintegrating, and just dissolving. Its head wouldn't turn, either. Its face was just lopsided, its face was just twisted. It couldn't look around. It talked at first, but senselessly. It was quickly dissolving in the water.

"It won't last," the mason and sculptor said then. "It seems to be dwindling away, so let it just dwindle. It can't walk and it can't multiply, so let it be merely a thought," they said.

Part IV: The Human Carved of Wood

So then they dismantled, again they brought down their work and design. Again they talked:

"What is there for us to make that would turn out well, that would succeed in keeping our days and praying to us?" they said. Then they planned again:

"We'll just tell Xpiyacoc, Xmucane, Hunahpu Possum, Hunahpu Coyote, to try a counting of days, a counting of lots," the mason and sculptor said to themselves. Then they invoked Xpiyacoc, Xmucane.

Then came the naming of those who are the midmost seers: the "Grandmother of Day, Grandmother of Light," as the Maker, Modeler called them. These are names of Xpiyacoc and Xmucane.

When Hurricane had spoken with the Sovereign Plumed Serpent, they invoked the daykeepers, diviners, the midmost seers:

"There is yet to find, yet to discover how we are to model a person, construct a person again, a provider, nurturer, so that we are called upon and we are recognized: our recompense is in words.

> Midwife, matchmaker,
> our grandmother, our grandfather,
> Xpiyacoc, Xmucane,
> let there be planting, let there be the dawning
> of our invocation, our sustenance, our recognition
> by the human work, the human design,
> the human figure, the human mass.

So be it, fulfill your names:

Hunahpu Possum, Hunahpu Coyote,
Bearer twice over, Begetter twice over,
Great Peccary, Great Tapir,
lapidary, jeweler,
sawyer, carpenter,
Maker of the Blue-Green Plate,
Maker of the Blue-Green Bowl,
incense maker, master craftsman,
Grandmother of Day, Grandmother of Light.

You have been called upon because of our work, our design. Run your hands over the kernels of corn, over the seeds of the coral tree, just get it done, just let it come out whether we should carve and gouge a mouth, a face in wood," they told the daykeepers.

And then comes the borrowing, the counting of days; the hand is moved over the corn kernels, over the coral seeds, the days, the lots.

Then they spoke to them, one of them a grandmother, the other a grandfather.

This is the grandfather, this is the master of the coral seeds: Xpiyacoc is his name.

And this is the grandmother, the daykeeper, diviner who stands behind others: Xmucane is her name.

And they said, as they set out the days:

"Just let it be found, just let it be discovered,
say it, our ear is listening,
may you talk, may you speak,
just find the wood for the carving and sculpting
by the builder, sculptor.
Is this to be the provider, the nurturer
when it comes to the planting, the dawning?
You corn kernels, you coral seeds,
you days, you lots:
may you succeed, may you be accurate,"

they said to the corn kernels, coral seeds, days, lots. "Have shame, you up there, Heart of Sky: attempt no deception before the mouth and face of Sovereign Plumed Serpent," they said. Then they spoke straight to the point:

"It is well that there be your manikins, woodcarvings, talking, speaking, there on the face of the earth."

"So be it," they replied. The moment they spoke it was done: the manikins, woodcarvings, human in looks and human in speech.

This was the peopling of the face of the earth:

They came into being, they multiplied, they had daughters, they had sons, these manikins, woodcarvings. But there was nothing in their hearts and nothing in their minds, no memory of their mason and builder. They just went and walked wherever they wanted. Now they did not remember the Heart of Sky.

And so they fell, just an experiment and just a cutout for humankind. They were talking at first but their faces were dry. They were not yet developed in the legs and arms. They had no blood, no lymph. They had no sweat, no fat. Their complexions were dry, their faces were crusty. They flailed their legs and arms, their bodies were deformed.

And so they accomplished nothing before the Maker, Modeler who gave them birth, gave them heart. They became the first numerous people here on the face of the earth.

Again there comes a humiliation, destruction, and demolition. The manikins, woodcarvings were killed when the Heart of Sky devised a flood for them. A great flood was made; it came down on the heads of the manikins, woodcarvings.

The man's body was carved from the wood of the coral tree by the Maker, Modeler. And as for the woman, the Maker, Modeler needed the pith of reeds for the woman's body. They were not competent, nor did they speak before the builder and sculptor who made them and brought them forth, and so they were killed, done in by a flood:

There came a rain of resin from the sky.

There came the one named Gouger of Faces: he gouged out their eyeballs.

There came Sudden Bloodletter: he snapped off their heads.

There came Crunching Jaguar: he ate their flesh.

There came Tearing Jaguar: he tore them open.

They were pounded down to the bones and tendons, smashed and pulverized even to the bones. Their faces were smashed because they were incompetent before their mother and their father, the Heart of Sky, named Hurricane. The earth was blackened because of this; the black rainstorm began, rain all day and rain all night. Into their houses came the animals, small and great. Their faces were crushed by things of wood and stone. Everything spoke: their water jars, their tortilla griddles, their plates, their cooking pots, their dogs, their grinding stones, each and every thing crushed their faces. Their dogs and turkeys told them:

"You caused us pain, you ate us, but now it is *you* whom *we* shall eat." And this is the grinding stone:

> *"We were undone because of you.*
> *Every day, every day,*
> *in the dark, in the dawn, forever,*
> *r-r-rip, r-r-rip,*
> *r-r-rub, r-r-rub,*
> *right in our faces, because of you.*

This was the service we gave you at first, when you were still people, but today you will learn of our power. We shall pound and we shall grind your flesh," their grinding stones told them.

And this is what their dogs said, when they spoke in their turn:

"Why is it you can't seem to give us our food? We just watch and you just keep us down, and you throw us around. You keep a stick ready when you eat, just so you can hit us. We don't talk, so we've received nothing from you. How could you not have known? You *did* know that we were wasting away there, behind you.

"So, this very day you will taste the teeth in our mouths. We shall eat you," their dogs told them, and their faces were crushed.

And then their tortilla griddles and cooking pots spoke to them in turn:

"Pain! That's all you've done for us. Our mouths are sooty, our faces are sooty. By setting us on the fire all the time, you burn us. Since *we* felt no pain, *you* try it. We shall burn you," all their cooking pots said, crushing their faces.

The stones, their hearthstones were shooting out, coming right out of the fire, going for their heads, causing them pain. Now they run for it, helter-skelter.

They want to climb up on the houses, but they fall as the houses collapse.

They want to climb the trees; they're thrown off by the trees.

They want to get inside caves, but the caves slam shut in their faces.

Such was the scattering of the human work, the human design. The people were ground down, overthrown. The mouths and faces of all of them were destroyed and crushed. And it used to be said that the monkeys in the forests today are a sign of this. They were left as a sign because wood alone was used for their flesh by the builder and sculptor.

So this is why monkeys look like people: they are a sign of a previous human work, human design—mere manikins, mere wood-carvings.

[The lengthy description of the hero journey of the hero twins that is included at this point in the original manuscript is presented below as one of the mythic texts in "Feathered Serpents and Hero Twins: The Mythic Structure of Rulership."]

Part V: The Creation of Humanity

And here is the beginning of the conception of humans, and of the search for the ingredients of the human body. So they spoke, the Bearer, Begetter, the Makers, Modelers named Sovereign Plumed Serpent:

"The dawn has approached, preparations have been made, and morning has come for the provider, nurturer, born in the light, begotten in the light. Morning has come for humankind, for the people of the face of the earth," they said. It all came together as they went on thinking in the darkness, in the night, as they searched and they sifted, they thought and they wondered.

And here their thoughts came out in clear light. They sought and discovered what was needed for human flesh. It was only a short while before the sun, moon, and stars were to appear above the Makers and Modelers. Broken Place, Bitter Water Place is the name: the yellow corn, white corn came from there.

And these are the names of the animals who brought the food: fox, coyote, parrot, crow. There were four animals who brought the news of the ears of yellow corn and white corn. They were coming from over there at Broken Place, they showed the way to the break.

And this was when they found the staple foods.

And these were the ingredients for the flesh of the human work, the human design, and the water was for the blood. It became human blood, and corn was also used by the Bearer, Begetter.

And so they were happy over the provisions of the good mountain, filled with sweet things, thick with yellow corn, white corn, and thick with pataxte and cacao, countless zapotes, anonas, jocotes, nances, matasanos, sweets—the rich foods filling up the citadel named Broken Place, Bitter Water Place. All the edible fruits were there: small staples, great staples, small plants, great plants. The way was shown by the animals.

And then the yellow corn and white corn were ground, and Xmucane did the grinding nine times. Corn was used, along with the water she rinsed her hands with, for the creation of grease; it became human fat when it was worked by the Bearer, Begetter, Sovereign Plumed Serpent, as they are called.

After that, they put it into words:

the making, the modeling of our first mother-father,
with yellow corn, white corn alone for the flesh,
food alone for the human legs and arms,
for our first fathers, the four human works.

It was staples alone that made up their flesh.

This is the first person: Jaguar Quitze.
And now the second: Jaguar Night.
And now the third: Mahucutah.
And the fourth: True Jaguar.
And these are the names of our first mother-fathers. They were simply made and modeled, it is said; they had no mother and no father. We have named the men by themselves. No woman gave birth to them, nor were they begotten by the builder, sculptor, Bearer, Begetter. By sacrifice alone, by genius alone they were made, they were modeled by the Maker, Modeler, Bearer, Begetter, Sovereign Plumed Serpent. And when they came to fruition, they came out human:
They talked and they made words.
They looked and they listened.
They walked, they worked.
They were good people, handsome, with looks of the male kind. Thoughts came into existence and they gazed; their vision came all at once. Perfectly they saw, perfectly they knew everything under the sky, whenever they looked. The moment they turned around and

looked around in the sky, on the earth, everything was seen without any obstruction. They didn't have to walk around before they could see what was under the sky; they just stayed where they were.

As they looked, their knowledge became intense. Their sight passed through trees, through rocks, through lakes, through seas, through mountains, through plains. Jaguar Quitze, Jaguar Night, Mahucutah, and True Jaguar were truly gifted people.

And then they were asked by the builder and mason:

"What do you know about your being? Don't you look, don't you listen? Isn't your speech good, and your walk? So you must look, to see out under the sky. Don't you see the mountain-plain clearly? So try it," they were told.

And then they saw everything under the sky perfectly. After that, they thanked the Maker, Modeler:

> *"Truly now,*
> *double thanks, triple thanks*
> *that we've been formed, we've been given*
> *our mouths, our faces,*
> *we speak, we listen,*
> *we wonder, we move,*
> *our knowledge is good, we've understood*
> *what is far and near,*
> *and we've seen what is great and small*
> *under the sky, on the earth.*
> *Thanks to you we've been formed,*
> *we've come to be made and modeled,*
> *our grandmother, our grandfather,"*

they said when they gave thanks for having been made and modeled. They understood everything perfectly, they sighted the four sides, the four corners in the sky, on the earth, and this didn't sound good to the builder and sculptor:

"What our works and designs have said is no good:

'We have understood everything, great and small,' they say." And so the Bearer, Begetter took back their knowledge:

"What should we do with them now? Their vision should at least reach nearby, they should see at least a small part of the face of the earth, but what they're saying isn't good. Aren't they merely 'works' and 'designs' in their very names? Yet they'll become as great as gods, unless they procreate, proliferate at the sowing, the dawning, unless they increase."

"Let it be this way: now we'll take them apart just a little, that's what we need. What we've found out isn't good. Their deeds would become equal to ours, just because their knowledge reaches so far. They see everything," so said

the Heart of Sky, Hurricane,
Newborn Thunderbolt, Raw Thunderbolt,
Sovereign Plumed Serpent,
Bearer, Begetter,
Xpiyacoc, Xmucane,
Maker, Modeler,

as they are called. And when they changed the nature of their works, their designs, it was enough that the eyes be marred by the Heart of Sky. They were blinded as the face of a mirror is breathed upon. Their eyes were weakened. Now it was only when they looked nearby that things were clear.

And such was the loss of the means of understanding, along with the means of knowing everything, by the four humans. The root was implanted.

And such was the making, modeling of our first grandfather, our father, by the Heart of Sky, Heart of Earth.

And then their wives and women came into being. Again, the same gods thought of it. It was as if they were asleep when they received them, truly beautiful women were there with Jaguar Quitze, Jaguar Night, Mahucutah, and True Jaguar. With their women there they became wider awake. Right away they were happy at heart again, because of their wives.

Celebrated Seahouse is the name of the wife of Jaguar Quitze.
Prawn House is the name of the wife of Jaguar Night.
Hummingbird House is the name of the wife of Mahucutah.
Macaw House is the name of the wife of True Jaguar.
So these are the names of their wives, who became ladies of rank, giving birth to the people of the tribes, small and great.

And this is our root, we who are Quiché people. And there came to be a crowd of penitents and sacrificers. It wasn't only four who came into being then but there were four mothers for us, the Quiché people. There were different names for each of the peoples when they multiplied, there in the east.

[The *Popol Vuh* concludes with a lengthy migration story that recounts episodes comprising the mythic and actual history of the Quiché people. Included is the brief section that follows, which accounts for the first sunrise and the appearance of the sun, moon, and stars, the final event in the story of the lives of the gods.]

Part VI: The Creation of the Sun and Moon

And here is the dawning and showing of the sun, moon, and stars. And Jaguar Quitze, Jaguar Night, Mahucutah, and True Jaguar were overjoyed when they saw the daybringer. It came up first. It looked brilliant when it came up, since it was ahead of the sun.

After that they unwrapped their copal incense, which came from the east, and there was triumph in their hearts when they unwrapped it. They gave their heartfelt thanks with three kinds at once:

Mixtam Copal is the name of the copal brought by Jaguar Quitze.

Cauiztan Copal, next, is the name of the copal brought by Jaguar Night.

Godly Copal, as the next one is called, was brought by Mahucutah.

The three of them had their copal, and this is what they burned as they incensed the direction of the rising sun. They were crying sweetly as they shook their burning copal, the precious copal.

After that they cried because they had yet to see and yet to witness the birth of the sun.

And then, when the sun came up, the animals, small and great, were happy. They all came up from the rivers and canyons; they waited on all the mountain peaks. Together they looked toward the place where the sun came out.

So then the puma and jaguar cried out, but the first to cry out was a bird, the parrot by name. All the animals were truly happy. The eagle, the white vulture, small birds, great birds spread their wings, and the penitents and sacrificers knelt down. They were overjoyed, together with the penitents and sacrificers of the Tams, the Ilocs.

And the Rabinals, Cakchiquels, those of the Bird House.

And the Sweatbath House, Talk House, Quiba House, those of the Yoke House.

And the Yaqui Sovereign—however many tribes there may be today. There were countless peoples, but there was just one dawn for all tribes.

And then the face of the earth was dried out by the sun. The sun was like a person when he revealed himself. His face was hot, so he dried out the face of the earth. Before the sun came up it was soggy, and the face of the earth was muddy before the sun came up. And when the sun had risen just a short distance he was like a person, and his heat was unbearable. Since he revealed himself only when he was born, it is only his reflection that now remains. As they put it in their own words:

"The sun that shows itself is not the real sun."

And then, all at once, Tohil, Auilix, and Hacauitz were turned to stone, along with the idols of the puma, jaguar, rattlesnake, yellowbite, which the White Sparkstriker took with him into the trees. Everywhere, all of them became stone when the sun, moon, and stars appeared. Perhaps we would have no relief from the voracious animals today—the puma, jaguar, rattlesnake, yellowbite—and perhaps it wouldn't even be our day today, if the original animals hadn't been turned to stone by the sun when he came up.

There was great happiness in the hearts of Jaguar Quitze, Jaguar Night, Mahucutah, and True Jaguar. They were overjoyed when it dawned. The people on the mountain of Hacauitz were not yet numerous; just a few were there. Their dawning was there and they burned copal there, incensing the direction of the rising sun. They came from there: it is their own mountain, their own plain. Those named Jaguar Quitze, Jaguar Night, Mahucutah, and True Jaguar came from there, and they began their increase on that mountain.

And that became their citadel, since they were there when the sun, moon, and stars appeared, when it dawned and cleared on the face of the earth, over everything under the sky.

AZTEC CREATION MYTHS

The Creation of the Sun and the Moon, from the *Florentine Codex*

A Franciscan missionary, Fray Bernardino de Sahagún, arrived in New Spain in 1529 just after the Conquest, and he died there in 1590. His contribution to our knowledge of the culture of the native peoples of Mesoamerica at the time of the Conquest is perhaps greater than that of any other single person. Anxious to know the ancient religion and to record the Aztecs' rich cultural heritage, he learned Nahuatl, the Aztec language, soon after he arrived. Through the use of native informants he systematically collected material about the ancient rites, gods, and myths as well as about the daily practices of the people. Much of this material is included in the best-known of his compilations, the *Historia General de las Cosas de Nueva España (General History of the Things of New Spain)*, which is also known as the *Florentine Codex*. This work, produced between 1575 and 1585, is particularly valuable since it contains both the Nahuatl texts of his informants and his often paraphrased Spanish translation and includes as well many images to illustrate the text. Although we do not know the identity of any of Sahagún's informants, it is clear from their work that they spoke both Nahuatl and Spanish and that they had been given something of a European education and Christian indoctrination.

Although the materials Sahagún gathered as well as his interpretation of Aztec culture provide an extremely valuable source for scholars, it is important to remember that his goal was primarily to create an appropriate instrument for preaching the Christian doctrine in New Spain, and therefore his comments often manifest his strongly pro-Christian bias, especially in his tendency to characterize the indigenous gods as demons and their images as idols.

This particular text narrates the events that transpired fifty-two years after the end of the first four suns, a time in which there was still only darkness. The story of how the gods gathered at Teotihuacan to create a new sun and by making great sacrifices found a way to put it in motion so that a new age could begin suggests both the central importance of the sun and the necessity of sacrifice.

THE CREATION OF THE SUN AND THE MOON

Translated from the Nahuatl by Arthur J. O. Anderson and Charles E. Dibble. Originally published in Bernardino de Sahagún, *General History of the Things of New Spain, Book 7: The Sun, Moon, and Stars, and the Binding of the Years.* Translated by Arthur J. O. Anderson and Charles E. Dibble (Santa Fe, NM: School of American Research, and Salt Lake City: Univ. of Utah, 1953), 3–9. Reprinted by permission of the publisher.

Behold the fable in which it is told how a little rabbit lay across the face of the moon. Of this, it is told that the gods were only at play with the moon. They struck his face with the rabbit; they wounded his face with it—they maimed it. The gods thus dimmed his face. Thereafter the moon came to arise and come forth.

It is told that when yet all was in darkness, when yet no sun had shone and no dawn had broken—it is said—the gods gathered themselves together and took counsel among themselves there at Teotihuacan. They spoke; they said among themselves:

"Come hither, O gods! Who will carry the burden? Who will take it upon himself to be the sun, to bring the dawn?"

And upon this, one of them who was there spoke: Tecuciztecatl presented himself. He said: "O gods, I shall be the one."

And again the gods spoke: "And who else?"

Thereupon they looked around at one another. They pondered the matter. They said to one another: "How may this be? How may we decide?"

None dared; no one else came forward. Everyone was afraid; they all drew back.

And not present was one man, Nanauatzin; he stood there listening among the others to that which was discussed. Then the gods called to this one. They said to him: "Thou shalt be the one, O Nanauatzin."

He then eagerly accepted the decision; he took it gladly. He said: "It is well, O gods; you have been good to me."

Then they began now to do penance. They fasted four days—both Tecuciztecatl and Nanauatzin. And then, also, at this time, the fire was laid. Now it burned, there in the hearth. They named the hearth teotexcalli.

And this Tecuciztecatl: that with which he did penance was all costly. His fir branches were quetzal feathers, and his grass balls were of gold; his maguey spines were of green stone; the reddened, bloodied spines were of coral. And his incense was very good incense.

And as for Nanauatzin, his fir branches were made only of green water rushes—green reeds bound in threes, all making, together, nine bundles. And his grass balls were only dried pine needles. And his maguey spines were these same maguey spines. And the blood with which they were covered was his own blood. And for his incense, he used only the scabs from his sores, which he lifted up. For these two, for each one singly, a hill was made. There they remained, performing penances for four nights. They are now called pyramids—the Pyramid of the Sun and the Pyramid of the Moon.

And when they ended their four nights of penitence, then they went to throw down and cast away, each one, their fir branches, and, indeed, all with which they had been performing penances. This was done at the time of the lifting of the penance; when, well into the night, they were to do their labor; they were to become gods.

And when midnight had come, thereupon the gods gave them their adornment; they arrayed them and readied them. To Tecuciztecatl they gave his round, forked heron feather headdress and his sleeveless jacket. But as for Nanauatzin, they bound on his headdress of mere paper and tied on his hair, called his paper hair. And they gave him his paper stole and his paper breech clout.

And when this was done, when midnight had come, all the gods proceeded to encircle the hearth, which was called teotexcalli, where for four days had burned the fire. On both sides the gods arranged themselves in line, and in the middle they set up, standing, these two, named Tecuciztecatl and Nanauatzin. They stood facing and looking toward the hearth.

And thereupon the gods spoke: They said to Tecuciztecatl: "Take courage, O Tecuciztecatl; fall—cast thyself—into the fire!"

Upon this, he went forward to cast himself into the flames. And when the heat came to reach him, it was insufferable, intolerable, and unbearable; for the hearth had blazed up exceedingly, a great heap of coals burned, and the flames flared up high. Thus he came terrified, stopped in fear, turned about, and went back. Then once more he set out, in order to try to do it. He exerted himself to the full, that he might cast and give himself to the flames. And he could in no way dare to do it. When again the heat reached him, he could only turn and leap back. He could not bear it. Four times indeed—four times in all—he was thus to act and try; then he could cast himself no more. For then he might try only four times.

And when he had ended, trying four times, thereupon they cried out to Nanauatzin. The gods said to him: "Onward, thou, O Nanauatzin! Take heart!"

And Nanauatzin, daring all at once, determined—resolved—hardened his heart, and shut firmly his eyes. He had no fear; he did not stop short; he did not falter in fright; he did not turn back. All at once he quickly threw and cast himself into the fire; once and for all he went. Thereupon he burned; his body crackled and sizzled.

And when Tecuciztecatl saw that already he burned, then, afterwards, he cast himself upon the fire. Thereupon he also burned.

And thus do they say: It is told that then flew up an eagle, which followed them. It threw itself suddenly into the flames; it cast itself into them, while still it blazed up. Therefore its feathers are scorched looking and blackened. And afterwards followed an ocelot, when now the fire no longer burned high, and he came to fall in. Thus he was only blackened—smutted—in various places, and singed by the fire. For it was not now burning hot. Therefore he was only spotted, dotted with black spots, as if splashed with black.

From this event, it is said, they took—from here was taken—the custom whereby was called and named one who was valiant, a warrior. He was given the name quauhtlocelotl. The word quauhtli came first, it is told, because, as was said, the eagle first entered the fire. And the ocelot followed thereafter. Thus is it said in one word—quauhtlocelotl; because the latter fell into the fire after the eagle.

And after this, when both had cast themselves into the flames, when they had already burned, then the gods sat waiting to see where Nanauatzin would come to rise—he who first fell into the fire—in order that he might shine as the sun; in order that dawn might break.

When the gods had sat and been waiting for a long time, thereupon began the reddening of the dawn in all directions, all around, the dawn and light extended. And so, they say, thereupon the gods fell upon their knees in order to await where he who had become the sun would come to rise. In all directions they looked; everywhere they peered and kept turning about. As to no place were they agreed in their opinions and thoughts. Uncertain were those whom they asked. Some thought that it would be from the north that the sun would come to rise, and placed themselves to look there; some did so to the west; some placed themselves to look south. They expected that he might rise in all directions, because the light was everywhere.

And some placed themselves so that they could watch there to the east. They said: "For there, in that place, the sun already will come to arise." True indeed were the words of those who looked there and pointed with their fingers in that direction. Thus they say, that those who looked there to the east were Quetzalcoatl; the name of the second was Ecatl; and Totec, or Anauatl itecu; and the red Tezcatlipoca. Also there were those who were called the Mimixcoa, who were without number; and four women—Tiacapan, Teicu, Tlacoyehua, and Xocoyotl.

And when the sun came to rise, when he burst forth, he appeared to be red; he kept swaying from side to side. It was impossible to look into his face; he blinded one with his light. Intensely did he shine. He issued rays of light from himself; his rays reached in all directions; his brilliant rays penetrated everywhere.

And afterwards Tecuciztecatl came to rise, following behind him from the same place—the east,—near where the sun had come bursting forth. In the same manner that they had fallen into the fire, just so they came forth. They came following each other.

And so they tell it; so they relate the story and repeat the legend: Exactly equal had they become in their appearance, as they shone. When the gods saw them, thus exactly the same in their aspect, then once more there was deliberation. They said: "How may this be, O gods? Will they perchance both together follow the same path? Will they both shine together?"

And the gods all issued a judgment. They said: "Thus will this be; thus will this be done."

Then one of the gods came out running. With a rabbit he came to wound in the face this Tecuciztecatl; with it he darkened his face; he killed its brilliance. Thus doth it appear today.

And when this was done, when both appeared over the earth together, they could, on the other hand, not move nor follow their paths. They could only remain still and motionless. So once again the gods spoke: "How shall we live? The sun cannot move. Shall we perchance live among common folk? Let this be, that through us the sun may be revived. Let all of us die."

Then it became the office of Ecatl to slay the gods. But they say thus: that Xolotl wished not to die. He said to the gods: "Let me not die, O gods." Wherefore he wept much; his eyes and his eyelids swelled.

And when he who dealt death was to overtake him, he fled from his presence; he ran; he quickly entered a field of green maize, and took the form of, and quickly turned into, two young maize stalks growing from a single root, which the workers in the field have named xolotl. But there, in the field of green maize, he was seen. Then once again he fled from him; once more he quickly entered a maguey field. There also he quickly changed himself into a maguey plant consisting of two parts called mexolotl. Once more he was seen, and once more he quickly entered into the water and went to take the shape of an amphibious animal called axolotl. There they could go to seize him, that they might slay him.

And they say that though all the gods died, even then the sun god could not move and follow his path. Thus it became the charge of Ecatl, the wind, who arose and exerted himself fiercely and violently as he blew. At once he could move him, who thereupon went on his way. And when he had already followed his course, only the moon remained there. At the time when the sun came to enter the place where he set, then once more the moon moved. So, there, they passed each other and went each one his own way. Thus the sun cometh forth once, and spendeth the whole day in his work; and the moon under-taketh the night's task; he worketh all night; he doth his labor at night.

From this it appeareth, it is said, that the moon, Tecuciztecatl, would have been the sun if he had been first to cast himself into the fire; because he had presented himself first and all his offerings had been costly in the penances.

Here endeth this legend and fable, which was told in times past, and was in the keeping of the old people.

The Creation of the World, from the *Historia de los Mexicanos por sus Pinturas*

The *Historia de los Mexicanos por sus Pinturas* was probably written between 1533 and 1540 by the Franciscan priest and linguist Andrés de Olmos. Its title reflects the fact that it was originally written as a commentary on a surviving codex to which it was attached. That codex, now lost, is generally thought to have set forth the "official" version of Aztec mythology and included what is perhaps the earliest account of the Aztec creation myths. It was probably written in the city of Mexico, or perhaps Tlatelolco, where Olmos, fluent in Nahuatl, was a lecturer between 1533 and 1539. Written for the use of the bishop of Cuenca, that cleric took it with him when he returned to Spain, and the manuscript remains today in Madrid.

This ancient account begins with the birth of the four sons of the primordial, "uncreated" high god Ometeotl (Tonacatecuhtli, rendered here as Tonacatecutli, in this version), and we learn that it is they who are responsible for the creation of fire, the sun, the underworld, the earth, corn, man and woman, and time itself. They

> constitute the primary forces that activate the history of the world and the symbolism of their colors—red, black, white, and blue—permits us to trace their identification with the natural elements, the directions of space, and the periods of time allotted to their influence. With the four sons of Ometeotl, space and time enter fully into the world. Both space and time are conceived not as empty stage settings, but as factors that combine to regulate the occurrence of cosmic events.[47]

The four elements—earth, wind, fire, and water—to which the four suns were related were associated also with the four time periods and the four directions and thereby the four cosmic divisions of the quadripartite universe.

After its narration of the creation of the four initial suns, the *Historia* recounts several of the events of the Fifth Sun, or present world, such as the raising and ordering of the heavens, the formation of habitable land, and the creation of the sun and the moon, but it does not include the story of the creation of mankind. Following the initial segment presented here, the narrative goes on to present its version of the origin and development of the Aztec state. It should be noted that we have excerpted the segment dealing with the rain god and presented it in the following section, "The Myths of Fertility."

THE CREATION OF THE WORLD

This is an original translation from the Spanish by Scott Mahler, prepared for this volume. In rendering the colonial account into modern English, the translator has omitted certain passages that attempt to explain, but do not contain, the creation myth and phrases such as "or so the Indians say" as well as the titles given each section. The editors have regularized the original's spelling of Tezcatlipuca to Tezcatlipoca and Tonacateuctli to Tonacatecutli.

I

There was originally one god named Tonacatecutli and his wife, Tonacacihuatl, who was also known as Cachequecatl. These gods created themselves and lived in the thirteenth heaven.

They had four children. The oldest was called Tlatlauhqui Tezcatlipoca, who was the principal god of the people of Huexotzinco and Tlaxcala, who knew him as Camaxtle. He was born with reddish skin.

The second son was called Yayauhqui Tezcatlipoca. He was the biggest and the worst and dominated the other three because he was born in the middle. He was born black.

The third brother was named Quetzalcoatl, who was also called Yohualli Ehecatl.

The fourth and smallest brother was called by the names Omitecutli and Maquizcoatl. The Mexicans called him Huitzilopochtli, because he was left-handed. He was the Mexicans' main god, as he was in the land from which they came, because he was the greatest god of war.

Of these four sons of Tonacatecutli and Tonacacihuatl, Tezcatlipoca was everywhere and knew the hearts and minds of others, so they called him Moyocoya, or the all-powerful and unequalled.

Huitzilopochtli, the youngest brother and god of Mexico was born without flesh—only bones—and lived that way for six hundred years.

II

Six hundred years after the four brothers were born, they got together and said that it would be good to organize what they had to do and what laws they had to have. Quetzalcoatl and Huitzilopochtli were assigned to do this on behalf of the others.

First they made fire, then a half-sun, which only cast a little light because it was not whole.

Then they made a man and a woman. They called the man Uxumuco and the woman Cipactonal. These two were commanded to work the land, and she was to spin and to weave. Uxumuco and Cipactonal gave birth to the macehuales, who worked constantly and were never idle.

To the woman the gods gave certain grains of maize so that she could cure, divine, and do magic with them.

Then they made the days and divided them into months, giving each one twenty days. There were eighteen months and three hundred and sixty days in a year.

Then the gods created Mictlantecutli and Mictecacihuatl, husband and wife and gods of the underworld, and settled them in their domain.

Then they created the heavens that join the thirteenth heaven. They made water, and they created a huge fish called Cipactli, from whom they made the earth.

[The narrative recounts here the creation of the god and goddess of rain, which we have included in the following collection of the myths of fertility.]

III

While these things were happening, before there was time and everything was one, a son named Piltzintecutli was born to the first man and woman. Because he needed someone to marry, the gods made a woman for him from the hairs of Xochiquetzal, and she became his first wife.

Then all four gods saw how the half-sun they created did not shine much, and so they decided that they should make the other half in order to cast enough light over the earth. On seeing what needed to be done, Tezcatlipoca turned himself into the sun so that there would be light.

Then the four gods created a race of giant men, so strong that they could pull up trees with their hands, who ate only acorns.

IV

After 676 years had passed, Quetzalcoatl struck Tezcatlipoca with a club and threw him into the water. Tezcatlipoca then turned himself into a tiger and devoured the giants who were created while he was the sun.

The macehuales ate only pine nuts at this time. Quetzalcoatl was the sun for 676 years until Tezcatlipoca, a god like his brothers and a tiger, ousted him and raised such a blast of wind that it carried him and all the macehuales away, except for a few that remained in the air, and who were turned into monkeys and apes.

Then Tlalocatecutli, the god of the underworld, became the sun for 364 years. During this time the macehuales had nothing to eat but acicintli, a seed like wheat which sprouts in the water.

After these years passed, Quetzalcoatl rained fire from the sky and kept Tlalocatecutli from being the sun. In his place he put his wife Chalchiuhtlicue, who was the sun for 312 years. The macehuales ate only cincocopi during this time, which is a kernel like corn.

V

In the last year that Chalchiuhtlicue was the sun, it rained so hard and so abundantly that the heavens fell, and the water carried away all the macehuales, who turned into every species of fish.

Seeing that the sky had fallen, the four gods ordained that they should make four roads through the center of the earth, in order to enter it and raise the sky. They created four men to help them. One they called Cuatemoc, another Itzcoatl, another Itzmali, and the last Tenexuchitl. Tezcatlipoca and Quetzalcoatl turned themselves into enormous trees; Tezcatlipoca into a Tezcacuahitl tree, or tree of mirrors, and Quetzalcoatl into a quetzalhuexotl tree. Then the men, trees, and gods raised the sky with the stars as they are today, and Tonacatecutli, their father, made them masters of the sky and stars. Tezcatlipoca and Quetzalcoatl walked through the heavens and made the Milky Way, where they dwell still.

VI

After the sky was raised, the gods gave life to the earth, which had died when the sky fell.

In the second year after the deluge, in the year called acatl, Tezcatlipoca changed his name to Mixcoatl, which means Cloud Snake.

That year he wanted to have a fiesta for the gods. He struck a light from some flint rods as he was accustomed to doing, and initiated the practice of starting a fire using flint. It was a great festival of many splendid fires.

In the sixth year after the deluge Cinteutl was born to Piltzintecutli, who was the son of the first man.

Two years later, the gods created the macehuales, just as they were before.

In the first year of the second cycle of thirteen years, all four gods got together and said that because the earth had no light except for the fires they had made, that they should make a sun, and that this sun should eat human hearts and drink human blood. So they had to make war wherever they could in order to get the hearts and blood.

Willing it so, the gods made war in the first year of the second cycle of thirteen, and it lasted three years.

During this time Tezcatlipoca created 400 men and 5 women, so that there would be people for the sun to eat. The men lived for only four years and the five women survived them.

In the tenth year of this cycle, Xochiquetzal, the first wife of Piltzintecutli and the bravest of all, died in war.

VII

In the twenty-sixth year after the flood, Quetzalcoatl wanted his son, who had no mother, to be the sun. Tlalocatecutli, the god of water, also wanted his son, whose mother was Chalchiuhtlicue, the moon, to be the sun.

They fasted and drew blood from their ears and from their bodies in their prayers and sacrifices.

Once this was done, Quetzalcoatl took his son and flung him onto a great fire, and from there he arose as the sun to cast light over the earth.

After the fire died down, Tlalocatecutli came and threw his son in the ashes, from which he arose as the moon, which is why he appears ashen and dim.

In this last year of thirteen, the sun began to shine, whereas before there had only been night, and the moon began to cross the sky, never to catch the sun. And so they both traversed the air, never reaching the heavens.

Myth of the Suns and the Toltec-Chichimec Origins of the Mexica People: The Entire *Leyenda de los Soles*

The *Leyenda de los Soles* contains what is probably the most ancient and most complete version of the Aztec creation myth. It was written in Nahuatl by a Spanish-educated Indian free of priestly direction who completed it in 1558, some time after the Conquest. León-Portilla, for one, believes that "the form of writing, which consistently juxtaposes such expressions as 'here is' to dates, indicates that it was used as a commentary on a native [pictographic] manuscript."[48] Willard Gingerich, the present translator, notes that the text "appears on internal linguistic evidence to be the redaction of a specific performance event, by an unknown Mexica Aztec speaker and recorded by an unknown amanuensis, from a lost pictographic codex (or codexes) on the date given in the first paragraph. Especially the first section gives repeated evidence of a speaker pointing to specific visual images." Supporting this conclusion is the fact that the number and order of the creations correspond very closely, although not exactly, to those on the Aztec calendar stone and to the account in the *Historia de los Mexicanos por sus Pinturas*.

The *Leyenda* version follows the pattern manifested in other Mesoamerican creation stories: each sun is given a name or an identification, usually related to the mode of its destruction; a number of years is given to indicate the duration of each sun; the particular food of the era is named; the means of destruction of the inhabitants is told, and the transformation of the inhabitants is described; and a date is given for the entire period of each sun. The fact that no two sources agree exactly on these matters suggests that it is this structure that is important within the tradition rather than the particular details. For the peoples of Mesoamerica the earth was not static; it was always in motion, but the constancy of that movement required a balance. The disturbance of the equilibrium of the forces within each era brought about cataclysmic destruction and the end of the period of that sun.

After narrating the creation and destruction of the first four suns, the *Leyenda* tells of several of the major events of the Fifth Sun: the discovery of fire and the raising of the heavens; the creation of mankind through Quetzalcoatl's shrewdness and creativity in overcoming the forces of death; the discovery of corn in a sacred mountain, thus assuring the subsistence of mankind in the present world of the Fifth Sun; the creation of the sun and the moon through the sacrifices of the gods. The *Leyenda* concludes with four sections loosely related to Quetzalcoatl, his parents, and the origin of the Mexica state.

This inclusiveness is typical of the mythic documents that remain, and it is for this reason that we present the whole of the *Leyenda* in this section despite the fact that the last six sections belong thematically with Part VI, "Feathered Serpents and Hero Twins: The Mythic Structure of Rulership," with the tenth section related also to fertility.

MYTH OF THE SUNS AND THE TOLTEC-CHICHIMEC ORIGINS OF THE MEXICA PEOPLE, OR TLAMACHILLIZTLATOLZAZANILLI ("THE WISDOM DISCOURSE OF FABLES")

This is an original translation from the Nahuatl, prepared for this volume by Willard Gingerich, of this manuscript, bound in the so-called *Codex Chimalpopoca* and traditionally titled *Leyenda de los Soles, Legend of the Suns,* or *Manuscript of 1558.*

I

Here is the wisdom-discourse of fables, how in ancient times it happened that the earth was established, and each individual thing found its place. This is the manner in which it is known how the sun gave rise to so many things, two thousand five hundred and thirteen years before today, the 22nd of May, 1558.

This sun, Nahui Ocelotl, 4 Jaguar, endured 676 years. Those who lived here first were eaten by jaguars on [the day] 4 Jaguar, of this sun. And they ate chicome malinalli, 7 Grass, which was their sun-sustenance, and so they existed 676 years until they were savagely devoured in 13 years, and so they completely perished and were abolished. And then the sun disappeared. And their year was the year Ce Acatl, 1 Reed. And they were first eaten under this same day-sign 4 Jaguar, so by just this means they were abolished and totally destroyed.

This sun is named Nahui Ecatl, 4 Wind. Those who lived in this second place were swept away by the wind; during the sun 4 Wind it was. And this way they were destroyed: they became monkeys. Their houses and even their trees were all swept away by the wind. This sun itself was carried away by the wind. Their sun-sustenance was matlactlomome cohuatl, 12 Serpent. And so they lived 364 years; thus they were utterly destroyed: in one day they were swept off by wind. Under the single day-sign 4 Wind they were destroyed, and their year was 1 Flint.

This is the sun Nahui Quiyahuitl, 4 Rain. And these are the ones who lived during the sun Nahui Quiyahuitl, which was the third. And thus they were destroyed, in a rain of fire; they were all transformed to birds. And the sun itself also burned; all their houses burned. And so they lived 312 years, and so they were totally destroyed by a rain of fire in only one day. They ate chicome tecpatl, 7 Flint; it was their sun-sustenance. And their year is 1 Flint, and in only one day-sign, 4 Rain, thus they were destroyed: they became the Pipiles, whose speech sounds like turkey-talk. This is why today children are called "little gobblers."

This sun is called Nahui Atl, 4 Water. And the water gathered for 52 years. These are the ones who lived in the fourth age, the sun of 4 Water. And so they lived 676 years and so they were destroyed, were inundated: they were transformed into fish. In only one day the heavens came down to inundate them, and they were destroyed. And they ate nahui xochitl, 4 Flower, it was their sun-sustenance. And their year was 1 House and on the single day-sign 4 Water they were destroyed; all the mountains were destroyed. And thus the water gathered for 52 years.

And so their years are finished.

‖

Then Titlacahuan, "Our Master," [Tezcatlipoca] called forth the one known as "Our Father" and his consort known as "Nene." He said to them, "You will want nothing more. Hollow out a large ahuehuetl log: you will enter it during the vigil of Toçoztli when the heavens will come crashing down." And so they entered it, and then he sealed them in. He said, "You will have a single ear of corn to eat and likewise your woman will have one." When they had finally consumed all the kernels, they heard the water outside declining. Their log no longer moved. Then they opened the log, they saw a fish, they struck a fire from the wood and cooked the fish for themselves. Then the gods Citlallinicue and Citlallatonac gazed down on them and said, "Who has made fire? Who is now smoking up the heavens?" And so then Our Master Tezcatlipoca descended; he scolded them and said to them, "What are you doing, Grandpa? What is this fire?" Then he struck off their heads and reattached them over their buttocks; they became dogs. And here at the sign 2 Reed [you can see] the way in which the heavens were smoked up.

Here are we ourselves, this was already us. Here the firestarting-sticks fell and here the heavens were inundated in the year 1 Rabbit. Here it is [shown] how the firestarting-sticks fell when fire appeared, and here how darkness covered everything for twenty-five years. And here the heavens came to a stop in the year 1 Rabbit. And while the heavens were arrested, then the "dogs" smoked them up, as already mentioned, off there in the distance.

And so finally the firestarting-sticks fell and Tezcatlipoca lit a fire, so that once again the heavens filled with smoke in the year 2 Reed.

III

And then the gods called an assembly; they said, "Who will be seated there, now that the heavens have come to a halt and the Earth Lord has come to a halt? Gods, who will be seated?" Then the gods

Citlallinicue, Citlallatonac;
Apanteuctli, Tepanquizqui;
Tlallamanqui, Huictlollinqui;
Quetzalcoatl, Titlacahuan;

were distressed.

And then Quetzalcoatl went off to Mictlan, the Region of the Dead, where he came before the Lord and the Lady of Mictlan. Then he said, indeed he did, "I come to take away the jade bones which you so honorably guard." And so then the Lord of Mictlan said to him, "What is it you will do, O Quetzalcoatl?" And again he said, indeed he did, "The gods are anxious to know who will be settled on the earth."

And so once again the Lord of Mictlan spoke, "Very well; Blow on my conch trumpet and carry it four times around my jade throne." But the conch trumpet had no holes for finger-stops. Then Quetzalcoatl called the worms who filled it with holes, and then bees and hornets quickly rushed inside and filled it with sound so that the Lord of Mictlan heard it.

And then once again the Lord of Mictlan said, "Very well, take them." And then the Lord of Mictlan said to his messengers, the Mictecans, "Tell him, O gods, that he must leave them." And Quetzalcoatl then came forward and said, "I will take them, once and for all." And then he said to his spirit-double, his nahual, "Go tell them that I will leave them." And the nahual came saying loudly, "I will leave them."

Then Quetzalcoatl went up quickly and took the jade bones, those of the man on one side and of the woman on the other. In this way he took them: he wrapped them in a bundle which he carried up with him.

And once again the Lord of Mictlan said to his messengers, "O gods, Quetzalcoatl is in fact carrying off the jade bones! Gods, go dig a pit." Then they went to dig it, so that Quetzalcoatl fell down into it. He was startled by a covey of quail and fell down as though dead, scattering the jade bones across the ground and the quail nibbled and pecked at them.

Soon Quetzalcoatl revived; he began to weep and said to his nahual, "How can this be?" His nahual answered, "As it must. Things have gone wrong but let us go on."

Then Quetzalcoatl gathered up the bones and made a bundle and carried them at once to Tamoanchan. And as soon as he brought them the goddess named Quilaztli, who is also Cihuacoatl, ground them in her jade bowl. And then Quetzalcoatl bled his penis over it.

Then all the aforementioned gods performed penance, Apantecutli, Huictlollinqui, Tepanquizqui, Tlallamanac, Tzontemoc, and the sixth, Quetzalcoatl. And then they said, "The gods have given birth to men, the common people," for certainly they performed penance in our behalf.

IV

So once more they spoke: "What shall they eat, O gods? Already they are searching for nourishment, a sun-sustenance." Then the ant went to take kernels of corn from within the Mountain of Food-Stuffs. Quetzalcoatl encountered the ant and said to it, "Tell me where you went to get it." Persistently he questioned the ant but it did not wish to tell him. Finally it said, "Over there," and led him to the place.

Then Quetzalcoatl transformed himself to a black ant, accompanied the first ant, and they went into the mountain together. That is, Quetzalcoatl followed the red ant to the storage bin, gathered up the corn and carried it quickly to Tamoanchan. There the gods chewed and ate of it and then fed it to us, to nourish and strengthen us.

And then they said, "What shall we do with this Mountain of Food-Stuffs?" Then Quetzalcoatl went and tried to pull it with ropes, but could not lift it. So then Oxomoco performed divination with the kernels and also Cipactonal, his wife, performed divination (Cipactonal is the woman). They said the kernels revealed that only Nanahuatl would be capable of breaking open the Mountain of Food-Stuffs. Then the attendant gods of Tlaloc, the Tlaloque, lords of rain, appeared: the Blue Tlaloque, the White Tlaloque, the Yellow Tlaloque, the Red Tlaloque, and Nanahuatl broke open the corn.

And the food-stuffs were all stolen away by the lords of rain; the white, black, yellow and red corn, beans, chia, amaranth, fish-amaranth—everything was stolen.

V

The name of this sun is 4 Motion. This is now our sun, the one under which we live today. This is its figure, the one here, because this sun fell into the fire at the sacred hearth in Teotihuacan. It is the same sun as that of Topiltzin, "Our Beloved Prince" of Tollan, Quetzalcoatl. Before becoming this sun, its name was Nanahuatl, who was of Tamoanchan. Eagle, Jaguar, Hawk, Wolf, 6 Wind, 6 Flower—all are names of this sun.

This thing is called the "sacred hearth," and it burned for four years. Tonacateuctli and Xiuhteuctli called to Nanahuatl and told him, "Now you shall become guardian of heaven and earth." He was much saddened and said, "What are the gods going about saying? I am only a sickly person." They also summoned there Nahuitecpatl, "4 Flint," who is the moon. Him the Lord of Tlalocan, Tlaloc, called upon, and also upon Napateuctli. Then Nanahuatl fasted in penance. He took up his maguey thorns and his pine branches upon which to offer them. The moon provided his own thorns. Nanahuatl was the first to offer sacrifice, then the moon sacrificed also. The moon used quetzal feathers for branches and jade for thorns, and incense.

When four days had passed, they coated Nanahuatl in chalk and down feathers and he went to throw himself into the fire. Nahuitec-patl made a kind of female song for him. Then Nanahuatl fell into the fire and afterward the moon fell also but only into the ashes. When Nanahuatl fell, the eagle lifted him and carried him off. The jaguar could not carry him, but only leapt into the fire and was spotted. Then the hawk smoked himself and the wolf was scorched. None of these three was able to carry him.

And so when Nanahuatl came to the sky, the high gods Tonaca-teuctli and Tonacacihuatl bathed him and sat him on a mat of fla-mingo plumes and wrapped his head with red bands.

And then he spent four days in the heavens; he stood still at the sign 4 Motion. For four days he did not move. The gods asked, "Why doesn't he move?" Then they sent Itztlotli to speak and inquire of the

Ƨ   THE FLAYED GOD

sun. He said to him, "The gods say, 'Ask him why he will not move.'"
The sun answered, "Because I require the blood of their legitimacy
and their reign."

Then the gods consulted with each other and Tlahuizcalpanteuctli, Lord of the House of Dawn, became angered and said,
"Why don't I put an arrow into him? He'll wish he had never been
detained!" Then he shot at the sun but missed him. For this the sun
shot Tlahuizcalpanteuctli; he shot him with the flaming plumes of the
cuetzalin-papagayo and suddenly covered over his face with the nine
heavens together. This was Tlahuizcalpanteuctli, the ice-god.

Then the gods Titlacahuan and Huitzilopochtli and the goddesses
Xochiquetzal, Yapaliicue, and Nochpaliicue gathered in council, and
from then on the gods in Teotihuacan began to die.

And when the sun rose into the sky, then the moon, which had
fallen in the ashes, went also. He had no sooner arrived at the edge of
the sky than Papaztac came to smash his face with a rabbit-jar. Then
the female demons and other demons came out to meet him at the
intersections of roads and said, "May you be welcome." Nevertheless
they stopped him there and clothed him in rags and came to make
offerings. And when the sun came to halt at 4 Motion it was also at
sunset.

VI

[At this point in the manuscript the scribe inserts a crude pictographic
sketch outlining the mythic precincts of Tula (Tollan) with Topiltzin
Ce Acatl Quetzalcoatl, "Our Beloved Prince 1 Reed Quetzalcoatl,"
standing at its center. Marking the four corners are his "four-part" temples: "Serpent House," "Gold House," "Jade House," and "Turquoise
House." (In the *Anales de Cuauhtitlan* these are called "his turquoise-
plank house, his coral-inlay house, his whiteshell-inlay house, and his
quetzal-feather house.") Under the sign for town, which appears to
bear the name "Xicococ," the names of Ce Acatl's parents, Mixcoatl
and Chimalman, are joined by what looks like a long umbilical, being
cut in the center by a detached arm and hand. Directly below the arm
stands Topiltzin. Mixcoatl's age at the time of his son Topiltzin's birth,
thirty-nine, is written in the upper-right corner of the pictograph,
above the date 1 Flint.]

And so Mixcoatl had lived 39 years. His wife was named
Chimalman. And Topiltzin lived 56 years [the drawing indicates fifty-
two, the figure given in other accounts]. In the same year 1 Reed in

which he moves, here he also leaves his city, Tollan. And here he died on 4 Rabbit in Tlapallan.

In the year 1 Flint the Mixcoa, "Cloud Serpents," were born, they were created. Iztacchalchiuhtlicue, "White Jade Skirt," bore the Four Hundred Cloud Serpents. They entered a cave and when they had entered the cave, again their mother gave birth; then "the Five" were born, also Cloud Serpents: this one is named Quauhtliicohuauh, "Eagle's Twin," this second is named Mixcoatl, "Cloud Serpent," this third, a woman, is named Cuitlachcihuatl, "Wolf Woman," this fourth is named Tlotepe, "Hawk Mountain," and this fifth is named Apanteuctli, "Lord of the River."

And when they were born they entered the water, they threw themselves into the water; then they emerged again and were nursed by Mecitli, she who is Lord [sic] of the Earth, Mecitli. And so it is that today we are "Mexica," not actually "Mexica" but "Mecitin."

And then the sun sent forth the Four Hundred Cloud Serpents. Giving them arrows, darts and shields, he said, "Here is that with which you will satisfy my thirst, with which you will serve my table." [He gave them] arrows, precious-feather arrows, fletched with quetzal plumes, heron plumes, troupial plumes, roseate spoonbill plumes, flamingo plumes, cotinga plumes. "And, furthermore," [he said,] "she is your mother, Lord of Earth."

But they did not perform their calling, they only shot at birds, they only enjoyed themselves; so it is that place is called "Bird Arrow." And occasionally they caught a jaguar; they did not offer it to the sun. When they did capture a jaguar, they decorated themselves with plumes and down, they slept with women, drank tzihuac liquor and wandered about completely drunk, wandered about completely intoxicated.

So the sun then called "the Five" who had been born later. He gave them tzihuac arrows and lords' shields and said, "Listen carefully now, my sons; you must destroy the Four Hundred Cloud Serpents who offer nothing to Our Father, Our Mother." So they gathered together in a large mesquite, from which the others saw them and said, "Who are these, so like ourselves?" And the time came to make war: Quauhtliicohuauh hid inside a tree; Mixcoatl hid within the earth; Tlotepetl hid within a hill; Apanteuctli hid in the water; and his older sister, Cuetlachcihuatl, hid in the ball court. And so when the Four Hundred came near, none of the Five were left in the mesquite tree. Then the tree cracked open and fell on them and out came Quauhtliicohuauh, the earth shook and out came Mixcoatl from within the earth, the hill erupted and fell down and out came Tlotepetl, the water boiled and out came Apanteuctli. So then they eliminated and destroyed the Four Hundred, and then served the sun at his table and gave him to drink. Others who had escaped came to supplicate and plead with them, saying, "We have been a great trouble to you. Please, won't your Honors go in to Chicomoztoc, 'Seven Caves'; certainly it is your beloved cave. Won't your Graces please go in, since it is your beloved home? Could it be that you have just now damaged your caves, your home? We will only sit outside the cave."

VII

Then there came down two deer, each with two heads, and also these two cloud serpents named Xiuhnel and Mimich, who hunt in the Sacred Lands.

Xiuhnel and Mimich pursued the two deer, trying to shoot them. A night and a day they pursued them and by sunset they were tired. They consulted each other and said, "You build a hut there and I'll build one here." The malicious ones had not yet arrived.

Then they came, they who were deer but had become women. They came calling, "Xiuhnel, Mimich, where are you? Come, come to drink; come to eat." And when they heard them they said to one another, "Hey, why don't you answer?"

Then Xiuhnel called to them and said, "You come here, sister." She came and said to him, "Drink, Xiuhnel." Xiuhnel drank the blood and then immediately lay down with her. Suddenly she threw him down and came face down upon him, then devoured him, tore open his breast.

Then Mimich said, "She has actually eaten my elder brother!" The other woman was still standing and calling, "Lover, come and eat." But Mimich did not call her. Instead he took the firesticks and lit a fire, and when it was lit, ran and threw himself into it.

The woman, pursuing him, also entered the fire. She followed him there the entire night, until noon of the following day. And then he descended into a thorny barrel cactus, fell into it, and the woman fell down after him. And when he saw the star-demon had fallen, he shot her repeatedly. Only then could he turn back.

Then he returned, parting and tying his hair, painting his face and weeping for his elder brother who had been eaten. Then the fire gods heard it and they went to bring the woman, Itzpapalotl, "Obsidian Butterfly."

Mimich went in the lead. And when they took her, they burned her and she burst into bloom. First she blossomed into the blue flint; the second time she blossomed into the white flint, and they took the white and wrapped it in a bundle. The third time she blossomed into the yellow flint, but no one took it, they only watched. The fourth time she blossomed into the red flint which no one took. And the fifth time she blossomed into the black flint which no one took.

Mixcoatl, Cloud Serpent, took the white flint for a god and wrapped it and carried it in a bundle, and then went off to make war in a place called Comallan. He went carrying his goddess of flint, Itzpapalotl. And when the Comalteca learned of it, they came out to meet Mixcoatl and placed food before him, and with this put his heart at rest.

And then he went to Tecanma where also his heart was rested. They said to him, "What does the Lord wish? May he be satisfied here. Bring him his beloved tzihuac, that I might here chop it up and serve him." And then he went to Cocyama where at once he came pulling down the high places [village temples]. And he conquered there in Cocyama then went to Huehuetocan and conquered in Huehuetocan, then went to Pochtlan and came there to conquer also.

And then when Mixcoatl went to conquer in Huitznahuac, the woman Chimalman came out to confront him. He spread out his shield and filled it with arrows and atlatl darts. She stood naked, without skirt or shift. When he saw her Mixcoatl shot his arrows: the first went over her and she only turned aside slightly; the second arrow passed by her side and she deflected it; the third she simply caught in her hand; and the fourth she passed between her legs. And being thus that Mixcoatl had shot four times, he transformed himself and immediately went away.

The woman fled away at once to hide in a cave among the canyons. And again Mixcoatl came to prepare and supply himself with arrows. And again he went to look for her but saw no one. So then he attacked the women of Huitznahuac, and the women of Huitznahuac said, "Let us go in search of her." They went to take her; they said, "Mixcoatl is searching for you. On your account he is mistreating your younger sisters." Then when they had gone to take her, they came to Huitznahuac. Then again Mixcoatl went and again met her, finding her exposed as before. Again he lay down the shield and the arrows and again he shot at her. Again the arrow went over her head, and one went by her side and one she caught in her hand and one passed between her legs.

And then when this had occurred, he took the woman of Huitznahuac, the one who is Chimalman, and lay with her and so she became pregnant.

VIII

And when he [Topiltzin, also called 1 Reed] was born, for four days he caused his mother to suffer. Then 1 Reed was born and as soon as he was born his mother died. And 1 Reed was then raised by [the divine women] Quillaztli and Cihuacoatl. And being already grown, he accompanied his father on campaigns. In this way he became exercised in arms, in a place called Xihuacan there he took captives.

The Four Hundred Cloud Serpents are uncles of 1 Reed; they despised and killed his father, and after killing him went to bury him in Xaltitlan. 1 Reed then went in search of his father; he said, "What is this about my father?" Cozcaquauhtli, "King Vulture," then said, "Well, they killed your father; he lies over there where they went to bury him." So he went and took him and seated him in his temple, Mixcoatepetl, "Mixcoatl Mountain." And the uncles who had killed his father were Apanecatl, Zolton, and Cuilton.

Then he said, "How will I dedicate the temple?" "If with only a rabbit, with only a snake, we will be angered; better would be a jaguar, an eagle, a wolf," [the uncles] said. 1 Reed spoke when they said this, "Very well, so it will be." Then he called the jaguar, the eagle, the wolf; he said to them, "Won't you come in, uncles? They say with you I must dedicate my temple. Certainly, you will not die. Instead you will eat men and with them indeed will I dedicate my temple." The ropes which tied the maneaters by their necks were rotten. And so then 1 Reed called the moles and said to them, "O uncles; won't you come here? We will tunnel into our temple." And the moles then promptly scraped down and tunnelled and 1 Reed entered into it and emerged at the summit of his temple.

And the uncles [who had killed his father] said to him, "We will light fire with the fire-starting stick there on the summit." The jaguar, the eagle and the wolf were most delighted to see them and thought them worthy of being wept for. And as they came reviving, returning to their senses, 1 Reed himself lit the fire with the fire-starting stick. Then the uncles became enraged, and they came up, Apanecatl rushing to the front. And then 1 Reed rose up and threw into his face a polished clay vessel so that he came falling down.

And then he quickly seized Zolton and Cuilton and whistled to the man-eaters, who proceeded to kill them. He brought them together and cut their flesh a little. And when they had tormented them then they cut open their chests.

And then 1 Reed conquered once more in a place called Ayotlan. And when he had conquered there, he went on to Chalco and Xicco where he conquered also. And having conquered there he went to Cuixcoc where he also conquered. And then he went to Zacanco where he also conquered; then he went to Tzonmolco where he also conquered; then he went to Maçatzonco where he also came to conquer; then he went to Tzapotlan where he also came to conquer; then he went to Acallan where he crossed a river and also there conquered well.

So he came to Tlapallan. And then in that place he became sick and was ill for five days until he died. And when he had died in honor there, they immolated him, he was burned.

And so then in Tollan no one remained. Huemac was installed as Speaker, and the second was this one named Nequametl, the third this one named Tlalchicatzin and the fourth this one named Huitzil-popoca. These four succeeded Topiltzin.

IX

The Speaker of Nonohualco is named Huetzin. . . . [text partially damaged] . . . They were startled and horrified; they saw the tlacan-exquimilli, the night-being without head or arms, the "long man." This then is the one who ate people. And then the Toltecs said, "O Toltecs, Who is this man-eater?" Then they guarded him, they seized him; and having seized this huge young man, toothless, lipless and filthy-faced, they killed him. And having killed him, they opened him up to look inside, and found no heart, no guts, no blood. Then he stank, and whoever smelled him died and even he who did not smell him but only passed by. And in this way many died. Then they dragged him but he would not move, and the rope broke. And those

PLATE 1

THREE EARLY FIGURINES FROM THE VILLAGE CULTURES OF THE BASIN OF MEXICO:

PLATE 1
A two-headed figurine from Tlatilco

PLATE 2
A female figurine from Chupicuaro

PLATE 3
A mother and child from Tlatilco

PLATE 2

PLATE 3

PLATE 4
"The Lord of Las Limas," an
Olmec stone sculpture from
Las Limas, Veracruz

PLATE 5
The Mixtec tree of
origin from the
*Codex
Vindobonensis*

PLATE 6
The Aztec Xiuhtecuhtli and
the four directions from the
Codex Fejérváry-Mayer

PLATE 7
The Aztec Tlaloc and the
four directions from the
Codex Borgia

PLATE 8

PLATE 9

LIFE IN DEATH, DEATH IN LIFE:

PLATE 8
A Mixtec ceramic figure of a face half-fleshed, half-skeletal from Soyaltepec, Oaxaca

PLATE 9
A Zapotec ceramic Xipe Totec from Monte Alban, Tomb 58

PLATE 10

LIFE IN DEATH, DEATH IN LIFE:

PLATE 10
The god of death, a
Teotihuacan stone
sculpture

PLATE 11
A decorated skull with a
flint sacrificial knife as a
nose from an offering at the
Aztec Templo Mayor
of Tenochtitlan

PLATE 12
A ceramic Xipe Totec from
Veracruz

PLATE 11

PLATE 12

PLATE 13

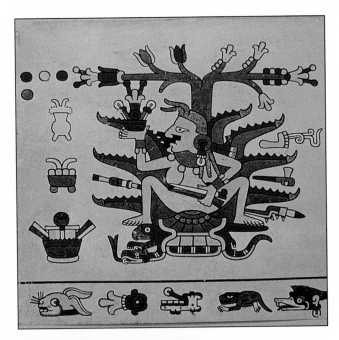

FERTILITY AND THE GODDESS:

PLATE 13
The Aztec Mayahuel from
the *Codex Laud*

PLATE 14
An Aztec ceramic corn goddess brazier from Tlatelolco

PLATE 14

who fell died where they fell. And when he did move, everyone died wherever he went, he devoured everyone. And when he did move along, everyone adorned him, the lineage-bearers, the elders, the princes' sons, the matrons. They tied him with eight ropes and dragged him along to Itzocan. And then he stood up. Those who dragged him did not let go of the ropes but were carried along dangling from them. And all who took hold of the ropes were lifted up and dragged along.

X

And so then Huemac played ball; he played ball with the lords of rain, the tlaloque. And the lords of rain said to him, "What shall we wager?" Huemac said, "My jade and my quetzal plumes." And again they said to Huemac, "None other than this shall you also win: our jade and our quetzal plumes."

Then they played and Huemac beat them. So the lords of rain went to transform that which they would give to Huemac, the ripe maize ear and their quetzal plumes, the green maize leaves in which the ear swells. But he would not accept them; he said, "Can this be what I have won! Was it not jade? Was it not quetzal plumes? Take this stuff away!"

So then the lords of rain said to him, "Very well; 'Give him the jade and the plumes and take away our jade and our quetzal plumes.'" And they took them and went away, then said to Huemac, "Very well, for now we are hiding our jade; the Toltecs will continue to work in suffering but only for four years."

And then the hail fell; it fell to the height of the knee, destroying all food-stuffs. The hail fell in the month of Teucilhuitl. And then especially on Tollan the sun shone; the trees, the nopal, the maguey all dried up; even the stones broke, everything disintegrated because of the sun.

And the Toltecs struggled and died of hunger. Then a sacrificial prisoner, who was probably kept guarded in some place by his uncle [his captor], miraculously, somehow bought himself a chicken, made himself tamales from it and ate them. And in a place called Chapolte-peccuitlapilco, on Mt. Chapoltepec, an old woman sat selling paper banners. He went and bought from her a banner and then went to be sacrificed on the stone known as techcatl.

And when the four years of famine had passed, the lords of rain again appeared there in Chapoltepec where there is water. Then suddenly to the surface of the water rose a green ear of maize that had been chewed upon, and a certain Toltec man happened to see it, took up the chewed ear, and chewed it himself. And then from out of the water came a priest of Tlaloc who said, "Mortal, have you learned something here?" The Toltec responded, "O most certainly, Our God. It has already been a long time that we lost it for ourselves." Then the other spoke: "Mortal, that is very good; sit here while I speak to the lord." And he returned once more into the water but did not tarry long; then once more he emerged bringing with him an armload of fully ripened ears. Then he spoke: "Mortal, deliver this to Huemac. And tell him the gods request the daughter of Tozcuecuex, the Mexitin [Mexica], for truly as they will eat this, little by little in a sacred manner she will be eating the Toltecs. For indeed the Toltecs will be destroyed and the Mexica will come to extend themselves. And over there at Chalchiuhcoliuhyan in Pantitlan they will go to deliver her."

And so then he went to tell everything to Huemac; thus he said just as Tlaloc had commanded it. And then Huemac was filled with contrition and wept; he said, "So it will certainly be; so the Toltecs will indeed depart; so Tollan will indeed be destroyed." Then he sent to Xicococ two messengers, Chiconcohuatl and Cuetlachcohuatl, to request of the Mexica the young woman named Ouetzalxochtzin who was not very old, still a little lady.

So then they went there to Xicococ, and they spoke: "Here have we been sent by Huemac; he says, 'the lords of rain have shown them-selves in a sacred manner. They request a young Mexica woman.'" And so the Mexica fasted for four days and fasted as for a death. And when the four days were completed, then they carried her to Panti-tlan; her father went with her. Then they sacrificed her.

Then again there the lords of rain appeared and spoke to Tozcue-cuex: "Tozcuecuex, don't be lost in your grief, for you will be with your young lady. Open your tobacco pouch." There they placed the girl's heart and all the many and varied foodstuffs. They said, "Here indeed is what the Mexica shall eat, for the Toltecs will certainly be destroyed."

And so then suddenly the clouds gathered and it began to rain furiously; for four days and four nights it rained without ceasing and the water was eaten by the earth. Then sprouted all the different green edible plants and all the herbs and grasses. And all the food-stuffs were created and brought to life.

And then the Toltecs planted; twenty and forty days passed and the young maize plants were full; very soon all the foodstuffs were produced. The year-sign under which all these foodstuffs were produced is 2 Reed.

In 1 Flint the Toltecs were destroyed. Then Huemac went into the cave at Cincalco. Some returned and others dispersed themselves in all directions.

XI

And then the Mexica came, traveling in this direction. 1. Tezcacoatl Huemac. 2. Chiconcohuatl. 3. Cohuatlayauhqui. 4. Cuitlachcohuatl. Thirteen years. 1 Reed. [The narrator is reading literally a picto-graphic text of some sort; then he explains:] And the names of the four protectors who led them in their departure are—name of the first lord, Cohuatlayauhqui; name of the second, Cuitlachcohuatl; name of the third, Chiconcohuatl; name of the fourth, Tezcacohuatl (this one was Huemac). They served as protectors for thirteen years, always wanderers.

And here they are coming from Colhuacan, from Aztlan; here the Mexica are fleeing, 58 years. 1 Flint. Here it shows they lived in Chapoltepec still in the time of Huitzillihuitl; they lived there forty years. 13 Rabbit. Here it shows they lived in Colhuacan, in Tizaapan, twenty-five years.

When the Toltecs departed in 1 Flint, the Mexica were arriving at the same time; they came from there, from Xicococ and it took them thirty-seven years to arrive at Chapoltepec. There they stayed, in Chapoltepec, for forty years. And then the Colhua rented them out as slaves; the Xaltocameca came to rent them. There the Mexica settled for a time, as the saying goes, "I'll only sleep here nearby you, be-cause I'm headed over yonder." So they "slept" there near the Colhua but in such a way that it seemed they went there only to guard them. And then they [the Mexica] suddenly fled from the Colhua; in this way the Mexica violated Colhua law: they said, "We will enter the Colhua houses" [i.e., marry Colhua women?].

And the Xaltocameca and the Quauhtitla were householders [i.e., former Chichimecs who now lived in permanent towns]; the Acolhua, the Tenayo, the Azcapotzalca, the Quahuaca, the Macahuaca, the

Xiquipilca, the Matlatzinca, the Ocuilteca, the Cuitlahuaca, and the Xochimilca; and others were there under protection of the Colhua.

These Colhua captured the Mexica chieftain Huitzillihuitl. Then the Mexica were robbed of their woman, the princess. And other Mexica escaped into the tule marshes at Acocolco and went to camp there for six days.

And here it shows the arrival on dry land here at Tenochtitlan, which was still nothing but tule marsh, still nothing but a reedy place; there the Mexica endured their labors for fifty years. No one was their Speaker.

The Mexica kept exclusively and singlemindedly to their own affairs. Year 51. 2 House: Colhuacan, Tenayocan. And here it was that the Mexica made their first conquests: only Colhuacan and Tenayocan.

1. And it was also there that Lord Acamapichtli was installed as The Speaker. He ruled twenty-one years. 20. 1 Flint: Xochmilco, Cuitlahuac, Quauhnahuac, Mizquic. And here are shown the conquests which he made: Xochmilco and Cuitlahuac and Mizquic and Quauhnahuac. In four places he conquered.

2. And here it is indicated that the son of Acamapichtli, named Huitzillihuitl, ruled for twenty-one years; here he ruled—21. 9 House: Xaltocan, Acolman, Otompan, Chalco, Tetzcoco, Tollantzinco, Quauhtitlan, Toltitlan. And here are shown the conquests which he made. Eight cities Huitzillihuitl conquered.

3. And here it is indicated that the son of Huitzillihuitl, named Chimalpopocatzin, ruled; for ten years he was The Speaker. Chalco, Tequixquiac. 10 years. 4 Rabbit. And here are shown the two cities which Chimalpopocatzin conquered.

4. And here it is indicated that the son of Acamapichtli, named Itzcohuatzin, was made The Speaker, and so he was Speaker for thirteen years. 13. 1 Flint. And here are all the conquests which Itzcoatzin made: Azcapotzalco, Tlacopan, Atlacuihuayan, Coyohuacan, Mixcohuac, Quauhximalpan, Quahuacan, Teocalhuiyocan, Tecpan, Huitzitzillapan, Quauhnahuac, Tetzcoco, Quauhtitlan, Xochmilco, Cuitlahuac, Mizquic, Tlatelolco, Itztepec, Xiuhtepec, Tzaqualpan, Chalco, Yohuallan, Tepequacuilco, Cuecallan.

5. And here it is shown that the son of Huitzillihuitl, named Ilhuicaminatzin Moteucçomatzin the Elder, was made The Speaker, and so he ruled for twenty-nine years. 29. 1 House. And here are the conquests which Moteucçomatzin the Elder made: Coaixtlahuacan,

Chalco, Chiconquiyauhco, Tepoztlan, Iyauhtepec, Atlatlauhcan, Totollapan, Huaxtepec, Tecpatepec, Yohualtepec, Xiuhtepec, Quiyauhteopan, Tlalcocauhtitlan, Tlachco, Quauhnahuac, Tepequacuilco, Cohuatlan, Xillotepec, Itzcuincuitlapilco, Tlapacoyan, Chapolicxitla, Tlatlauhquitepec, Yacapichtlan, Quauhtochco, Cuetlaxtlan.

6. And here is indicated how the grandson of both Speakers Moteucçomatzin the Elder and Itzcohuatzin, named Axayacatzin, was made The Speaker; he ruled for twelve years. 12. 4 Rabbit. And here are all the places which Axayacatzin conquered: Tlatilolco, Matlatzinco, Xiquipilco, Tzinacantepec, Tlacotepec, Tenantzinco, Xochiyacan, Teotenanco, Callimayan, Metepec, Ocoyacac, Capolloac, Atlapolco, Qua . . .

[The manuscript ends here at the bottom of page 10; the rest has been lost.]

MIXTEC CREATION MYTHS

The Mixtec Creation Myth, from the
Origen de los Indios del Nuevo Mundo e Islas Occidentales

This version of the Mixtec creation myth was transcribed by Fray Gregorio García in 1607 from an original written in the Mixtec language that was preserved by a vicar in the monastery of Cuilapa, an original that had been compiled from indigenous codices and oral accounts of Mixtec elders. Although the original is no longer extant, Miguel León-Portilla feels that the rhythm and forceful expression of García's account substantiate his claim that pre-Conquest beliefs "were preserved in the hearts and minds of the people" and found their way into such accounts as this. He notes that "the rhythm of expression in parallel phrases, describing the same idea with different shades of meaning," is particularly reminiscent of pre-Conquest practice.[49]

Jill Furst, struck by the obvious overlap between this colonial period narrative and the pictorial version in the pre-Hispanic *Codex Vindobonensis,* also believes that García's account reflects the pre-Conquest mythological tradition.[50] Although it begins at a time before the present world came into being, which sounds "suspiciously Judeo-Christian," the indigenous nature of the narrative is clear from its use of calendrical names, such as 1 Deer for both the male and female first gods, who, like their counterparts in Maya and Aztec creation myths, are also dual entities, and from its use of personal names, such as "Lion Serpent" and "Jaguar Serpent" for them. Although a number of the episodes in García's version have no counterpart in the codex, Furst concludes that the two versions of the myth may merely emphasize different aspects of the story. The most obvious difference between the two versions is that the narrative myth ends with the establishment of a garden, perhaps betraying another Judeo-Christian influence, whereas there is only "a vague hint of a garden" in the codex, where "a tree, probably the birth tree of the Mixtec kings and nobles at Apoala, is visited by the progeny of the 1 Deer pair." Thus it seems clear that to the extent that "the recorded legend and the manuscript overlap, [they do so] only to a point."

THE MIXTEC CREATION MYTH

This is an original translation from the Spanish by Scott Mahler, prepared for this volume.

In the beginning, before there were days and years, when the world was dark and everything in it was in chaos and confusion, the land was covered with water, and the face of the earth was covered with only mud and slime. At that time there appeared a god named One Deer, who was also known as Lion Serpent, and a very beautiful goddess named One Deer, who was also known as Jaguar Serpent.

As soon as these two gods appeared in human form, omnipotent and wise, they made a huge mass of rock on which they skillfully built a very sumptuous palace for their seat and dwelling on earth. At the highest point of their house was a copper axe, the blade turned upward under the sky.

The rock and the palace were on a high hill, near the village of Apoala in the province of Mixteca Alta. This rock was called Place Where the Heavens Were. It was a paradise for the gods and they spent many centuries in repose and contentment there, while the rest of the world was in darkness.

These two gods, father and mother of all the gods, had two very handsome sons who were prudent and wise in all the arts. The first was named Nine Serpent Wind, after the name of the day on which he was born. The second was named Nine Caverns Wind, after the day of his birth. These two children were raised in great luxury. The older, when he wanted to amuse himself, would turn into an eagle, and soar to the heights. The other turned himself into a small animal, in the form of a winged serpent, and flew through the air with such agility and craft that he could enter into boulders and walls and make himself invisible. The noise they made was heard by those below. They took these forms to show that they had the power to transform themselves.

While enjoying the tranquility of living in their parents' house, these two brothers agreed to make an offering and a sacrifice to their parents the gods, so they took a clay incense burner with some live coals in it and threw some ground tobacco on it. This was the first offering made in the world.

Then the two brothers made a garden for their enjoyment, in which they planted many flowering trees, fruit-bearing trees, roses, and many fragrant herbs and spices. They amused themselves in the garden almost every day, and next to it they made a very beautiful field with everything they needed for all the offerings and sacrifices they would make for their parents. After the brothers left their parents' house, they lived in the garden, taking care to water the trees and plants and making offerings of ground tobacco. They also made prayers, vows, and promises to their parents, and asked if by virtue of the sacrifices and offerings they had made their parents might create the earth, form the waters and the sky, and bring light into the world, since they had no place to rest but in their small garden. And in order to oblige their parents more to do what they asked, they pierced their ears with stone lancets and let a few drops of blood. They did the same with their tongues, and the blood was scattered in the branches of the trees and plants with a willow wand. Busying themselves this way, they waited for those things they had asked for, all the while showing their submission to their parents the gods and attributing to them far greater power and divinity than they had themselves.

Later, there was a great flood, in which many gods were drowned. After the flood, the god called Creator of All Things began the creation of the heavens and earth. The human race was restored, and this is how the Mixtec kingdom was populated.

The Tree of Origin, from the *Codex Vindobonensis*

The birth of the founders of the Mixtec people, metaphorically the original human beings, from a tree at Apoala is depicted on page 37 of the pre-Hispanic Mixtec *Codex Vindobonensis* (see also Color Plate 5). The codices of the Mixtecs, in addition to being remarkable works of art, provide an almost unique sense of the scope of the mythic-historic vision of the people of Mesoamerica, re-telling Mixtec history from its primordial beginnings. Claiming descent from the feathered serpent, the Mixtecs, who by 1350 A.D. occupied an area of southern Mexico that now comprises the western section of the state of Oaxaca and the adjacent regions of Puebla and Guerrero, believed that their founding fathers were born from trees, both a metaphoric reference to their close ties to the land and to their cosmic relationship to the world axis, since the world tree stands in the center of the cosmos uniting the lower, middle, and upper worlds and thus also suggests the continuing nature of the process of creation.

Following the detailed interpretation of this image by Jill Furst,[51] we see a tree with a cleft in its crown from which emerges a nude male covered with red body paint. A nude female stands above him. On either side of the tree, identified by their signs, appear 7 Rain on the right, holding a cutting implement in his right hand while touching the tree with his left, and 7 Eagle on the left side, holding a clawed implement in one hand and similarly touching the tree with his other hand. They seem to be cutting into the trunk of the tree, which appears to grow from a feathered carpet, a Mixtec symbol for a plain. At the base of the tree there is a female head with an extended tongue, a fang in the corner of her mouth, and long hair with what appear to be red "bangs," both probably generative signs, the color suggesting one of the possible colors of corn. Together with the male figure at the top of the tree, this female figure at the base indicates the male-female nature of the birth tree, a metaphor similar to the male-female nature of the Aztec creator god, Ometeotl. The blue tubular earplug she wears is a male characteristic and thus suggests again the dual sexuality of the tree, as does the fact that the left side of the tree has a row of white circles—female symbols—while the right side has three arrows—masculine symbols—increasing in size toward the bottom. The body of the tree itself is swollen, indicating perhaps that the offspring will be removed by cutting into the "pregnant" trunk, which is divided on top by a V-shaped cleft before being separated in half vertically along the center by a thin red line that thickens as it reaches the bottom.

On either side of the tree there are groups of five branches, the arrangement of which strongly suggests a quincunx, with all its cosmic implications concerning the space-time continuum that is the created world, the world into which humanity, in the persons of the nude male and female, is emerging. Such an image, of course, would suggest that this tree is the world tree at the cosmic center, and in that connection the possibility of seeing this image as both an upright tree and an inverted female figure links cosmic creation to human procreation. That link is one of the primary concerns of the narrative myths of human creation throughout Mesoamerica since it is through procreation, the uniting of the created male and female, that the process of creation becomes cyclical and continuous.

As Furst points out, several aspects of the creation myth depicted here are similar to the Mixtec myth of creation as retold by Fray Gregorio García about ninety years after the Conquest,[52] but instead of the tree birth depicted in this scene, García's legend emphasizes the establishment of a garden.

AN IZAPAN CREATION MYTH

IMAGE 7

An Izapan Creation Myth: Izapa Stela 5

This stela with its complex narrative scene is typical of the stelae of Izapa whose unique features have been variously described. Michael Coe, for example, calls it a baroque, cluttered style with a wealth of ideographic symbols from which Maya art developed,[53] whereas V. Garth Norman notes "the apparent convention at Izapa of depicting different motifs in direct or overlapping contact to express specific interrelationships. The Izapa sculptures appear to record mythical and historical events as well as religious and cosmological concepts."

Stela 5 (ca. 100 B.C.) is without doubt the best example in Izapa art of the "optimum communication" derived from the "maximum utilization of the limited space"[54] on a stone; it contains by far the most complex scene of any on the Izapa stelae. Gareth Lowe, after a lengthy calendrical analysis of the stela, suggests that this scene presents an original creation myth similar, though not identical, to the one presented in the later *Popol Vuh.* He argues that "the old creator couple, very many supplementary personages, numerous plant and animal motifs, the flood or sea, mountain peaks, and the 'birthing' of clouds or sky symbolized by the small sprouting 'spirit' in the huge scroll at upper right all support a general parallel" with that myth of the later Maya.[55]

Norman, in an eighty-page study of this stela, points out that crowded into this one scene there are from twelve to fifteen human figures, another twelve animals, over twenty-five plants and inanimate objects, and nine stylized deity masks, making a total of over sixty separate figures, and "many of the motifs, particularly the human figures, the raised 'serpents,' and the tree, contain additional symbolic elements."[56] Much wider than it is high, this not-quite-symmetrical arrangement includes standing and seated figures, a large tree, and large compound dragon creatures all carved in very shallow relief. The tree in the center of the carving, with roots extending into a mound of earth at the base and branches that reach into a sky panel, obviously representing the tree of life and thus the central world axis, dominates the design.

A water scroll design is carved beneath the base panel, and the seven human figures seated on that panel seem to be involved with religiously symbolic objects. Two larger, bird-masked, godlike figures appear on either side under the branches of the tree, and all of the other figures, particularly those on the right side of the tree, seem to relate to the tree through them. At the top of the scene are two stylized serpents with bare tooth sockets and prominent scroll headdresses. Two fish, clearly water symbols, hang above the left serpentlike composite creature, and a pelican-type bird, possibly a symbol characterizing the carrying back of the rainwater from the heavens to the earth, is perched above that on the right, thereby relating the two. Other bird and fish figures are associated with the personage in the center of the left scene. In addition to the large, bird-masked individuals and the sky panel, there are on the stela nine other "deity" masks of varied styles.

The complexity of the scene allows for many different interpretations, but Norman sees it as "an extremely detailed 'road-of-life' portrayal of both this and the next life which includes concepts of cosmology, religion, [and] myth."[57] He suggests that the theme of immortality is central, expressed both in terms of the rain, and thus the agricultural life cycle, and of the human life cycle. Because he believes that most of the Izapa stelae seem to be concerned with the life cycle of man, with each illustrating a specific phase of the cycle, he concludes that Stela 5 synthesizes all of these, revealing the full cycle of human life in both the world of nature and the world of the spirit. Thus humanity's origin and life on earth are essentially the subject of this scene.

IMAGE 8

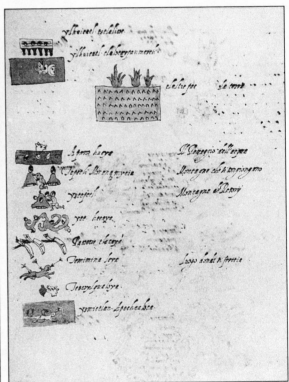

The Vertical Dimension of the Cosmos, from the *Codex Vaticanus A*

The post-Conquest pictographic manuscript known as *Codex Vaticanus A* is one of the prime sources of ritual-calendrical, historical, and ethnographic material from the Basin of Mexico, but it also contains information essential to the mythologist. Dating from about 1566–89, it is virtually identical to the *Codex Telleriano-Remensis,* and both are believed to be copies of a single original, the lost *Codex Huitzilopochtli.* It is invaluable for the study of creation myths since one of its seven major sections includes cosmogonic images with detailed explanatory glosses, images such as these from the first two pages of the codex.

As we have already seen, the Aztec image of the vertical dimension of the cosmos, the tiers of heavens and levels of the underworld, was complex. This is the only extant pictorial representation of the thirteen heavens, and it differs considerably in detail from the prose description in the *Historia de los Mexicanos por sus Pinturas.* It is possible that a nine-tiered celestial heaven may be more ancient in conception, and this would, of course, give the upper world the same number of tiers as the underworld and serve to make them parallel. The highest or thirteenth level is shown here as Omeyocan, the "place of duality," referred to in the codex in a variant spelling, "Homeyoca," and described as "the place of the creator of all, or the first cause." Portrayed as the lords of this tier are the figures of the creator god Ometecuhtli, the god of duality, he who lives in the "place of duality," and his spouse, Omecihuatl.

Codex Vaticanus A is also the only pictorial source showing the nine tiers of the underworld. Again, this source differs from other descriptions. In the *Florentine Codex* Sahagún's account focuses on the "tests" that confronted the spirits of the dead on each level before they finally arrived at the ninth tier and attained eternal rest. This image assigns no such metaphoric functions to the various levels.

The Vertical Cosmos

Level	Nahuatl Name	Translation[58]	Level	Nahuatl Name	Translation
13	Omeyocan	Place of Duality	1	Tlalticpac	The Earth's Surface
12	Teotl Tlatauhcan	The God Who Is Red	2	Apanohuayan	The Place of Water Passage
11	Teotl Cozauhcan	The God Who Is Yellow	3	Tepetl Imonamiquiyan	The Place Where the Hills Clash Together
10	Teotl Iztacan	The God Who Is White			
9	Itztapal Nanatzcayan	Where the Stone Slabs Clash Together	4	Itztepetl	The Place of the Obsidian Mountain
8	Ilhuicatl Xoxouhcan	The Heaven That Is Blue	5	Itzehecayan	The Place of the Obsidian Wind
7	Ilhuicatl Yayauhcan	The Heaven That Is Black			
6	Ilhuicatl Mamalhuazocan	The Heaven of the Fire Drill	6	Pancuecuetlayan	The Place Where Banners Are Flourished
5	Ilhuicatl Huixtotlan	The Heaven of the Salt-Fertility Goddess	7	Temiminaloyan	Where Someone Is Shot with Arrows
4	Ilhuicatl Tonatiuh	The Heaven of the Sun			
3	Ilhuicatl Citlalicue	The Heaven of the Star-Skirted Goddess	8	Teyollocualoyan	Where People's Hearts Are Eaten
2	Ilhuicatl Tlalocan Ipah Meztli	The Heaven of the Rain God and Moon	9	Iz Mictlan Opochcalocan	The Place of the Dead, Where the Streets Are on the Left

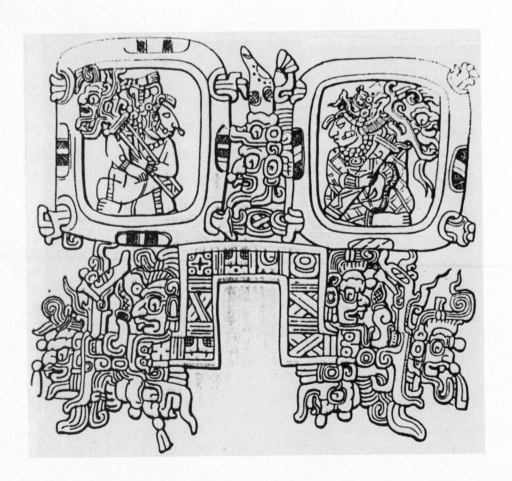

THE FLAYED GOD

The Image of Time: An Architectural Detail from Palenque and Yaxchilan Stela 10

The upper portion of the Classic period Stela 10 at Yaxchilan (Image 10) demonstrates the Mesoamerican preoccupation with time itself as a primordial reality. While time manifested itself in many different guises, representing various periods and cycles of time, it was itself the unitary reality behind all of these manifestations. Because of the identification of time with space, those guises, those cycles, also represented aspects of space.[59] On this stela is depicted the essential nature of time. The face of the old lord of *kin* (time) is portrayed in the center with his characteristic solar eye and prominent eyetooth. On either side of him, set within squares are, according to Miguel León-Portilla,[60] two deities representing the sun and the moon, each with a scepter crowned with a mask that also represents the sun. On either side and below each of those gods and on either side of the center arch that is formed from the body of the celestial monster and covered with symbols related to the sky are three faces, each with the solar eye and prominent eyetooth that we see in the central figure. They are obviously variations of it that also represent *kin*. The two faces extending outward on the extreme sides seem to be parts of that monster.

The celestial monster, an icon that frequently functioned as a cosmological frame in the art of the Maya of the Classic period, provides an important clue to the meaning of this image. As can be seen from the example given here as Image 9, an architectural detail from Palenque, that monster typically has an elongated body with a crocodilian head at either end, with the body, often decorated with sky symbols, itself forming the skyband. The front head, on the left, has a long snout and teeth, lids on the eyes, a deerlike ear, and the sign of Venus. The body clearly belongs to this front head, while the second head, on the right, is that of the quadripartite god hanging upside down and seeming to be a burden borne by the celestial monster. It has a blunt snout and a skeletal lower jaw, and as Schele and Miller point out, "atop the forehead is a deep bowl with an inverted rim fused with the glyphic sign of the sun, *kin*. Atop the bowl rest three symbols: crossed bands, a stingray spine and a shell. This four-part configuration is known as the Quadripartite Badge."[61] The two heads represented here forming what we recognize as the celestial monster suggest Venus as the morning star leading the sun into the day, while the sun appears behind it, with its head inverted, at the time of its setting. Together these two heads thus exemplify the dualistic conception that invests each deity with diametrically opposed qualities, in this case, the celestial and underworld roles of the sun.

Returning now to Image 10 and the larger image below this skyband, we can see that the images in the squares on either side of the sun deity repeat the sense of those on the celestial band by suggesting again the movement of time from day to night, in this case from the solar to the lunar modes. We have here then the amazingly unified image of time itself: the deity of time "creating the cycle of the days: he appears in the heavens; then, on one side, he enters the fangs of the monster, journeys through the regions below, finally reappearing, on the other side, from the same monster's fangs. The universe of the faces and masks of *kin* thus achieves its most perfect expression."[62]

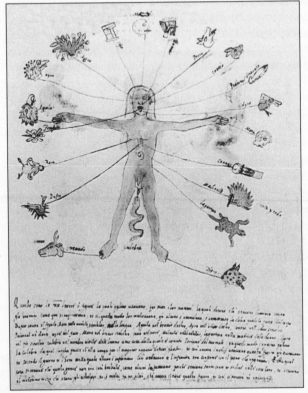

THE FLAYED GOD

Time, the Gods, and Man, from the *Codex Borgia* and the *Codex Vaticanus A*

Page 17 of the *Codex Borgia* contains this image of Tezcatlipoca (Image 11) showing the twenty day signs of the sacred calendar arranged in such a way as to indicate the powers specifically associated with him. Recognizing him by his missing foot, which has been replaced with a smoking mirror, by the yellow and black horizontal bars on his face, and by the untied umbilical cord, suggesting that he was born fully armed, we see him here as a paragon of the warrior,[63] with the image as a whole focusing on the sharpness of his death-dealing spear, his swift movement, and the steadfastness of his eye. The day sign for "movement" is placed on his tongue near his cheek, and the symbol for word or speech pictured as the day name "flower" comes out of his mouth. The "snake," representing potency, protrudes from his loins. The "eagle" at his head and the "jaguar" at his foot are symbols of the two military orders of the Aztecs, although the latter may also suggest that his foot touches the earth, just as "Cipactli" or "Earth Monster" placed at the other foot recalls the loss of that foot to the Earth Monster. On his breast is the sacrificer's "flint knife," and on the top of his banner is "rabbit" with "death" below it, indicating that the captive was taken. His shield protects and is therefore the "vulture," emblem of merchants and trade, and behind him the "house" or symbol of the community is defended. Hunt sees a note of humor in having "wind" placed behind his body.

In addition to the specific meanings associated with the placement of the various day signs, the figure as a whole suggests that Tezcatlipoca *is* the sacred calendar, the most hallowed cycle of time. Each day is actually a transformation of a portion of his "body," his identity. This view accords with the basic nature of Tezcatlipoca, which we have explained above, as the unfolding of the creative essence that is Ometeotl into the world of space and time. Here, then, we have a picture of Tezcatlipoca as a cycle of time.

Interestingly, plate lxxiii of the post-Conquest *Codex Vaticanus A* (Image 12) similarly portrays a nude man surrounded by the twenty day signs, each connected by a line to a specific part of the body, suggesting most literally the relationships that could be used in curing illnesses. But there is also the suggestion of a mystical relationship between man and time. A fundamental premise of Mesoamerican spiritual thought involved the interchangeability through transformation of the inanimate, the human, and the divine, since all were ultimately transformations of the same unchanging essence, the life force. Through these symbolic transformations the very structure and order of the universe could be understood, and human life could be harmonized with the sacred order. Since man and Tezcatlipoca are both manifestations of the divine essence, albeit on different planes, and since that divine essence is also reflected in the twenty day signs, which are symbolic of the mystery and order of time, their juxtaposition in these metaphoric portrayals provides an assurance of their relationship and imbues both man and the god with the mystical power associated with time and the sacred calendar.

It is not surprising that in Mesoamerica, where time was considered to be a revelation of the fundamental order of the universe and where the 260-day calendar provided a basic key to its understanding, we would find the twenty day signs of the sacred calendar[64] distributed over the bodies of various sacred and natural beings in at least six illustrations from the codices.[65]

THE FLAYED GOD

Huehueteotl and the Quincunx

This striking Classic period ceramic brazier from Cerro de las Mesas, Veracruz, depicts the old god of fire, Huehueteotl, bearing on his head a large brazier that was used for the ritual burning of copal incense, the offering to the gods of the essence of the copal in the smoke that rose from the brazier, a process symbolizing the spiritualization of matter. Huehueteotl was conceived as the god of age, of the last phase of the cycle of life, whose symbolic lines and wrinkles pointed beyond the grave to the permanence of the cycle within which human beings live their lives, another aspect of the spiritualization of matter.

From the time of the earliest village cultures fire was the center of both the domestic and the spiritual realms of Mesoamerican life, so it is not surprising that the deity associated with fire was the first to appear (Image 5) in the conceptual development of named deities representing aspects of a world of the spirit that were to be called "gods." The final manifestation of this spiritual concept was the very complex god of fire known to the Aztecs as both Huehueteotl and Xiuhtecuhtli, whose alter ego was Xiuhcoatl, the fire serpent[66] (see Figure 15).

What is particularly striking on this image is the symbolic device that decorates the brazier. It is a Greek cross, a cross with arms of equal length, but the circle marking the center is recognizably and uniquely Mesoamerican. That circle makes the cross a quincunx, which emphasizes five points, the four at the ends of the arms, and the one at the center, the place of meeting. Throughout the mythic art of Mesoamerica this five-point figure is used to symbolize the essence of reality, the fundamental nature of space-time, and it is fitting that the symbol of the quincunx here accompanies the image of Huehueteotl, as it suggests the fact that the god of fire was seen as the driving force behind all cosmic movement, the god of the center around which all revolves.

As we have already demonstrated,[67] the daily path traced by the sun's passage can be visualized as exactly this figure, with one of the arms representing a line connecting east (the point of sunrise) and west (sunset) and the other connecting south (or the zenith, high noon) and north (or the nadir, midnight). The point at which the arms meet locates the cosmic center, but in addition, the two intersecting lines define two other mythically crucial dimensions. On the one hand, they mark the central axis of the universe, which brings together the great cosmic regions of the sky, the earth, and the underworld and creates the symbolic "opening" through which the gods are able to move from one level to another. On the other hand, they mark the sun's path, defining this world of the earth's surface, man's world of life and eventual death, which is bounded by the point at which the sun "dies" in the west and passes into the underworld, the necessary prelude to its rebirth at the opposing point on the eastern horizon, from which it will once again arise. Since those lines are simultaneously symbolic of both the space that the sun traverses and the time that it takes to do so, we have evidence once again of the Mesoamerican concern with the "shape" of time and its complex relationship to space. Thus this geometric figure in its several variations is ubiquitous in Mesoamerica precisely because it symbolizes the earth and the cosmos, life and motion, and the endless cyclic whirling of time.

The Aztec Calendar Stone

The Aztec calendar stone is without doubt the most important of the extant Aztec monuments. A thirteen-and-a-half-foot, mandala-shaped, once-polychromed basalt relief weighing twenty-five tons, this masterpiece combines a graphic representation of the Aztec creation myth with an image of the Mesoamerican conception of cyclical time and space.[68] It is extremely complex iconographically, and there is some dispute about the meaning of a number of the particular features, but however each symbol is interpreted, the combination in its entirety reveals the cosmological vision of the society by and for whom it was made, a people for whom "the universe was seen as a reflection of relationships between life-forces."[69] It provides what may be the best single image of the Mesoamerican view of the equivalence of space and time in its depiction of the four suns encircling the Fifth Sun at the center, an image that unifies time and space as "both the synthesis and the 'center' of the history of the world."[70]

The face portrayed at the center of the stone is generally interpreted as the Aztec sun god, Tonatiuh, wearing nose and ear pendants with claws grasping the earth and a tongue represented by a flint knife suggesting sacrifice.[71] That central face is depicted within the glyph meaning movement and symbolizing the Fifth Sun, 4 Movement. The four quadrants spaced around the central figure represent the preceding four suns, or world ages,[72] and each contains a representation of the name of the particular age derived from the sign of its last day, a name that indicates as well the method of its destruction. The first, on the upper right, designates the First Sun, 4 Jaguar, followed in counterclockwise, or sunwise, order by the Second Sun, 4 Wind; the Third Sun, 4 Rain; and the Fourth Sun, 4 Water. By encircling the Fifth, or present, Sun, they form a quincunx suggesting the centrality of both the sun itself and of the present world age, the Fifth Sun.

The ring encircling all of this contains the glyphs of each of the twenty day signs of the tonalpohualli, the 260-day sacred calendar,[73] again arranged in counterclockwise order, and the outer rim is formed by two fire serpents, Xiuhcoatls, whose tails come together at the top of the stone, while their heads, from whose open mouths emerge two anthropomorphic heads with skeletal jaws, meet at the bottom. These are the carriers of the sun across the sky, and Townsend explains that they should be seen here as "metaphoric pictograms" representing the qualities of the sky rather than as mythological animals. Eight V-shaped forms (four larger and four smaller) denote the rays of the sun and probably the four directions, the most prominent at the top indicating the east, the place of the sun's emergence.

Here, then, is a mandalalike image that places the sun and the present world age at the center and relates all of time and space to them. It illustrates remarkably well that "in that immensely magic world [of myth], perceived objects were automatically translated into another level: the boundaries between objective and perceptive become blurred, dream and reality are one, and everything is alive and intimately relatable."[74]

Xiuhtecuhtli and the Four Directions, from the *Codex Fejérváry-Mayer*

The opening page of the pre-Conquest *Codex Fejérváry-Mayer* contains a fascinating cosmological model of the Mesoamerican spatial-temporal universe conceived horizontally as a "complex topological-visual metaphor"[75] (see also Color Plate 6). It is a quadripartite diagram, a quincunx, so remarkable in its conception that the archaeoastronomer Anthony Aveni claims that its construction parallels "the unifying aspects of Einstein's equations in the modern world."[76]

The basic design of the image combines two systems of spatial arrangement: a Maltese cross with a square in the center forms a quincunx, and a St. Andrew's cross in the form of an X with diagonal arms appears at a forty-five-degree angle forming a second quincunx between the arms of the first. In addition, the temporal dimension is expressed by the 260 small circles of the border design, representing the 260 days of the sacred calendar, which are divided into thirteen sets of twenty days each. Uniting space and time in still another way, each of the diagonal arms forming the St. Andrew's cross contains a particular plant and bird and is topped with the glyph of one of the four year bearers, Acatl (Reed) being the year bearer of the east, Tecpatl (Flint Knife) of the north, Calli (House) of the west, and Tochtli (Rabbit) of the south. These arms thus represent a quadripartite division of time.

The arms of the Maltese cross represent the spatial dimension of the created world; they are the four cardinal directions, each having its sacred tree topped with its particular bird. Gods or goddesses stand on either side of each tree, and the quadrant of each direction is bordered with its representational color. At the center of the quincunx, and thus at the center of the cosmos, is the fire god, Xiuhtecuhtli, armed with spears and the recipient of four streams of blood. The quadrant at the top of the diagram represents east and the gods Itztli (Flint Knife) and the sun as Piltzintecuhtli (Young Corn). In the quadrant on the left representing south we find Tepeyollotl (Heart of the Hill) and Tlaloc (Rain), while the bottom quadrant, west, contains the two goddesses Chalchiuhtlicue (Skirt of Jade) and Tlazolteotl (Earth). The remaining quadrant, representing north, contains the corn goddess, Cinteotl, and Mictlantecuhtli, lord of the underworld. In addition, some scholars see the body parts—hand, ribs, leg, and head—of a dismembered Tezcatlipoca in the four corners. The spiked disk in the east represents the sun rising in the east, with the north and south on either side and facing the west, where it will come to rest, symbolized by the head of death, suggesting its disappearance in the underworld. It has also been suggested that the spatial division corresponds to the four divisions of the city of Tenochtitlan and that from each of the four cardinal points sacrificial blood flows toward the ceremonial center, representing the "nourishment" that will enable the gods, that is, the world of the spirit, to continue to maintain life in this world.[77]

A careful consideration of this remarkable pre-Conquest drawing reveals the ability of an image not only to illustrate the complexity of the space-time continuum but also at the same time to relate that continuum to the various corresponding facets of the world of the spirit. This image is, thus, a "map" of the cosmos that includes all of its possible dimensions. As such, it serves as a "guide" to the multileveled, quadripartite order of the universe as it was understood in the Mesoamerican mythological system.

Tlaloc as the Four Quadrants of Space and Time, from the *Codex Borgia*

The *Codex Borgia* is widely considered to be "the most important, detailed, and complex pictorial source extant for the study of Central Mexican gods, ritual, divination, calendar, religion and icon-ography"[78] (see also Color Plate 7). Characterized by its intricate symbolism and a divinatory content related to the 260-day cycle of the sacred calendar, it has been both a mine of information and a bewildering enigma for scholars. Page 27 of this screenfold manuscript reveals five images of the rain god, Tlaloc, one in each corner and one in the center, each with that god's characteristic goggled eyes and curving upper lip and fangs, suggestive of their descent from similar images at Teotihuacan and their ultimate relationship to the Olmec were-jaguar. Like the Zapotec Cocijo, Tlaloc was essentially related to lightning and through lightning to both power and the orderly passage of time. From one hand each of these Tlalocs pours water from a vessel that is itself Tlaloc, and in the other each holds an adze and a lightning serpent.

Together, these five portraits illustrate the Mesoamerican identification of time, space, and the gods in the person of Tlaloc. Seen as a spatial image, they depict each of the four directions and the center; seen as a temporal image, they depict each of the four points in the daily cycle of the sun and the center, around which the sun symbolically moves; and seen as a "spiritual" image, each of the four directional Tlalocs wears a mask helmet representing another god. The Tlaloc of the center, who represents the all-important vertical axis of the spirit, however, does not wear such a mask. He is the essential Tlaloc, the "thing itself," as close as man can come to depicting the essential reality of the world of the spirit.

The temporal interpretation is further strengthened by the function of this page within the codex, which, according to Seler, is to represent the quadripartite divisions of the 260-day sacred calendar and of the fifty-two-year cycle.[79] The four Tlalocs thus represent the year bearers, the gods who "carry" each of these four divisions.

> To the ancient seers it must have seemed marvelous that of the twenty day-signs, only four fell on the initial days of the years, but we can imagine that they considered as a veritable mystery the division of the 52 year cycle . . . into four quarters, each of which had as its initial day a day numbered 1 which had one of those same four day-signs in the proper sequence. Thus the 52 year cycle was automatically ordered in accord with the four cardinal points in the same way that the *tonalamatl* . . . organized itself into four sections similarly corresponding to the four directions. And this division of the 52 year cycle in accord with the four cardinal points is what is represented on page 27 of our manuscript.[80]

On this page is recorded, then, the central mystery of the division of the essential unity of the cosmos into the quadripartite form of the world of man. The images here reproduce the essential "shape" of the space-time continuum as perceived by the sages of Mesoamerica.[81] Once again we see the image of the quincunx,[82] in this case with Tlaloc as the fifth point, the very center and power of the vertical axis.

IMAGE 17

IMAGE 18

THE FLAYED GOD

Time Turning into Space: Two Mesoamerican Pyramids

The fundamental relationship of space to time is most abstractly expressed in the symbol of the quincunx, the four-part symbol representing both the cardinal directions and the "cardinal" points on the sun's daily path.[83] Significantly, a pyramid, viewed from above, forms a quincunx with the top, the site of the temple elevated into the realm of the spirit, as its center. This is fitting since the primary function of the Mesoamerican pyramid was to raise the temple along the vertical axis of the cosmos into the heavens, the realm of the spirit. Both the Pyramid of the Niches at El Tajin and the Temple of Quetzalcoatl in the Ciudadela at Teotihuacan complement this spatial concept with a temporal element, providing in that way mythic images of "time turning into space."[84]

IMAGE 17: The Pyramid of the Niches at El Tajin

The Pyramid of the Niches is located at the site of El Tajin in the north-central part of the state of Veracruz. The pyramid must have been a focal point of that tremendous city, which reached its height between 600 and 900 A.D. and was occupied until about 1200. The name it carries today is derived from the Totonac word for "lightning" and is also the name of the Totonac rain god. The four sides of the pyramid are covered with tiers of deeply recessed niches that are generally thought to have numbered 365, the number of days in the solar calendar, indicative almost certainly of its symbolic calendric association. The dynamic visual quality of the pyramid is the result of the play of light and shadow as the sun travels through the sky so that the pyramid is, in this way as well, a symbol of the movement of time.

IMAGE 18: The Temple of Quetzalcoatl at Teotihuacan

At the very center of the sacred city of Teotihuacan, at the intersection of the main east-west avenue with the north-south Avenue of the Dead, is the Ciudadela, and in the center of that quadrangular complex lies the Temple of Quetzalcoatl, a small pyramid that displays a frieze described by Nicholson as "one of the greatest *tours de force* of monumental stone sculpture in world history."[85] Divided into six bands, one on each of the pyramid's six levels, are huge projecting serpent heads with feathered collars alternating with stylized geometrical masks that are unique variants of the mask of the rain god, Tlaloc.[86] These heads and masks are superimposed on the undulating bodies of feathered rattlesnakes sculpted in bas-relief, and additional serpents are depicted beneath them. The empty spaces are ornamented with seashells realistic enough "to permit precise zoological identification."[87] All of these symbols suggest fertility, while the pyramid's location suggests a connection with rulership,[88] but the probability that the frieze originally displayed from 360 to 365 composite masks and was the setting for the celebration of calendric rituals substantiates its calendric significance.

V

FLAYED GODS
SNAKE WOMEN
AND
WERE-JAGUARS

THE MYTHS OF FERTILITY

INTRODUCTION

When we turn our attention from the myths describing the initial creation to those that delineate the ongoing processes through which life in the created world is maintained, we find before us relatively few texts, but a great body of images portraying the actors in the vast cyclic drama of death and regeneration, the drama that is life on the earthly plane as it was perceived by the peoples of Mesoamerica from the earliest of times. The principal actors on this stage are the gods and goddesses associated with what we know as fertility. While many of them are connected with the processes of fertility in its most obvious form, referring to the fecundity of the earth and of the various life forms that inhabit it, fertility, especially in Mesoamerican terms, is more than that. It denotes the constant transformation of spirit into matter through which life is regenerated and maintained and is thus really a fecundity of the spirit, the unending ability of the forces at work in the realm of the spirit—that is, the gods—to keep the cosmos in motion.

In terms of the myths of the Aztecs this distinction between creation and fertility can be seen in the differences between Ometeotl, the generative force in the cosmos who is responsible for the initial creation, and Tlaloc, for example, the god of rain and storm whose seasonal efforts are instrumental in the regenerative process through which life in the created world is maintained. Ometeotl, as we have seen, manifests himself in an initial series of acts, through Tezcatlipoca, as the quadripartite created world, the world of the Fifth Sun. Tlaloc, in contrast, appears cyclically from the world of the spirit as the life-sustaining water during the course of each year's season of rains. While Ometeotl can be conceived of as an act, albeit a prolonged one, Tlaloc must be seen as a part of an ongoing cyclical process in which he periodically *becomes* the nurturing rain.

XIPE TOTEC AND THE NECESSITY OF SACRIFICE

That god of rain and storm, known by various names throughout the development of the mythological tradition of Mesoamerica, is the oldest god associated with fertility by the various cultures making up that tradition, originating, as we will demonstrate through a series of mythic images, with the Olmecs. But the most compelling and most direct embodiment of this process that we are calling fertility is not the ancient Tlaloc but the god known to the Aztecs as Xipe Totec, "Our Lord, the Flayed One," a god whose nature is described in one of the

FIGURE 15

An Aztec stone sculpture
of Xiuhcoatl

most beautiful and metaphoric of Aztec hymns. It opens with a description of the god's donning his "golden cape," an act that refers, on
a number of mythic levels, to the spiritually driven, regenerative cycle
of life. On the most literal of these levels that action signifies the arrival
of the harvest, with the cape becoming the metaphor for the ripened
corn, and the donning of the cape equating the god who is so clothed
with the corn within the kernel, the ear within the husk, so that the
corn, which sustains mankind and from which humanity was formed,
is actually the substance of the god. As many scholars have noted, the
donning of that cape may also denote the coming of the spring rains,
the time when the earth puts on the new clothing of spring growth.

From that image symbolic of transformation, the poem turns to
the process of cyclical conception and growth through which spirit becomes matter. The seasonal cycle brings the rains, turning aridity into
lushness as the dead covering of the earth in the dry season of winter,
the time of the "fire serpent," Xiuhcoatl (Figure 15), gives way to the
new vegetation bursting forth in spring, the time of the "quetzal serpent," Quetzalcoatl (see Figure 19). In this way the cycle provides sustenance in plenty as the seeds sprout, the tender corn matures, if the
rains continue, and ultimately ripeness is achieved, literally the
ripeness of the corn but by extension the "ripeness" of human maturity and of that of all life on the earthly plane. That ripeness includes as
well the "coming of age" of Aztec society under the tutelage of the "war

chief," their patron god and god of the sun, Huitzilopochtli. Implicit in this reference to that god and to war is the reality of death, especially sacrificial death, through which the cycle will renew itself. And all of this, the poem continually asserts, is the cyclic work of the gods, of the world of the spirit, specifically, in this case, of Xipe Totec. Through this eternal cycle, as the hymn suggests, the inner becomes outer, and spirit thereby manifests itself in the world.

But the poem clearly refers as well to the macabre Aztec ritual of Tlacaxipehualiztli, the flaying of men, one of the cycle of veintena festivals that marked the end of each of the "months" of the solar year. Of these festivals Johanna Broda has said that "the richness of the array of the participants, with the lavish use of gold, splendid feathers, and beautifully woven materials, combined with the dramatic power of the ceremonies, must have had an overwhelming effect upon the spectator, an effect that cannot be grasped in modern secular terms. In this tense atmosphere the human sacrifices were performed. Myth was enacted and became reality in an overwhelmingly theatrical setting."[1] And the festival of Tlacaxipehualiztli, celebrated immediately before the time of sowing, must have had an atmosphere so dramatic and intense as to exceed our power to imagine, for in the annual enactment of this rite, prisoners were not only sacrificed, their beating hearts torn from their bodies and offered to the gods as the people simultaneously offered ears of corn, but their very skin was flayed from their bodies and donned by priests so that those priests might in this way impersonate the god Xipe Totec, the skins becoming his "golden cloak." So closely is this ritual tied to the identity of the god that the depiction of Xipe Totec in art is almost always as a ritual performer so costumed (see Figure 7, Image 19, and Color Plates 9 and 12). Following the ritual, the skins were donned in turn by ritual beggars, who roamed through the city for twenty days begging alms in the name of the god. Finally the skins were returned to the temple, where they were placed in a special repository in the earth of that sacred space.

Even such a brief description of the ritual as this suggests its metaphorical complexity and subtlety. At the heart of its meaning lies the key Mesoamerican idea of the necessary complementarity of inner and outer. As the Mesoamerican mythological tradition demonstrates at every turn, outer reality—the world of man and nature—is finally nothing more than a manifestation of inner reality—the realm of the spirit, the world of the god. Xipe Totec's ritual is the most graphic, the most compelling, the most basic rendering possible of this metaphor. Here inner is physically separated from outer in a series of actions, and in every action of the series it is demonstrated that it is the inner that is life; in every case the function of the outer is to cover—that is, to manifest, to make visible—the inner.[2] The ritual thus makes clear that the return of spirit, now separated from matter, to the realm of the gods is one of the primary functions of sacrifice. That return is the ritual acknowledgment of the essential cyclicity of life.

The great German scholar Eduard Seler's interpretation of this ritual as a metaphor for the living seed bursting forth from within its dead covering resulting in the "new skin" of vegetation placed upon the earth by the coming of the rainy season[3] has been generally accepted, since it seems to explain the timing of the calendrical ritual dedicated to Xipe in terms of the reference in the hymn to the god's donning his golden cape. As Seler suggests, the ritual, like the hymn, may on one very clear, fairly literal level be seen as referring simultaneously to the sowing of the seed and to the harvesting of the corn, thus embodying the agricultural cycle from "birth" to "death." According to this interpretation, Xipe can be seen as a god of the earth whose essential concern is fertility and man's sustenance, a god who is the embodiment of the sustenance provided from the world of the spirit for humanity.

An American scholar, H. B. Nicholson, among others, objects to this interpretation on the grounds that we have no native informant's testimony to support it, although he does agree "that fertility promotion was the central purpose" of the ritual. His interpretation is somewhat more general: "By donning such a terrible garment the ritual performer thereby *becomes* the deity into which the victim had earlier been transformed, literally crawls into his skin, so to speak—or, at least more directly partakes of his divine essence than by merely attiring himself with the god's insignia."[4] Such an interpretation of the ritual accords quite well with the idea of fertility as the metaphorical movement of the life force from the world of the spirit *into* the now-living plant or animal or human being. Thus such a view does not conflict with Seler's interpretation; rather, they approach the ritual on different levels. This seems a perfect example of the multivocality of ritual and myth, expressive as they are of a single reality on a multitude of levels of metaphoric interpretation while remaining themselves transparent to transcendence.

Interestingly, the French scholar Laurette Séjourné provides still another level of interpretation, which, we would argue, conflicts with neither of these. Calling Xipe "the most hermetic of all Nahuatl divinities," she sees the symbolism of his ritual as one in which the victim

> is relieved (by flaying) of his earthly clothing and is freed forever from his body (an act represented by the dismembering of the corpse). The mystical significance of these rites is emphasized by the behaviour of the owner of the sacrificed prisoner. Not only does he dance, miming the various stages of the [ritual] combat and death; he also behaves towards the corpse as if it were his own body. This identification suggests that the slave represents the master's body offered to the god, the former being merely a symbol for the latter. The drama thus unfolds on two planes: that of the invisible reality, and that of finite matter, a mere projection of the former.[5]

Such an interpretation accords perfectly with the most fundamental assumptions of Mesoamerican mythic thought, and while it is probably true that the ordinary citizen caught up in the observation of this ritual was most aware of its gruesome fertility implications, it is just as probably true that the priest saw in its series of oppositional relationships between inner and outer and living and nonliving the acting out of the most profound mystery recognized by Mesoamerican seers, that mysterious entry of the spiritual essence of life into the world of nature. In the ritual myth did indeed "become reality."

Sahagún indicates clearly the validity of such an interpretation of the ritual. In his account he spends a great deal of time delineating the relationship between the captor of the prisoner of war, who is to become the sacrificial victim, and his captive. The captor did not kill the captive but offered him "as tribute," the actual sacrifice being consummated by the priests. Furthermore, "the captor might not eat the flesh of his captive. He said: 'Shall I, then, eat my own flesh?' For when he took the captive, he had said: 'He is as my beloved son.'" And that identity between captor and captive is made explicit in still another way:

> They named the captor the sun, white earth, the feather, because he was as one whitened with chalk and decked with feathers.
> The pasting on of feathers was done to the captor because he had not died there in the war, but was yet to die, and would pay his debt in war or by sacrifice. Hence his blood relations greeted him with tears and encouraged him.[6]

Thus the captive is simultaneously the god whom he impersonates and the alter ego of the all-too-human captor; in the captive the human and divine identities of the human being merge, and it becomes agonizingly clear that the human skin is but a mask hiding the divine essence, which is revealed in the most literal and striking manner possible in the course of the ritual.

In this ritual the impersonator of the god is stripped of his human covering to reveal the essence of life, which is then ritually consumed so that it—literally—can sustain human life. Thus it becomes clear that Xipe Totec, although obviously a complex and multivocal symbolic entity, is essentially the metaphoric embodiment of the cyclical pattern of all life, a pattern that promises the rebirth of man and man's sustenance, the corn, but requires death for the accomplishment of that rebirth. Xipe was the divine embodiment of life emerging from the dead land, of the new plant sprouting from the "dead" seed. In the cyclical pattern death is always a beginning, a rite of passage, a transition to a spiritual mode of being,[7] and an essential stage preceding regeneration in the transformational process. Thus the development of the life force within each human being paralleled the sacred movement of time. The rhythms of life on earth as manifested in the succession of the seasons, the annual cycles of plant regeneration, and the individual life that encompassed birth, growth, procreation, and death were intimately parallel to those of the heavens, a parallelism that gave a divine aura to human processes. In his mythic emergence from the dead skin of that sacrificed prisoner, Xipe demonstrated, as graphically as can be imagined, that life inevitably emerged from death in the cyclic round of cosmic time, an emergence that suggests in yet another way the centrality of sacrifice to Mesoamerican mythic thought and ritual practice.

SACRIFICE AND FERTILITY

Observed closely, Xipe's ritual reveals that the essence of sacrifice is transformation, the means by which the realm of the spirit enters human space and man can enter the domain of the spirit. A variety of means were used by the peoples of Mesoamerica to move from one plane of existence to another, to move from the surface of life inward, and sacrifice was central to many of them. We know that for the Maya, and probably for all of the other cultures of pre-Columbian Mesoamerica, bloodletting served this purpose in the transformational process; loss of blood produced visions that brought kings and priests into direct contact with their ancestors and with the gods. The Hauberg stela (Figure 16) provides a fascinating example of this process in its depiction of the ritual bloodletting preceding by fifty-two days the accession of Bac-T'ul to the throne. The soon-to-be-installed ruler is shown not drawing his own blood but rather "in the midst of his vision, frozen between the natural and supernatural worlds,"[8] or, as we might put it, transformed from his physical being into spirit.

The act of blood sacrifice provides the most dramatic illustration of the use of ritual to incarnate the supernatural (Images 20 and 21). A great deal has been written about sacrificial practices in pre-Columbian Mesoamerica, especially among the Aztecs, and it seems clear that the mythological equation represented by the sacrificial act is an integral part of the transformative relationship between matter and spirit. So fundamental is sacrifice to this conception that the creation myths of pre-Columbian Mesoamerica all charge mankind with the ritual duty of sacrifice. An Aztec myth, as we have seen, depicts man's creation as the result of an autosacrificial act by Quetzalcoatl. That this idea is fundamental to the Aztec conception of Quetzalcoatl is demonstrated by his being depicted in the codices holding a bone or a thorn used to draw blood, a clear reference to his sprinkling his own blood on the bones of past generations he had gathered in the underworld to transform them into the first man and woman, thereby creating mankind. The myth demonstrates the dependence of mankind on the sacrifice of the god for its existence and suggests the reciprocal human duty of sacrifice, a duty that is the reenactment of the gods' sacrifice in the creation of the sun: "This was the voluntary sacrifice of the assembled gods, to provide the freshly created sun with nourishment. In performing this self-immolation, the gods set an example for man to follow for all time."[9]

FIGURE 16
The Hauberg stela

That the same reciprocal relationship was seen by the Maya is illustrated in both their buildings and their myths. Speaking of Structure 22 at Copan, Schele and Miller point out that within the temple was "a room probably designed for ritual bloodletting. While the nobility let blood in the inner sanctum, maize flourished on the exterior of the building, suggesting that the king's most potent substance, his blood, flowed to fertilize and regenerate nature itself."[10] Thus the king, or priest, entered symbolically into the world of the spirit to give his blood so that the gods would respond with man's sustenance. The same motif appears in the *Popol Vuh*, where the gods' intention is to create "a giver of praise, giver of respect, provider, nurturer." The import of this is made quite clear when man is finally created and begins to proliferate: "And this is our root, we who are the Quiché people. And there came to be a crowd of penitents and sacrificers," a "crowd" made up of the historic Quiché lineages, which are then enumerated.

The Mixtec creation myth, brief as it is, makes the ritual duty of sacrifice equally clear. In that account two gods, male and female, who share the name 1 Deer "appeared" and ultimately became "father and mother of all the gods." They created "two very handsome sons" who, among other things, pierced their own ears and tongues in order to let "a few drops of blood," which they then offered as a sacrifice to the gods who created them. These actions provided a model of proper conduct for the human beings who were then restored to life. The various creation myths thus agreed that sacrifice of human blood was a ritual duty. Metaphorically the sacrifice of life's blood, that is, returning life to its spiritual source, was necessary for the continuation of the endless cycle of transformations through which life was constantly created and maintained. Human beings, helpless without the gods, must sacrifice their blood in return for the continuation of the rains, the growth of the corn, and the healing of illnesses. As Jacques Soustelle points out, there was surely no doubt that "the machinery of the world, the movement of the sun, the succession of the seasons cannot continue and last unless they [the gods] are nourished on the vital energy contained in 'the precious water,' chalchiuatl; in other words, human blood."[11]

Reading any account of Mesoamerican ritual activity makes chillingly clear that the blood needed to maintain the universal system was provided. There seem to be endless numbers of sacrificial rituals running the gamut from symbolic bloodletting and animal sacrifice to autosacrifice to the ultimate sacrifice of human life itself. Autosacrifice, as depicted in the Aztec and Mixtec creation myths, was most common. Throughout Mesoamerica the bleeding of ears, tongues, and genital organs by members of the priesthood was a daily ritual occurrence, sometimes reaching ghastly proportions. "In a certain Mixtec province," for example, "the bleeding of the genital organ was practiced by passing cords as long as fifteen to twenty yards through it."[12]

While such forms of self-sacrifice were quite common, the most sacred form of sacrifice was surely the offering of human life, for that offering involved the sacrifice of life to life. Today, we see such sacrifice as the killing, or even slaughter, of human victims for the gods, but to understand human sacrifice in Mesoamerican terms, we must see it, for the moment at least, as they did, and their intent "was to sacrifice an image of the god to the god."[13] A vital part of the sacrificial ritual, therefore, involved a symbolic transformation of the sacrificial victim into the god, a transformation metaphorically possible because man was both spirit and matter and could, through ritual, "become" spirit. "Accordingly, not only was the correct godly attire important, but also the sex, age, physical condition, and proper emotional attitude of the deity impersonator. . . . All the sixteenth century reports make it clear that the victim *became* the god to whom he was sacrificed,"[14] costume and the physical body functioning as the ritual mask in making the inner reality outer, spiritualizing the physical. The actual sacrifice was the logical final step; the "mask" of the physical body was removed, leaving the spirit to travel to its proper home, the realm of the gods. Thus, to return for a moment to Xipe Totec, that god is "the Flayed One," the inner reality now separated from its outer covering, revealing graphically the "logic" of sacrifice.

These fundamental ideas grew from the shamanic base of Mesoamerican religion, with its emphasis on transformation, and that shamanic worldview included the idea that "the essential life force characteristically resides in the bones. . . . [Consequently] humans and animals are reborn from their bones,"[15] which, like seeds, are the very source of life. Thus Jill Furst contends that in the Mixtec *Codex Vindobonensis* "some, if not all, skeletal figures . . . were deities with generative and life-sustaining functions," and her reading of the codex shows that skeletonization "symbolizes not death, but life-giving and life-sustaining qualities."[16] This, of course, is the same metaphoric message carried by Xipe Totec: death is properly seen as the precursor, or perhaps even the cause, of life. The striking visual image on Izapa Stela 50 (Image 22), depicting what appears to be a small human figure attached to an umbilical cord emerging from the abdomen of a seated, masked skeletal figure, puts this idea in its clearest possible symbolic form.

There are, of course, many other manifestations of the belief that life is born from death. There is a scene on page 52 of the *Codex Borgia,* for example, showing the copulation of the god and goddess of death, a depiction of death in the act of creating life, a fitting image for a world that sees death as another phase of the cycle of life. The same message is conveyed by images on Maya funeral vessels; one, for example, shows "a young male rising from a skull, an event that can only mean emergence from death to life."[17] Still another connection between bones and rebirth can be seen in the fact that in many areas of

Mesoamerica, from the earliest times, red pigment was used to cover bones and funerary offerings because red was associated with the east and the daily rebirth of the sun. Significantly, Xipe Totec was the red aspect of the quadripartite Tezcatlipoca. Ancestor worship provides yet another manifestation of the concept. Among the Maya, dead members of the elite, especially rulers, were apotheosized as divinities, and this belief was shared by those in central Mexico, as can be seen in a passage from Sahagún's *Codex Matritensis*:

> *For this reason the ancient ones said,*
> *he who has died, he becomes a god.*
> *They said: "He became a god there,"*
> *which means that he died.*[18]

The life force never dies; it moves in a cycle from ancestors to descendants, joining them in a spiritual pattern essentially the same as the one traced by the sun as it moves from its zenith to the underworld below and rises again as well as the one manifested in the "dead" seed's sprouting new life. Sacrificial death was thus seen as a necessary part of that cyclical movement, the human work necessary to maintain that motion; in that sense, human blood fueled the cosmic motion, and, by providing that blood through willing sacrifice, humanity played its part in maintaining the cyclical life of the cosmos.

THE NOURISHING CORN: LIFE AND SUSTENANCE

For all of the peoples of Mesoamerica the corn plant was the living manifestation of this cyclical process of regeneration, living proof that the life force never dies. It was essential for man's survival. MacNeish and Linn point out that for Mesoamerica the discovery of corn, as "a source of energy, is comparable to our discovery of the energy within the atom. . . . [It] enabled man to carve his empires in the jungle . . . [and was] indeed the grain that built a hemisphere."[19] As Aztec mythology attests, it was the gift of sustenance from the gods, bestowed by Quetzalcoatl himself, the god who gave man life. Several individual myths recount this event. The version in the *Leyenda de los Soles,* presented above, depicts the god's accomplishing this feat after an encounter with a red ant, who told him that he would find the precious kernels he was carrying—the corn—hidden in Tonacatepetl, the mountain of foodstuffs. Changing himself into a black ant, Quetzalcoatl went to the mountain, found the corn, and took a sample back to the gods in Tamoanchan, who joined him in tasting and enjoying it. He then returned to the mountain for more but failed in his attempt to return with the entire mountain. Nanahuatl was dispatched in his place by the primeval couple, Oxomoco and Cipactonal, and Nanahuatl broke the mountain apart, allowing the Tlalocs to carry the precious corn and other foods to the gods to be given to mankind in reciprocation for human blood sacrificed to the gods.

In the somewhat different version retold in the *Histoyre du Mechique,* Pilzintecuhtli, the son of the primeval couple, and his wife, the goddess Xochiquetzal, make their home in a cave. In that cave, their beautiful son Centeotl had been buried in the earth, whereupon cotton grew from his hair, two wild seed-bearing plants from his ears, sweet potato from his fingers, a special kind of corn from his nails, and other important foods from the rest of his body. Descending into the cave, the gods discovered these staple foods, which they could then provide for the sustenance of humanity. Although this tale differs remarkably in detail from the story in the *Leyenda,* it is significant that in both myths the sustenance is hidden within the earth and in both cases the efforts of the gods must be complemented by those of the primeval human couple. These similarities suggest both the elemental nature of corn and its fundamental connection with human life.

It is not surprising, then, that among the Aztecs, and presumably among their predecessors in the Basin of Mexico, corn was represented by not one but a complex of deities—each representing one of the various stages of maturation in the cyclical process of its growth. Because corn was in fact the essential sustenance of man, the Mesoamerican staff of life, the process of its growth provided a symbolic pattern through which humanity could make sense of the basic cycle of all life: the birth from a dead seed, then the regular stages of growth to the point of maturity, followed by the harvest and the cutting and burning of the dead stalks, followed then by the planting of the "dead" seed to begin the cycle anew. This cyclical pattern of the corn promised the immortality of regeneration, and it was precisely this fundamental cycle that was imaged forth in the various corn gods and goddesses (Color Plate 14) of the Basin of Mexico and of the rest of Mesoamerica.

Maya myths relating the creation of corn are similar to those of the Aztecs. According to the version in the *Popol Vuh* a fox, coyote, parrot, and crow brought the news of the finding of the yellow and white ears of corn at Broken Place, Bitter Water Place. They then showed the creator gods how to reach those places, whereupon the gods created the present human race from the grain that was to be man's essential food. In the *Annals of the Cakchiquels* only the coyote and the crow knew where the food was hidden, but when the coyote was killed and quartered, the corn was found in his body. Then it was kneaded with the blood of the tapir and the serpent to make men. As both of these myths suggest, corn was inseparably linked to the life of the Maya. For that reason, no doubt, it was often used symbolically in their art to represent the cycle of life. At Palenque on the lid of the sarcophagus covering the tomb of Pacal (Image 49), for example, that ruler is depicted at the base of the world tree, down which he seems to be sliding into the underworld, Xibalba, which will be the scene of his combat with death and his eventual resurrection. That depiction of the world tree bears an unmistakable resemblance to a stalk of corn and thus suggests in that metaphoric way as well the rebirth that is to come.

A contemporary Maya myth retold by Thompson is strikingly similar to the Aztec myth. In it an army of ants, having made a tunnel to the place where corn was stored within the rock under a mountain, was carrying the grain on their backs when a fox stopped them and tasted it. Then other animals and finally man discovered it and asked the rain gods to help him obtain it for himself. Three of the rain gods, however, were unable to break the rock open, even with the use of their axelike thunderbolts; finally, the oldest—the chief rain god—sent a woodpecker to tap the rock and find a weak spot. He then hurled his thunderbolt at the place designated by the woodpecker and finally split the rock. But the intense heat of the thunderbolt burned some of the white corn, discoloring it so that four kinds came into being—black, red, yellow, and white. As Thompson points out, this legend is retold in more allegorical language in the *Book of Chilam Balam of Chumayel,* a suggestion of its antiquity. As in other allegorical tales, the ear of corn before it ripens is here equated with the precious jade, which is found, as is the corn in the myth, hidden within rock.[20] Similarly, the Aztec myth from the *Historia de los Mexicanos por sus Pinturas,* which we discuss and present below in connection with the rain god, suggests corn's preciousness by comparing it to the precious jade and quetzal feathers.

In fact, the importance of corn throughout Mesoamerica, as indicated by these mythic references to its preciousness, cannot be overestimated. As Miguel León-Portilla points out, the Nahuatl word for corn is "tonacayotl," which

> can be translated into "our support," [and] connotes not only the basic cereal in the Mesoamerican native diet, but a cluster of related concepts that goes beyond its character—acknowledged by other authors—of sacred symbol. . . . Besides having meanings associated with the sacred, it is understood and experienced as something primordial, and it becomes a dominant factor in the totality of the whole culture, it provides new forms of coherence, and it becomes an essential key in the conformation of the world view and ethos of the community.[21]

For the peoples of Mesoamerica, then, the myths demonstrate not only that corn was a staple food but also that it had a mystic value. It was a living thing worthy of reverence, an object of worship, and a god, all inseparably linked to their lives and all expressive of the essential pattern of life itself.

MAGUEY AND MAYAHUEL

Interestingly, the maguey plant was almost as useful and as important to the people of Mesoamerica as was corn. According to various Aztec sources, Quetzalcoatl was also responsible for the creation of the maguey or the pulque, a liquor often used in ritual, that is made from it and that was believed to be powerfully regenerative, providing mankind with pleasure from its intoxicating effects and the ability to experience other levels of reality. This liquor was made from the plant's fermented juice, but that juice had many medicinal uses in its unfermented state, and the plant itself had still other uses: its fibers were used for weaving cloth and making rope; its thorns were used for needles; its leaves for paper making, roofing, and even for food.

In the account of its creation given in the *Histoyre du Mechique*, Quetzalcoatl, in his form as Ehecatl (Image 26), was instrumental in causing the death and burial of Mayahuel (Color Plate 13), a virgin goddess, and that burial brought the blessing of the pulque. Again, death causes life in the essential cycle of the cosmos, but this time that cycle operates through the female. It is thus quite significant that, according to Thelma Sullivan, Mayahuel means "powerful flow," and that the commentary in the *Codex Vaticanus A* tells us that she was given this name "because they believed that she was a woman who had four hundred [i.e., innumerable] breasts and that because she was so fruitful, the gods transformed her into a maguey, which is the life of this land."[22] Mayahuel, who personified the prolific maguey plant, which produces shoots seemingly endlessly after it has been pruned, was thought to be the epitome of female reproductivity and was therefore associated mythically with all the fundamental characteristics of the feminine principle, such as weaving and the moon,[23] creativity and the irrational, the mystery dimension of life and death, as well as the earth and its fertility, all of which were embodied in the concept of the Mother Goddess. Similarly, among the Mixtecs, the goddess 11 Serpent is the personification of the maguey, and in the *Codex Vindobonensis* she is depicted wearing her own decapitated head on her back, for "the maguey plant is decapitated and has its heart cut out for the extraction of *agua miel*, 'the honey water' that ferments into the sacred pulque."[24] As in the Aztec myth, the giving of life demands the sacrifice of the gods: life lives on life as life invariably comes from death in the endless cycle of fertility.

THE GREAT GODDESS: THE MOTHER, THE EARTH, AND THE MOON

No mythic figure, however, is more clearly and fully illustrative of this truth than that of the Great Mother Goddess, associated often with the earth and with the moon, whose varying manifestations are as ubiquitous in the mythic thought of Mesoamerica as were the painted and sculpted images of those goddesses. According to H. B. Nicholson, "of the many deities portrayed by the surviving stone images, more probably represent the fertility goddess than any other single supernatural."[25] This is surely not surprising, for since the time of the early village cultures of Mesoamerica, as we have seen, the maternal, female figure has been omnipresent in mythic art, suggesting always the fundamental importance of the association between the feminine principle and the fertile earth. These early figurines are in that sense directly ancestral to the bewildering array of earth goddesses elaborated in the mythologies of the high cultures. Humanity continued, from that early time, to be seen metaphorically as the child being nurtured by the earth, by the Great Mother Goddess.

Both the human female and the female earth thus remained, metaphorically and literally, the mystery vessel of life, the birth from which enabled spirit to enter the world of nature. Ultimately the focus was on the miracle of rebirth, through which the dead seed, invigorated by the spiritual energy of the earth, sprouted anew from that earth. When the sprouting took place under the aegis of archaic man, he saw it as an action that must be "storied" in myth[26] and accompanied by the ritual that would recognize and reciprocate the spiritual energy that drove the cycle of regeneration. And in such disparate cycles as those of the growth of the corn, the waxing and waning of the moon, and the span of a human life, generation, death, and regeneration were seen to form the essence of the mystery—the mystery most fully expressed in the mythic image of the Great Mother.

It is important to realize that the mythic quality of this cyclical process was embodied in the *conception* of the Mesoamerican Mother Goddess and was therefore to be seen in all of her fantastically varied manifestations. She was the earth goddess, the fundamental creator and destroyer of life, both nourisher and protector of humanity, but simultaneously the embodiment of the forces of decline and death. Always closely associated with spinning and weaving, which represent the cyclical process of life, death, and rebirth, the Mother Goddess weaves the masculine, vertical principle represented by the warp—the active, direct principle associated with the light of the sun—into the feminine, horizontal principle represented by the woof, the temporal and variable principle. The crossing of these two forms a union of opposites suggesting the duality of all life, a duality that grows from, depends upon, and will return to the underlying and essential unity of spirit.[27] Thelma Sullivan suggests in this connection that "spinning goes through stages of growth and decline, waxing and waning, similar to those of a child-bearing woman. The spindle set in the spindle whorl is symbolic of coitus, and the thread, as it winds around the spindle, symbolizes the growing fetus, the woman becoming big with child."[28]

The Mother Goddess is also closely associated with the moon, which, in its waxing and waning, is one of nature's most striking images of the process of growth, decline, death, and rebirth. As Joseph Campbell reminds us, this process has specifically feminine connections. "The moon," he says, "is the lord and measure of the life-creating rhythm of the womb, and therewith of time, through which beings come and go; lord of the mystery of birth and equally of death—which two, in sum, are aspects of one state of being."[29] Fundamentally analogous to the feminine principle, the moon is evocative of many of its aspects: the dark side of nature with its unseen, inner knowledge, the mystery of the intuitional and the irrational; the enigmatic essence of time that is measured out in the heavens by lunar phases and in women's bodies by the equivalent menstrual cycle. The Goddess is therefore the bringer of change—of birth and growth as well as of suffering and decay. She is thus fundamentally associated with the process of becoming in all its forms. As moon goddess she represents perpetual renewal: she is the bringer of the seasons, the measurer of time, and thus the weaver of fate. In this aspect she controls the life-giving waters, the tides, the rains and floods, and is fundamentally associated with the seasons. Because the phases of the moon include birth, death, and resurrection and manifest the most basic rhythm of cyclic time, the moon goddess is also associated with the span of life and the idea of perpetual renewal.

These aspects of the feminine principle—all of them integral parts of the Great Mother Goddess—are responsible for the tremendous similarity and overlapping of attributes of the multitudinous specific goddesses of the Mesoamerican mythological tradition. The paucity of information remaining to us about most of them makes it extremely difficult to differentiate clearly among them. In many cases they seem to be interchangeable, and scholars often disagree as to their specific functions and relationships, although most would agree that the many specific goddesses represent different aspects of a single goddess.

As the Aztec Tlazolteotl, who is also known as Tlazolteotl-Ixcuina, since one of her manifestations is named Ixcuina, the Great Goddess manifests herself most basically as the great spinner of the thread and weaver of the fabric of life. She is a fertility goddess, a life giver, and as such seems to have represented the Mother Goddess in her totality, including both her negative and positive aspects. To complicate matters, she had many aspects, each known by a different name. Sometimes portrayed as a corn goddess who was the mother of the corn god Centeotl and therefore closely affiliated with Mayahuel, goddess of the maguey, she is often depicted wearing a flayed human skin and is thus closely associated with rituals of spring, fertility, and renewal similar to those involved with Xipe Totec. As the great conceiver, she is portrayed in the *Codex Borbonicus* (Color Plate 18) giving birth to a child that resembles herself, suggestive of Tlazolteotl's generative and regenerative powers. In addition, she was a moon goddess, and as Ixcuina was the wife of Mictlantecuhtli, lord of the underworld.

As Teteo Innan she was seen as the "Mother of the Gods," who "appears in the sixteenth century . . . texts as the female component of Huehueteotl, Xiuhtecuhtli" and is thus fundamental in importance. Willard Gingerich traces the ancient cult of Teteo Innan back to the figurines of the period of the village cultures and contends that she "represented a mother and earth numen of considerable antiquity and authority in the Valley of Mexico."[30] As the ritual hymn "Teteo Innan, Her Song," which we present in his translation below, demonstrates, the conception of Teteo Innan was basic to the Aztec understanding of fertility on all its levels of meaning.

As Toci, an aspect of the Goddess closely related to Teteo Innan, the Great Goddess was "Our Grandmother," the older aspect of the female principle, and was both male and female, thus emphasizing the creative powers that resulted from the union of the two opposed genders in the same way that that union was emphasized in the supreme deity, Ometeotl, "Our Father, Our Mother." In a fascinating argument, Susan Gillespie contends that although Huitzilopochtli refers to Toci as "my mother, my grandmother," she was much more than that: she was to become his wife and sister after her death. She played all the female roles in opposition to the archetypal maleness of Huitzilopochtli in the myth. "Toci is a goddess and the wife of a god, so she is not constrained by mortal prohibitions against holding mutually contradictory roles."[31] This multifaceted nature can be seen clearly in the most important ritual dedicated to her, the Aztec veintena festival of Ochpaniztli, held at the time of the harvest. The name means "sweeping of the roads" and suggests the clearing of the way for the passage of the gods associated with agricultural fertility, just as Ehecatl represented the storms that cleared the roads for the passage of the rain god. The festival celebrated both the earth's provision of sustenance and the return of the dead stalks to the earth so that the renewal of life in the spring might take place.

For this festival a woman was chosen to represent Toci, our grandmother, mother of the gods, heart of the earth, and was transformed into that goddess not only by being "garbed exactly as the goddess" but also by being made godlike in other ways. After being "purified and washed," she was "given the name of the goddess Toci, . . . consecrated to avoid all sin or transgression, [and] locked up and kept carefully in a cage" for twenty days to ensure her abstention from all carnal sin. In addition, "she was made to dance and rejoice" so that "all could see her and worship her as a divinity"; she was encouraged to be joyful and happy in the manner of the gods. In fact, "the people held her to be the Mother of the Gods and revered her, respected and honored her as if she had been the goddess herself," as, ritually, she was.

After her sacrificial death, the culmination of her transformation into the goddess, a further transformation took place. The skin was removed from her dead body "from the middle of the thigh upward as far as the elbows. A man appointed for this purpose was made to don the skin so as to represent the goddess again." Still later in the ceremony he who was transformed into the goddess stripped himself and bestowed his goddess regalia on a straw figure, which resulted in the transformation of that figure into the goddess—a total of three incarnations of the goddess through transformation in a single festival.[32] And each transformation of the goddess marked a stage in the all-important transformation of the ripened corn from the earth to man and back to the earth in the continuation of the cycle, ensuring the renewal of life in the spring. It was through the ritual's serving as the necessary catalyst that the energy from the heart of the cosmic realm was transformed into the natural world. That transformative force is the power of the Great Goddess in her aspect of Toci.

As Xochiquetzal, which according to Thelma Sullivan means "Flowery Quetzal Feather,"[33] she manifested herself as the young, fecund mother goddess related to procreation, pregnancy, and childbirth. One of the remaining mythic fragments recounting her exploits[34] illustrates her sensuous femininity and her association with lust, voluptuousness, and carnal pleasure. It tells of an ascetic named Yappan who resolved to leave his worldly existence and win the favor of the gods by leading a chaste, penitent life as a hermit atop a great cylindrical (phallic?) rock dedicated to penitential acts. The gods doubted his resolve and sent various women to tempt him, but he remained steadfast. Finally, however, Xochiquetzal decided to try her seductive ways, and Yappan was sufficiently lured by her enticement to descend in order to assist her in climbing up the cylindrical rock to his place of penitence. She tempted him, and he fell, after which she left him, having accomplished her purpose. In disgrace, he was decapitated by Yaotl, his enemy, and then transformed by the gods into a scorpion, an insect that lives under rocks and not atop them. Díaz Cíntora tells us that this myth is still invoked by the shaman to cure the sting of this insect. Because she was affiliated with the moon and weaving, Xochiquetzal was often portrayed in mythic art with her loom, weaving the patterns of life with the thread of destiny, a conception not unrelated to her effect on Yappan.

As Coatlicue (Image 23), the Great Goddess plays a role in the only complete surviving Aztec myth relating to the Goddess.[35] A focal point of the myth is her relationship with another aspect of that goddess, Coyolxauhqui (Image 24), her daughter in this case. The pious Coatlicue, innocently sweeping the temple, becomes pregnant when "a ball of fine feathers" falls on her. She has conceived Huitzilopochtli, and although this is an immaculate conception, her children, the goddess Coyolxauhqui and the four hundred (i.e., countless) gods of the south, see it as shameful and resolve to kill their mother.[36] They fail in the attempt because Huitzilopochtli springs fully armed from his mother, decapitates his female sibling, and routs her followers.[37] It has been pointed out by scholars that Coatlicue can be understood as the earth, Coyolxauhqui as the moon, Huitzilopochtli as the sun, and the four hundred as the stars, suggesting that the myth is an astronomical allegory referring to the daily ascent of the sun, whose rays at dawn remove the moon and the stars from sight. But it is also apparent that the myth focuses on rebirth in other ways. Coatlicue's pregnancy brings life into the world from the female, but a female must die as a result. In addition, Coyolxauhqui's decapitation and ultimate dismemberment have often been seen as relating to the gradual disappearance of the moon in the night sky, a disappearance whose cycle parallels the female menstrual cycle, which is, of course, intimately related to pregnancy and, thus, rebirth.

But Coatlicue is associated not only with birth. Like most of the goddesses, she was closely connected to the idea of death as well. Because the earth is both the womb and the tomb of all life, it is certainly not surprising that symbols of death would be prominent in the iconography associated with fertility goddesses such as Coatlicue. In this sense Willard Gingerich describes Coatlicue as "one of mankind's definitive expressions of the 'Terrible Mother' . . . who both feeds and devours her children."[38] However, these seemingly contradictory roles made sense in a culture that saw death as the necessary precondition for birth, a culture that saw bones as seeds. As Gillespie observes in another context: the goddess "is immortal, not because she does not die, but because she does age and die but is then reborn. She is the earth and the maize that grows from it to sustain mankind in its seasonal permutations of conception, growth, maturity, and death—that is, planting, nurturing, harvesting, and eating."[39] Again, death is the prelude to rebirth.

Toci, Xochiquetzal, and Coyolxauhqui were all associated by the Aztecs with the moon, so it is interesting to note that among the Maya, the moon goddess, Ix Chel (Figure 17), was doubtlessly the most important moon divinity. Her name, according to Eric Thompson, means "stretched out woman" and "recalls that incident in the moon's life on earth when she was made to stretch herself on the ground so that the deer, by trampling on her, might restore her generative faculties. . . . In connection with a goddess of procreation that incident was naturally of paramount importance."[40] Considered to be the wife, or sometimes the sister, of the sun as well as earth goddess and mother of the corn god, there was a widespread devotion to her at the time of the Conquest. Thompson indicates that her four main roles portray her as the dispenser of fate, the erotic patron of marriage, the guardian of children and of childbirth, and the patron of various diseases and their cures.[41]

But as Schele and Miller suggest, her

two aspects in Classic Maya depictions [are] both associated with making cloth. At times she appears as a demure, young weaver; at other times, she is a sexy, comely courtesan associated with spinning. . . . Frequently, a bird is perched on her loom, recalling illustrations of the Central Mexican goddess Xochiquetzal, who is also associated with the moon and weaving. . . . A second female type is the courtesan who wears unspun cotton in her headdress. In spite of the association with spinning, we never see this woman at work, in contrast to the industrious weaver. She sometimes wears a cape, but generally she is depicted wearing no garment over her breasts, which is the custom of many Maya women today when they are at home. Like the erratic moon, this woman is not a model of constancy. In paintings and clay sculptures she is paired with

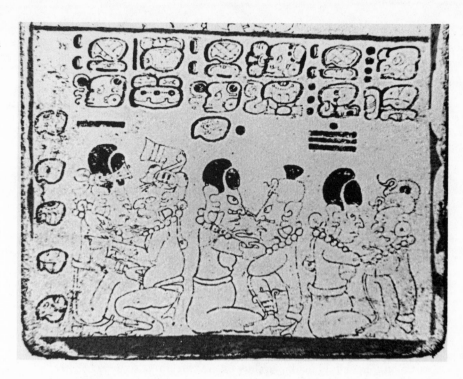

old men, deities, and even large rabbits, as if she wandered from one to
the other. Often she is depicted with companions who hug her or fondle
her breasts.[42]

A tale of Ix Chel's infidelity told by his Maya workmen to Eric
Thompson earlier in this century has been shown by Norman Hammond's convincing study of the scenes on several Maya vases to have
been in existence as early as 300 and not later than 450 A.D.[43] In it the
moon goddess is married to the sun, who has built her a house where
they live in the company of his brother, the future morning star. Sun,
suspecting her infidelity with his brother, puts them to the test by
preparing a tamale for them. When they eat it they both vomit, and
Sun knows they are guilty. Very unhappy, Ix Chel is sitting alongside
the river when she is confronted by a vulture, who induces her to leave
Sun and live with his master, the king vulture, in a palace (his nest)
white from vulture droppings. Sun manages to find her, and after out-
witting the vultures to gain access to his wife, he convinces her to return home with him so they can resume their duties in heaven. Once
there, Ix Chel shines as brightly as the sun and people cannot sleep, so
"Sun took out one of her eyes, and since then she has given only a soft
light."[44]

But as Arthur Miller points out in a discussion of the murals at the
Maya site of Tulum, Ix Chel held "the power to transform darkness into
light and to cause birth and rebirth."[45] In that, she typifies the power of

the Great Goddess; while the daytime sun might be seen as defeating the nighttime moon from a male, day-oriented point of view, the opposite female-centered view is also possible. The night and the moon will vanquish the sun at the close of day. It is that invincible, mysterious power of the night, symbolized in the ever-changing moon, that is the power of the Great Goddess.

THE EARTH MONSTER

As we have seen in numerous cases, however, it was not unusual for goddesses to have a male counterpart or aspect, nor, conversely, was it out of the ordinary in Mesoamerican mythology for gods to have female manifestations, and one of the manifestations of Tlazolteotl, the most fundamental Aztec aspect of the Great Goddess, was the sometimes-male, sometimes-female Tlaltecuhtli, a representation of the earth itself, who is depicted in mythic images as a huge, rapacious toad—the Earth Monster (Image 25)—who

> was conceived of as a giant, reputedly amphibian, creature afloat in the center of a large ocean where her body formed the surface and bowels of the earth. Her upturned head, with wide open jaws, rested at the western horizon, her hind quarters presumably at the eastern horizon. All vegetation sprang from her body; thus she was the direct source of all life and its nourishment. As the archetype of fertility, birth, and nurture, she was logically conceived of as a female and a mother; such a concept accounts for the consistent appearance of the goddess in the displayed posture of parturition.[46]

Alana Cordy-Collins suggests that

> in female guise the goddess was the Earth Mother, the source of life. As the great toad with its fanged and gaping jaws and the epitome of the Mesoamerican belief that the underworld existed in the bowels of the earth, she was also the Earth Monster, the taker of life and therefore accompanied by symbols of death. Thus was the earth personified during Aztec times; it was that from which all life came and that to which all life returned.[47]

In the myth included in the *Histoyre du Mechique,* which we present below, the earth is formed from her body, with all the earth's features arising from various parts of it. The same idea is expressed, as we have seen earlier in connection with the myths involving the creation of the earth and the mythic explanation of Tezcatlipoca's missing foot, in a panel from the *Codex Fejérváry-Mayer* (see Figure 11), which illustrates the myth of Tezcatlipoca's tempting Tlaltecuhtli to come up from the deep water by enticing her with his tremendous foot. But she swallowed his foot, whereupon he tore off her jaw so that she could not return to the primeval sea from which she came, and thus the earth where man was to live was created from her body. Since Tlaltecuhtli's giant head was placed to the west, her womb opened to the east, so that the heavenly bodies were believed to pass through the Earth Monster in the process of making their daily cycles. Even her placement, then, is directly metaphoric of her regenerative function.

The Maya, as we have seen in our discussion of Itzam Na above, conceived the earth as the continuation of the iguana house, the four archetypal iguanas reaching from the zenith to the horizon, where they turned to form the surface of the earth. But there was also the belief among the Maya, similar to that of the Aztecs, that the earth was the back of a gigantic crocodile floating on the cosmic waters. The various depictions of these Maya earth monsters from which life springs[48] combine to suggest that the earth gives life, thus sustaining the cyclical pattern as it was created in the beginning. Since death was the prerequisite for rebirth and continued fertility within that cosmic pattern, the earth monsters required nourishment in the form of human hearts and blood in order to continue to supply mankind with sustenance.

Thus it is interesting that while corn and the maguey were the ultimate products of the rituals and myths dedicated to fertility, the goddesses and the earth monsters were the epitome of the process of fertility. Their conceptual makeup embodied every facet of the Mesoamerican view of that process: the stages of growth and decay; the processes of creativity, including the union of the male and female principles; the respect for the earth, from which all life comes and to which it inevitably returns; and the promise of cyclical rebirth like that of the corn and the sun itself. And as we have seen, the various goddesses were all aspects of and unfolded from the Great Goddess. They were called by metaphoric names characterizing their attributes, "not as they were seen by the physical eye, but as . . . conceived in terms of a spectrum of life-forces." And they appeared in metaphoric guise, for in Mesoamerica, to an extent not always seen in other areas of the world, "items of ritual attire are descriptive of cosmic phenomena, not of the personality of an anthropomorphic god";[49] consequently the great art and myths of Mesoamerica portray in the language of metaphor the magnificent mystery that both provided the stage for and filled every corner of that world.

It is significant, then, that although "the conscious world view of the Aztecs was 'patriarchal' [and] by the time of the conquest the power of the Goddess had grown almost invisible and the male principle of the light and the sun is dominant, . . . a closer analysis yields a very different psychological picture. . . . Here there is no doubt that an originally matriarchal constellation was overlaid by patriarchal institutions."[50] The magnificence and power of the goddess were so much a part of the mythological structure of the culture that alongside the king there governed a figure that, though always represented by a man, bore the name of the earth goddess, Cihuacoatl, "Snake Woman." Thus the Great Goddess of Mesoamerica, like William Faulkner's Dilsey in *The Sound and the Fury*, is at "the beginning and the end." "Her many manifestations correspond to the four stages of life—youth, fecundity, middle age, and old age, [the approach] to death—as a metaphor for the cyclical nature, and hence immortality, of the cosmos."[51] That concept was indelibly ingrained as the mythic basis of the Mesoamerican worldview.

THE GODS OF STORM AND RAIN

While plants grow from the fertile earth, represented in the mythic consciousness of Mesoamerica by the Great Goddess, to sustain the life of mankind, their growth depends upon the timely provision of water from the heavens. The upper and lower realms of the spirit must thus cooperate in the maintenance of earthly life. The heavenly component of the process involves the storms, which deliver the rains at the proper times and in the proper amounts. In the Aztec conception, as Sahagún presents it, these storms were, fittingly, the manifestations of two male gods working in tandem. Quetzalcoatl, in his fertility aspect as the bird-billed Ehecatl (Image 26), "was the wind; he was the guide, the roadsweeper of the rain gods, of the masters of the water, of those who brought rain. And when the wind increased, it was said, the dust swirled up, it roared, howled, became dark, blew in all directions; there was lightning; it grew wrathful."[52] And the god for whom he swept the roads was "Tlaloc, the provider. To him was attributed the rain; for he created, brought down, showered down the rain and the hail. He caused the trees, the grasses, the maize to blossom, to sprout, to leaf out, to bloom, to grow. And also were attributed to him the drowning of people, the thunderbolts"[53] (Images 31–38).

Although no narrative texts remain in which Ehecatl's efforts are recounted, we do have two rather brief descriptions of the function and methods of Tlaloc. The first of these, found in the *Historia de los Mexicanos por sus Pinturas,* is the most straightforward. In it Tlaloc is described as living in a quadripartite dwelling where he has four urns in which are stored the rains—some beneficent, some destructive—which he will ultimately provide. These rains are distributed by his diminutive assistants, the Tlaloque, and the manner of their distribution causes the lightning and thunder that we associate with the rainstorm. The second text, from the *Leyenda de los Soles,* connects the activities of Tlaloc with the fall of the Toltec empire, suggesting thereby the importance of the god. In it Huemac, the last Toltec ruler, defeats Tlaloc in a game of tlachtli and wins armfuls of green-husked, ripe corn rather than the precious jade and quetzal plumes—also green, of course—that he had expected. Enraged, he orders the messengers, who are the Tlaloques, to take the corn away. This they do, and with a vengeance; no corn will grow in the kingdom for four years, a punishment that is instrumental in destroying the Toltec kingdom. Huemac learns what is truly precious.

Interestingly, both of these myths continue beyond these fundamental stories, and in both cases the continuation stresses the connection between Tlaloc and sacrifice. This connection is clearest in the *Leyenda* tale. In it the four years of deprivation were ended when one of the Tlaloques, after a consultation with the god himself, offered to renew the provision of sustenance on two conditions. First, rulership must be transferred from the Toltec ruler, Huemac, to the Mexica, and second, the Mexica must provide the daughter of Tozcuecuex, whose name was Quetzalxochtzin, as a sacrificial offering. After these two conditions were fulfilled, "then sprouted all the different green plants and all the herbs and grasses. And all the foodstuffs were created and brought to life." Although the transfer of power required here seems, on one level, a transparent attempt on the part of the Mexica tellers of this story to legitimize their rule by depicting themselves as the rightful successors to the Toltecs, the equation of fertility and sacrifice strikes a far deeper chord in Mesoamerican thought.

Similarly, the tale in the *Historia* continues with a brief account of the comparable attempt by the ruler of Chalco to deal with the god of rain. After placing a humpback within a cave atop a mountain, then sealing the entrance to the cave so that the victim will die as an offering to the Tlaloques, the ruler, upon returning later, is amazed to find that the victim has not died but has traveled in a vision to the dwelling of Tlaloc and there discovered, first, the nature of the god, and second, the fact that the ruler would soon be defeated by the Mexica. Again, the Mexica are clearly using the story of Tlaloc to legitimize their rule, but again, that surface interpretation of the story does not obscure the fact that its primary metaphor involves the necessity of sacrifice as a means of communing with the realm of the spirit.

It is thus doubly significant that sacrifice is the focal point of the two other remaining Aztec texts relating to Tlaloc. These are both ritual texts—prayers and invocations of the god—rather than myths, but they clearly refer to the basic myth. One of these texts is rather long, the other brief. One is fairly straightforward, the other enigmatic. In the lengthy, straightforward "Prayer to Tlaloc," in fact, sacrifice provides the pivot on which the myth turns. The prayer begins with a statement, in mythic terms, of the situation—a drought:

> The gods, Our Lords, the Providers,
> the Lords of Rubber, the Lords of the Sweet-Scented Marigold,
>   the Lords of Copal,
> have sealed themselves in a coffer, they have locked themselves
>   in a box.
> They have hidden the jade and turquoise and precious jewels
>   of life,
> they have carried off their sister, Chicomecoatl, the fruits of the
>   earth,
> and the Crimson Goddess, the chile.

Then follows an enumeration of the disastrous effects of the gods' withdrawal, effects felt by the land, the people, especially the children, and the birds and animals.

After this doleful listing comes the first half of the mythic equation requiring sacrifice:

> *It is the jade, the armlet, the turquoise—*
> *the most precious, the only precious thing there is;*
> *it is the sustenance, the substance, the life of the world,*
> *whereby those who are alive, live*
> *and talk and rejoice and laugh.*

The "it" is, of course, the growing plants, but by extension the rain, the precious fluid without which there can be no life, and as the hymn makes quite clear, the rain is provided from the world of the spirit as the gods' means of maintaining life in the world of nature. It is "the life of the world" because it is a transformation of the essence of spirit into the essence of life.

The Aztec audience would have realized two key facts about this transformation. First, it was systematic, a *regular* part of the annual cycle of the seasons in their Valley of Mexico home, where the rains came, and still do, during their regular season. The cycle's regularity was one of many indications of the order underlying the seemingly chaotic world of nature, an order of the spirit. It was an order related in its regularity to the fundamental cycle of creation, according to which the Aztecs were living their lives during the fifth such cycle. The prayer connects the two in its suggestion that the disruption of the seasonal cycle may presage the end of the larger cycle when "the demons of the air shall descend and come to destroy the earth and devour the people." Neither the earth nor its beings nor even the seasonal cycle is permanent; the only permanence is to be found in the underlying order of the world of the spirit, from which all these contingent realities are derived.

Second, the seasonal cycle, as long as it would last, required reciprocal participation on the part of human beings, the second half of the mythic equation. In Aztec terms the fundamental metaphor for this human participation in the cosmic scheme describes human blood as the food for the sun, the nourishment that alone can provide divine energy. It is not coincidental, then, that following the hymn's expression of fear at the possible ending of the earth and its enumeration of possible means through which that destruction might occur, the final means of potential destruction is to let the sun "do his work," charring the people of the earth, scattering their hair, whitening their bones, and splitting their skulls open. This death is specifically likened to the sacrificial death of the warrior, either in battle or on the sacrificial stone of his captors, a death that is followed by the warrior's apotheosis, his going to the house of the sun.

FIGURE 18

The old god of fire,
Huehueteotl, an Aztec
stone brazier imitating
the Teotihuacan form,
but in this case the old
god of fire wears the
"goggles" of Tlaloc (see
Figure 12)

In one sense this reference to sacrificial death and apotheosis seems strange in a prayer to Tlaloc, since those who were sacrificed to that god were generally thought to have gone to Tlalocan, the heaven of the rain god, rather than the house of the sun, but Thelma Sullivan, in her note to the present translation, suggests that "like the gods who hurled themselves into the fire to put the sun in motion, the blood of the warriors gloriously consumed by the fire of battle provided nourishment for the sun so that it could make its daily journey through the skies and be victorious in its combat with the night."[54] This suggestion makes clear that what is at stake here is not merely an end to the drought but the cosmic order itself, for the cyclical provision of water is fundamental to the maintenance of life.

Perhaps the prayer's reference to the charring of the people as they perish from the drought, like the earlier, striking allusion to "a monstrous serpent" within those suffering from the drought, a serpent that burns, shrieks, and howls, is meant to suggest the necessary suffering brought about by aridity, a suffering that must be complemented and relieved by the gods' sending water, "the riches that are theirs alone." This union of fire and water is intriguing from a mythic point of view since it is precisely the same union suggested by Teotihuacan's much earlier Tlalocan mural (Color Plate 19) as well as by an Aztec Huehueteotl who wears the mask of Tlaloc (Figure 18), a sculpture presumably contemporary with the composition of the prayer.

Interestingly, the "brazier" that this figure bears is not open at the top, and on the flat surface that is its top are symbols relating to water precisely in the spot where the mind expects fire. Fire and water are thus the polar points between which the cycle of fertility constantly moves, and both are necessary.

Laurette Séjourné has applied this fertility-related concept to an even larger reality in the mythic thought of Mesoamerica:

> The dynamics of the union of two opposites is at the basis of all creation, spiritual as well as material. The body "buds and flowers" only when the spirit has been through the fire of sacrifice; in the same way the Earth gives fruit only when it is penetrated by solar heat, transmuted by rain. That is to say, the creative element is not either heat or water alone, but a balance between the two.[55]

And that union is also suggested by the lightning serpent often held by images of Tlaloc (see, for example, Color Plate 7). In later Aztec mythic thought that serpent was known as Xiuhcoatl (see Figure 15) and was intimately related to Xiuhtecuhtli, the god of fire. And Xiuhtecuhtli, of course, was the Aztec manifestation of the Teotihuacan fire god (see Figure 12) on whose brazier the diamond-shaped eyes of the god of the Tlalocan mural (Color Plate 19) are found. Significantly, this is the same fire serpent referred to in the song of Xipe Totec discussed above:

> My god, thy precious water hath come down from Coapan. It hath made the cypress a quetzal. The fire serpent hath been made a quetzal serpent. Want hath gone from me.

The reference to sacrifice that follows this one in the "Prayer to Tlaloc," the death of "the little child, the tot," of whom it is said, "a perfect jade, a perfect turquoise, a smooth and lustrous turquoise, is the heart he shall offer the sun," relates the feared end of the present order with the drought in yet another way, since throughout Mesoamerica, children were the sacrificial offerings to the gods of rain. Following these references to the destruction of the present order, with their oblique allusion to the sacrifice of human life, which should be reciprocated by Tlaloc, the prayer makes its plea to the god directly: "Oh, with a sprinkle, with a few drops of dew, may you succor, may you aid, Tlaltecutli, Lord of the Earth, who feeds and nourishes man." Thus the mythic equation is completed. Tlaloc, the rain, and Tlaltecuhtli, the earth, must provide sustenance for man if life in the present sun is to continue (see below and Image 43). And that provision of sustenance must be reciprocated through the sacrifice of human blood, the nourishment of the sun.

While the statement of that mythic equation in the "Prayer to Tlaloc" is relatively clear and unambiguous, the same cannot be said for the hymn entitled "Tlaloc, His Song." Even for those whose careers have been devoted to the study of Nahuatl literature, the twenty sacred hymns, of which "Tlaloc, His Song," as well as the "Song of Xipe Totec Iouallauan," forms a part, are difficult. Willard Gingerich, a noted translator of Nahuatl and the translator of the hymn presented here, for example, says that they "form a genre of Nahuatl poetry unique in its obscurity and hieraticism" and that "these texts remain among the most confusing in the language."[56] And for those not devoted to the study of that literature, the songs are even more difficult. The first difficulty one encounters is the fact that this song is, in part, a description of a ritual action. But because that description was meant for those intimately familiar with the ritual, we are given only the isolated details that Aztec citizens would have been able to fit into the picture they knew so well from a series of experiences we have not shared.

Gingerich summarizes the extant accounts of that ritual:

According to Durán this festival was called *Huey Tozoztli* (Great Perforation), and it fell on the first day of the month of that name, which he identifies as 29 or 30 April. Sahagún, however begins this month on 14 March. It was the purpose of this feast, Durán notes, to request a good growing season, since all the new maize had by then sprouted. The ceremonies were divided into three sequences, of which the first took place on the summit of a mountain on the east wall of the valley named Tlalocan. This valley was identified with the mythic paradise of the god. On this summit was a large courtyard enclosed within an eight-foot wall, one corner of which contained a covered shrine with an image of the god. Here, just after dawn on the day of the festival, the *tlatlatoani* (rulers) and lords of all the cities of the valley, Mexica and otherwise, came in procession to deck the idol with expensive and elaborate robes, jewels, and feathers, and to present offerings of food. The central feature of this ritual was the sacrifice of a child by slitting its throat in an enclosed litter; the blood was sprinkled over the food-offerings and smeared on the idol.

Meanwhile, back in Tenochtitlan, all the people were participating in the second aspect of the ceremonies, which involved an artificial "forest," erected in the main temple courtyard for this occasion. It consisted of a single large tree with foliage intact that had been brought from a Hill of the Star (where the New Fire ceremonies were enacted every fifty-two years and where the mythic Ce Acatl Quetzalcoatl had built a temple to his father Mixcoatl) and surrounded by four smaller ropes known as *nezahualmecatl* or "ropes of fasting and penance." The central tree was addressed as *Tota* or "Our Father." (Only one other ceremony in the Nahuatl year demonstrates a more overt phallic symbolism—in the month of Xocotl Huetzi a naked tree trunk was erected in the temple courtyard in honor of Huehueteotl Ixcozauhqui, the ancient yellow-faced god of fire who is associated directly with the supreme Ometeotl. In this festival young men held a contest in which they raced to the top of the pole, pulling down the image of *tzoallia* dough placed there.) On the morning of the ceremony a small girl was brought into this artificial grove in a covered litter and there addressed by all the people with songs to the accompaniment of a single drum, but without dancing, until the lords came down from the ceremonies on the mountain. These songs undoubtedly included the hymn here presented.

[In the third segment of the ritual] both tree and girl were then carried by canoe to a large whirlpool, sinkhole, or spring—Durán was unable to specify which—in the lake some distance from Tenochtitlan. Here the tree was erected in the muddy bottom (where it remained until it rotted), the girl's throat was cut, and her body thrown to the whirlpool along with numerous offerings of jewelry and precious stones. "In grave silence all returned to the city. In this way the festival ended, but the ceremonies did not, since the peasants . . . continued them in their tilling and sowing in the fields, in the river, springs, and streams."[57] At the University of Mexico I was told that it is believed that occasionally, in the mountains, a child succumbs to the memory of Tlaloc even today. Sahagún, in his account of the same ceremonies, notes that it was considered a good omen of rain if the victim wept excessively.

Thus the song's opening references to paper flags and festive handfuls of bloodied thorns are details drawn from the ritual observance, the bloodied thorns, bloodied through autosacrifice, are "the penitential 'collateral' required by the theology of the Five Suns myth (see above) and referred to in the opening line of the Song: 'Mexico seeks a loan of the god.'" Here we see again the mythic equation of human sacrifice with the gods' provision of sustenance, the realization that it is human blood that drives the cosmic cycle that makes life possible on the earthly plane. The third stanza expresses the ritual abasement of the participants before the god and offers their condemnation of the human failings of their followers; even with the sacrifice of their own blood, they are unworthy. But in the fourth stanza they are reassured by the god.

The second segment of the song, stanzas six to eleven, dwells on the role of the child victim of the sacrificial ritual as the parent of the child, Tozcuecuexi, "the mythic type of all parents whose children are taken as payment on the 'loan' of Tlaloc, a parenthood which the city as a whole ritually takes on itself," bemoans the loss of his child. This Tozcuecuexi is, of course, the same character who appears in the *Leyenda de los Soles* account to which we have referred above, and here he is used to make precisely the same point regarding the regrettable necessity of sacrifice. That sacrifice sends the victim to Quenamican, the place "where somehow we continue to exist." This is the appellation applied generally to the afterlife, and it refers in this case specifically to Tlalocan, the paradise of the rain god, but, as Gingerich suggests, its generality "invokes the quality of unknowability which no doctrine of the afterlife can ever quite dispel, of Hamlet's 'undiscovered country, from whose bourn no traveler returns.'"

Again according to Gingerich, the penultimate stanza of the song contains the essential kernel of the myths of fertility:

[In] "the Place of the Fleshless, House of Quetzal" . . . a transformation of human bodies does indeed take place, not into new human bodies but into the flesh of the earth's fruits. . . . What this hymn identifies is the equation in Nahuatl doctrine between man's literal, physical flesh and the various plant bodies on which he lived. It is an equation whose mechanics are identical to our modern understanding of the organic cycle with an important limitation: the transformation of man's life into the life of his food plants is here implied to be as direct and exclusive as the digestive process by which the plant is eaten and becomes man. The hymn glorifies this natural process, the inverse of man's digestion, as the means whereby new food plants will be given life—the "loaning" referred to in the first line, now clearly more than a simple trade of blood for rain and vice versa. The "stomach" where this inverse digestion of the victims of Tlaloc takes place is "the Place of the Fleshless, House of Quetzal," epithets for Tlalocan and Mictlan. . . . This equation of human and plant life, mystical to us but scientific to the Nahuas, is subsumed in the word *tonacayotl.* The word can be literally understood as both "our flesh" and "the things of the sun's warmth," i.e., fruits of the earth or man's sustenance. In the work called the *Historia de los Mexicanos por sus Pinturas,* the Supreme God of Duality, [Ometeotl], is identified as Tonacatecutli, "Lord of Our Flesh" or "Lord of Earthly Fruits" and in the present hymn Tlaloc is told, "Yours is our flesh, you its maker."

These four surviving Aztec texts—two myths and two ritual hymns—in which Tlaloc is the focus, then, are essentially similar in their fundamental concern with the cyclical provision of the sustenance upon which human life depends and the reciprocal provision of the human sustenance that nourishes the gods. We have no texts from the other cultures of Mesoamerica relating to the rain god, nor do we have them from earlier times in the Basin of Mexico, but the tremendous number of images of that god that do remain, from the earliest times of the urban tradition in Mesoamerica to the latest and from every culture area, provide a great deal of evidence that they must have been accompanied by narrative myths similar to those that remain. We present below a selection of these images to illustrate both their range and the clear pattern of development they evidence (Images 27–42). In those images the various rain gods are related to the mythic structures of rulership and of time and space. Often connected metaphorically with fire images, the rain god images are consistently used as a way of understanding the cyclical progression of the seasons and of the life of the corn, man's essential sustenance.

All of these abstract relationships in which the god of rain is seen were built on his primary function, and that function is emphasized consistently in all of the cultures in which his images are found. As can be seen from the "gallery" of images at the end of this part, among the Aztecs (Image 38), as among the various "Toltec" cultures (Image 35), among the Teotihuacanos (Images 31–33), and among the Zapotecs (Images 28–30), the god of rain is consistently depicted on the "face" of urns, which were clearly representative of those from which he and his assistants dispensed the life-sustaining waters in the myth. A number of such urns were found among the offerings at the Aztec Templo Mayor, and they are iconographically identical to those depicted a thousand years earlier in the murals of the initial high culture in the Basin of Mexico, that of Teotihuacan. The earliest representation of

Tlaloc, in fact, is on exactly such an urn from the earliest phase of the development of Teotihuacan (Image 31).

Significantly, in the Basin of Mexico and in the Valley of Oaxaca ceramic sculptures have been uncovered in which Tlaloc or Cocijo is attached to a cluster of four or five vessels, making the connection with the myth even clearer. In the mural representations from Teotihuacan (Color Plates 19 and 20) Tlaloc is depicted holding similar urns with water flowing from them, and the Tlalocan mural makes clear that these are the nourishing waters that will sustain life, since a portion of that mural shows corn plants growing from such streams before they ultimately flow into the mouths of earth-monster figures.

The two myths we present show Tlaloc directly associated with rulership, and that same connection is apparent in the images. The first hint of such a relationship is Olmec, as can be seen in the two images we present in connection with the mythic structure of rulership (Images 44 and 45). These images depict rulers seated within cave mouths bearing the features of the Olmec were-jaguar, visual metaphors for the sanctioning of rule by the rain god. Among the Maya, the ruler is often depicted costumed and masked in impersonation of Chac (Image 48), another metaphoric way of making the same mythic point. Among the Zapotecs a substantial number of the rulers whose names we know included the name of the rain god Cocijo in their own names, and at Teotihuacan the structure most closely associated with the rulers of that fabled city, the Temple of Quetzalcoatl (Image 18), alternates heads related to the rain god with heads of the feathered serpent on its magnificent frieze. That this beginning at Teotihuacan was continued in the Basin of Mexico is shown not only by the myths we present but also by the monumentally important fact that Tlaloc's temple shared the summit of the pyramid known as the Templo Mayor with Huitzilopochtli's, the temple of the tutelary god of the Aztec state.

And this, of course, brings us full circle back to Tlaloc and his connection with caves and mountaintops in the provision of the regularly timed rainfall upon which life on the surface of the earth depends. But the significance of timing in the provision of the needed water also suggests another connection fundamental to the god of rain. Returning to our preceding presentation of the myths of creation, we have seen that time and space were consistently depicted in images of the gods (Images 9–15). One of those images, found in the *Codex Borgia,* shows Tlaloc as the quadripartite reality of time and space and as the center uniting the four quadrants (Image 16). In keeping with that graphic relationship between Tlaloc and time, it is not surprising that we find numerous instances in which the god of rain is depicted wearing a headdress composed of the interlocking "trapeze and ray" symbol of the year or otherwise associated with that symbol (Images 34 and 37). Among the Maya precisely the same mythic relationship between the rain god, Chac, and the four quadrants into which the reality of space and time is divided can be seen in the image from the *Dresden Codex*

(Image 40), in which the first four Chacs are seated in the trees of the four directions of time and space, while the fifth is in the cave of the center, the point of penetration to the world of the spirit. The Zapotecs connected Cocijo with time in another way: the four basic divisions of the sacred calendar of 260 days were each called *cocijo*. This division seems to have no obvious basis in Cocijo's function as a rain god, and for that very reason it reveals clearly the power attributed to him: just as he was the operative force in providing the rain, he was also the force that moved the calendar, i.e., time, through its endless cycles, a fundamental relationship to time clearly shared by Tlaloc and Chac.

Cocijo also illustrates another mythic connection between the rain god and time. The Zapotecs divided the 365-day solar year in several ways, the most common being a contrast between a dry season, *cocijobaa,* and a rainy season, *cocijoquije*. In this case the reason for the designation *cocijo* seems clear since the distinction between the seasons relates to rain. Significantly, this is the same mythic division described in the "Song of Xipe Totec Iouallauan," which speaks of the fire serpent (Xiuhcoatl) becoming a quetzal serpent (Quetzalcoatl). Of the two, one would normally connect the rain god with the quetzal serpent, symbol here of the green, rainy season. But in the art of the Basin of Mexico from the time of Teotihuacan up to the point of the Conquest, numerous images of Tlaloc are found in which the god holds a fire or lightning serpent, Xiuhcoatl (Color Plate 7 and Image 36). The metaphor seems clear, and it is the metaphor underlying the Tlalocan mural (Color Plate 19): the combination of fire and water—whether it be lightning and rain or the dry season and rainy season—is necessary for fertility. And the existence of that fertility and its resulting human sustenance require the god of rain and storm.

One last image is significant in this respect, and that image ties together a number of the mythic strands that make up our consideration of fertility. Among the Aztecs, a number of strange images relating to Tlaloc have been found (Image 43). They are peculiar in a number of ways, not the least of which is the fact that they are generally carved on the base of major monuments. On the underside of the base of the monolithic Coatlicue, for example, a carved block of basalt roughly ten feet high and four feet wide, such an image exists. Clearly, the Aztec sculptor could not have created that relief carving to be seen by the populace. For whom was it designed? The gods? The earth itself? In addition, the image itself is a strange one. The body is that of the generally female Earth Monster, Tlaltecuhtli, as a comparison of this image with that of Tlaltecuhtli (Image 25) will readily show. But the head of this image is just as unmistakably that of the male Tlaloc, and he is gazing not upward but straight ahead at the viewer, whoever that viewer was imagined to be. While we certainly cannot explain the reasons the Aztec sculptors might have had for the creation of such images as these, we can appreciate their blending, in typical Mesoamerican mythic fashion, the images of two of the most important forces in the process that we call fertility.

THE FLAYED GOD

Song of Xipe Totec Iouallauan, from the *Florentine Codex*

"Xipe Totec Iouallauan" is one of the ancient hymns preserved in Sahagún's *Codex Matritensis* and in his *Florentine Codex*. Although
these hymns were not recorded until sometime about 1550, their archaic language suggests they are among the most ancient texts in
Nahuatl. As one can see from the detailed analysis of this hymn to the
god Xipe Totec and the ritual with which it was involved in our discussion of fertility, the text is extremely confusing and difficult to explicate completely. Of its background, we can surmise that "it was sung at
the Yopico temple, which stood where the western tower of the Cathe-
dral of Mexico now stands. It was sung at the Tlacaxipehualiztli festival
before sowing-time"[58] to beseech of the god a rich harvest.

Additionally, however, it is important to note that Xipe Totec,
also known as Yopi, clearly a complex and multivocal symbolic entity,
was essentially the metaphoric embodiment of the cyclical pattern of
all life, a pattern promising the rebirth of man and man's sustenance,
the corn, but requiring sacrificial death for the accomplishment of that
rebirth. It is no wonder then that Barlow suggests that the power of the
piece comes "not from its structure but its function."[59] As our analysis
above indicates, however, its structure is certainly noteworthy. But the
real power of this hymn to the flayed god comes from neither its function nor its structure; lying behind these words is the ancient power of
centuries of belief in the cyclical nature of reality and its promise not
only of the coming harvest but also of the certainty of rebirth.

SONG OF XIPE TOTEC IOUALLAUAN

Translated from the Nahuatl by Arthur J. O. Anderson and Charles E. Dibble. Originally published in Bernardino de Sahagún, *General History of the Things of New Spain, Book 2: The Ceremonies.* Translated by Arthur J. O. Anderson and Charles E. Dibble (Santa Fe, NM: School of American Research, and Salt Lake City: Univ. of Utah Press, 1959), 213. Reprinted by permission of the publisher.

O Iouallauan, why dost thou mask thyself?
Put on thy disguise.
Don thy golden cape.

My god, thy precious water hath come down from Coapan.
It hath made the cypress a quetzal.
The fire serpent hath been made a quetzal serpent.
Want hath gone from me.

Mayhap I shall die and perish—I, the tender maize.
Like a precious green stone is my heart,
yet I shall see gold in it.
I shall be content if first I mature.
The war chief is born.

My god, give me in part plenteous tender maize.
Thy worshipper looketh toward thy mountain.
I shall be content if first I ripen.
The warrior chief is born.

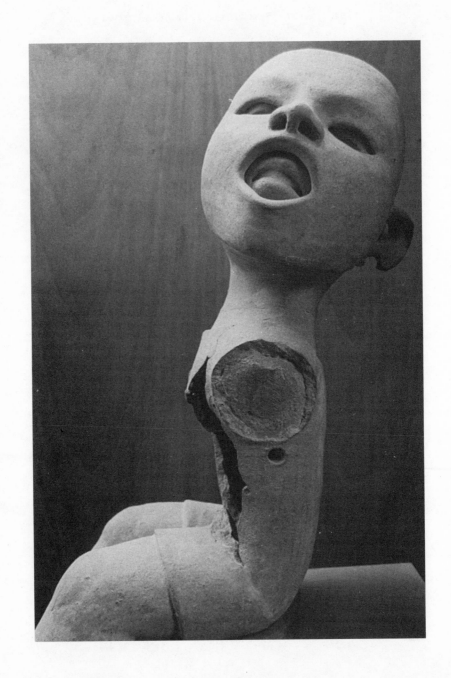

THE FLAYED GOD

Xipe Totec: The Flayed God:
A Ceramic Image from Veracruz

The Aztec god Xipe Totec, "Our Lord the Flayed One," although clearly a complex and multivocal symbolic entity, is, as we have seen, most fundamentally an embodiment of the concept of renewal and the promise of regeneration. He is depicted in this ceramic sculpture from Palma Cuata, Veracruz, a sculpture probably created in the Postclassic, with his face covered by a mask made from the taut skin of a sacrificial victim, a mask through which we can see the wearer's own living eyes and mouth, and he also wears the skin of the flayed one as a garment over a large part of his body. This is the typical "costume" of this god to whom the ritual and the hymn were dedicated at the time of the planting of the corn, and the costume refers directly to the ritual.

In that ritual a priest donned the skin of a victim, representing in this sense the dead covering of the earth in the dry season of winter before the new vegetation bursts forth in spring. Xipe Totec, then, was the divine embodiment of life emerging from the dead land, of the new plant sprouting from the "dead" seed. Death is not an end, but always a beginning; the dead seed *is* the promise of the corn. Although certainly a typical depiction of this god, this Postclassic portrayal is particularly striking because of its impressive simplicity and the intensity that results from its striking combination of boldness and delicate beauty.

THE FLAYED GOD

The Ritual Act of Sacrifice:
Two Scenes from the Ritual Ball Game

There seems to be no doubt that some kind of ball game was played in Mesoamerica since the second millennium B.C. We do not know exactly how it was played but images in the mythic art of Mesoamerica, such as these panels from ballcourts, and various objects, such as representations of the protective yokes ballplayers wore on their hips in order to hit the very hard rubber ball, provide clues to the nature of the game.[60] Evidently it was very difficult to play because the ring through which the ball had to pass was not much larger than the heavy ball itself, because that ring was attached high up on the side of the ballcourt wall, and because the players could not touch the ball with their hands but used their hips and shoulders to hit it. More important from a mythological point of view, we know that the game was often, perhaps always, played as a ritual enterprise and that it often, perhaps always, ended with the sacrifice of a player, presumably a loser, as these panels depict. The Maya version of the ball game is an important element of the *Popol Vuh*. The hero twins, like their father and uncle before them, are summoned to Xibalba because of their playing the game, and one of their most important trials in the underworld is to play the ball game against the lords of Xibalba.[61] This suggests that the mortal players of the game, when sacrificed, were themselves beginning the hero journey first undertaken in the *Popol Vuh*.

IMAGE 20: Ballcourt Scene from El Tajin

This scene from a ballcourt at the site of El Tajin in northern Veracruz depicts the moment of that sacrifice. The sacrificial victim is seated in the lower center, his arms held by the figure at his left, and the figure in front of him at the right is raising the sacrificial knife in his right hand. Intriguingly, a large human skeleton appears to be seated on or emerging from a round vase in the separate panel to the left, a motif that is repeated in the skeletal figure who is hanging upside-down over the victim's head. Kampen observes that the panel has a "highly complex formal structure in which all the elements . . . point to the center of the panel, the head of the sacrificial victim,"[62] and one might also observe that the denizens of the underworld—the skeletal figures in this scene comparable to the lords of Xibalba in the *Popol Vuh*—seem anxiously to be awaiting the removal of that head.

IMAGE 21: Ballcourt Scene from Chichen Itza

In this macabre scene from the Great Ballcourt at Chichen Itza in the Yucatan we see what would seem to be the next stage in the ritual process. Here the kneeling sacrificial victim on the right has been decapitated and is now surrounded by blood scrolls, while six snakes and an elaborate tree arise from his severed neck, suggesting, perhaps, the fertility resulting from that sacrifice. Standing in front of him, his decapitator holds the victim's head in his left hand and the sacrificial knife in his right. Here the presence of death in the form of a skull can be seen in the image of the ball that lies between them, recalling the episode in the *Popol Vuh* in which the lords of Xibalba introduce a skull to be used as a ball, perhaps suggesting metaphorically that the ball itself is the catalyst of death.

Life Born from Death: Izapa Stela 50

The very early Stela 50 found at the pre-Maya site of Izapa in Chiapas has an extremely strong impact, but in a very different way from Izapa Stela 5 (Image 7), which we discussed above. Here, instead of a crowded field of figures, we encounter four very clear, very bold images. They include a base panel, a seated skeletal human figure with the right leg slightly raised, a smaller sky-borne human or deity figure whose legs appear to be in motion, and a very prominent cord connecting the two figures. But these are not separate images; the sculptor is able to establish a strong sense of the unity of these varied forms. As we have seen, "reading" the narratives inscribed imagistically on the Izapa stelae is generally extremely difficult because of their unusual complexity and because they seem not to fit the narrative sequence of any mythology we know. Stela 50, however, provides the exception to that rule; in addition to any culturally specific meaning it might have had for the people by and for whom it was carved, it seems clearly to have a universal message that transcends its more specific implications.

The prominent umbilical cord connecting the skeleton to the creature on the upper left seems obviously to express the belief we have seen over and over in our presentation of the images and texts of the Mesoamerican mythological tradition: life comes from death. This belief that man and all other living things are "born" from the bones of the dead is fundamental to the Mesoamerican view of life as a cyclical process. The cyclical symbolism of rebirth inherent in the umbilical cord stresses that renewal of life in what would otherwise be a deathly scene. Here death is depicted in the very process of giving birth to life, which is in turn nourished by death.

THE GREAT GODDESS

The Myths of Tlaltecuhtli and Mayahuel, from the *Histoyre du Mechique*

The myths of Tlaltecuhtli, the Earth Monster, and of the fertility goddess Mayahuel are told in the *Histoyre du Mechique,* a sixteenth-century manuscript that the French cosmographer André Thévet translated from a Spanish document now lost. First published in 1905, the work is a diverse compilation of materials that includes mythological material relating to creation and the four suns, to some of the major gods such as Tezcatlipoca and Quetzalcoatl, to the calendar, as well as various episodes in the history of the Mexica. Actually, as Thévet says in his introduction, the title of the work fails to describe its contents accurately; it is less a historical text and more a mythological one. After the French translation was published in 1905, two Spanish translations were done (1961, 1965), but as yet the entire work has not been published in English.

As we know from other myths and images, the Aztecs conceived of the earth as crocodilian or toadlike. This myth of the earth goddess Tlaltecuhtli, goddess of fertility, of birth and nurture, tells the story of an immortal being sacrificed to produce the temporal world, and it is told with the clear implication that living in this world demands reciprocal sacrifice. Joseph Campbell points out that "throughout the ranges, not only of the early planting cultures, but also of all those archaic high civilizations whose mythologies were inspired by the idea of the earth and its biosphere as a self-sustained living entity, two complementary themes are outstanding. One is of death as the generator of life; the other, of self-offering as the way to self-validation. In the symbolism of the sacrifice both are comprehended."[63] This myth is illustrative of that fundamental conception, as is the other myth from the *Histoyre* included here. In that case it is a goddess, Mayahuel, who is sacrificed and from whom the divine pulque comes.

THE MYTH OF TLALTECUHTLI

This myth and the myth of Mayahuel that follows are original translations from the French by F. M. Swensen, prepared for this volume. The editors have regularized the spelling of Mayahuel, Tezcatlipoca, and Tlaltecuhtli in both myths.

Some say that the earth was created in this fashion: Two gods, Quetzalcoatl and Tezcatlipoca carried down from the heavens the goddess of the earth Tlaltecuhtli, who was filled up at all joints by eyes and mouths with which she bit like a wild beast. Before they came down, there was already water, which they do not know who created and upon which this goddess made her way down. Which upon seeing, the gods said to one another: "There is need to make the earth"; and saying this they changed themselves into two large snakes, of which one seized the goddess from the right hand to the left foot, the other from the left hand to the right foot, and they pulled so much that they broke her in half, and from the half towards the shoulders they made the earth and carried off the other half to heaven, and by this the other gods were greatly angered.

After this deed, in order to recompense the goddess of the earth for the damage that the two gods had done to her, all the gods came down to console her, and ordered that from her would come all the fruit necessary for the life of men; and in order to do this, they made from her hair trees and flowers and grasses, from her skin the very fine grass and small flowers, from her eyes wells and fountains and small caverns, from her mouth rivers and great caverns, from her nose mountain valleys, and from her shoulders mountains. And this goddess sometimes wept at night, desiring to eat men's hearts, and would not be quiet until they were offered to her, nor would she bear fruit unless she was watered with the blood of men.

THE MYTH OF MAYAHUEL

The gods said amongst themselves: Now man will be quite sad if we do not do something to gladden him so that he will enjoy living on earth and praise us and sing and dance. This was heard by the god Ehecatl, god of the air, who pondered in his heart where he could find some liquor to give to man to cause him to rejoice. While pondering upon this, he remembered a virgin goddess called Mayahuel, who was guarded by her grandmother, a goddess called Cicimitl, and he went off immediately to them and found them asleep. He awakened the virgin and said to her: "I have come to get you to take you to the world." To which she immediately agreed and so the two of them went down, he bearing her upon his shoulders; and as soon as they arrived on earth, they transformed themselves into a tree with two branches, of which one was called Quetzalhuexotl, which was the one of Ehecatl, and the other Xochicuahuitl, which was the one of the virgin.

Now, when her grandmother, who was sleeping, awoke and did not find her niece, she immediately summoned the other goddesses, who are called Cicime, and they all came down to earth to search for Ehecatl. At this point, the two tree branches separated from each other and the one of the virgin was immediately recognized by the old goddess who took it and broke it and offered a piece of it to each of the other goddesses who ate it; but the branch of Ehecatl they did not break, but left it there; which, as soon as the goddesses had gone back up to heaven, turned back into its first form of Ehecatl, who gathered up the bones of the virgin whom the goddesses had eaten and buried them, and from there a tree arose, which they call *metl,* from which the Indians make the wine that they drink and in which they rejoice; but this is not because of the wine, but for some roots that they call *ucpatli* which they put into it.

Teteo Innan, Her Song, from the *Florentine Codex*

This is another in the series of the sacred hymns recorded by Sahagún in both the *Codex Matritensis* and the *Florentine Codex,* a series that includes the "Song of Xipe Totec Iouallaun" presented above. Willard Gingerich, translator of this poem and a distinguished interpreter of Nahuatl poetry, indicates that "by Aztec times Teteo Innan represented a mother and earth numen of considerable antiquity and authority in the Valley of Mexico. Toci, 'Our Grandmother' is the name of her specifically Mexica hierophany," who by the time of the Aztecs can be seen as reflecting their "sacrificial concerns and imperial preoccupations."[64] The ritual context of the hymn, however, described in detail by Sahagún[65] and discussed briefly below in connection with Toci, certainly demonstrates the hymn's concern with earthly fertility as well as those "imperial preoccupations." It is for that reason that Teteo Innan was addressed as "Our Mother, Lord of the Earth."

Gingerich contends that "the identification of Tamoanchan [an earthly paradise] as the goddess's place of origin . . . affirms that god and man have a common place of origin, since it was to Tamoanchan that Quetzalcoatl brought the 'precious bones' from which the first men were made by Quetzalcoatl and the goddess Quilaztli ['she who makes things grow,' an aspect of Coatlicue]."[66] The line "you emerge from Tamoanchan" suggests, then, that "the goddess appeared first among men from that chthonic womb" and that Teteo Innan links humanity back to the "venerable legitimate mother numen," Quilaztli. Thus "Teteo Innan, Her Song," is concerned with fertility on the deepest of levels.

This fundamental concern is suggested by the first stanzas in at least two ways. First, the mask referred to "is the mask of human thigh-skin donned in the ritual by Teteo Innan's 'son' Cinteotl, a god of corn who seems to have represented the ripe ear." Second, the hymn's opening is marked "by the flower symbolism so pervasive in Nahuatl lyrical poetry. The yellow and white flowers which 'had opened the blossom' evoke the creative, fecundive powers of the mother earth-spirit throughout the world. . . . They are first the literal flowers of spring which festoon the earth to announce the rebirth of life. They are also the 'flowers of our flesh,' and sacred, therefore to Chicomecoatl, 'Seven Serpent,' goddess of the vegetables on which our flesh depends—maize most specifically."

The hymn's second section refers to a complex mythic tale, one neither wholly preserved nor fully understood, in which the goddess Itzpapalotl, "Obsidian Butterfly," as an aspect of Teteo Innan, is involved with the initiation of sacrifice among the desert peoples who were to become the Aztecs. "With new chalk and new plumage she is anointed as in our first sacrifice of her on the desert. . . . She herself becomes the deer, the two-headed or paired were-deer who seduced Xiuhnel and consumed him, and who pursued Mimich through the fire until she fell into the barrel cactus and became our sacrifice." This myth of Xiuhnel and Mimich to which the last line of the hymn refers is presented in the myths of creation above as section VII of the *Leyenda de los Soles*. It involves the transformation of Itzpapalotl into a two-headed were-deer who seduces and consumes Xiuhnel, a cloud serpent, and then, in the process of chasing the other cloud serpent, Mimich, is caught in the barrel cactus and sacrificed.

Interestingly, "the rituals of Toci blending fertility, growth, harvest, parturition, and patriotic warfare all grow (mytho)logically from the elements found initially together in the little charter narrative of Xiuhnel, Mimich and the goddess Itzpapalotl." And that narrative strikes the deepest of the chords relating to fertility in Mesoamerica: the necessity of sacrifice in reciprocation for the bounty of the earth.

TETEO INNAN, HER SONG

Translated from the Nahuatl by Willard Gingerich. Originally published in "Three Nahuatl Hymns on the Mother Archetype: An Interpretive Commentary" by Willard Gingerich in *Mexican Studies/Estudios Mexicanos* 4 (1988): 191–244. Reprinted by permission of the translator.

Ahuiya! Yellow flowers open the blossom;
She, Our Mother with the sacred thigh-mask:
You emerge from Tamoanchan.

Ahuiya! Yellow flower is your flower:
She, Our Mother with the sacred thigh-mask
You emerge from Tamoanchan.
Ahuiya! White flowers open the blossom;
She, Our Mother with the sacred thigh-mask;
You emerge from Tamoanchan.

Ahuiya! White flower is your flower;
She, Our Mother with the sacred thigh-mask;
You emerge from Tamoanchan.
Ahuiya! Goddess upon the barrel cactus,
Our Mother, Aya, Itzpapalotl.
Ao, We had seen her;
on the Nine Plains
With hearts of deer she will nurture herself.
Our Mother, Aya, Lord of the Earth.
Ao, ye, With new chalk, new plumes,
She is anointed;
in the four directions arrows are broken.

Ao, To the deer transformed.
across the Divine Land to behold You
come Xiuhnel and Mimich.

Cihuacoatl, Her Song, from the *Florentine Codex*

This is yet another in the series of the sacred hymns recorded by Sahagún in both the *Codex Matritensis* and the *Florentine Codex,* a series that includes the "Song of Xipe Totec Iouallauan" and "Teteo Innan, Her Song," both of which are presented above.

Generally considered an aspect of Tlazolteotl, "Mother of the Gods," Cihuacoatl's name means "snake woman," and it is generally agreed that she was one of the most important Aztec gods at the time of the Conquest. The stone images depicting her or manifestations of her outnumber those of any other Aztec god. In another sense Cihuacoatl was probably an aspect of Teteo Innan, although as is the case with most Mesoamerican deities, she had her own individual identity as well. That identity was particularly important because it provided the Aztecs "the direct antecedent for their own image of Huitzilopochtli's mother, Coatlicue, culminating avatar of the devouring woman."[67]

The hymn contains a great deal of imagery related to fertility, some of it directly tied to rituals devoted to agricultural fertility. The "sweeping of the roads" is an obvious reference to the festival of Ochpaniztli, which in fact means "sweeping of the roads," a festival dedicated to Toci, "Our Grandmother," and to the promotion of fertility. The hymn itself was sung as a part of the festival devoted to Cihuacoatl, a festival culminating in a fire sacrifice that was essentially a firstfruits ceremony celebrating the arrival of the first flowers after the renewal of the rainy season.

But it is important to note that "the imagery of agricultural process is invoked in this Hymn in terms of human sexuality" in such images as the "timbrelled staff" and "the cactus shaft, his glory," which will "fill" the goddess. Gingerich suggests that this "filling of the goddess" was probably understood as a reference to her insatiable appetite for sacrificial victims,[68] and once again we have a suggested relationship between fertility—on all its levels—and sacrifice.

Essentially, the hymn describes "the supposedly intimate relation between earthly fertility and human acts of war and sacrifice: the earth-fertility numen, Quilaztli, towering protectress of the Chalmeca who maintains the precious maize erect in its mythic holy field is one and the same as the sacrificial eagle, the consuming and warring sun, the were-deer of Colhuacan, consumed and consuming—in short, Our Mother Yaocihuatl, 'Enemy Woman.'" And all of these—Quilaztli, Yaocihuatl, and Cihuacoatl—are aspects of the Great Goddess, simultaneously the guarantor of fertility and receiver of human sacrifice. She surely is, as Gingerich calls her, the "Terrible Mother."[69]

CIHUACOATL, HER SONG

Translated from the Nahuatl by Willard Gingerich. Originally published in "Three Nahuatl Hymns on the Mother Archetype: An Interpretive Commentary" by Willard Gingerich in *Mexican Studies/Estudios Mexicanos* 4 (1988): 191–244. Reprinted by permission of the translator.

The Eagle, the Eagle, Quilaztli,
of snake-blood circled face,
emplumed,
in eagle plumes, she comes.

She comes sweeping the roads,
Protectress of Chalma and spreading tree
over the Colhua, Huiya!
In the place of Sun's acxoyatl tree,
in the Divine Fields the maize ear
is supported on the timbrelled staff.

Thorns, thorns fill my hands;
Thorns fill my hands.
In the Divine Field the maize ear
is supported on the timbrelled staff.

The grass broom fills my hands;
In the Divine Field the maize-ear
is supported by the timbrelled staff.

13-Eagle, Our Mother, Aya,
Ruler of the Chalmeca.

"His cactus shaft, his glory;
Let him fill me, He
my Prince, Mixcoatl, Aya."

Our Mother, Enemy Woman, Aya;
Our Mother, Enemy Woman, Aya;

The Deer of Colhuacan
in her costume of feathers, Aya.
Ahuiya!
Already had Sun declared his war:
"Aya! Let men be dragged forth,
All shall be destroyed!"

The Deer of Colhuacan
in her costume of feathers.
Ahuiya!
She of the eagle plumes, unmasked;
Ahuiya!
The rising one, unmasked.

Coatlicue

Coatlicue was one of the most important aspects of the Great Goddess, the mother of the gods, goddess of the earth, of the sun, the moon, and the stars. Having given miraculous birth to Huitzilopochtli, who sprang from her womb fully grown and armed, Coatlicue represents the birth giver from whom all life comes and to whom all life must return in the eternal cycle of death and rebirth. We see her depicted here in a colossal sculpture of the fifteenth century (in both a photograph and a drawing of that sculpture) as a goddess embodying simultaneously the seemingly contradictory ideas of birth and death. In place of her own head two serpents' heads confront each other in striking position suggesting both the idea of sacrifice by decapitation in the ritual dedicated to her (see Image 21) and her relationship to the moon, Coyolxauhqui (see Image 24), whose head, having been cut off by Huitzilopochtli, the sun in this case, was born again. This idea of death and resurrection can be seen also in the symbolic skull that hangs from her necklace strung with hearts and hands. Beside the necklace her raised, clawed hands suggest her nature: "She granted everything with her generous hands and took it all back with her implacable claws."[70]

True to her name, "She of the Serpent Skirt," she wears a skirt of interwoven serpents, and she has fanged faces at her elbows, suggesting her connection with Tlaltecuhtli. Beneath her clawed feet, on the underside of the base of the monument, is another evocation of Tlaltecuhtli, this time with the face of Tlaloc (Image 43). On the rear of the sculpture, at the center of her back, there is another skull similar to the one she wears on the front. The human female skin that she wears, also a symbol of regeneration, is reminiscent of the one worn by Xipe Totec and clearly identifies her as a fertility goddess.

Her pyramidal form "created principally by a large appendage which hangs down the back, from the waist almost to the ground, composed of thirteen leather braids on two distinct levels,"[71] anchors her to the earth, suggesting a rising from the depths of the earth and the land of the dead to Omeyocan, the highest of the heavens.[72] Townsend notes that the image "can be called anthropomorphic only in a general structural sense, as it is primarily an assemblage of ritual attire from various related sources."[73]

But it is much more than that. Scholars long familiar with the massive stone sculpture as well as first-time visitors to the Museo Nacional de Antropología in Mexico City are awed by the experience of confronting this massive, masterly work, for as Justino Fernández says, its "originality of form has no rival or parallel in the works of the ancient indigenous world [of Mesoamerica], with its variety of cultures, or outside Mexico in the classical cultures of the Orient or the West. It is a gem of world art."[74] But there is no doubt that the greatness of this piece goes beyond its formal aspects. Considering its symbolic implications, Caso finds that "the whole figure is an admirable synthesis of love and destruction which corresponds to the earth."[75]

Many have marveled at the simultaneously exalted and terrifying conception of the universe it conveys and have felt as well the mystery of the cosmic vision it expresses, but Fernández's insightful analysis and his passion for the sculpture are worth special note. Pointing out that this magnificent figure of a goddess contains within its features the whole of Mesoamerican cosmology,

Fernández says it "becomes much more than just the Goddess of Earth or the Goddess of the Serpent Skirt. In effect it symbolizes the earth, but also the sun, moon, spring, rain, light, life, death, the necessity of human sacrifice, humanity, the gods, the heavens, and the supreme creator: the dual principle. Further, it represents the stars, Venus; Coatlicue, then, is a complete view of the cosmos carved in stone. . . . To me this is the most genuine and profound of all the beauties created or imagined by man because it makes one conscious of the mystery of life and of death."[76] Armillas comments on the universality of the work, seeing it "as manifesting in its imagery the vital inner force to be found in all human beings or animals, as well as in those abstract works which possess mysterious strength."[77] Ultimately, Coatlicue's majestic calm emerges powerfully as a brilliant expression of the complexity and mystery of all existence.

THE FLAYED GOD

Coyolxauhqui

This incredible image was carved in 1469 but discovered only by chance in 1978, when it was encountered by a worker when his shovel struck a carved stone. That is not an unusual occurrence in Mexico City since the modern city is superimposed on the Aztec capitol of Tenochtitlan, but this particular discovery had far-reaching consequences, leading, as it did, to the most important archaeological project ever undertaken by the Mexican government in Mexico City. Proyecto Templo Mayor unearthed a number of major works of mythic art, a number of rich caches of offerings, and, most important, the superimposed series of main temples of the Aztec nation, one of them still intact.

What that worker had discovered was one of the largest (eleven feet at its widest point) and most striking Aztec monuments ever found, a gigantic oval relief sculpture of Huitzilopochtli's dismembered sorceress sister, the goddess Coyolxauhqui. In the myth of Huitzilopochtli's birth from Coatlicue on the hill of Coatepec, when Coyolxauhqui learned of her mother's pregnancy, she incited her four hundred siblings and led them into battle against their mother. Huitzilopochtli was born at that moment, fully grown and armed, and in defense of his mother he killed his sister and cut off her head. As her body rolled down the slope, it fell to pieces. It is precisely that decapitated and dismembered Coyolxauhqui that we see depicted on this massive sculpture. Symbolically, the killing of Coyolxauhqui memorialized here paradoxically guarantees the rebirth of Huitzilopochtli and the continuation of the cosmic cycle of life, manifesting once again the cyclical alternation from life to death and the return to life that lies at the basis of Mesoamerican fertility.

The original placement of the relief in the ground at the base of the staircase leading up the steep pyramid to the temple of Huitzilopochtli, a staircase lined with undulating serpents, suggesting its symbolization of Coatepec, serpent mountain, reinforces this interpretation, for it was down those very stairs that the bodies of innumerable sacrificial victims were tumbled after their chests had been opened on the sacrificial stone in Huitzilopochtli's temple and their still-beating hearts torn out and offered to the gods so that the eternal cycle of life might continue. Her image at the foot of the pyramid, representing her death at the hands of her brother, whose temple crowned the pyramid, thus was seen to provide a charter for human sacrifice, to explain, in mythic terms, the terrible necessity of the offering of blood and life.

This aspect of the myth is emphasized in this awesome sculpture as it shows each dismembered limb, like the decapitated head, in deep relief as part of a strikingly complex design. Adding to its fascination is the fact that while the head and legs of this goddess figure are shown in profile, the torso is seen from the front, displaying dramatically Coyolxauhqui's large pendulous breasts in the visual center of the massive stone. Even in death, the nurturing quality of the Great Goddess is thus emphasized. Her head, depicted with one eye open, is turned upward, with her left hand reaching up toward her face while the other hand falls limp in death beside the body from which it has been dismembered. At her waist she wears a double snake belt that has a skull seemingly tied to it, and these are but two of the eleven snakes intertwining over and around the broken body and providing tremendous energy to the entire conception. There is, paradoxically, "something vigorous and abundant in the totality" of the effect of the relief.[78] Again, death and life, stillness and vigor are seen as cyclical realities.

Tlaltecuhtli, the Earth Monster

Tlaltecuhtli is the generally female Aztec Earth Monster from whom all life comes. A variant of Coatlicue, she too was inevitably accompanied by symbols of death because she had the function of "receiving and housing the dead in exchange for the regeneration of life throughout time."[79] We see her depicted in this relief originally discovered in the area of the Templo Mayor in Mexico City. Similar images of Tlaltecuhtli were often carved on the undersides of the bases of Aztec monuments, so that the image of the Earth Monster faced directly the surface of the earthly plane it symbolized, and this relief is a good example of its type since it, too, was originally carved on the underside of a large monument but was removed in colonial times when Aztec monuments served the Spanish as a quarry.

The earth goddess is portrayed here in a squatting position with her knees bent, the position assumed by native women in childbirth, thereby distinguishing her from the male earth deity Cipactli, a spiny monster with an extended snout resembling a crocodile. Here she is depicted with her "head flung back, facing upward, and [her] bent arms similarly upraised. The hair is characteristically twisted and tangled, intertwined with malinalli grass. 'Demon faces' appear on the elbows, knees, and claws, the upper claws clutching skulls. . . . Instead of the stylized monster head, this example shows the face of the earth goddess. . . . Small concentric circles appear on her cheeks, a common feature of earth goddesses. A sacrificial stone knife-tongue [see Color Plate 11] protrudes from her fleshless mouth with rows of teeth exposed."[80] The stone knife, a symbol of sacrificial death and in this form itself a deity, is also a symbol of the bloody, primeval Great Mother, who is herself dismembered in her aspect of Coyolxauhqui and thus becomes the source of all life, thereby providing yet another demonstration of the fact that she embodied the concept of fertility always associated with the earth goddesses.

In our discussion of the myth of this earth goddess we explained how the earth came to be conceived of as a crocodilian or toadlike monster surrounded by the primeval sea. The open jaws of the monster were envisioned as the entrance to the underworld, and heavenly bodies were thought of as passing through the Earth Monster in their daily cycles. Since the underworld is enclosed in the earth, the earth goddess is related to death as well as to life, and often death symbols appear on the images of Tlaltecuhtli. In this case a skull-and-crossed-bones motif can be seen on the skirt, which protrudes from behind the goddess, and a large skull, viewed in profile, hangs from the back of her belt. While all of these symbols represent death, her position suggests birth. But because death was a prerequisite for rebirth, it is not surprising to find the concepts of life and death intertwined in the image of the monster who images forth the female earth. The Great Goddess, in her identity as Coatlicue (Image 23) and in her identity here as Tlaltecuhtli, generates life and all living things but also takes them back into herself.

Ehecatl

This unusual image of Quetzalcoatl in his manifestation as the god of wind, Ehecatl, was found in Mexico City in 1900 along with another piece almost identical to it. Nicholson suggests that "the posture of the pair [slightly bent over with arms raised high alongside their heads, while the tops of their heads and hands form a flat, horizontal upper surface] indicates that they served as a type of figure called atlantean, that appears in Mesoamerica as early as the Olmec era . . . but is particularly diagnostic of the Early Postclassic or Toltec period (ca. 900–1200 A.D.). . . . While the Toltec figures stand upright with their arms held rigidly overhead, the stooped posture, slightly bent knees, and flexed arms of the Aztec statues convey an impression of the weight of the load being borne. These two sculptures are the only Aztec atlanteans known."[81]

Although the relationship between Ehecatl and Quetzalcoatl, the feathered serpent, is not entirely clear, there is no question that the former is the particular aspect of the latter that represents the wind and, by extension, both fertility and the human breath, symbol of human life. Conceived in quadruple form and associated with the winds of the four cardinal directions, he was the most important aspect of Quetzalcoatl. Typically, as we see him here and as he is shown in the codices (see Figures 9 and 10), he wears a unique mask that covers the mouth, with the rest of the face exposed above it. It was through this bird mask that Ehecatl blew the wind with which he swept the roads for the coming of the rain and caused the storms to blow, working thus in tandem with Tlaloc. The headdress he wears is similar to Quetzalcoatl's typical "zigzag band, to the front of which is attached a quadruple bow device knotted in the center."[82]

The God and Goddess of Water, from the
Historia de los Mexicanos por sus Pinturas

This explanation of the origin and nature of the rain god, here called Tlaltecutli rather than Tlaloc, has been excerpted from the portion of the *Historia* presented above in the "Myths of Creation." The shift in the rain god's name is particularly interesting in the light of the identification of Tlaloc with Tlaltecuhtli in such sculpted reliefs as that presented as Image 43 below.

THE GOD AND GODDESS OF WATER

This is an original translation from the Spanish by Scott Mahler, prepared for this volume. In rendering the colonial account into modern English, the translator has omitted certain passages that attempt to explain, but do not contain the creation myth and phrases such as "or so the Indians say," as well as the titles given each section.

In order to create the god and goddess of water, all four gods got together and made Tlaltecutli and his wife Chalchiuhtlicue, whom the people asked for water when they needed it.

The water god's dwelling has four rooms and a large courtyard in the middle, where there are four large earthenware bowls of water. The water in one of these is good, and makes the seeds and grains grow. The water in another is bad and blights the fields. The third bowl rains ice. And when it rains from the fourth, nothing produces seed and nothing dries out.

The water god created many servants to make it rain, and they lived in the rooms of the water god's dwelling. In one hand they carry little collection boxes in which they catch the water from the earthenware bowls, and in the other hand they have various rods. When the rain god commands them to go and water somewhere, they take their rods and go make rain. When they strike the boxes with their sticks, it thunders, and lightning flashes.

Eighty years passed before a man from Chalco wanted to sacrifice his hunchback to the water god's servants. They carried him to a volcano on a mountain always covered with snow and put him in a cave and blocked the entrance. Having eaten nothing, he became drowsy and was carried to the water god's palace to see how he lived. Later some servants of the man from Chalco came to see if the hunchback was dead, but they found him alive and carried him away, and he told them what he had seen. In this very year the people of Chalco were defeated and enslaved by the Mexicans, and it was said that their defeat resulted from this incident.

A Prayer to Tlaloc, from the *Florentine Codex*

Just as she says that she can do no better than to quote Sahagún (though she does do considerably better), we cannot do better for the introduction to this beautiful and moving hymn than to present Thelma Sullivan's introduction to her translation of "A Prayer to Tlaloc":

> The prayer to Tlaloc, god of rain, that follows . . . occurs in the Florentine Codex, *Historia General de las Cosas de Nueva España,* by fray Bernardino de Sahagún. . . . By way of introduction I can do no better than the heading for the text written in Nahuatl by Sahagún: "The prayer they delivered with great feeling when they invoked Tlaloc to whom they attributed the rain. They said he ruled over Tlalocan, which they regarded as a sort of Garden of Eden, where other gods, called Tlaloque, also dwelled, and a goddess, their sister, called Chicomecoatl, who is similar to Ceres. The fire priests made their supplication when there was drought and they asked for rain. It is a remarkable prayer, and in it are revealed many of the false notions that existed in the past."
>
> A moving and eloquent plea for the survival of man and beast, and the vegetation upon which both depend, this prayer sharply etches the physical anguish that man, animal, and the earth suffer as a result of drought and famine, and, in addition, a deeper anguish regarding the fate of the world, a fear the people lived with daily and which motivated much of their thinking: whether, as predicted in ancient times, the cataclysm that was to eventually destroy the world was now imminent. This impassioned and mellisonant appeal to the god of rain takes us into the mind of the believer, bringing to life for us Tlaloc, the Tlaloque, Chicomecoatl, the various hereafters, and numerous other Nahuatl concepts, with an immediacy that few other texts have. . . . As for the authenticity of the texts, the final word on this was said by Sahagún four hundred years ago: "what is written in this book is not possible for a human mind to invent, nor is there a man living capable of inventing the kind of language contained in it."

A PRAYER TO TLALOC

Translated from the Nahuatl by Thelma Sullivan. Originally published in "A Prayer to Tlaloc," translated by Thelma D. Sullivan, in *Estudios de Cultura Nahuatl* 5 (1965): 41–55. Reprinted by permission of the publisher.

O Lord, Our Lord, O Provider, O Lord of Verdure,
Lord of Tlalocan, Lord of the Sweet-Scented Marigold, Lord of
*   Copal!*
The gods, Our Lords, the Providers,
the Lords of Rubber, the Lords of the Sweet-Scented Marigold,
*   the Lords of Copal,*
have sealed themselves in a coffer, they have locked themselves
*   in a box. They have hidden the jade and turquoise and*
*   precious jewels of life,*
they have carried off their sister, Chicomecoatl, the fruits of the
*   earth,*
and the Crimson Goddess, the chile.

Oh, the fruits of the earth lie panting;
the sister of the gods, the sustenances of life,
feebly drags herself along,
she is covered with dust, she is covered with cobwebs,
she is utterly worn and weary.

And behold, the people, the subjects, are perishing!
Their eyelids are puffy, their mouths dry as straw,
their bones are desiccated, and they are twisted and gaunt,
their lips are thin, their necks pale and scrawny.

And the children, the little ones—
those who barely walk, those who crawl,
those still on the ground making little piles of earth and broken
*   bits of pottery,*
and the infants lashed to their boards and slats
all of them are hollow-eyed.

Everyone knows anguish and affliction,
everyone is gazing upon torment;
no one has been overlooked.

All living things are suffering.
The troupial and the roseate spoonbill drag themselves along,
they topple over and lie prostrate on their backs,

weakly opening and closing their beaks.
And the animals: the dogs of the Lord, of the All and the
       Everywhere are reeling;
they take refuge among us, vainly they lick the earth.
Man and beast alike are crazed for want of water,
they die for want of water,
they are perishing, they are wasting away, they are vanishing!

The breast of our mother and father, Lord of the Earth, is dry;
no longer can she nourish, no longer can she feed,
no longer shall she suckle what sprouts, what comes forth,
what is the very life, of the people, their food and their
       sustenance.

Oh, the sustenances of life are no more, they have vanished;
the gods, the Providers, have carried them off,
they have hidden them away in Tlalocan;
they have sealed in a coffer, they have locked in a box,
their verdure and freshness—
the cuphea and fleabane, the purselane and fig-marigold—
all that grows and puts forth,
all that bears and yields,
all that sprouts and bursts into bloom,
all vegetation that issues from you
and is your flesh, your germination and renewal.

It is the jade, the armlet, the turquoise—
the most precious, the only precious thing there is;
it is the sustenance, the substance, the life of the world,
whereby those who are alive, live
and talk and rejoice and laugh.

Oh, the fruits of the earth, the green and growing things have
      gone,
they have hidden themselves away!

O Lord, Our Lord, Lord of Tlalocan, O Provider!
What does your heart will?
By chance, have you let this fall from your hand?
Is it to be thus? Is this all? Is this the end?
Are the people, the multitude, to die out, to vanish from the
      earth?
Is the city to be left empty and desolate?

Is this all? Is it to be thus?
Was it so ordained Above and in the Region of the Dead?
Was it so decreed for us? Was it so determined?

But all the little ones suffer—
those who barely walk, those who crawl, those on the ground
    still,
and the infants lashed to their boards and slats,
who are sensible of nothing—
give them, at least something to eat,
at least provide them with something,
for as yet they do not reason.

If we have vexed the Above and the Region of the Dead,
if our foulness and corruption rose up,
if it wafted up to the Above, to the heavens,
then, perhaps, this is all; perhaps, this is the end.
Perhaps, at this very moment darkness shall come
and all shall perish, all shall disappear from the earth.
What can we say? What is the use? To whom can we appeal?
It has been ordained.

At least let the common people have fullness and abundance;
let them not know total dissolution.
Their hearts and bodies are in torment,
day and night their hearts burn, their hearts are on fire!
A monstrous serpent is within them
slavering and panting and shrieking;
it is terrifying how it burns, how it shrieks, how it howls!

Perhaps now is coming true, now is coming to pass,
what the men and women of old knew, what they handed
    down:
that the heavens over us shall sunder,
that the demons of the air shall descend
and come to destroy the earth and devour the people,
that darkness shall prevail, that nothing be left on earth.
Our grandmothers and grandfathers knew it,
they handed it down, it was their tradition
that it would come to pass, that it would come to be.

And now to the ends of the earth, to the outermost bounds of the
    earth,
the land is devastated.
It is all over now, it is the end;
the earth's seeds have withered,
like old men and women they have shriveled,
and nothing has food, no one shall give food and drink to
    another.

O, Our Lord, let it not go on like this,
let there be fullness and abundance for all!
Or, let pestilence seize the people in its grip,
let the Lord of the Region of the Dead do his work, take up his
    duties.
Then, perhaps, Chicomecoatl and Cinteotl shall sustain them,
    shall succor them a little;
perhaps, into their mouths she shall put a drop of corn gruel, a
    scrap of food, as provisions for their journey.
Or let the Sun, the Eagle Ascendant, the Precious Child, the
    Valiant One,
the Brave Warrior, the Everlastingly Resplendent One, do his
    work.

Then the people, and the Eagle and Jaguar Knights shall
    rejoice,
for in the middle, in the center, of the battlefield they shall be
    charred,
and their hair shall scatter, their bones whiten, their skulls
    split open.
And they shall know the House of the Sun,
where the sun is amused, where his praises are sung,
where the nectar of the sundry sweet and fragrant flowers is
    sipped,
where the Eagle and Jaguar Knights,
the brave and valiant who die in battle, are glorified.

And the little child, the tot,
still a chick, still a mite, not sensible of anything,
as jade, as turquoise, he shall go to heaven, the House of the
    Sun;

a perfect jade, a perfect turquoise, a smooth and lustrous
     turquoise,
is the heart he shall offer the sun.

And your sister Chicomecoatl shall sustain him,
the sister of the gods, the Providers, shall enter his belly,
and thus he shall be provided for his journey;
she shall lift him to that far-off place.
For she alone is our flesh and bones,
she alone is our staff and support,
she alone is our strength and fortitude;
she is man's entire recompense.

O Lord, Our Lord,
the people, the subjects—the led, the guided, the governed—
now behold, now feel, now are filled to bursting
with the searing pain of affliction.
Their flesh and bones are stricken by want and privation,
they are worn, spent, and in torment;
indeed, the pain reaches to the heart of them.
Not only once, or merely twice
do they behold, do they suffer death!
And the animals, also.

O Lord, O King,
Lord of Verdure, Lord of Rubber, Lord of the Sweet-Scented
     Marigold!
May it be your will,
may you, at least, cast a sidelong glance at the people.
They are going, they are perishing, they are vanishing,
they are breaking and crumbling,
they are disappearing from the earth,
the suckling infants are wizened and dying,
the little ones that crawl are wasting away!

May it be your will, O, Our Lord,
may you grant that the gods, the Providers,
the Lords of the Sweet-Scented Marigold and the Lords of Copal
     do their work,
that they see to their tasks on earth.
May bounty and good fortune be unleashed,

may the sweet-scented marigold rattles shake,
may the rattle boards of the mist clatter,
may the gods don their rubber sandals!
Oh, with a sprinkle, with a few drops of dew,
may you succor, may you aid, Tlaltecutli, Lord of the Earth,
who feeds and nourishes man!
And may you comfort the anguished fruits of the earth,
beloved child, sister of the gods,
who feebly drags herself through the rows,
who is wilting and withering in the rows!

Let the people be blessed with fullness and abundance,
let them behold, let them enjoy, the jade and the turquoise—the
       precious vegetation
the flesh of Our Lords, the Providers, the Gods of Rain,
who bring, who shower down, the riches that are theirs alone.
And let the plants and animals be blessed with fullness and
       abundance,
let the troupial and the roseate spoonbill sing,
let them flutter their wings, let them sip the sweet nectar.

Oh, let not the Gods of Rain loose their wrath and indignation,
for the people are enfeebled
and they shall frighten them, they shall strike terror into them.
Let them not lash themselves into a fury,
but let them only take, let them only strike the one who is theirs,
who was born, who came into the world, marked for Tlalocan,
who is their property, their possession.
Let them not deceive the people
that inhabit the forests and open plains,
that dwell in the wild, untilled fields.

Neither let them do this;
let them not blight the trees, the magueys, the prickly pears,
      and all that grows,
for they are the root and the life of the people,
the sustenance of the poor and hapless,
those living in misery and want, the destitute,
who have nothing to eat in the morning, nothing in the evening,
who go about empty, their stomachs rumbling.

O Lord, Beloved Lord, O Provider!
May it be in your heart to grant, to give, to bring comfort to
    the earth
and all that lives from it, all that grows on it.
And you who inhabit the four quarters of the universe,
you the Lords of Verdure, you the Providers,
you the Lords of the Mountain Heights, you the Lords of the
    Cavernous Depths,
I call out, I cry out to you:
come, bring yourselves here,
comfort the people, slake the thirst of the earth;
the earth and the animals, the leaves and stalks
are watching and waiting and crying out.
O gods, Our Lords, make haste!

Tlaloc, His Song, from the *Florentine Codex*

"Tlaloc, His Song" is still another in the series of sacred hymns recorded by Sahagún in both the *Codex Matritensis* and the *Florentine Codex*, a series that includes the "Song of Xipe Totec Iouauallan," "Teteo Innan, Her Song," and "Cihuacoatl, Her Song," all of which are presented above.

This hymn to Tlaloc is third among those hymns. As one can see from the analysis of this sacred hymn in our discussion of fertility, this text, like the other sacred hymns we have presented, is extremely confusing and difficult to explicate completely. Willard Gingerich, whose sensitive translation follows, tells us that this hymn "was sung in the festivals of Tlaloc and the present version is specifically from Tenochtitlan since 'Mexico' is mentioned as its locale. The worship of Tlaloc as a god of agriculture was universal throughout Mesoamerica from ancient times. Every successive empire rested directly on an agriculture base and none ever forgot it; cults came and went, but Tlaloc never waned."[83]

TLALOC, HIS SONG

Translated from the Nahuatl by Willard Gingerich. Originally published in "Tlaloc, His Song," by Willard Gingerich, in *Latin American Literatures* 1 (1977): 79–88. Reprinted by permission of the translator.

> *Ahuia! Mexico seeks a loan of the god;*
> *paper-flag places in the four directions;*
> *men stand forth;*
> *finally the time of its weeping.*
>
> *Ahuia! I am creation of my god.*
> *With festive handfuls of bloodied thorns*
> *I fill the sacred patio.*
>
> *Ahuia! My over-lord, Magic Prince:*
> *though in truth*
> *our flesh is yours and you make us,*
> *though you are foremost,*
> *they only shame you.*
>
> *Ahuia! "If some cause me shame*
> *they know me not well;*
> *but you are my fathers,*
> *my priesthood, Jaguar-Serpent."*

Ahuia! In Tlalocan of the turquoise boat
he who appeared there is no longer seen—
Acatonal.

Ahuia! Look to all points;
Ahuia! Go forth in Poyauhtlan.
With the timbrelled mist staff
is it carried to Tlalocan.

Ahuia! 0 my elder Tozcuecuexi:
I send him forever
to his place of weeping.
Ahuia! "Send me to Quenamican,
where somehow we continue to exist."
His word has been given,
and I have already said
to the Prince of Horrific Omens,
"I send him forever
to his place of weeping."

Ahuia! In the fourth year
comes over us the wind—
unknown to any, innumerable;
to the Place of the Fleshless, Quetzal House,
We are carried across:
It is a benefice of man's reviver.

Ahuia! Look to all points;
Ahuia! Go forth in Poyauhtlan.
With the timbrelled mist staff
is it carried to Tlalocan.

A PROCESSION OF RAIN GODS

As we have indicated in our discussion of the myths of fertility, the Mesoamerican god of rain and storm has the longest history of any of the named gods of the Mesoamerican mythological tradition, although we do not know the name bestowed upon him by his Olmec creators. What we do know are his features, the characteristic "mask" in which he manifested himself for the Olmecs, a "mask" from which the features of all of the succeeding rain gods of the Mesoamerican cultures to come were derived. The case for this continuity was made quite early; in 1946 Miguel Covarrubias, a Mexican artist and anthropologist, constructed a chart showing precisely this derivation. Since then much has been learned about the Olmecs and the cultures that followed them in Mesoamerica, but Covarrubias's fundamental intuition still seems sound, although the reality of the influences at work was far more complex than he could have imagined.

Those complexities are far too intricate even to summarize here,[84] but it must be said that the complex system of Olmec supernaturals was far beyond the ken of Covarrubias or of anyone else in 1946. But if we limit his insight to a discussion of the rain god and if we realize that new discoveries have complicated even that picture, his fundamental idea will serve us well. It will help us understand the development of the rain god in all of his manifestations—as the Olmec were-jaguar, the Cocijo of Monte Alban, the Tlaloc of the Valley of Mexico, the Tajin of coastal Veracruz, and the Chac of the Maya—and it will help us to understand as well that the Mesoamerican mythological tradition was really one tradition with each member culture modifying the fundamental mythic idea to fit its own circumstances.

The Olmec Were-Jaguar: San Lorenzo Monument 52 (ca. 1200–900 B.C.)

The large body of Olmec stone sculpture created between 1200 and 500 B.C. in the Olmec heartland on the Gulf coast and in tributary areas throughout Mesoamerica can be divided into three types. There are a number of essentially realistic depictions of the human form and face, depictions so striking in their beauty and grace as to suggest the ultimately spiritual nature of humanity. Such a sculpture as that of Las Limas (Color Plate 4) provides a beautiful example of this type. A second category depicts realistic human beings costumed—and often masked—in ritual regalia (see Image 46). A third type, and Monument 52 clearly belongs in this category, consists of biologically impossible creatures incorporating features of humans and animals. These are not natural beings but the fantastic creatures of myth, metaphors expressing the Olmec view of the world of the spirit.

Many of these combine the features of men and jaguars,[85] a fitting combination when one realizes that the jaguar was the natural lord of the Olmec's jungle home, a creature so powerful as to have no natural enemies. He was man's equal opposite, the wild counterpart to the civilized human. By combining the features of these two powerful creatures, the Olmecs created a metaphor for the provision by the all-powerful world of the spirit of the water—in normal and orderly fashion—on which settled human life, tied as it is to agriculture, depended. There has been some debate as to whether the were-jaguar depicted on Monument 52 and in many, many other figures was in fact related to water, but in the case of this sculpture there can be no doubt.

This were-jaguar was discovered at the head of a system of artificial drains constructed by the inhabitants of San Lorenzo. It was no doubt used in the ritual reenactment of the gods' provision of water not by rain but perhaps in the manner of a spring filling a cenote, the large sinkholes prevalent in the Yucatan, or in the annual flooding of the river levees, which created a floodplain of great fertility, as in the ancient Nile valley, enabling the San Lorenzo Olmecs to produce two bountiful crops a year. That drain system was fashioned from blocks of basalt hollowed out to form the units of a channel. These blocks were then covered with basalt slabs and buried, thus creating what was essentially a network of large "pipes" joining several artificial ponds in the ceremonial center of San Lorenzo. The compelling case for the water-relatedness of this were-jaguar rests not only on its discovery at the crucial point in this network but also on the fact that the back of the figure is hollowed out in exactly the same fashion as the "pipe" stones. This figure is thus both literally and figuratively a conduit for the provision of water to man by the gods.

Cocijo: The Zapotec Rain God

A discussion of the rain god of the Zapotecs, Cocijo,[86] must be based on the urns decorated with human or supernatural faces or figures that these people placed with their honored dead from very early times at and around the mountaintop site of Monte Alban. The mythic importance of these burials, interments of the ancestors who had been deified, is indicated clearly by Paddock in his characterization of Monte Alban at the end of its very long period of importance in the Valley of Oaxaca: "No matter that it was already in ruins, nearly abandoned. No matter that Zaachila had already replaced it as the functioning administrative capital of a severely shrunken domain. In the tombs of Monte Alban lay the remains of already legendary, deified ancestors; under its disintegrating late buildings were layered more than a thousand years of earlier ones, accompanied by the rich and reverent offerings that dozens of generations had placed in honor of many rebuildings; the ceremonials of some 1,500 ritual 'years' of 260 days had concentrated unimaginable supernatural power there."[87]

Those offerings included the urns characteristic of Zapotec culture. It was once thought that all of the figures on the urns were gods,[88] but it has become clear that most of the figures are human beings, often wearing masks and costumes in impersonation of one or another of the gods. On those urns the face and figure or the regalia of Cocijo occurs more frequently than that of any other. That fact reinforces other indications of the importance of the god: the names of the basic divisions of the sacred calendar incorporated Cocijo, and many of the rulers whose names we know from the lists compiled by the friars after the Conquest also incorporated the name of the god. That mythic figure, then, was of extreme importance to the tradition of Monte Alban.

IMAGE 28: Monte Alban I Funerary Urn (ca. 400 B.C.)

This tiny urn, not too much larger than its reproduction here, carries in its features the certain evidence of the early Olmec influence on Monte Alban but evidences as well the Zapotec contribution to the identity of the rain god. Even the most cursory comparison of this face with that of San Lorenzo Monument 52—the Olmec rain god—reveals the same puffy, squarish face and the same jutting upper lip surmounted by a pug nose. But there is one striking, incredible difference: the Olmec were-jaguar has been given teeth and the bifid tongue of the serpent. And the tongue on this urn is not to be missed. Not only is it disproportionately large, but its inverted form is repeated in the face's headdress. The Olmec form had been translated by the Zapotecs into their own reality. What Paddock said of three other urns roughly contemporary with this one applies equally well to our Cocijo: "Somebody in the Valley of Oaxaca had a total understanding of Olmec style [and, presumably, Olmec mythology] in a setting that was no longer Olmec."[89] And for the first time we know the name given the god of rain and storm. This is Cocijo.

IMAGE 29: Monte Alban II Funerary Urn (ca. A.D. 100)

This urn, discovered in the excavation of Building I at Monte Alban, and the following one illustrate clearly the development over time of the funerary urns in general as well as those depicting Cocijo in particular. Describing that development, Covarrubias said: "The art style of the second period is characterized by sober nobility, refinement, and grandeur in sharp contrast to the archaic simplicity of the first period and the formalistic, purely decorative quality of the later periods."[90] This Cocijo from the second period, with its simple headdress, earflares, necklace, and cape functioning to set off and thus emphasize the symbolic face, illustrates well the artist's concentration on the myth he was conveying. And the rich simplicity of the apparel, decorated with chalchihuites (circles of precious jade) and ornaments fashioned of conch, suggests both the importance of the person entombed with this urn, a person whose spirit was perhaps destined for the paradise of the rain god, and the importance of the myth.

IMAGE 30: Monte Alban III Funerary Urn (ca. A.D. 600)

On this urn, as Covarrubias has suggested, the decorative elements overwhelm the representation of the god. The headdress, rising above and behind the face and sweeping down around it, features a centrally placed Glyph C, an enigmatic Zapotec sign associated with Cocijo. This version is a later development of the glyph as it appears on the urn from Monte Alban I. The figure's earflares have become ornate and gigantic, and it wears a heavily decorated pectoral composed of a face mask and tinklers.

Tlaloc: The Rain God of the Basin of Mexico

IMAGE 31

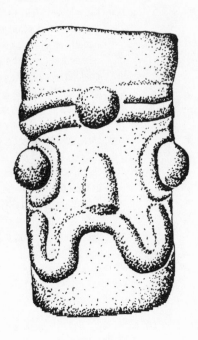

IMAGE 33

IMAGE 32

THE FLAYED GOD

The Teotihuacan Tlaloc

The development of Tlaloc, the rain god of the Basin of Mexico, took place later than that of Cocijo, his Zapotec "brother," and that development at Teotihuacan was more complex than the development at Monte Alban. Cocijo, as we have seen, is always easily recognizable from the Olmec-derived treatment of his mouth as well as from his bifid tongue. Tlaloc's mouth is also clearly derived from an Olmec model, perhaps with a Zapotec intermediary, but rather than a single mouth treatment, Tlalocs are found with a series of variations on the basic theme. There have been a number of discussions of the differences between them, notably those of Pasztory, but the situation is still far from clear.

An additional problem in understanding the Teotihuacan Tlaloc is caused by the fact that that god's features are sometimes merged with those of other gods, as in the "Tlalocs" of the frieze on the Temple of Quetzalcoatl (Image 18) and in the central figure of the Tlalocan mural (Color Plate 19). But it is clear, we feel, that the Teotihuacan Tlaloc was always fundamentally associated with rain. This association is amply demonstrated by the existence in all the phases of Teotihuacan's development of urns bearing the features of the rain god, the only decorated urns found at Teotihuacan, in contrast to the wide variety of figures found on the urns of Monte Alban. These Tlaloc urns are clearly connected with the myth: these are the urns in which the god of rain stores the waters he provides and the urns from which those waters will be dispensed by the Tlaloques.

IMAGES 31 AND 32: Two Early Tlaloc Urns

These two tiny urns, the first (Image 31) from the initial phase of development at Teotihuacan, ca. A.D. 100, and found in the fill of the Pyramid of the Sun, and the second (Image 32) from the following phase, perhaps a hundred years later, encompass in their features all that was to come in the development of the rain god's image in the Valley of Mexico. The earlier urn is rudimentary but contains the two essential features of one version of Tlaloc, a version that would survive until the Conquest: the so-called goggle eyes and the handlebar moustache mouth. The later urn couples the goggle eyes with a different mouth, this one an oval with protruding fangs, a mouth clearly reminiscent of Cocijo.

IMAGE 33: The "Plancarte" Urn

Presented to Archbishop Francisco Plancarte y Navarrete by the citizens of Nanchitla, this urn carved from a block of jadeite probably dates from about A.D. 500 and in its complexity makes clear the development of the form since the earliest urns. Not only is the face of Tlaloc, with a variation of the handlebar moustache mouth, depicted, but the lower-front portion of the urn displays the rain god's hands, and behind them, on the sides of the vase, can be seen his legs and feet.

Tlaloc after the Fall of Teotihuacan

The fall of the great city of Teotihuacan about A.D. 750 caused great turmoil throughout the Valley of Mexico, as competing centers of power sought to dominate the entire area. Eventually that domination seems to have been achieved by the Toltecs of Tula, but there were other important cities in the valley throughout the period. From the point of view of mythology, it is significant that Tlaloc remained an extremely important mythic figure throughout this period; his images are found in significant contexts everywhere. These two are illustrative.

IMAGE 34: Xochicalco Stela 2

This stela from Xochicalco, one of Tula's rivals after the decline of Teotihuacan, is fascinating in its varied depictions of Tlaloc. In the center we see the face of the rain god in a depiction almost identical to that of the Tlaloc in the border of Teotihuacan's Tlalocan mural (Color Plate 19). It has the same eyes, the same fanged mouth from which dangles the same water lily. But its earflares and headdress differ, and the difference in the headdress is very significant. This Tlaloc wears on his head a symbol often associated with the rain god. Known among Mesoamericanists as the "trapeze and ray" symbol because of its form, it is the sign associated at least from the time of Teotihuacan with the solar year, the annual cycle in which Tlaloc, of course, plays a vital part. Beneath the face of Tlaloc, with its oval mouth, the stela presents the other mouth of Tlaloc, the handlebar moustache variety. While the stela is clearly related to fertility, the year sign headdress, which is repeated in two versions on the back of the stela, and the numerous glyphs on all four sides of the stela suggest that here Tlaloc's fertility is directly related to the calendrical cycle of time.

IMAGE 35: Cacaxtla Mural Figure

Like Xochicalco, the mountaintop site of Cacaxtla also vied with Tula for supremacy. Long neglected, this site came powerfully to public attention when a series of murals were recently discovered there. The murals forced a total rethinking of intercultural contact during this period since they contained figures delineated in the Maya fashion within borders typical of Teotihuacan art. This combination had never before been known to exist. From our point of view here, one of these murals is particularly fascinating. Found on the north jamb of a doorway is a figure whose face and posture are those of a man but whose hands and feet are those of the jaguar skin he is either wearing or emerging from. He truly seems a were-jaguar in the literal sense. But he is also Tlaloc, for in one hand he holds a traditional Tlaloc effigy urn and in the other a serpent, precisely the same accoutrements as the typical "lightning Tlaloc" of Teotihuacan (Color Plate 20). And even more fascinating, his fertility association is compellingly demonstrated by the flowering vine that seems to grow from his navel. Here Tlaloc is literally providing man's sustenance.

IMAGE 36

IMAGE 37

The Aztec Tlaloc

These three pieces come from very late in the development of Aztec culture, probably after
A.D. 1450, and illustrate several important facts about the rain god. First, Tlaloc remained undiminished in importance until the moment of the Conquest. Second, he remained connected with the
rains and thus with fertility, but third, he was directly associated with philosophical speculation
regarding time and with the imperial power of the Aztecs.

IMAGE 36: Castillo de Teayo Relief Sculpture

The Aztec site of Castillo de Teayo, not far from El Tajin in the state of Veracruz, has yielded a
number of striking stone carvings, none more interesting, however, than this one. On it we see
Tlaloc depicted in profile with his handlebar moustache mouth, in an image identical to one in the
Codex Magliabechiano, in what might well be a scene from a myth. He confronts a goddess, whom
Seler identifies as Xochiquetzal on the basis of her paper crown bearing a flower (xochitl) and
quetzal feathers. Both figures hold corn stalks with ripened ears of corn, while Xochiquetzal holds
"in her left hand the rattlestick chicauaztli, the sign of fertility and the magic instrument with which
the priest conjured the rain from . . . Tlalocan."[91] Although no narrative myth remains that recounts
such a confrontation, its fertility implications are obvious.

IMAGE 37: Castillo de Teayo Tlaloc Sculpture

Also from Castillo de Teayo and also probably carved after 1450, this image of the rain god is a
significant one for it incorporates a number of his most important Aztec features. This is a frontal
view of Tlaloc with the handlebar moustache mouth, but his nose and eyebrows are fashioned from
entwined serpents, adding the serpent symbolism to the rain god that the Zapotecs had suggested
with the bifid tongue of Cocijo. Here, as in Xochicalco Stela 2 (Image 34), Tlaloc is wearing the
"trapeze and ray" headdress symbolizing the solar year, and for that reason we may relate this
image to that on page 27 of the *Codex Borgia* (Image 16), a representation of the mystery of time.

IMAGE 38: Tlaloc Urn, from the Templo Mayor

Discovered during the recent excavation of the principal pyramid of the ceremonial center of Tenochtitlan, the Aztec capital, this urn, one of an almost identical pair, each discovered in a different offering cache, is one of the most spectacular unearthed by Proyecto Templo Mayor. Except for Tlaloc's headdress and fangs, the urn is basically blue, with Tlaloc's oval mouth, goggle eyes, and serpentlike nose and eyebrows "decorated with lines and dots that, in the *Codex Borgia,* indicate preciousness when they are on a blue ground."[92] This suggests the preciousness of the rain that Tlaloc's great urns would hold, but the beauty of this particular urn and the care with which it was wrought suggest as well the importance of Tlaloc at the Templo Mayor, the very center of the Aztec imperial state.

Indeed, the pyramid of the Templo Mayor was constructed in order to lift two great temples, those of Huitzilopochtli and Tlaloc, into the heavens. Before the recent excavations were undertaken, Huitzilopochtli, the tutelary god of the Aztecs, was thought to have been the more important of the two, but now the picture has changed. The ancient god of the Valley of Mexico, Tlaloc, has taken his rightful place since, as Eduardo Matos Moctezuma, director of the excavations, has affirmed, "the majority of the objects [excavated] represent Tlalocs or objects associated with him," while fewer are associated with Huitzilopochtli. "Significantly, not a single literal stone image of Huitzilopochtli has been found."[93]

Izapa Stela 1 (ca. 200 B.C.)

While it is certainly clear that the art of Izapa is not Maya and that the gods and myths portrayed on the numerous stelae found at that site (see also Images 7 and 22) are not those of the later Maya, though they show some similarities, a majority of scholars believe that the images on these stelae provide the "missing link" between the Olmec "mother culture" and her Maya descendant. To make the metaphor explicit, the art of the Maya would be the grandchild of the Olmec matriarch.

Stela 1 makes that line of descent apparent in terms of the rain god. Here we see the transitional stage between the Olmec were-jaguar, with his protruding upper lip, and the Maya Chac, characterized by a greatly extended upper lip or nose. The main figure here is "a human figure impersonating a water god—a forerunner or variant of the Classic period rain gods (Maya Chac, Mexican Tlaloc, Zapotec Cocijo)." On this figure, "in place of the human head is a variant of the long-lipped deity mask" often found in Izapan art.[94] As the drawing indicates clearly, the stela incorporates a number of other such deity masks.

The scene, which might well portray an incident in a myth now irretrievably lost, makes clear that these deity masks are to be associated with water. At the base of the scene fish swim in a border, reminiscent of those on the later Tlalocan mural at Teotihuacan (Color Plate 19), flowing from two deity masks. The figure on the stela has just netted one of the fish, and water streams down from the net, paralleling the water streaming from the deity mask at the base of the urn strapped to his back. That the bounty derived from the stream is meant to suggest the bounty to be expected from the rain is suggested by the clouds surrounding the water urn, clouds that will release the needed rain from the mouth of the deity, a clear metaphor for their mythic point of origin in the world of the spirit.

On the basis of a complex argument, Norman suggests that the scene at the top of the stela suggests "that the central 'water of life' theme below also goes beyond the struggle to support mortal life" and "may be symbolizing man's life and death cycle."[95] The band separating this scene from the scene below is reminiscent of the jaguar mouth from which the seated figure emerges on the Olmec Altar 4 from La Venta (Image 45) and of the skybands on later Maya stelae, thus establishing another possible link between the Olmec, Izapa, and the Maya.

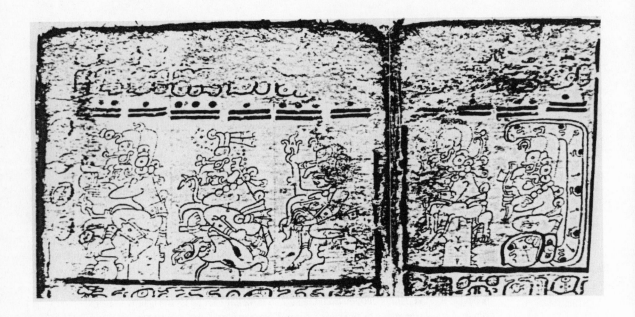

The Chac of the Codices

In the Maya codices, presumably from the Postclassic Yucatan, Chac, the god of rain and storm, is portrayed with "a long pendulous nose, a scroll beneath the eye (the pupil of which is represented by a volute), a peculiar projection above the nose ending in a curl, and a mouth which is usually toothless but sometimes shows normal teeth. . . . A thin, ribbonlike object with backward curve projects from a corner of the mouth, and frequently a similar object dangles from below the center of the upper jaw." In these last two features Eric Thompson is "inclined to see . . . the flickering tongue of the serpent,"[96] features that would relate Chac to Cocijo. And it is surely likely that either the pendulous nose or the projection above it, or perhaps both, is the final development of the Olmec were-jaguar's protruding upper lip.

While those features can be seen in certain Classic period images of the god, such as the mask worn by the ruler depicted on Yaxchilan Stela 11 (Image 48), other Classic period images of Chac are different. On the painted funerary pottery that accompanied the Classic period Maya elite to their graves, a body of painting to which Robicsek and Hales have referred as "the ceramic codex" since the painting resembles that of the later codices, Chac appears in somewhat different form in his manifestation as Chac-Xib-Chac, the Chac of the east, a direction associated with regeneration and therefore with fertility in all of its aspects.

IMAGE 40: The Quadripartite Chac from the *Dresden Codex*

This codex, the finest of the four Maya codices that survive and probably the oldest, is a ritual-astronomical work made up of almanacs that probably dates from A.D. 1200–1350, although much of its material was no doubt copied from earlier works. These illustrations of the Chacs are included in a section that Thompson sees as farmers' almanacs dealing "with the problems of farmers—the weather and crops. Not unexpectedly, it is dominated by Chacs, the rain gods."[97] Here we see five images of the god. The first four are the Chacs of the four world directions, each seated on the tree symbolically associated with his direction. The fifth Chac, the Chac of the center position, sits within an enclosure, perhaps a cave mouth, and holds an axe, a symbol associated with the Chacs for it was with this axe that they caused thunder and lightning. Although utterly different in appearance from the image on page 27 of the *Codex Borgia* from the Valley of Mexico (Image 16 and Color Plate 7), this image, roughly contemporary, presents the quadripartite nature of the rain god in much the same way, with the rather serpentine axe of the Chac of the center replacing Tlaloc's lightning serpent, Xiuhcoatl.

IMAGE 41: Painted Pottery Funerary Plate (ca. A.D. 700)

The image on this plate,[98] probably representing a scene from a myth now forgotten, depicts the Classic period Chac-Xib-Chac, the red Chac of the east, rising up through the waters that separate the underworld from the world of nature (see also Color Plate 21). From Chac's head grows the world tree, which reaches up toward the celestial monster painted on the rim of the plate and thus links this world to the upper world of the spirit. In one hand Chac holds an axe symbolic of his rain-making function, while his other hand is missing, lost to some unknown sacrifice, blood streaming from the place where it should be. Regeneration, as we know, requires sacrifice; blood must be exchanged for the water
of life.

Although Arthur Miller was not referring to this scene in writing of the Maya connection between regeneration and the east, his discussion fits it perfectly:

> The east, for the Maya, was a place of rebirth, where astronomical bodies such as the sun, which they had seen descend and disappear in the west, reappeared after a period out of view (literally under the world) or after passage through the world of the dead, the Underworld. The understanding that the west was associated with death in the Maya mind, and the east with rebirth, comes from written sources of Maya cosmogony such as the Popol Vuh, from recent research on Maya funeral pottery, and from the texts and iconography at Palenque. It also comes from a simple structural analysis of their cosmology, aspects of which are common in several parts of the world at different times. For example, ancient Egyptian followers of Akhnaton conceived of the death of their Pharaoh as the sun's passage into the Underworld at night, visually expressed by the image of the Pharaoh Tutankhamen being carried through the Underworld on the back of a black leopard. The Maya believed that the sun was transformed into a jaguar at night. Even our own culture has reference to the "dying sun" and "newborn sun," as for example, with Joseph Conrad's ominous metaphor [in his novel *Victory*] for imminent death: "Faint puff of wind, a mere sign from the west, where Venus casts her rays on the dark edge of the horizon, like a bright lamp hung over the grave of the sun."[99]

THE FLAYED GOD

The Architectural Chac

One cannot visit the archaeological sites of the Yucatan without being confronted constantly by the huge architectural masks of Chac peering down from above. At the site known today as Labna (Maya for "old ruined buildings"; the original name is unknown), located in the west-central part of the state of Yucatan, Mexico, one finds the mask depicted here surmounting a doorway on the west façade of the east wing of the richly embellished building known as the Palace, a large two-story structure set magnificently on an extremely long terrace.

Throughout Mesoamerica, but especially in the Maya Yucatan, many of the structures that housed rituals were profusely decorated with masks, often over the doorways or even forming the doorways, the entrance being through the gaping mouth as if to indicate in the most tangible possible form the movement from the mundane world to that of the sacred. This point of entrance into the body of the god marked the liminal path or transition to another level of existence. When the masks appear on the façades, they signify the sacred function of the building, symbolizing the underlying cosmological purpose of the structures that served "to dramatize the cosmogony by constructing on earth a reduced version of the cosmos."[100] Both mask and structure, then, were metaphors.

This particular mask of Chac is typical of many found throughout the Yucatan, with the notable exception that this one bears a date, corresponding to A.D. 862, inscribed on its elongated proboscis. The precise reason for the appearance of this date is, of course, unknown, but it may well indicate a connection between Chac and the movement of the cycles of time comparable to Tlaloc's basic identification with that movement (Images 16 and 37). In this image the Maya god of rain and storm is portrayed with a long pendulous nose that ends in a curl, a scroll beneath his eye, a mouth that shows teeth, and fangs curving backward from the corners of his mouth. These fangs are interesting to one fluent in the imagery of rain gods, for while they clearly resemble those that characteristically emerge from the sides of Chac's mouth, their placement is also reminiscent of Tlaloc's handlebar moustache mouth, indicating, perhaps, an influence from the Basin of Mexico. On the whole, however, the features of this image fit well Thompson's description of the Chacs of the codices, probably also Yucatec, which we quoted in connection with the previous image.

THE FLAYED GOD

Tlaloc as Tlaltecuhtli or Tlaltecuhtli as Tlaloc

This particular relief, which shows the head of Tlaloc, the rain god, on the body of Tlaltecuhtli, the Earth Monster, appears under the base of a stone sculpture of the feathered serpent, but other such reliefs are found on the undersides of other monumental Aztec sculptures, notably the massive Coatlicue (Image 23). In our discussion above of the Templo Mayor relief on which Tlaltecuhtli is depicted (Image 25), we noted that figures of the Earth Monster, with her own proper head, were frequently carved on the undersides of Aztec monuments so that the image of the Earth Monster faced directly the surface of the earthly plane it symbolized, but here we have the strange combination of Tlaltecuhtli's female body with Tlaloc's male head. Such a combination surely suggests that their multifaceted, unified existence relates to fertility in a very basic and far-reaching sense.

On this relief we see Tlaltecuhtli in her typical position, portrayed frontally with her knees bent and outstretched in the position of giving birth in the manner assumed by Aztec women, but the head atop this body is looking forward instead of being flung back and facing upward, and it is clearly that of Tlaloc with his characteristic goggle eyes and handlebar moustache mouth with its protruding fangs. The central emblem on the torso is the symbol for turquoise, which signifies preciousness, and significantly, that symbol is a quincunx. That quincunx in this all-important position suggests the cosmic center, and the combination of these two gods—the earthly and heavenly forces of fertility—suggests the omnipresence of that spiritual force that we call fertility. That force is, of course, at the center of the cosmos, for it is the conduit whereby energy moves from the realm of the spirit to sustain life on the earthly plane.

There could be no more fitting image than this one, an image meant only for the eyes of the gods, to end this presentation of the myths of fertility.

FEATHERED SERPENTS
AND
HERO TWINS

THE MYTHIC STRUCTURE OF RULERSHIP

INTRODUCTION

The third and last of the broad categories of myths of the Classic period that we will present is characterized by Joseph Campbell as one in which the cycle of creation is no longer carried forward by the gods nor by the timeless mythological processes originating in the realm of the spirit, "but by the heroes, more or less human in character, through whom the world destiny is realized."[1] The Mesoamerican myths of this kind thus provide a transitional stage between the invisible realm of the spirit and the manifest world of human life. In so doing they fulfill almost exactly Campbell's description of comparable Old World myths in which "creation myths begin to give place to legend—as in the Book of Genesis, following the expulsion from the garden. Metaphysics yields to prehistory, that is dim and vague at first, but becomes gradually precise in detail. The heroes become less and less fabulous, until at last, in the final stages of the various local traditions, legend opens into the common daylight of recorded time."[2]

Campbell's reference here to the recording of time is particularly apt for our application of his insight to the mythological tradition of Mesoamerica because, as we have seen in connection with the myths of creation and fertility, the calendrical recording of the cycles of time within that tradition provides the foundation on which its fundamental mythic structures are erected and provides as well one of the primary means of linking historical events to their mythic counterparts. It is now known, for example, that the Maya, in addition to recording the dates of presumably historical events, also recorded, in the same context as those historical dates, the dates of what can only be mythic occurrences. One such date on three stelae at the Yucatan site of Coba records the elapsing of "142 nonillion years or, in our number system, 142 followed by thirty-six zeros." Such a comparison of Maya dates with ours suggests the awesome and necessarily mythic scale of that vision of time, for "in our world view, the Big Bang took place only fifteen billion years ago."

These mythic numbers were used by the Maya

> to set a prescribed distance between a date in historical time and one occurring in a previous [mythic] era, . . . [a distance] deliberately calculated so that both dates fell at exactly the same position in one or more of the repetitive cycles—including astronomical ones, such as the eclipse and Venus cycles, so important to Maya thought. . . . By showing that the two dates had the same shape in time, the Maya declared that the actions and the actors associated with those dates—gods for the mythical dates, kings for the historical ones—were also the same. By

indicating that these historical dates are made from the same symmetry as the mythological dates, the Maya declare the actors to be made of the same fabric: the human king was god, and his substance was intimately linked to the symmetrical order and matter of the previous creation.[3]

This discussion of the interweaving of history and myth by Linda Schele and Mary Ellen Miller suggests two fundamental truths about the Mesoamerican mythic conception of rulership. First, the heroes to whom Campbell refers generally are, in the mythology of Mesoamerica, rulers or function to provide a paradigm of rulership rather than the warrior heroes, such as Achilles and Sargon, or the saintly heroes, such as Christ and the Buddha, whom we are accustomed to find in the mythologies of the Old World. Although the heroes of Mesoamerica may possess a number of the qualities of these Old World figures, the Mesoamerican hero emerges from the realm of the spirit to fulfill a particular function: the provision of the ultimately spiritual order on which a settled society depends. Second, that spiritual order was conceived as cyclical, with each cycle repeating, in its own fashion, the fundamental structure of all the cycles, a structure metaphorically revealed in myth. As the mythic images and texts gathered in this section clearly show, it was this structure that provided the framework within which the rulers of Mesoamerica, from the time of the Olmecs to that of the Aztecs and for all of the civilizations between the two, were conceived as being manifestations of the spirit who, in the exercise of profane power, spoke for the gods and thus provided an essentially spiritual order for human society.

As recent studies of the mythic elements in the tales of Topiltzin Quetzalcoatl, ruler of Toltec Tula, for example, make clear, the seers of Mesoamerica saw their rulers as avatars of the gods entering and exiting the world of time and space at regularly timed intervals,[4] basing this mythic conception of rulership on the cyclic reality most clearly and abstractly charted in their intricate calendrical system. Thus each "separate" ruler was really not the individual he seemed but rather, in some mysterious way, a new manifestation of the abiding world of the spirit sent to perform the ages-old tasks of rulership. Like the sun, with whom he was often identified by Mesoamerican societies, he would rise, reach the peak of his powers, decline, and then return to the world of the spirit whence he came, only to rise again as a new manifestation of the eternal force:

> The Maya believed that while rulers die, kingship does not. Emphasis was on the office, not the person. The visual metaphors for rebirth of Maya rulership were the primordial Maya gods who had ruled over the earth in a continuous cycle since the beginning of time: images of the sun and other celestial bodies rendered in stone, stucco and paint on Tikal Early Classic architecture. Rulership, then, was clearly related to the calendar, for Maya rulers reigned over repeating periods of time as did the gods.[5]

And what Arthur Miller says here of the Maya was equally true of the other Mesoamerican civilizations. This unique system of myth and ritual, centered on the ruler, functioned to bring the peoples of Mesoamerica into accord with the sense of order they intuited in the cosmos, an order underlying the struggle and strife they experienced in their mundane lives.

Thus among the Yucatec Maya at the time of the Conquest, and probably among earlier peoples throughout Mesoamerica, this cyclical conception of rulership extended well beyond its application to individual rulers. One of the more fascinating revelations of the enigmatic *Books of Chilam Balam* suggests that the calendrical cycle of the katuns was used to "rotate" the seat of rule from one "heavenborn" capital to another every twenty years; at the end of each katun cycle of twenty years, the previous capital city was ritually abandoned in favor of the new capital, and a new ruler representing a different lineage came to power.[6] It has even been suggested that the so-called "collapse" of Classic period civilizations throughout Mesoamerica was a similar response to the ending of a cycle.

MYTH AND HISTORY

Accustomed as we are to think of rulership within the framework provided by history and politics, we must bend our minds to capture the Mesoamerican conception. The identification of the ruler in each of the Mesoamerican high cultures with a bewildering plethora of gods (among the Aztecs, for example, the ruler was identified, in one way or another, with Tezcatlipoca, Quetzalcoatl, Xiuhtecuhtli/Huehueteotl, Huitzilopochtli, and Tlaloc) suggests in yet another way that for all of the high cultures of Mesoamerica, the basic conception of rulership was cast in uniquely Mesoamerican mythic terms. For those peoples, reality was to be understood as the constant interpenetration of the planes of spirit and matter, and "history" was, for them, a record of the workings of the world of the spirit as it manifested itself on the earthly plane. As Serge Gruzinski puts it in his study of the Aztecs, " 'myth' and 'history' interweave here so inextricably that one ends up wondering if these Western categories do not contribute to obscuring the idea that the Nahua were forming of their past."[7] Since what had been would be, the proper function of "history" was as much to comprehend the underlying spiritual structure of the present and the future as it was to understand the past.

Rather than reading the mythic and legendary Mesoamerican "historical" accounts as revelatory of what actually occurred in the past, then, we must understand that for the seers of Mesoamerica myth was used to interpret history, and history was seen as the realization of myth. There is no clearer example of this reality than the reaction of Motecuhzoma to the arrival in the east in 1519 of Cortés and his men in the incredibly coincidental year of 1 Reed, as the Aztecs reckoned

PLATE 15

FERTILITY AND THE GODDESS:

PLATE 15
A depiction of the Aztec ritual Ochpaniztli. In the center is a priest wearing the skin of a sacrificed woman who had impersonated (i.e. *become*) the goddess Toci. From the *Codex Borbonicus*

PLATE 16
An Aztec stone sculpture of a fertility goddess

PLATE 16

PLATE 17
A Cihuatateo, a deified
woman who had died in
childbirth. A ceramic sculpture from El Cocuite,
Veracruz

PLATE 18
The Aztec Tlazolteotl from
the *Codex Borbonicus*

PLATE 19

The Tlalocan patio mural from Teotihuacan, a reproduction in the Museo Nacional de Antropología in Mexico City. The mural is an incredibly complex series of mythic and ritual allusions to the provision of water to the earth by the world of the spirit. The upper register depicts a costumed and masked male or female priest flanked by subordinate priests. The lower register depicts Tlalocan, the paradise of the rain god, Tlaloc.

PLATE 20

THE RAIN GOD AT TEOTIHUACAN AND AMONG THE MAYA:

PLATE 20
The "lightning Tlaloc" mural from Tepantitla, Teotihuacan, showing the goggle-eyed rain god of the Basin of Mexico, Tlaloc, holding a lightning serpent

PLATE 21
One of the aspects of the Maya god of rain and lightning, Chac, rising from the underworld with the world tree growing from his head, Maya painted funerary plate

PLATE 21

THE DUALITY OF THE GODS:

PLATE 22
The Aztec Quetzalcoatl and
Tezcatlipoca from the
Codex Borbonicus

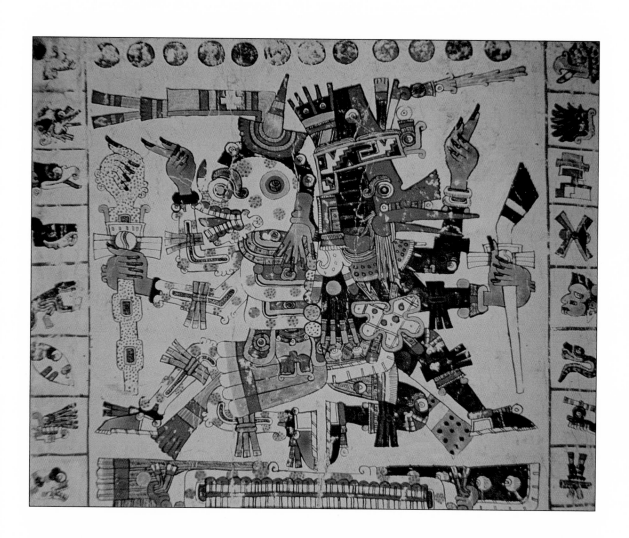

PLATE 24
Chicomoztoc, the Aztec
cave of origin, from the
Historia Tolteca-
Chichimeca

time, the year of the birth, in an earlier fifty-two-year cycle, of Topiltzin Quetzalcoatl, that same Quetzalcoatl who had, at the end of that
earlier cycle, vanished into the east with the understanding that he
would return in a later year 1 Reed. For Motecuhzoma, the cycle had
come round again, and Quetzalcoatl, the fair god, had returned from
the realm of the spirit to reclaim his earthly kingdom. What else could
the Aztec ruler have done but send his emissaries to greet the returning god with the mask and costume that would allow him to manifest
himself in his full glory?

"O our lord," Motecuhzoma is reported by Sahagún to have said
to Cortés on their first meeting,

> thou hast arrived on earth, thou hast come to thy noble city of Mexico.
> Thou hast come to occupy thy noble mat and seat, which for a little time
> I have guarded and watched for thee. . . . Lo, I have been troubled for a
> long time. I have gazed into the unknown whence thou hast come—the
> place of mystery. For the rulers of old have gone, saying that thou
> wouldst come to instruct thy city, that thou wouldst descend to thy mat
> and seat; that thou wouldst return. And now it is fulfilled: thou hast re-
> turned. . . . Arrive now in thy land. Rest, lord; visit thy palace that thou
> mayest rest thy body. Let our lords arrive in the land![8]

The shaping power of myth within the consciousness of ancient
Mesoamerica, as revealed in Motecuhzoma's words and actions, com-
pels us to temper the excitement in Mesoamerican scholarship today
now that the fog that has shrouded the ancient past is gradually being
lifted through our growing ability to read the Maya glyphs and our increasing archaeological sophistication. Our rapidly developing understanding of the names and careers of Maya rulers and the material
cultures of all of the ancient civilizations seems capable of allowing
"history" to emerge from that fog, but we must be careful to keep in
mind the Mesoamerican understanding of the essential nature of reality. As Peter Mathews puts the problem from a twentieth-century Maya
scholar's perspective: although the "decipherment of Maya hieroglyphic writing has reached the stage where we can be confident of
correctly understanding 70% or more of the inscriptions, we cannot
always be so sure of the historical accuracy of what the Maya themselves wrote."[9]

And in speaking of the "historical accuracy" of the events
recorded in the Mixtec *Codex Vindobonensis*, Gordon Brotherston
again emphasizes the calendrical basis of Mesoamerican myth and the
mythic nature of the calendar, pointing out that we must recognize

> the intense ritual patterning that the story has undergone. . . . Again and
> again over its length the Tepexic narrative of Tula [i.e., the *Codex Vindo-
> bonensis*] records time intervals whose primary significance lies in ritual,
> calendrics and the cycles of astronomy. Nonetheless, ideal as they may
> seem, such time-calculations are inseparable from the stuff of history: in
> both iconographic and hieroglyphic texts it is not a matter of opposing
> two kinds of time-measurement, ideal (astronomical-numerological) and

material-historical, but of seeing how both are integrated within one holistic calendrical system. Hence for native scribes, recording the history of Tula from early on in the Era was not so much a matter of spurning brute material fact as of selecting calendar names, dates and periods which could resonate numerically within the Era system as a whole.[10]

It is within that resonance that we can "hear" the mythic consciousness of the seers of Mesoamerica.

All of this is not to say that a number of details that are historical in our sense cannot be gleaned from the "historical" narratives of Mesoamerica and that a "historically accurate" account of the pre-Columbian Mesoamerican past could not eventually be worked out from them, but such a historical account is neither our concern here nor the primary concern of those who created and retold the narratives. That concern is to reveal the mythic structure that supported the institution of rulership throughout Mesoamerica, the structure through which the peoples of Mesoamerica saw the world of the spirit providing, in calendrically predictable cycles, earthly rulers, those "heroes, more or less human in character," as Campbell termed them or "man-gods," in the terminology of the Mexican scholar Alfredo López Austin.

RULER AS GOD

A key text in understanding the precise nature of the Mesoamerican mythic attribution of deity to its rulers is the formal speech delivered by each Aztec ruler upon the occasion of his accession to the position of rulership, a position symbolized throughout Mesoamerica by the reed mat upon which the ruler sat, the Mesoamerican equivalent of the throne that we still use as a metaphor for rulership. This remarkable ritual entreaty, which we will present in the collection of myths gathered below, outlines for us the mythic structure of rulership in the process of delineating the Aztec ruler's relationship to Tezcatlipoca, a patron deity of rulership. In it the newly installed ruler represents himself as one who will "pronounce for thee," i.e., Tezcatlipoca, and simultaneously "pronounce for" the progenitor of Tezcatlipoca, who is none other than Ometeotl, the embodiment of the creative principle in its most abstract form. Significantly, however, the speech goes on to make clear that the new ruler is not to be seen as a human being speaking for a god from whom he is essentially separate. Rather, he is one of a line of rulers who, in some mysterious sense, shelters the god: "thou [i.e., Tezcatlipoca] wilt hide thyself in them; from within them thou wilt speak."

That last sentence gives a somewhat more precise, if equally mysterious, Mesoamerican meaning to Joseph Campbell's characterization of heroes as "more or less human" with which we began this discussion. For a fuller explanation we might turn to two fascinating recent studies of the nature of the Mesoamerican ruler/hero. In *Man-Gods in the Mexican Highlands,* Serge Gruzinski asks the question, "What was power for the Nahua?" In his answer we get a sense of both the complexity and the profundity lying behind that metaphoric "hide thyself in them." "The source of that power," Gruzinski says, "was a divine force infused into the nobles, into the ranks of the pipiltin—a vocation for leadership that came from the gods Quetzalcoatl and Xiuhtecuhtli and sealed the nobles' authority. . . . The higher one went in the hierarchy, the more irresistible was the force. . . . Thus, in the course of the rites of enthronement and divinization, the sovereign was literally inundated with that divine and protective energy that his body soon diffused."[11]

Linda Schele and Mary Ellen Miller, in *The Blood of Kings,* in contrast, see in ritual the key to an understanding of the Maya sovereign's "ability to host the supernatural": "The power of ritual to incarnate the supernatural," they say, "may . . . explain why the king could appear in so many different guises. It appears that the king was conceived to be a vessel of sorts and that through ritual, a god was brought into his body." This kingly ability to shelter the god was shared, they believe, by others who impersonated the gods in ritual.[12] As such essentially metaphoric statements suggest, Gruzinski, Schele and Miller, and we ourselves are all dealing with the same problem: how to transpose the Mesoamerican metaphor into our terms, how to clarify in our language the Mesoamerican ruler's ability to mediate between the essential reality of the world of the spirit and the contingent reality of this world.

Although he is not writing specifically of Mesoamerica, Theodore Gaster understands the archaic sensibility that sees men and gods and ancestors as varying manifestations of the same essential reality and therefore capable of such kaleidoscopic ritual change, and he provides the structure for what is perhaps the best solution to our problem:

> In the case of divine kingship . . . the conventional idiom has been taken at face value, and on this basis elaborate theories have been constructed in which the king is represented to be the actual offspring of a "sacred marriage" or a human being specifically selected and delegated by a superior deity. The truth is, however, that he is nothing other than the deity himself in his punctual aspect, the imagery of physical descent or special selection and designation being simply a concession to empirical forms of articulation.[13]

Thus the "god" mysteriously enters into and exists through the corporeal form of each successive king, providing in that way a spiritual ordering of the lives of his people on the natural plane, and the language of the myth struggles, as myths always must, to express that mystery metaphorically.

Such a conception, in Mesoamerica and elsewhere, would seem to be the natural outgrowth of an earlier shamanism, retaining as its basis the shaman's ability to penetrate the barrier dividing matter from spirit. However, this ability is now institutionalized in the lineage of kings rather than having to rely on the visionary trance of the individual shaman.[14] It is thus no mere coincidence that one of the principal divine patrons of rulership among the Aztecs, Tezcatlipoca, can be described as the "archsorcerer, associated with darkness, the night, and the jaguar, the were-animal *par excellence* of the Mesoamerican sorcerer-transformer," a god whose shamanic origins are suggested by his primary symbol, "the obsidian mirror, an instrument used for divinatory scrying."[15] And among the Maya, the "ruler was one of the multiple incarnations of God K, the first ancestor, through the cycles of time."[16] Michael Coe has demonstrated that God K is the Maya equivalent of Tezcatlipoca, and in a recent study Karen Bassie-Sweet takes that identification a step farther, suggesting that "God K was the lineage and patron god of the Classic Maya."[17]

A fuller understanding of the significance of the identification of the ruler with Tezcatlipoca/God K requires us to return our attention to the speech by the incoming Aztec ruler, for in that speech the ruler is careful to specify that the particular function of Tezcatlipoca to which he refers belongs to the god as the result of his descent from Ometeotl. As the manifestation of Ometeotl accessible to man through ritual, Tezcatlipoca is to be seen as the creative force itself, and thus the ruler is "sheltering" none other than the generative principle that creates and maintains all reality, a force so abstract and inaccessible to the human mind that it must be approached, even by the deified ruler, through its manifestation. The deified ruler, in his turn, brings that force to a point of accessibility to ordinary humanity, mediating in this way between the essence of the life force and the common man and woman.

There remains no record of the comparable speeches delivered by Maya rulers on the occasion of their accession to the mat of rulership, their "enthronement and divinization," but we do have a detailed visual record from a number of Classic period cities of the lengthy ritual that accomplished that accession. Those images, accompanied by rows of glyphs specifying occasions and dates, were chiseled into upright stone slabs that we call stelae but that the Maya called *te-tun*, literally "tree stones"[18] (Image 48). These man-made trees rose from the sacred ground of the lowland Maya ceremonial centers in front of artificial mountains, the pyramids that raised the temples into the heavens and provided symbolic caves in their inner reaches to serve as the final resting place for the deified kings who presided in the temples and whose images graced the tree stones. So ubiquitous are these symbolic stones that they have been seen as one of the primary diagnostic traits of the Classic period of Maya civilization. It is no surprise, then, that, taken collectively, they image forth the Maya myth of divine rulership, a myth incorporating gods, deified ancestors, ritual blood sacrifice, and the hero journey into a single coherent structure, a structure that unifies time and space, matter and spirit. This mythic conception, distinctly

Maya, no doubt once found expression in narrative myths, now irretrievably lost except for those preserved within the structure of the *Popol Vuh,* but it remains for us in the images on the stelae as well as in a wealth of comparable images carved into other stone surfaces within the sacred precincts of Classic period Maya ceremonial centers.

CYCLES

That moment of accession, that moment of "enthronement and divinization," is a focal point of the concern with rulership manifested in the Aztec ruler's speech and in these images because it is the moment on which the whole system pivots—the highly liminal moment of the beginning of a new cycle, a new repetition of the essential pattern. It is the moment at which the man or woman who is to rule *becomes* the god—or, to put it the other way around, as it would have been understood by the peoples of ancient Mesoamerica, the moment at which spiritual reality manifests itself anew in material form in the world of space and time. Thus it is simultaneously a moment of continuity and of renewal, dual themes of equal importance on each of the individual stela.

Although the dynastic art of the Maya contains a multitude of images related to this crucial moment, no image presents these elements more clearly and forcefully than the one engraved on the rear face of the *te-tun* we know as Stela 11 at Yaxchilan (Image 48). There we see depicted the man who ruled that celebrated city from A.D. 752 to 771, Bird Jaguar by name, literally encased within the regalia of the god Chac-Xib-Chac. Above him, engaged in conversation, are shown his dead parents, Shield Jaguar and Lady Evening Star, and before him kneel three bound captives destined for sacrifice as a part of the lengthy ritual of his accession to the mat of rulership. While his parents' presence clearly testifies to the dynastic legitimacy of Bird Jaguar's reign and thus stands for continuity, the blood that will be shed in the sacrifice of the bound captives provides a chilling metaphor for the cosmic energy necessary for the renewal of the cycle; what was true for the Aztecs was equally true for the earlier Classic Maya: it was human blood that fueled the cyclic movement of the cosmos.

This dual theme of continuity and renewal at the pivotal point in the cycle can be seen even more clearly in the figure of Bird Jaguar himself. The "X-ray convention" used here to depict him, a convention of Mesoamerican art since Olmec times (see Image 46), enables us to view the man within the mask of the god, and the god, of course, is the embodiment of continuity. Insofar as each successive ruler is seen as the manifestation of Chac-Xib-Chac, he is the same ruler, cycle after cycle, individual after individual; as Gruzinski points out, "the fire was one and the man-gods were many."[19] But, this image insists, the ruler truly is individual. The lineaments of the face of Bird Jaguar, the actual human offspring of Shield Jaguar and Lady Evening Star, testify eloquently to the particularity of his identity. But he is Chac-Xib-Chac as well, for with the shedding of the blood of the captives kneeling before him, Bird Jaguar will assume the mantle and the mask of rulership for the duration of his life, mysteriously *becoming* the god, and his individual life will become one of the cycles of rulership that make up a larger cosmic cycle. This tree stone marks that very particular moment in the "histories" of Bird Jaguar and Yaxchilan, and the "X-ray convention" it uses seems particularly suited to imaging forth the dual themes of continuity and renewal.

To understand the full significance of this artistic convention and of this particular image, one must understand the multifaceted metaphoric nature of the mask for the peoples of Mesoamerica. As we have suggested throughout this book,[20] the most fundamental aspect of Mesoamerican spiritual thought is its view of essential reality as that of the spirit, the inner, as opposed to the contingent reality of the material world, the outer covering of spirit. The mask, when worn in ritual, as Bird Jaguar wears it here, allows that inner, spiritual reality to be made outer, allows the "accidental" natural face of the wearer to be replaced by his more fundamental spiritual identity. Essential reality thus emerges from the spirit into the contingent world of nature through ritual.

But the reverse is also true. By animating the lifeless mask, the wearer takes on the function of the god, the life force within all animate beings. Thus the man "becomes" the god in a double sense: he is both the particular divine identity and the animating force. That image of Bird Jaguar, ruler of Yaxchilan, that through the conventions of Maya art shows his natural features inside his real, spiritual features—those of Chac-Xib-Chac—makes the metaphorical nature of the mask instantaneously clear. And it makes equally clear the fact that Bird Jaguar both "shelters" and "pronounces for" the inner spiritual reality that is the god he manifests. Upon his accession to the mat of rulership, he thus becomes "the deity himself in his punctual aspect." In Mesoamerica that "punctual aspect," as was the case with everything related to time, was seen as a cyclical phenomenon: the ruler, born human, would become the god upon his accession and at death would complete the movement from nature to spirit. For what is involved in such a death "is not (as is all too commonly supposed) a process of *deification*—that is, of *conversion* into a superior type of being—but rather a *reversion* of the avatar to that more comprehensive essence which it temporally and temporarily embodied. In other words, the punctual and actual recedes at death, and being then continues only in the aspect of the eternal and ideal."[21] At that point in time, of course, a new manifestation of the spirit would assume the mask of rulership; the fire would pass into a new man-god, as the cycles continued their eternal movement.

While the mask provided an important metaphor throughout Mesoamerica for the relationship between worldly power and the life of the spirit, among the Maya the mythic image of the tree became a metaphor as important as that of the mask in the presentation of the spiritual essence of rulership. The very form of the *te-tun* on which the images of the god-kings were inscribed in itself suggests the basic identification of the living king with the world tree, which stood as a metaphor for the vertical axis of the cosmos.[22] That axis, according to the shamanistic view of the relationship between spiritual and material realities characteristic of Mesoamerica, both unites and allows communication between the physical reality of the earth's surface and the enveloping realm of the spirit, metaphorically identified with the heavens and the underworld. Gaining access to those realms of the spirit through the visions induced by blood sacrifice, through the communion with deified ancestors, through "becoming" the god in ritual, the ruler serves to enable the order of the world of the spirit to flow into the chaotic, cyclical world of nature. As Schele and Freidel put it, "In the rapture of bloodletting rituals, the king brought the great World Tree into existence through the Middle of the temple and opened the awesome doorway into the Otherworld."[23] Through that opening flowed the bounty of the spirit.

The metaphorical identification of ruler and tree is understandable if we think of the majestic ceiba, the epitome of the plant kingdom as man is of the animal kingdom, growing from the surface of this earth into the heavens, providing there a vast canopy, like the sky,[24] under whose shelter earthly life exists. But penetrating downward from the earth's surface, the tree's roots draw nourishment from the underworld, a sustenance coupled with that provided from the heavens in the form of rain and sunshine to maintain the tree's life. Like man, the tree is a physical being that draws its life from the enveloping spiritual realm, but unlike man, the tree reaches physically into both the upper and lower realms of the spirit, thus uniting them with the earth's surface, creating precisely the union achieved by the ruler on another level.

Most striking, most complex, and most profound of all the Maya images "telling" the myths that link rulers and trees is the one carved into the stone that was to become the lid of the sarcophagus of Pacal, ruler of Palenque from A.D. 615 to 683[25] (Image 49). Functioning to seal the king's final resting place within the soaring pyramid constructed to house the sarcophagus, the mythic imagery on that massive stone records Pacal's fall into Xibalba, the underworld, the realm of the dead, in the context of the powerful central presence of the world tree, which grows in this image from the head of the Earth Monster, whose jaws represent here the maw of death, providing certain assurance that death is but a stage of the cyclical process of life rather than an end. As the narrative myth of the hero twins, which we will discuss below, makes clear, the Maya ruler would "triumph" over death, continuing an existence of the spirit as a "god," a divine ancestor validating and sustaining the rule of the later kings of his lineage in precisely the same way that Bird Jaguar's parents, for example, continued to function after their death.

Pacal, like all Maya rulers, "was, after all, the living manifestation of the Hero Twins who had set the example of how to defeat the Lords of Xibalba,"[26] as was recounted in the *Popol Vuh*. Just as he is represented as falling down the world tree at his death, the vertical axis of the cosmos along which movement into the realm of the spirit is possible, so the hero twins begin their hero journey by entering Xibalba, the underworld realm of the spirit ruled by the lords of Xibalba. In his discussion of the paradigmatic hero journey in world mythology, Joseph Campbell says of that crucial moment that Pacal and the hero twins face: "The hero goes forward in his adventure until he comes to the 'threshold guardian' at the entrance to the zone of magnified power. Such custodians bound the world in the four directions—also up and down—standing for the limits of the hero's present sphere, or life horizon. Beyond them is darkness, the unknown, and danger."[27] It is the task of the hero to journey beyond the known world and to find in those outer reaches the boon that will bring harmony and fulfillment to that known world. The hero twins accomplish precisely that by following the Black Road into Xibalba, as does Quetzalcoatl in his own way in his hero journey, central to the mythology of the Basin of Mexico. It is precisely this moment that is symbolized by Pacal's fall into the maw of the Earth Monster, which serves here as the "threshold guardian" of the entrance to the realm of the spirit.

The task of the mythical heroes was therefore the hero task of the ruler:

> For the Maya, the world was a complex and awesome place, alive with sacred power. This power was part of the landscape, of the fabric of space and time, of things both living and inanimate, and of the forces of nature—storms, wind, mist, smoke, rain, earth, sky and water. Sacred beings moved between the three levels of the cosmos: the Overworld which is the heavens, the Middleworld where humans live, and the Underworld or Xibalba, the source of disease and death. The king acted as a transformer through whom, in ritual acts, the unspeakable power of the supernatural passed into the lives of mortal men and their works.[28]

It was, then, the transformative power located in the person of the king, "the deity in his punctual aspect," that enabled the sun to shine, the rain to fall, the crops to grow, children to be born and to flourish, the armies to prevail. It was that power, in short, that enabled the cycle of life on all its levels to continue.

THE HERO JOURNEY

Thus it is abundantly clear that the Mesoamerican ruler was seen as functioning within a mythic reality characterized by cycles within cycles, some calendrical, some related to his particular society and his lineage, and it is also clear that each ruler was himself a cycle within those larger cycles. Like all of the cycles, his was a repetition of the basic pattern or paradigm, and that paradigm was set forth for all time in the myths, most especially in portions of the two major narrative myths that have been preserved from the Mesoamerican past. One, the *Popol Vuh,* which contains the story of the hero twins, has come down to us in a single narrative; the other, the adventures of Quetzalcoatl, exists in a large number of variant manuscripts, both verbal and pictographic. Although the two narratives are substantially different in detail, they are surprisingly similar in both structure and function. Both, as we have seen in the earlier chapters of this book, are parts of larger narrative structures that contain creation cycles and fertility myths, and both contain the exploits of more-or-less human heroes whose symbolic journeys serve as mythic paradigms for rulership.

Similar hero cycles are to be found throughout the mythologies of the world, and Campbell, among others, has studied their general features and structure coming to the conclusion that "the standard path of the mythological adventure of the hero is a magnification of the formula represented in the rites of passage: *separation—initiation—return.*" He goes on to describe the paradigmatic adventure: "A hero ventures forth from the world of common day into a region of supernatural wonder: fabulous forces are there encountered and a decisive victory is won: the hero comes back from this mysterious adventure with the power to bestow boons on his fellow man."[29] Although Campbell has worked out the variant possibilities of this pattern in great detail, those details are of less importance to our concern with the Mesoamerican myths than is the general pattern. It is that pattern, with one major modification, that links the two great Mesoamerican hero myths to the cycle of rulership.

The modification is of the greatest significance. Both Quetzalcoatl and the hero twins of the *Popol Vuh* are "called," as are all the heroes of world mythology, by a supernatural figure to leave their normal lives and enter an initiatory alien world in which they must confront a series of trials and accomplish the hero deeds proper to that realm. But following their initiation they die to that world to become heavenly bodies rather than returning to their former world with the boon they have won, which is the more usual pattern. Their apotheosis is a merging—what Campbell often calls an "at-onement"—with the world of the spirit, or, more precisely, a merging with the fundamental cycle of reality represented most basically by the sun. Their "return," in Campbell's sense, is thus the cyclical return of the heavenly body each becomes—the sun, moon, or Venus—a return that symbolizes the renewal of the cycle. The hero has become one with the cycle that he manifested earlier, and so it will be with the ruler. While the particular ruler will not return, the spiritual force of which he is but a manifestation will "rise again" in the person of his successor to the mat of rulership, just as life will inevitably return after death. That cyclic return that allows the energy of the world of the spirit to flow into the world of human life is the boon bestowed by the original heroes.

THE HERO TWINS

Of the two great Mesoamerican hero myths, it is the Maya myth of the hero twins contained within the *Popol Vuh* that most closely follows the worldwide pattern of the hero journey. As with many Native American versions of the hero journey, this myth presents us with twins—two sets of twins, in fact—rather than a single hero. Their exploits take place in that liminal time after the creation of the world but before the creation of the sun and moon, the time in which the Maker, Modeler was still trying, unsuccessfully, to create a viable humanity. The exploits are recounted in three segments. First we see the hero twins, Hunahpu and Xbalanque, vanquishing Seven Macaw and his offspring Zipacna and Earthquake "on the face of the Earth," as the narrative puts it. Then the story flashes back to its second segment, "the telling and accounting of the begetting" of the twins, a description involving the exploits in Xibalba, the underworld, of an earlier set of twins, One Hunahpu and Seven Hunahpu, the father and uncle, respectively, of Hunahpu and Xbalanque. The final segment relates the adventures of the hero twins in Xibalba, adventures that culminate in their apotheosis as the sun and the moon.

That this tripartite tale is to be seen as a cycle, in the order in which it is narrated, becomes clear when, keeping that final apotheosis in mind, we return to the beginning of the story, a time when "the face of the sun-moon" was still "clouded over," and read the claim of "the one who magnified himself," Seven Macaw: "I am their sun and I am their light." In that first segment the hero twins demonstrated that he was only an impostor, and their final apotheosis at the end of the tale allowed their own inner strength to show the true sun and moon. That they are the heroes who will set things right is suggested by beginning their story with this defeat of the false sun, which they will finally replace. Only after that beginning *in medias res* are we given the cyclic account of their lives.

And that account begins, in its turn, with the exploits of their supernatural father and uncle, sons of the original creator couple, Xpiyacoc and Xmucane, who had themselves set out on a hero journey into Xibalba. In their encounter with the lords of Xibalba they failed the hero task, but their failure was a prelude to success as it served to establish the task to be achieved by their sons and nephews. Great ballplayers, One Hunahpu and Seven Hunahpu had disturbed the lords of Xibalba with the noise created by their playing on the earth. Summoned to the underworld to play against the lords, they failed to surmount the various trials they encountered on the way. They could not distinguish between wooden manikins and the true lords of Xibalba sitting as guardians of the underworld; they could not foresee that the bench they were themselves to sit on was red hot; they could not preserve intact the torches and cigars given them at the beginning of the night. In consequence, they were sacrificed and buried by the lords of Xibalba.

But before burial One Hunahpu's head was cut off and, at the direction of the lords of Xibalba, "put . . . in the fork of the tree that stands by the road." This was the road, of course, that led to Xibalba, the Black Road they had taken and the same Black Road the later hero twins would follow, and the tree inevitably recalls to us the world tree that sustains life in the earthly realm and that links the upper and lower worlds of the spirit to this middle realm. Through a series of miraculous events, the now-fleshless head of One Hunahpu, which had become identical with the fruit of the tree, impregnated a maiden named Blood Girl, causing her to bear the hero twins after fleeing her home in Xibalba and overcoming a series of her own trials on earth while pregnant with them, trials that already suggest the twins' hero nature. It is significant, of course, that these trials take place in the cyclical context of death in the process of generating life.

Passing the threshold of birth, Hunahpu and Xbalanque began their adventures as children, even as infants, by vanquishing the jealous sons of their father's earlier marriage, turning them into monkeys in an echo of the earlier attempt at the creation of humans through the creation of wooden dolls. Following further childhood exploits, the twins were led to discover the ball game gear of their father and uncle—that is, their heritage and, in that important sense, their identity as heroes. As the sons of One Hunahpu, the nephews of Seven Hunahpu, their future course was set. True to that destiny, they too played the ball game, angered the lords of Xibalba, were summoned to Xibalba, and confronted the trials their predecessors encountered, undergoing what Linda Schele calls "an Underworld rite of passage."[30]

These exploits constitute the third segment of the story, a segment in which Hunahpu and Xbalanque succeed where the earlier twins failed. They succeed by using their wits against the superior power of the lords, but the reader cannot help but feel that their triumph is due as well to "a benign power everywhere supporting" them.[31] Ultimately, after what seems to be their sacrificial death, they vanquish death itself and finally take their leave, having completely conquered all of Xibalba. "And then the two boys ascended this way, here into the middle of the light, and they ascended straight on into the sky, and the sun belongs to one and the moon to the other. When it became light within the sky, on the face of the earth, they were there in the sky."

Their death is not a death but an apotheosis, a merging with the life force itself, or, put another way, an identification with or a becoming of the cycle that their lives had manifested. In the paradigmatic course of their lives, as that final statement indicates, Hunahpu and Xbalanque move along the vertical axis of the cosmos, traversing all of the realms and uniting all of the oppositions of matter and spirit: sky, earth, and underworld; life and death; day and night. In so doing they share the essence of the heroes of all mythology, for as Joseph Campbell points out, "The hero's sphere of action is not the transcendent but here, now, in the field of time, of good and evil—of the pairs of opposites. Whenever one moves out of the transcendent, one comes into a field of opposites."[32] Having moved into that field of opposites, the hero twins accomplish there a complete cycle, for it is the wholeness of the cycle that ultimately unites what would seem, from any partial view, to be opposed states; in fact, it is that very unity and wholeness within Mesoamerican spiritual thought that *is* the transcendent.

Schele and Freidel comment on the remarkable structural parallels between the two sets of twins and the Maya ruler:

> The first descent and sacrifice was of [One Hunahpu and Seven Hunahpu], the first set of twins. The second descent into Xibalba, which resulted in the sacrifice, was made by the Hero Twins, Hunahpu and Xbalanque. They sacrificed each other in order to trick the Lords of Xibalba into defeat. The third descent is that of the king in his guise as the avatar of the Hero Twins. This descent can be accomplished by two means—his own ecstatic journey through bloodletting or by the decapitation of a captive who goes as his messenger.[33]

In the same vein Arthur Miller applies this cyclical pattern of the hero journey undergone by the hero twins to the institution of rulership among the Maya, saying that it

> can be interpreted as a Maya explanation of why and how certain individuals become rulers, characterizing them as cyclically passing through the Underworld to emerge, reborn, as the next generation of a ruling family. In the *Popol Vuh,* the Hero Twins, probably representatives of rulers in general, emerge from the Underworld caves as the sun and Venus. It seems likely that the sun and Venus become astronomical symbols for rule itself, symbols which appear to have been invoked in the imagery of royal funerary contexts at Tikal and elsewhere in the Maya lowlands. . . . [Thus] rulers, as in the myth of the Hero Twins, were not subject to death in the Underworld. Rather they emerged in the form of their legitimate heirs.[34]

While this formulation certainly captures the connection between the hero twins and the ruler, from the Maya perspective it is perhaps not so much that the previous rulers "emerged in the form of their legitimate heirs." Rather, the spirit that animated the parents has now passed to the children, who now "shelter the god." Like the ball game gear symbolic of the hero twins' heritage and destiny, this spirit will enable the new ruler to traverse, for himself and for his people, the trials he will face in his journey to his own apotheosis. Thus the essential meaning of the tale of the hero twins echoes that of the imagery on the stelae we discussed above. Serge Gruzinski conveys this mythic reality in his discussion of comparable figures in the Basin of Mexico and their relationship to the mythic paradigm established by Quetzalcoatl. In the lives of these man-gods,

> all became a ritual, a liturgy, a predestined and mystical journey. "The man-gods completed on earth an obligatory trajectory, fixed in the divine world before the beginning of this time,"[35] for their lives were subject to a pre-established scheme whose beginning and often whose end were determined once and for all. . . . Did the man-god die? He left. He was not born; he returned. . . . Some man-gods arrived, others went away: the fire passed into new human receptacles according to the ineluctable rhythm of the cycles.[36]

QUETZALCOATL

The idea of the mystical, cyclical journey provides the essential link between the mythic heroes of the Maya and of the Basin of Mexico. Both are "more-or-less human" heroes of paradigmatic tales set in a liminal time between the age of the gods prior to the creation of the earth and man in the present age, and both ultimately merge with "the ineluctable rhythm of the cycles." But when we deal with the myths embodying Quetzalcoatl, we encounter a problem not presented by the hero twins of the Maya. The story of the mythic hero of the Basin of Mexico exists in a large number of variant tales, all telling what is clearly the same story but varying the details of that story substantially. From the host of surviving versions of the myth,[37] we have selected two rather different tellings to give a sense of the variety that confronts the scholar in search of *the* story of Quetzalcoatl. Both of these versions, it must be remembered, were actually recorded some time after the Conquest, as were all of the extant narratives of Quetzalcoatl, and we must therefore expect to find a certain degree of interplay between the indigenous and the Christian traditions and worldviews. Which of the two versions we present is closer to the original conception it is difficult to tell, although the version from the *Florentine Codex* seems less indebted to the European narrative tradition in the telling of the ancient tale.

An additional problem presented by Quetzalcoatl is that in these variant tales he has several identities and functions, of which the hero who serves as a paradigm of the ruler is but one. In presenting the myths of creation we have already seen Quetzalcoatl as a creator god, the white aspect of the quadripartite Tezcatlipoca and therefore an aspect of Ometeotl. And in our presentation of the myths of fertility we have seen that Ehecatl, the divine force of the wind in its fertility function (see Image 26), is an aspect of Quetzalcoatl (or, as the archaeological evidence suggests, Quetzalcoatl is an aspect of Ehecatl). Within the Mexican mind, however, all of these seemingly disparate identities were somehow resolved into the figure of the feathered serpent (Figure 19), a fact that in itself testifies to the spiritual significance of rulership in its bringing to a focus such varied aspects of the creative force.

The Quetzalcoatl who provides the mythic paradigm of rulership is distinct from those first two, distinct in name and distinct in function and story. Only this aspect of Quetzalcoatl is called Ce Acatl and Topiltzin. Ce Acatl, meaning 1 Reed, is the date on which the hero was reputedly born, and that date, a year bearer and one of the four that could begin a quarter of the fifty-two-year cycle, suggests that Quetzalcoatl, who not only was born on that date but also died on the same date fifty-two years later, was somehow identical in the Mesoamerican mind with the concept of the fifty-two-year cycle, arguably the most important of all the calendrical cycles. Topiltzin, actually more a title than a name, means "our prince" and clearly designates Quetzalcoatl as the mythic paradigm of the ruler. The battle continues to rage among scholars over whether this Topiltzin whose story we will consider was an actual Toltec ruler who had taken the name of the god, as the narratives read "historically" would indicate, or whether that heroic figure is essentially mythic. Until recently the "historical" contingent had the upper hand, but today's scholarship seems to be tending again toward the "mythic."[38] From our perspective, though clearly not from others, this is a distinction without a difference. All would agree that the tales of Quetzalcoatl functioned to provide a model of

FIGURE 19
The feathered serpent,
an Aztec stone sculpture

THE FLAYED GOD

rulership for the Basin of Mexico at the time of the Conquest. His three names are a sufficient demonstration of that fact in their unification of the calendrical cycle (Ce Acatl), rulership (Topiltzin), and the cosmic creative force (Quetzalcoatl). As Gillespie puts it, Quetzalcoatl was "the source and legitimator of kingship and dynasties."[39]

But as we have suggested, the story of the hero journey of Topiltzin Quetzalcoatl differs substantially from that of the Maya hero twins. Compared to the *Popol Vuh,* the tales of Topiltzin Quetzalcoatl seem relatively simple and uncomplicated. This is true in part because there is only a single hero, and in part because that hero undergoes fewer trials and adventures. Perhaps his story has been pared to the essentials as a result of the circumstances under which it was retold in the present versions, or perhaps his struggles are more internal than the adventures of the hero twins.

But while Quetzalcoatl's is basically a simple tale, its key episodes have tremendous symbolic depth, a depth not so immediately apparent in the hero twins section of the *Popol Vuh.* This is true, at least in part, because Quetzalcoatl's hero journey clearly repeats on a heroic scale the stages of a normal human life and in so doing suggests, in very human terms, the cyclical movement of the ideal world of the spirit into this world in all its carnality and then its return to the spirit. This is the journey of all our lives, the journey from the protected world of childhood into the world of adult disillusionment that may finally result in the attainment of an understanding of the true nature of life. Thus Quetzalcoatl's story unites the stages of a normal human life with the paradigmatic tale of a ruler-priest, using both to exemplify the movement of spirit into nature. His adventures are not fantastic exploits in Xibalba but rather a magnified version of those common to humanity. Here we deal with Oedipus's inner journey rather than Ulysses's outer one.

The depth of the tale arises also from its tragic component. While both the hero twins and Quetzalcoatl suffer an initiatory fall, a reversal of fortunes, Quetzalcoatl's seems real, while the circumstances surrounding that of the hero twins persuades us that their difficulties and ultimate death are only apparent; we know they are gods who will succeed where their father and uncle failed, who will survive where their predecessors died. But there is no comparable prelude to the tale of Quetzalcoatl and no such sense of assurance for us, since, as we know, many fail to overcome the adversities he faces. It is thus important that the machinations of the sorcerers who bring about Quetzalcoatl's fall may be seen on another level as failings of the divine hero, "human" weaknesses that cause his undoing. While the hero twins "fall" into the underworld, where their trials will take place, Quetzalcoatl "falls" from an ideal, divine life into a human one, with all of its attendant suffering.

The pattern of separation—initiation—return in the tale of Quetzalcoatl is thus different in detail from that of the hero twins, but it is equally clear. After a miraculous birth, the details of which vary from tale to tale, Quetzalcoatl grew up, living a penitent, sheltered life, and became ruler-priest of Tollan. He ruled wisely, abjuring human sacrifice, and created a utopian kingdom reminiscent of those of the Golden Age of Old World tales. The myths make it clear that Tollan was an expression of its ruler: all of its wisdom and art "started and proceeded from Quetzalcoatl." The mythic city and its ruler were "a symbolic complex of ideal harmony, . . . less a historical city than a paradigm of perfectly blended individual piety and public statecraft."[40] That life of peace and plenty, however, was not an end but a beginning. The insight of Joseph Campbell that we quoted above indicates why: "The hero's sphere of action is not the transcendent but here, now, in the field of time, of good and evil—of the pairs of opposites. Whenever one moves out of the transcendent, one comes into a field of opposites."[41] As a hero, Quetzalcoatl must leave that "ideal harmony" to confront the forces operative in the field of opposites.

And his initial virtue there finds its opposite in Tezcatlipoca, who takes the shape of one or more sorcerers in various versions of the tale. Although it would be easy to characterize this conflict as one between the good Quetzalcoatl and the evil Tezcatlipoca—a characterization that is certainly true on one level—it must be remembered that Quetzalcoatl and Tezcatlipoca are, on another level, complementary parts of the unity that is Ometeotl, as we have seen in our consideration of the myths of creation, and that Tezcatlipoca, far from being merely an evil antagonist to the pure Quetzalcoatl, is, on that level, the generative force made manifest. Thus the fact that these sorcerers are Tezcatlipoca is of monumental significance, for all who heard the tale knew that "if ever there was an Aztec supreme god, it was Tezcatlipoca; patron not only of sorcery but of warriors and the ruling dynasty, he was the giver and taker away of life, like the Hindu god Shiva. With his magic mirror, he could look into the hearts of men."[42]

The sorcerers, alter egos of Quetzalcoatl in various ways in the variant tales, conspire to make him aware of both his physicality and his darker side, both of which had played little role in his life to that point. In the most metaphoric of the tales, exemplified here by the version from the *Anales,* that physicality is presented to him through a mirror brought by Tezcatlipoca, whose name means "smoking mirror," in order to "give him his body to see." And in that magical mirror this man-god, whose life had been up to now one of the spirit, saw, as if for the first time, his *physical* being, his own mortality, and in stark contrast to his spiritual being, it appeared ugly, gross, disfigured; seeing himself darkly through the mirror of Tezcatlipoca, he "was filled with fear." His response, at the urging of the sorcerer, was to cover his body with plumed finery and his face with a wondrous mask, thereby using the logic of the mask whereby the inner becomes outer to restore his appearance and his confidence.

This is his first initiation into the depths of the world of nature, in which each state finds its opposite. But it is only a beginning, for appearance and reality coexist on many levels. That magical mirror that revealed his distorted body leads next to the revelation of a distorted soul, as Sahagún's version of the tale makes clear. This time the sorcerers bring him pulque as a healing, liberating potion, "good, soothing, and intoxicating. If thou shalt drink of it, it will relieve and heal thy body." But it will also precipitate him further into the field of opposites, the world of nature: "Thou shalt weep; thy heart will become troubled. Thou shalt think upon thy death. And also thou shalt think upon where thou shalt go." These thoughts of mortality suggest both the most fundamental initiatory revelation and the way to what Campbell calls the "culminating insight." As Sahagún's informants put it in relating the sorcerer's answer to Quetzalcoatl's question, "Where am I to go, old one?": "Thou shalt go there to Tollan Tlapallan. A man there standeth guard, one already aged. Ye shall consult with each other. And when thou shalt return here, thou shalt again have been made a child."

Marvelously simple, that reply stands as a metaphor for all that the hero journey of Quetzalcoatl has to reveal. In it we see the essentially cyclic nature of life in which death is not an end but the prelude to rebirth. We see the necessity of paying the heavy price of passing through the sometimes seemingly unrelieved pain and ugliness of life to come to wisdom, a necessity that forms the essence of the tragic nature of life, "the sense of ancient evil, of 'the blight man was born for,' of the permanence and the mystery of human suffering. . . . By most men it must be learned, and learned through direct, immediate experience; that is, through suffering."[43]

According to Willard Gingerich, that tragic sense lay at the heart of the Nahuatl conception of the nature of man:

> The individual, infused with a moral energy in the timeless chaos of preternatural darkness before birth, is turned loose to survive or perish according to his own devices in a cut-throat, vicious reality. He may at any moment be confronted with violence of personal, social, or divine origin. He is morally independent but may be doomed; he is freighted with fate but must work out his own destiny in fear and humility. Tragedy . . . is simply the normal condition of everyday affairs.[44]

The liberating draft of pulque, actually a carefully specified four drafts to mirror the quadripartite nature of reality and a final fifth to unlock the center, leads to further, deeper suffering, a deeper immersion in the destructive element. In an episode handled very discreetly by all the texts that include it, the drunken Quetzalcoatl calls for his sister to share his pulque-caused liberation, and after drinking together, they fall from their divine, spiritual state into a grossly physical one symbolized most clearly by their implied sexual relationship. Truly Quetzalcoatl has been given "his body to see." This is an initiation into a very different reality from the one he had lived earlier.

Following this multifaceted initiatory experience, the various versions of the tales play out the consequences in a variety of ways. It is in this segment of the hero journey that the version of the tale told by Sahagún's informants fascinates, especially as it is related to rulership. The events that constitute Quetzalcoatl's fall occur in the second section of Sahagún's narrative.[45] In an abrupt shift, section three begins a series of six sections telling of other mischief caused by Tezcatlipoca in his manifestation as Titlacahuan, but it is striking that these episodes do not deal with Quetzalcoatl. Rather they begin with the story of the sexual temptation of the daughter of Uemac and continue with various other problems suffered by the Toltecs during Uemac's reign. Why, we must wonder, do the narrators shift their focus from Quetzalcoatl to Uemac, an illustrious Toltec ruler mentioned in all of the historical accounts? Why does Quetzalcoatl not reappear until the tenth section, which deals with his leaving Tollan in disgrace after the events narrated in section two?

These are difficult questions to answer unequivocally. Some scholars contend that Quetzalcoatl and Uemac are the same person, while others see them as contemporaries—Quetzalcoatl as high priest, Uemac as ruler. No single explanation, however, is able to account for all the evidence in the various tales. Two things, however, seem clear. First, the implications of Quetzalcoatl's fall are specifically related through these episodes to his function as the paradigmatic ruler. Second, his fall not only causes his personal suffering but also causes his city and his people to suffer. Perhaps the tale also suggests that Quetzalcoatl's fall has consequences going beyond his immediate time, consequences reaching into the later history of his people, conceived here not only as Toltecs but also as the Aztecs who succeeded them and who were telling and hearing the tale,[46] consequences that surely mark the story of Quetzalcoatl as a Mesoamerican rendition of the tragic vision, a vision generally exemplified in a tale of a person of high position who undergoes a fall due, in significant part, to his own human weakness.

But that tragic vision in general is not one of unrelieved suffering. Rather it is the double vision that sees both suffering and reconciliation, what Campbell calls in another context "the paradox of the dual focus" characteristic of myth.[47] If one can accept the existence of human weakness—as one surely must—and the suffering that results from that weakness, one may also see the greatness that coexists with that weakness. Quetzalcoatl is the man-god who cannot deal with the weaknesses of his body, but he is also the man-god who in the opening portion of his story established a kingdom of the spirit here on earth. Now, in the concluding segment of the tale, he will renounce this world to return to the spirit whence he came. Calling for the destruction of the grandeur that was Tollan, he leaves his city on his fated journey "there to Tollan Tlapallan," to the sunrise. Significantly, this progression leads toward the Gulf coast, and his death or disappearance occurs in many of the variants only when he reaches the regenerative primal water of the sea after a series of symbolic episodes. Despite the fact that the death of Quetzalcoatl occurs in a number of ways and at a number of places in the various versions,[48] that death is an apotheosis: "He had gone to the sky, he had entered the sky. The old people say that he was changed to the star that appears at dawn. Therefore they say it appeared when Quetzalcoatl died, and so they called him Lord of the House of Dawn."

Like the hero twins of the Maya, he has merged with the cycle he manifested in his life on earth. His is the complex cycle of Venus: "When he died [as the evening star] he disappeared for four days," a period in which his descent into death was imagined to have continued. Then, the beginning of resurrection: "For four days also he made himself arrows. And so in eight days he appeared," now reborn as the morning star to symbolize and herald the reentry of the world of the spirit into human affairs with the rising of the sun.[49] But those arrows he made in the first four days of his rebirth before becoming visible are vital to an understanding of Quetzalcoatl and his relationship to the paradigm of rulership. As the description of his rebirth in the *Anales* indicates, it was believed throughout Mesoamerica that the rays of Venus as morning star as it rose immediately before and thus heralded the rebirth of the sun were tremendously powerful and terribly dangerous. They were direct emanations from the world of the spirit and carried with them the awesome power associated with that realm. In this way the tragic aspect of the life of Topiltzin Quetzalcoatl manifests itself in the cyclic reality for which that life stands as a metaphor. The fact that rebirth can come only after catastrophic destruction and after a return to the spirit is a fundamental and tragic truth of the world of nature. But the ruler, as the god before him, can use his life as a guide through this world, in which "tragedy . . . is simply the normal condition of everyday affairs," a world that Sahagún's informants characterize elsewhere in the following way: "On the earth we walk, we live, on the ridge of a mountain peak sharp as a harpoon blade. To one side is an abyss, to the other side is another abyss. If you go here, or if you go there, you will fall, only through the middle can one go, or live."[50]

Judging from the evidence unearthed by archaeologists, the tragic tale, in some form, must be ancient. From perhaps as early as 900 B.C. we find carved in stone an Olmec plumed serpent whose arching body forms a sheltering womblike enclosure for a seated figure bedecked with symbolic regalia (Image 47). His towering, intricate headdress is reminiscent of much later Maya creations and may well signify his status as ruler and even his identity. While the satchellike bag he carries in his extended right hand is the mark of the religious functionary throughout Mesoamerican history, it was also carried by rulers on ceremonial occasions. Thus, like the Topiltzin Quetzalcoatl of our tales, this figure seems to be specifically identified as both ruler and priest. But ruler or priest or ruler-priest, he must certainly be seen as an expression of that powerful plumed serpent who rears above him, and to make that truth doubly clear, the human figure's face is depicted as emerging from the mouth of a mask/helmet identical to the serpent's head. Symbolically, this image insists that its central figure functioned to allow the sacred order residing in the realm of the spirit to enter the mundane world of that society. In so doing the Olmec image connects, in paradigmatic fashion, the plumed serpent with rulership in the first of the great civilizations Mesoamerica was to produce.

Although the Olmecs penetrated into the Basin of Mexico and left there compelling evidence of the mythic connection between their rulers and the gods, it is in the art of the first great center of civilization native to the Basin of Mexico, Teotihuacan, that we find the prototypical images of the plumed serpent (see Image 18) as that image existed among the later Toltecs and Aztecs. It is significant that in that fabled city, those images were chosen to adorn the staircase of the pyramid that served as the base for the temple within what is now known as the Ciudadela, the compound thought by archaeologists to have been the seat of the government of Teotihuacan and of the far-flung empire it ruled. That staircase lined with the masks of the god must have been of immense importance, for the stairways of pyramids throughout Mesoamerica provided ritual access to the temples crowning them. According to Mircea Eliade, "The act of climbing or ascending symbolizes *the way towards the absolute reality.*"[51] Those images of plumed serpents lining the stairway of what has come to be known as the Temple of Quetzalcoatl at Teotihuacan are a visual metaphor for the function of the ruler of that great city. He was himself the deity (i.e., absolute reality) in his punctual aspect, and in his ascending those stairs in ritual he channeled the energies of the realm of the spirit into the daily lives of his people, his city, and his empire.

At what is thought to have been the capital of the successor state in the Basin of Mexico to the power of Teotihuacan, Toltec Tula, relatively little remains to remind the visitor of that god symbolized by the feathered serpent. This is strange, since in the myths that have come down to us, Quetzalcoatl is presented, as we have seen, as the ruler of the Toltecs. Or perhaps this is not so strange since the battle between scholars over the proper identification of the Tollan of the myths and of Topiltzin Quetzalcoatl as a particular ruler of that city continues to rage. The basic positions are relatively simple. The myths depict the Toltecs, whose capital was Tollan, as the bringers of culture to the Basin of Mexico. Larger than life, these Toltecs provide an image of "the ideal city and sovereign ruler in Mesoamerica."[52] One group of scholars, until recently a large majority, sees these depictions of the Toltecs as history, exaggerated perhaps, but an essentially accurate record of the doings of the historical people known as Toltecs. For these scholars the mythical Tollan is Tula, the ancient city located in the present state of Hidalgo, and Ce Acatl Topiltzin Quetzalcoatl was one of its rulers. For them, his name suggests that he was a man who identified himself with the god symbolized by the feathered serpent.

Other scholars, however, take an opposed position. Seeing the myths as essentially similar to the Old World tales of a Golden Age, these scholars see Tollan as a mythical construct, perhaps identified in later years with Teotihuacan, that served to image forth the ideal state in its paradigmatic form. For them, Ce Acatl Topiltzin Quetzalcoatl is a creature of myth—in Old World terms, a legendary figure—comparable in function to King Arthur, for example. It is not necessary, of course, to hold either position in its extreme form, and Quetzalcoatl and his capital, Tollan, have often been seen as quasi-mythical or quasi-historical. From our perspective in this presentation of the myths of Mesoamerica, the "historical accuracy" of the tales is of secondary importance. That they functioned as myths to set forth in metaphoric terms the paradigm of rulership is clear and would be granted by even the most hardened historian.

THE MIGRATION MYTHS

The merging of history and myth that we find in the tales of Topiltzin Quetzalcoatl and the consequent battles among scholars as to their "historical accuracy" are even more pronounced in the final category of myths we will present. These myths of origin, often called migration myths, recount the genesis and development through time of a people. This development is always characterized as a series of movements, a purposeful migration from the place of origin through a series of trials undergone in a number of places to a destined place of settlement where they will prosper. Whatever the "historical accuracy" of any of the individual tales, the pattern remains constant and is clearly reminiscent of the hero journey, in these cases applied to a people rather than an individual, like those we have discussed in the tales of the hero twins and of Quetzalcoatl.

In all of them the land of origin is far away, usually in the north (Image 52). The people depart from that northern land as the result of a dramatic event, often at the direction of a god, and this departure is always recorded as taking place on a date that marks the beginning of a new era. They leave the original homeland in the company of other groups, but those groups split off during the southward trek. That trek follows a route pointed out by a god or a messenger from the world of the spirit or by leaders who are manifestations on earth of that world of the spirit, and the destination of these chosen people is identified by a series of supernatural signs. These characteristics, taken together, delineate the mythic pattern of the migration journey, which defined a people and explained their relationship to close and distant neighbors and to the world of the spirit, the ultimate place of origin.

From the point of view of our concern with the mythic conception of rulership in Mesoamerica, it is of great significance that these migration tales bring together, almost to a point of fusion, the people, their ruler, and the god whom they conceive as their patron. This patron god, often called a tutelary god, at times appears in human form, especially at moments of crisis, but more typically is represented by his image or by a sacred bundle, usually carried by a "god bearer" who mediates between the god and his people, serving as a conduit of sorts for instructions that came to him shamanistically in dreams or visions. This three-way relationship between god, leader, and people embodied in the myth describes the Mesoamerican conception of rulership from a different angle of vision from that employed in the paradigmatic myths of Quetzalcoatl and the hero twins, but the ultimate identity of the two can be seen in the *Popol Vuh.* The migration of the Quiché that is described in the final segment of that work takes place under the guidance of Tohil, their patron god, and Jaguar Quitze, their original leader. According to Tedlock, this migration was probably conceived "as a reenactment of the adventures of Hunahpu and Xbalanque in Xibalba."[53]

THE AZTEC MIGRATION MYTH

While any of the extant migration myths might have been presented to illustrate the fundamental pattern they all follow, we have selected the Aztec variant of the basic myth both because it exists in the most varied forms and because it is the most celebrated and best known. In all of its versions it traces the movement of the Mexica, the particular Aztec group about whom we know most, from the place of their humble origins, a place to the north associated with an island or a series of seven caves or both, to Tenochtitlan, the island site of their imperial splendor and their ultimate conquest by Cortés and the Spaniards. In the course of that movement, they journey from place to place, each place associated with an event of symbolic significance, a movement closely associated, in most of the tales, with their tutelary god, Huitzilopochtli (Figure 20). He directs their course, prophesies their final destination, and, like Athena among the Greeks, materializes at critical moments to help them surmount the formidable difficulties that arise.

FIGURE 20
The Aztec Huitzilopochtli from the *Codex Borbonicus*

Such myths testify eloquently to the correctness of Alfredo López Austin's description, taken from an ancient source, of the tutelary god as the heart of the people, "el 'corazón del pueblo,' *altepetl iyollo,*" and to his interpretation of that description as meaning more precisely "spirit or soul" than "heart."[54] Thus we must see such gods as Huitzilopochtli in a twofold manner. On the one hand they clearly act as a guiding force, the embodiment of the destiny of their people; but on the other hand, they image forth something even more basic—the essential nature or spirit of their peoples, the quality that determines or fits them for that destiny. Gaster's definition of their role throughout the world clarifies this concept as it relates to the role of the ruler:

> The king and the tribal god . . . are two aspects of the same phenomenon, viewed respectively from the standpoint of the real and of the ideal. The *king* personifies or epitomizes the "spirit" or character of a living community, as it exists in a particular moment of time. The *tribal god,* on the other hand, personifies or epitomizes the "essence" of that community conceived as an ideal, transcendental entity of which the living generation is but the present phase.[55]

The Aztec ideal may thus be seen through the image of their tutelary god, Huitzilopochtli, "the divine embodiment of the ideal Mexica warrior-leader: young, valiant, all-triumphant,"[56] and that ideal is the focal point of the myth of his birth. A good deal of evidence, much of it unearthed recently by archaeologists working at Tenochtitlan's Templo Mayor in the heart of today's Mexico City, suggests that the Aztecs placed that myth at the very center of their own magnificent city and of their ritual life, just as it formed the center of their consciousness as a people.

According to the myth, Huitzilopochtli was said to have been miraculously conceived by Coatlicue, the earth goddess (Image 23), when "a ball of fine feathers," fell on her one day as she was performing penance by sweeping near her home on Coatepec, Serpent Mountain. Her "husbandless" pregnancy was seen as shameful by her children, Coyolxauhqui (Image 24) and the Centzonuitznaua, the four hundred (i.e., countless) gods of the south, and they resolved to kill her. Still in her womb, Huitzilopochtli vowed to protect his mother. As the four hundred led by Coyolxauhqui approached, Huitzilopochtli, born at that moment, struck her with his fire serpent and cut off her head. Her body "went rolling down the hill, it fell to pieces," and her destruction was followed by Huitzilopochtli's routing her four hundred followers and arraying himself in their ornaments.

Such a story has many levels of implication. Scholars have seen it as an allegory depicting the cyclical "routing" of the moon and stars by the rising of the daytime sun, and they have dealt at length with the series of male/female oppositions it embodies, seeing them as revelatory of the fundamental dualism at the heart of Aztec spiritual thought. In addition to those views, however, and more to the point of our concern (and that of the Aztecs, one suspects), the story has a great deal to suggest to us about the Aztec conception of rulership. According to Gillespie, "The origin of the dynasty is mirrored in the preceding origin of the tutelary deity, a celestial god, out of the earth, his mother." Thus "the mother of the Tenochtitlan kings was also the mother of the gods and is the earth that gives birth to all life."[57]

Since the tutelary god embodies as well the spirit of the people, the myth deals also with the nature of and relationship between the Aztecs and the world, in their view an essentially spiritual one, they inhabited. They were a warrior people who saw their destiny in the same way as did their predecessors in the Basin of Mexico, the peoples of Tollan and Teotihuacan. As the migration myth makes clear, battle was their "work"; they would "await the peoples from the four directions" and "join battle with them," bringing together these "diverse peoples" through conquest. This destiny, however, a destiny expressed metaphorically in the nature of their divine patron, was not merely the formation of a secular empire. More important, they were destined to bring together again all of the peoples who had formed the original unity, a unity split asunder through the events of the migration, thus restoring the perfection of the world of the spirit.

Because the myth deals, on another level, with the cyclical return of the sun, it would seem to insist that we see that Aztec destiny as part of a larger cyclical pattern, the pattern that saw their predecessors, the peoples of Teotihuacan and of Tollan, undergo the same migration and rise to preeminence, only to fall from that position and disappear into the "night" or "death" of the past. This is, of course, precisely the pattern of the hero journey that we have traced in the life of Topiltzin Quetzalcoatl, ruler of Tollan. In that connection the Aztec migration tale told by Sahagún's informants, a tale that differs markedly from those found elsewhere, is fascinating in its relating the migration of the Aztecs, and specifically the Mexica, to those preceding peoples. Although not divided by its narrator, the myth falls clearly into three segments. The first, rather brief, section details the arrival of the first people "in this land" from a place "over the water." Led by priests who spoke for their god, they settled in Tamoanchan, the mythical site of the creation of humanity in other tales. In this story, however, it is also the place where humanity shall dwell: "That which lieth here, that which spreadeth germinating, that which resteth in the earth, is your merit, your gift." So saying, the priests, "those who carried the gods on their backs," departed, taking with them "the writings, the books, the paintings, . . . the song books, the flutes," that is to say, "the knowledge" that constitutes the world of the spirit, leaving mankind bereft in the new world of nature.

The second segment of the tale details humanity's beginnings in this brave new world. Four wise men who remained, two of them bearing the names of the creators of present-day humanity in other tales, established the fundamental and enduring relationship this world was to have with the essential world of the spirit through the reestablishment of the sacred texts on which that relationship was founded. "They devised the book of days, the book of years, the count of the years, the book of dreams. They arranged the reckoning just as it has been kept." After this beginning, the tale recounts three successive departures from Tamoanchan, but since no returns are even suggested, it is apparent that these travels are to be read metaphorically as cyclical episodes, the returns taking place in time rather than space. The first episode recounts the building of Teotihuacan; the second, remarkably reminiscent of the myth of Topiltzin Quetzalcoatl, tells of the discovery of pulque and the ritual accompanying its use; the third describes the establishment of the ruling lineages and the beginning of the migration of each lineage group to its present home, the splitting apart of the original unity, the making of the one into the many.

At this crucial point in the tale, the point at which mythic time shades gradually into historical time, the various groups make their way to Chicomoztoc, the place of seven caves and the archetypal place of origin in many other tales (Image 53). After making offerings there, they depart. "They say that they were created at Chicomoztoc, that from Chicomoztoc they came forth." But as the tale itself points out, this emergence is to be read metaphorically as the moment of the creation, of the welding together, of the particular group rather than literally as a moment of creation of life. Beyond this, Sahagún's tale provides little more than a bare outline of the specific migration of the Mexica or the other groups. It suggests, in fact, that if one wants more detail one should consult "the Mexican accounts," for in them "the places by which the Mexica passed, exist, are painted, are named."

For that account we will turn to the migration tale retold by Tezozómoc, but before examining that lengthy narration of the wanderings and eventual settlement of the Mexica Aztecs, we should think for a moment about the essence of Sahagún's tale. In it the emphasis is clearly on the long, detailed second segment, which, like the hero journeys of Quetzalcoatl and the hero twins, narrates a series of crucial events taking place in a period of mythic time before the era of historical time. That this is the case is clearly suggested by the explicit linkage of that section to the tale of Quetzalcoatl and through its concern with Teotihuacan, the mythic site of the origin of life and of the present order of reality in many other tales. In this segment we find, in order, the establishment of the basic structure of time, the foundation of the paradigmatic city, and the establishment of the nature of ritual, in the case of pulque, and the awareness that the bounty of nature must be used properly, in accord with the dictates of ritual. Only after these fundamental parameters of reality are fixed is the final requirement for civilized life, rulership, instituted. Only then, the tale suggests, can the life of historical time begin.

And Tezozómoc's tale deals with those "historical" beginnings. After a very brief description of the Mexica Aztec's beginnings in Aztlan, a description focusing brilliantly on the symbolic identification of the people, their god, and their destiny in the figure of the eagle, the story begins the episodic delineation of the adventures undergone by the Mexica in the realization of that destiny. Cast in the mold of a migration, the story focuses on five episodes, separating them with summary accounts of the migratory movements of the Mexica, which suggest that the central episodes are to be seen as taking place sequentially, each in a different locale. It is apparent, however, that such a linear, "historical" reading of the tale is meant to be complemented by a cyclical, "mythic" reading, for each of the central episodes repeats in varying form the essential details of the myth of Huitzilopochtli's birth.

The first of these central episodes is exemplary. In it is told the story of Huitzilopochtli's abandoning his sister, Malinalxoch. On the historical level, this abandonment accounts for the separation of the Mexica Aztecs, the people of Huitzilopochtli, from another group of Aztecs, the people who settled at Malinalco whose tutelary deity was Malinalxoch. On another level, however, this episode sets forth the nature of Huitzilopochtli as a warrior god whose ultimate destiny it is to reverse the historical splitting apart of groups by bringing "together the diverse peoples . . . from the four directions" through conquest, and by doing so to recreate the perfection of the original cosmic unity. Significantly, this unity is described in terms reminiscent of the paradise ruled over by Quetzalcoatl before his fall, suggesting that it must be seen metaphorically as a unity of spirit rather than as a worldly empire. But there is another mythic level here as well, one that figures centrally in each of the episodes. This story of internecine conflict is surely meant to recall to the Aztec mind the myth of Huitzilopochtli's birth, for here, as in that other myth, Huitzilopochtli's warlike nature is demonstrated in his struggle against an "evil" sister. In both cases male-female opposition is stressed, and the male, warlike Huitzilopochtli is associated with good, while the female, sorcerer sister is associated with evil. Both myths have clear astronomical implications, and both suggest the identity of the Aztec nature with the Aztec destiny.

Once that destiny has been defined, the myth moves to its second episode, in which the Mexica settle at Coatepec, a barren site that they convert to a lush island paradise by damming the river, thereby creating a settlement reminiscent of Aztlan and prefiguring Tenochtitlan. When the Mexica people and their leaders, the Centzonhuitznahua, make clear that they think Coatepec is their destined home, Huitzilopochtli reacts violently, slaying and devouring "his uncles, the Centzonhuitznahua," and decapitating his mother, Coyolxauhcihuatl, and devouring her heart. Following this destruction, he destroys the dam that had made Coatepec what it was and recommits his people to their journey to "the place off there" where they will realize their destiny. Significantly, as the Aztec listener would have known, Coatepec figured prominently in another myth dealing with Huitzilopochtli. The tale recounting that god's birth takes place at Coatepec: it is there that he is conceived, there that he is born, and there that he routs his evil sister and her followers.

The striking fact that emerges in the comparison of the myths of the birth of the god and of the migration is that while the identities of the characters change, the basic structure remains intact. Now it is the mother, Coyolcihuatl, who is sacrificially decapitated, whereas before it was the sister, Coyolxauhqui. Now the defeated Centzonhuitznahua are his uncles, the semihistorical leaders of the Mexica people, whereas before they were not leaders but the followers of his sister. Now Coatepec is the prototypical site of the settlement of the Mexica, whereas before it was the mythical site of Huitzilopochtli's conception and birth. Such kaleidoscopic shifts in identity suggest strongly that what is really important is the structure, and that structure suggests in turn that each of the specific characters and places is to be seen not as a discrete historical entity but as a manifestation of the spirit. Just as the underlying world of the spirit manifested itself in the multitudinous elaborately costumed ritual performers depicted in painted books and spiritual art throughout Mesoamerica, so that same spiritual realm is manifested variously in the characters and places of the myths.

It is thus not coincidental that the myths we are discussing consistently show Huitzilopochtli sacrificing a relative, either a female one or the offspring of a female relative. In the cyclical movement of the cosmos, creation is accomplished through the union of opposed forces such as male and female; it follows that the destruction that is the necessary complement to creation would have the opposite cause, the dissolution of that union between opposed forces. In the same way it is not coincidental that an island place of settlement is consistently associated with the Mexica, whether it be the mythic Aztlan from whence they came or the quasi-historical Coatepec, the midpoint on their journey from spirit to empire. One must remember in this connection that the world itself was conceived by the peoples of Mesoamerica as a gigantic island. Clearly the Mexica homeland was seen metaphorically as a microcosm of the world itself as well as the mythic center of that world, the point where the world of the spirit could enter human space. The Mexica were, therefore, the people through whom the cosmic destiny would be realized, the people destined through warfare and sacrifice to act as the force driving the cyclical cosmic movement.

Thus to complement the mythic Aztlan and the quasi-historical Coatepec, the main pyramid of the ceremonial center of Tenochtitlan was constructed as an artificial, but very real, Coatepec. So we have three Coatepecs, each of them situated to allow movement between spirit and matter. We might therefore see the Coatepec of the migration myth as a "middle ground" between the wholly spiritual place of origin and the very real place of settlement. Gillespie deals with this mediating function at great length,[58] showing that Coatepec links the world of the spirit to the world of nature on a number of different levels. In terms of our concern here, however, it is primarily important to note that the events at Coatepec signify *both* a continuation of the original journey *and* a new beginning. That sense of a new beginning emphasizes the cyclical nature of the tale that in turn underlies the linear, progressive story that dominates the surface level of the myth with its account of the continuing journey. It is extremely important to note that the cycle begins anew only after violence, destruction, and sacrifice. Death is the necessary precondition for rebirth in life, and ritual death—sacrifice—must precede spiritual rebirth, just as the creation of the Fifth Sun was preceded by the sacrificial death of the gods.

Putting the events of Coatepec behind them, the Mexica, led by Huitzilopochtli, journey onward. Meanwhile at Malinalco, the son of Malinalxoch, Copil, comes to maturity and vows to avenge the abandonment of his mother by her brother. He will "destroy him, . . . devour him," and ultimately replace him in the divine quest for the place of settlement, the earthly paradise. But his ambitions are dashed, and he is destroyed in the ensuing battle with Huitzilopochtli. After killing him, Huitzilopochtli opens his chest and removes his heart, directing one of his priests to take the heart and cast it away at a particular place associated in legend with Quetzalcoatl's journey to the east.

In this episode we have a further series of variations on the themes first enunciated in the myth of the birth of Huitzilopochtli. But the implications of these variations differ from those of the Coatepec episode. Here the emphasis is clearly on warfare and the institution of heart sacrifice. As is well known, warfare and its concomitant heart sacrifices, mind boggling in their reported numbers, were a central fact of Aztec communal life. But, the myth insists, they must be seen in a spiritual context. Through these means the Mexica sought to spiritualize matter, to get beyond the vicissitudes of life to the essence of it. It is significant, therefore, that the myth explicitly associates the heart sacrifice of Copil with Quetzalcoatl's journey to the east, the scene of his apotheosis, the land of the spirit.

Elizabeth Boone suggests that the central structure in Tenochtitlan's ceremonial center, the artificial Coatepec, was the site of ritual that made the same metaphoric association: "The Templo Mayor was . . . conceived iconographically to express an analogy between the mythic victory of Huitzilopochtli over his sister following his miraculous birth and the success of the Mexica over their enemies. Each war captive dispatched on the sacrificial stone before the shrine of Huitzilopochtli thus repeated symbolically the god's own victory over his adversaries."[59] Such a statement refers even more clearly to the mythic sacrifice of Copil, from whose heart, as we shall see, "grew" both the city of Tenochtitlan and that very Templo Mayor. Life, as the Aztecs knew, grew from death.

After this sacrifice the Mexica resume their journey, coming to Tizaapan, where they learn to cook and eat the snakes that were thought to make the place uninhabitable. This might seem a rather straightforward "adventure," but when one realizes the extent of the symbolism associated with snakes in connection with Huitzilopochtli, its significance becomes clearer. Born on Coatepetl, "Serpent Hill," to a mother named Coatlicue, "She of the Serpent Skirt," he immediately destroys his sister with his Xiuhcoatl, "Lightning Serpent." All of this suggests the intimate relationship of the serpent with sacrifice that we have seen in the previous section, further underscores the essential part sacrifice plays in suggesting cyclical renewal in the migration myths, and in still another way links the birth myth to the migration myth.

Sacrifice is again the focus of the ensuing events that precipitate the Mexica's leaving Tizaapan. Read on a literal level, their horror seems senseless, but mythically the flaying of Achitometl's slain daughter allows Yaocihuatl, the "grandmother" of Huitzilopochtli, to manifest herself. What we have here is precisely the same separation of inner essence from outer covering that we have discussed above in connection with Xipe Totec and with Toci. The living human being who is the daughter of Achitometl shelters the goddess within her body, and when the outer covering of that body is removed and worn as a mask by the priest, he *becomes* the god at the ritual moment.[60] The tale emphasizes this duality by registering the horror of her father, who must necessarily see his daughter, the human being, in the midst of the ritual through which the spiritual essence, Yaocihuatl, can manifest herself. After the institution of sacrifice in the earlier episode, this one "explains" its meaning. And, like each of the earlier sacrificial episodes, this one propels the Mexica forward in their quest for Tenochtitlan, their destined place of settlement.

The final episode of the myth details their finding of the destined place. The leaders of the Mexica, who bear the idol of the god, have been directed to look for certain signs that will identify their place of settlement. When they see the first of these—white cypresses, white willows, white reeds, white rushes as well as white aquatic creatures—all reminiscent of Aztlan, their place of origin, they begin to hope. "Perhaps it is to be here," they think. Huitzilopochtli then appears in the night to one of the idol bearers, providing more precise instructions. They are to seek out a cactus on which will stand an eagle eating the heartlike fruit of the cactus. Soon, "in among the rushes, in among the reeds," they find the cactus and the eagle, and when that great bird acknowledges their approach, they realize that they have indeed found the site of "the city that shall be ours." It is of the utmost importance to the meaning of the myth that the cactus on which the eagle stands is growing from the heart of Copil, which had been cast away at the direction of Huitzilopochtli at that very spot in the earlier episode. From that sacrificial act the new era, the new cycle, can begin. The Mexica are now a settled people leading a communal life through which they will realize the mandate of their god. As the leaders say, echoing the cry of Huitzilopochtli in the opening stages of the myth, "There we shall be, we shall keep guard, we shall await, we shall meet the diverse peoples in battle." Their actual battles with their "brothers" and "sisters," and the ensuing sacrifices, will reenact the episodes of the myth, keeping the cosmic cycle in motion, ceaselessly turning matter into spirit.

Gillespie emphasizes this cyclical pattern in her interpretation of the myth:

> The reality faced in Aztec cosmology was that death was essential for the completion of a cycle, thereby paving the way for the birth of a new cycle and the continuance of life. The deaths of the women [as well as the death of Copil] propelled the Mexica onward in a cyclical fashion, for although they ostensibly traveled to different cities prior to finally founding Tenochtitlan, they were actually returning each time to the metaphorical promised land—Aztlan, Coatepec, Chapultepec, Tizaapan, Tenochtitlan—which was both the beginning and the end of the cycle.[61]

Each repetition of the pattern emphasized the spiritual birth and the spiritual nature of the Aztec state. Because the migration "began in the realm of the gods and moved slowly to the Basin of Mexico, the realm of secular kings, it thereby recapitulated the cosmogony—the origin of the cosmos—within Mexican phylogeny—the development of society."[62]

One last myth, this one retold by Durán, emphasizes even more strongly the spiritual nature of the Aztec state. It tells of the expedition sent by the emperor Motecuhzoma I, the ancestor of the later Motecuhzoma, who saw the cycle's end in his encounter with Cortés, to seek out and learn more about the place of origin, Chicomoztoc, the Seven Caves (Color Plate 24, Image 53). He is advised that he cannot expect warriors to find such a place but that he must send sorcerers instead for only they will be able to find a place of the spirit. And soon enough, after traveling normally as far as Coatepec, and from there traveling magically through the world of the spirit to the place of origin, they find Coatlicue, still grieving for her missing son, and a people who remember the events and people surrounding the origins of the Mexica but who know nothing of the present Mexica reality. For the inhabitants of Chicomoztoc, time does not pass as it does in this world. The Mexica envoys also find that they do not have the strength or the energy of these inhabitants of the world of the spirit, a lack that is to be attributed to their worldly nourishment. "Such food and drink, my children, have made you heavy and they make it difficult for you to reach the place of your ancestors," an elder advises them in a statement that is itself heavy with metaphoric import. He continues, "The wealth you have we know nothing about; we live poorly and simply," obviously implying that the world of the spirit values another sort of wealth.

This interchange is repeated, and thus emphasized, when the envoys meet Coatlicue, who sends with them a simple mantle and loincloth for her son, clearly to remind him of his origins. She commands the envoys to tell him that as soon as his time comes, he is to return; she is awaiting that return. The message here would seem to be twofold. First, all the power and splendor of the Aztec state are but one point on the cyclical journey that it must undergo; it will eventually crumble and return to its origins in the only way that that return can be made—through death. Second, that power and splendor are ultimately insignificant. Only a material people could be "nourished" by material things. For "true" people, such as the Aztecs, whose real nature is spiritual, such nourishment is actually destructive: "You have become old, you have become tired because of the chocolate you drink and because of the foods you eat. They have harmed and weakened you. You have been spoiled by those mantles, feathers and riches that you wear and that you have brought here. All of that has ruined you."

The Aztec Ruler's Entreaty to Tezcatlipoca, from the *Florentine Codex*

Once again we rely on Sahagún and his native informants to provide us with the material necessary to our understanding of the beliefs and rites of the Aztec people.[63] Here we have the prayer that the ruler addressed to Tezcatlipoca, the god who ruled over the destiny of men, on the occasion of his installation, entreating that all-powerful god to help him meet the requirements of his newly acquired duties. This remarkable ritual entreaty outlines one of the transformational processes, in this case involving rulership, through which Ometeotl, the divine essence, referred to here as "thy progenitor," that is, the creator of Tezcatlipoca, manifests himself in human life. That divine essence, seen here in two of its aspects, is the creative principle—"the mother of the gods, the father of the gods"—as well as the life force itself represented by Ueueteotl, the old god who is "life-giving warmth, the vivifying principle, . . . the sacred perpetual fire."[64]

The outline of that transformational process is suggested in the newly installed ruler's depiction of himself as one of those who will "pronounce for thee," that is, for Tezcatlipoca, and simultaneously "pronounce for thy progenitor," that is, Ometeotl. Significantly, it is Tezcatlipoca, the manifestation of the divine essence approachable through ritual, who is addressed, but it is also significant that the new ruler is not to be seen as a human being addressing a god from whom he is essentially separate. Rather, he is one of a line of rulers who, in some mysterious sense, shelters the god: "Thou wilt hide thyself in them; from within them thou wilt speak." Thus "thy progenitor," who is located at the "center of the hearth, in the turquoise enclosure," a metaphoric reference to what is elsewhere referred to as "the navel of the earth," the symbolic center of the earth from which the primary axes of time and space radiate, manifests itself successively *and* simultaneously as the all-powerful Tezcatlipoca, as the earthly plane itself, and as the earthly ruler.

It is important to note that the ritual entreaty takes care to indicate that this transformational process functions systematically. Rulers were not selected on the whim of a capricious god; rather, "their day-signs [in the ritual 260-day calendar, the *tonalpohualli*] were such that they would become lords, would become rulers." Thus the gods, the earthly realm in all of its spatial-temporal complexity, and the earthly ruler are all to be seen as systematic transformations of the essence of divinity.

HERE ARE TOLD THE WORDS WHICH THE RULER SPOKE WHEN HE HAD BEEN INSTALLED AS RULER, TO ENTREAT TEZCATLIPOCA BECAUSE OF HAVING INSTALLED HIM AS RULER, AND TO ASK HIS HELP AND HIS REVELATION, THAT THE RULER MIGHT FULFILL HIS MISSION. VERY MANY ARE HIS WORDS OF HUMILITY.

Translated from the Nahuatl by Charles E. Dibble and Arthur J. O. Anderson. Originally published in Bernardino de Sahagún, *General History of the Things of New Spain, Book 6: Rhetoric and Moral Philosophy.* Translated by Charles E. Dibble and Arthur J. O. Anderson (Santa Fe, NM: School of American Research, and Salt Lake City: Univ. of Utah, 1969), 41–45. Reprinted by permission of the publisher.

"O master, O our lord, O lord of the near, of the nigh, O night, O wind, thou hast inclined thy heart. Perhaps thou hast mistaken me for another, I who am a commoner; I who am a laborer. In excrement, in filth hath my lifetime been—I who am unreliable; I who am of filth, of vice. And I am an imbecile. Why? For what reason? It is perhaps my desert, my merit that thou takest me from the excrement, from the filth, that thou placest me on the reed mat, on the reed seat?

"Who am I? Who do I think I am that thou movest me among, thou bringest me among, thou countest me with thy acquaintances, thy friends, thy chosen ones, those who have desert, those who have merit? Just so were they by nature; so were they born to rule; thou hast opened their eyes, thou hast opened their ears. And thou hast taken possession of them, thou hast inspired them. Just so were they created, so were they sent here. They were born at a time, they were bathed at a time, their day signs were such that they would become lords, would become rulers. It is said that they will become thy backrests, thy flutes. Thou wilt have them replace thee, thou wilt have them substitute for thee, thou wilt hide thyself in them; from within them thou wilt speak; they will pronounce for thee—those who will help, those who will place on the left, who will place in obsidian sandals, and who will pronounce for thy progenitor, the mother of the gods, the father of the gods, Ueueteotl, who is set in the center of the hearth, in the turquoise enclosure, Xiuhtecutli, who batheth the people, washeth the people, and who determineth, who concedeth the destruction, the exaltation of the vassals, of the common folk.

"O master, O lord of the near, of the nigh, thou hast inclined thy heart, thou hast shown me mercy. Perhaps it is because of the weeping, the sorrowing, of the old men, the old women, those who have gone beyond to reside; perhaps it is because of their spines, their maguey which they left planted deep.

"May I not regard myself. May I not consider myself worthy of the favor, may I not consider myself deserving of that of which I dream, which I see in dreams. It is the load, the burden on the back, heavy, intolerable, insupportable; the large bundle, the large carrying frame which those who already have gone to reside beyond went assuming when they came to guard for thee, when they came to reign.

"It is all, O master, O our lord, O lord of the near, of the nigh, O night, O wind, O Teyocoyani, O Teimatini, O Techichiuani. Poor am I. In what manner shall I act for thy city? In what manner shall I act for the governed, for the vassals? For I am blind, I am deaf, I am an imbecile, and in excrement, in filth hath my lifetime been; and my desert, my task, is greens, is wood.

"And here my real desert, my real merit, my real gift is blindness, paralysis, rottenness. And the tatters, the miserable cape are my desert, my merit, my gift. And I am that which should be carried, I am that which should be borne upon the back; for there are thy friends, thy acquaintances.

"However, thou hast determined it; thou art provided with laughter on earth. May thy spirit, thy word be regarded; may they be satisfied.

"Perhaps thou mistakest me for another; perhaps thou seekest another in my stead. Behold, thou wilt take unto thyself, wilt move unto thyself, wilt hide unto thyself thy wonder, thy glory. Thou hast become tired, thou art vexed. Behold, thou wilt give it to thy real friend, thy real acquaintance, the weeper, the sorrower, the sigher, the deserving one.

"Do I dream? Do I see in dreams?

"Thou who art here, thou who art Teimatini, thou who art Teyocoyani, thou who art Techichiuani, do not conceal, do not hide thy spirit, thy word.

"For hardly are we given explanation. What is the road I shall follow? What way shall I make? Do not conceal, do not hide the mirror, the torch, the light. May I not carry things into dangerous places. May I not direct, introduce the governed into the forest, to the cliff. May I not cause one to encounter, to see the way of the rabbit, of the deer. And may something evil not move upon me; may warfare not move, unfold upon me. May hunger, may famine not befall me.

"To what purpose, in what manner shall I deal with the governed? Where shall I take them? Where shall I introduce them? Wretched have I become. What can I do, I who am untrained, ignorant?

"And may sickness not unfold upon me, not spread upon me. What will result when already thou, lord of the near, of the nigh, makest thy city a place of desolation? What will result when already it lieth abandoned, lieth darkened? And what will result when filth, when vice have come upon me? What will result when I have ruined the city? What will result when I depart leaving the governed asleep, when I gladly leave them? What will result when I cast the common folk into the torrent; cast them from the crag?

"O master, O our lord, O night, O wind, do not depart completely. Come passing by here; know the humble reed enclosure, the mound of earth, for I await thee at thy humble home, at thy humble waiting place. I do what I can for thee, I place my trust in thee. I request, I seek, I expect, I ask of thee thy spirit, thy word, with which thou hast possessed, with which thou hast inspired thy friends, thy acquaintances, who ordered things for thee on thy reed mat, on thy reed seat, thy place of honor. It is where thou art given a proxy, where thou art replaced by another, where thou art substituted, where there is pronouncing for thee, where there is speaking for thee, where thou usest one as a flute, where thou speakest from within one, where thou makest one thy eyes, thy ears; where thou makest one thy mouth, thy jaw.

"And there thou art provided with laughter; there thou selectest one, thou screenest one out; there thou livest, thou rejoicest among thy real friends, thy true acquaintances. There thou takest possession of, thou inspirest the weeper, the sorrower, the sigher, those who truly deliver their minds, their hearts to thee. And there thou dost bequeath them, there thou arrayest them with, there thou givest them the broad mirror, the two-faced mirror wherein we commoners appear. There thou givest them, thou settest up for them the thick torch, the clear one which lighteth, illumineth the world.

"And there thou dost bequeath them, thou arrayest them with, thou placest upon them, thou honorest them, glorifiest them with the peaked hat, the turquoise diadem, and the earplug, the lip plug, the head band, the arm band, the band for the calf of the leg, the necklace, the precious feather.

"And there thy heat, thy warmth, thy freshness, thy tenderness, thy sweetness, thy fragrance come from thee; and there is received as merit the peace, the contentment, the peaceful life, the moment of well-being by thy grace. And there are received as merit paralysis, blindness, the miserable cape, rags. And there is demanded of thee, there is hastened thy time of destroying one, thy time of hiding one: death.

"O master, O Teyocoyani, O Teimatini, O Techichiuani, is it perhaps of my own doing, I being a commoner, the manner in which I shall live, what I shall do, what I shall perform? Thou wilt determine the way on thy reed mat, on thy reed seat, thy place of honor. And howsoever thou wilt require of me, that I shall do, that I shall perform. Whichsoever road thou wilt show me, that one I shall follow; whatsoever thou wilt reveal unto me, that I shall say, that I shall pronounce.

"O master, O our lord, I leave myself, I place myself completely in thy hands, for I cannot govern myself; for I am blind, I am darkness; I am the corner, I am the wall. May thou incline thy heart; require that I deserve, that I merit a little, a bit, a firefly-flash of thy torch, thy light, thy mirror, in order that, as if in dreams, as if seeing in dreams, I endure for a while, a day. I shall bring about for thee the ruination of government, the laughable, the folly on thy reed mat, on thy reed seat, on thy place of honor.

"O master, O our lord, come passing by here, that I be not ruined, that I be not endangered, and that I be not murmured against.

"O master, O our lord, verily I am thy backrest, I am thy flute; not by my desert, not by my merit. I am thy lips, I am thy jaw, I am thy eyes, I am thy ears. And me, a commoner, a laborer, thou hast made thy teeth, thy fingernails. Insert, place within me a little of thy spirit, of thy word; it is that which is ever heeded and is irrefutable."

This he prayed standing, standing bowed, standing head bowed, placing the feet well together. And the very devout stood naked. Perhaps he first offered copal in the fire or offered incense. And when someone stood, cape tied on, he placed his knot in front. And when someone squatted—placed himself as a man—he placed his knot over his shoulder.

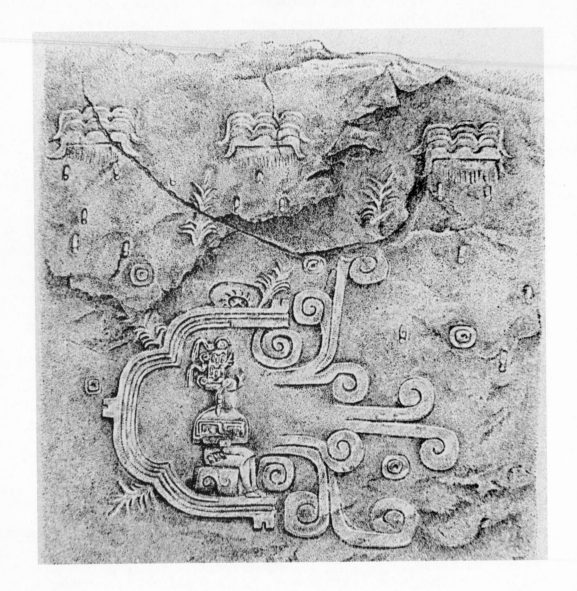

"El Rey": Chalcatzingo Monument I

Monument I, "El Rey," from the Olmec fertility shrine at Chalcatzingo, Morelos, depicts a figure holding a ceremonial bar signifying rulership seated within a stylized cave mouth that lies under three stylized clouds from which raindrops are falling. The clouds themselves bear a striking resemblance to the heavy upper lip of the were-jaguar mouth, which was the symbol *par excellence* of rain and fertility (Image 27), and the cave is that same mouth represented in profile, as is made clear by the appearance above it of an eye bearing the typically Olmec St. Andrew's cross on its eyeball, the same cross often associated with the Olmec rain god. A further indication that this cave is to be seen as a mouth are the "speech scrolls" issuing from it in typical Mesoamerican fashion.

This monument clearly manifests the thematic interweaving of high politics and high worship, of the ruler and the rain god, a fact recognized even by today's villagers, who have given the monument its name, "El Rey." On the one hand, the seated figure is clearly associated with the rain god by the stylized raindrops, identical to those falling from the clouds, decorating his costume and headdress, and by his location within the mouth of the cave/jaguar; on the other hand, he is identified as a ruler by the ceremonial bar he holds and, perhaps, by the headdress he wears, thus identifying ruler and rain god. David Grove and Susan Gillespie claim the relief "depicts a person seated within a cave, source of both water and supernatural power," and they think that person "was a revered ancestor rather than merely a generalized 'rain god.'"

The location of the relief "above the site on the main rainwater channel," which would cause "the torrent of water rushing down the mountain" to appear "to come directly from this revered ancestor," and the evidence of the symbols on the relief suggest overwhelmingly that the "revered ancestor"[65] or, perhaps, current ruler is to be equated metaphorically with the rain. The speech symbolized by the scrolls emanating from the cave mouth would seem to be either his speech or speech concerning him, and that speech is symbolically equated with the issue of the mouthlike rain clouds—the raindrops—with which his costume and headdress are also decorated. The ruler depicted here is symbolically equivalent to the rain, as is the "speech"—his rule—that issues from him, and thus from the gods. That speech sustains the life of the ruled, as does the rain, which gives life to the corn that nourishes man. While the relief was no doubt intended by its creators to commemorate a particular ruler or to indicate their reverence for the supernatural power that provided the rain or, perhaps, to do both, its primary significance for us is to indicate the identification in the Olmec mind of those two motifs.

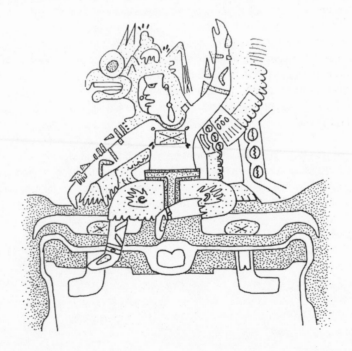

The Olmec Throne: La Venta "Altar" 4 and Oxtotitlan Mural C-1

Throughout the area of the Olmec heartland on the Veracruz coast, curious monoliths are found. Shaped like large tables with pedestal bases containing a niche from which often emerges a human figure, these monoliths were originally thought to be altars and were thus given the appellation they still bear. An Olmec painted mural discovered at Oxtotitlan in Guerrero, however, clearly reveals their original function, for it depicts a masked and costumed figure seated atop one of these monuments. Because the figure is probably a ruler, we can conclude that the monument is the Olmec equivalent of a throne, the seat of power. This interpretation makes sense of the scene carved into the pedestal, revealing that it depicts the ruler emerging from a spiritual realm often equated metaphorically with both a cave and the mouth of a composite creature, a god.

IMAGE 45: La Venta "Altar" 4

This is the most striking of the remaining thrones. On its pedestal is shown a seated figure at the point of emergence from a large niche. Above the niche is the upper jaw of the jaguar-related figure from whose mouth the ruler is emerging. Wearing a symbolic headdress, cape, and pectoral ornament in the fashion of the remaining portraits of Olmec rulers, he is bent forward slightly, grasping a rope that runs along the base of the altar and is tied to realistically portrayed human figures on either side. Those familiar with later Maya symbolism would be inclined to see the figures on the sides as captives, suggesting the dominance of the lord seated in the niche. But the figures on the side are not bound, as captives typically are in Maya art, and may symbolize kinship ties resulting in alliances with the domains of other lords[66] or the common Maya theme of accession. In any case it seems clear that the symbolic meaning of the rope is related in some way to earthly rulership and equally clear from the throne as a whole that the ruler is to be thought of as emerging from the world of the spirit.

IMAGE 46: Oxtotitlan Mural C-1

The large polychrome mural found on the face of a cliff above a cave at Oxtotitlan, Guerrero, relates directly to the La Venta throne. Here the central figure, also a ruler, is depicted frontally so as to display the symbolic regalia in which he is dressed, but his face is depicted in profile within a cutaway mask. His placement atop the upper jaw of a jaguar, which forms the niche on a throne similar to "Altar" 4, is a conventional way of indicating his status to the viewer. As is the case with Yaxchilan Stela 11 (Image 48), the ruler is depicted in X-ray fashion, allowing the viewer to see the person and his role, the man and the god, simultaneously. He is an expression of the gods, and his personal identity is to be understood as coexistent with his divine status. For that reason symbols of fertility are predominant here, and it is likely that Oxtotitlan served originally as a fertility shrine. Even in recent years, water is reputed to have cascaded out of the cave into the land below, suggesting that Oxtotitlan continues to be seen as a "mystical source of water"[67] emanating from the world of the spirit.

The Ruler and the God: La Venta Monument 19

The Olmec sculpture that is now known as La Venta Monument 19, probably carved by 900 B.C., depicts a ruler or priest or priest-ruler, identifiable as such by the valiselike bag he carries in his extended right hand and by his intricate headdress, seated within the womblike, enveloping body of a powerful, protective serpent. The precise relationship between the priest-ruler and the serpent is suggested by the fact that his head is shown within the open jaws of a mask headdress identical to the serpent's head. Clearly, the human figure metaphorically emerges from and is therefore a ritual expression of the composite serpent figure, whose head, repeated in the mask helmet of the seated man, combines features of serpent, jaguar, and bird of prey, a combination that, when viewed in the context of the crest or plume above the serpent's head, leads us, along with many other scholars, to conclude that this figure represents a supernatural being, a god. The particular god is a prototypical plumed serpent, perhaps the first of those that would later become the Mexican Quetzalcoatl and the Maya Kukulcan.

It is also significant that this bas-relief epitomizes the depiction of liminality, the condition of being "betwixt and between" the world of spirit and the world of nature, in Mesoamerican ritual art. In the jaws of the serpent mask, the priest-ruler can be seen as metaphorically midway between earthly reality and the world of the spirit, emerging from the "womb" formed by the serpent, in much the same way that the serpent emerges from the sheltering, fertile earth. Thus the masked priest, whose curved back clearly echoes the line of his cape and of the snake's body, is perilously close to the world of the spirit—whose danger is here indicated by the fact that this particular serpent is a rattlesnake—and yet is protected by ritual from the danger of being absorbed totally into the spiritual realm.

It seems quite clear that the ruler-priest is depicted here as a catalyst through which the realm of the spirit can enter the mundane world, just as the composite figure of the bird-serpent-man represented in the later figure of Quetzalcoatl, known to the Aztecs as the legendary ruler of Tula, bridged those two worlds.

The Ruler as the God: Yaxchilan Stela 11

Stela 11 at Yaxchilan is a stunning example of an image capturing the highly liminal moment of the beginning of a new cycle, the moment when the man or woman who is to rule *becomes* the god, when spiritual reality manifests itself in material form in the world of space and time. Engraved on the rear face of this stela, shown here, is Bird Jaguar, the man who ruled Yaxchilan from A.D. 752 to 771, depicted in the regalia of the god Chac-Xib-Chac. Although the image is essentially a frontal view of the splendidly arrayed figure of the ruler, his face is shown in profile, and depicted in front of his face is a mask that is an integral part of, and extends downward from, his elaborate symbolic headdress. It is important to note that this image, for all the realism of its depiction of the facial features of Bird Jaguar and the three bound captives kneeling in front of him, ready to be sacrificed, is the result not of an attempt by the carver to portray natural reality but rather of his application to the stone of an elaborate set of artistic conventions designed to permit the symbolic communication of spiritual reality. The frontal view of the body allows the viewer to see—and "read"—the symbolic details of the ruler's costume, while the profile view of the head is surely designed to afford the viewer the revelation of the ruler unmasked. What has been called an X-ray view of the face within the mask allows the simultaneous depiction of the masked face of the costumed ruler, which was presented to his subjects on this ritual occasion, and the human face of the man within the mask. He is a particular man who rules in a particular time and place, but he is also the god. The god has entered into him, and he displays the features of that god whom he now shelters over those of his natural face.

In thus becoming the god depicted by the mask, Bird Jaguar has entered the liminal realm, in which he can be simultaneously human and divine; he is, at this precise point in time and space, "manifesting the sacred,"[68] demonstrating that only through such symbols can the sacred be made manifest. Thus the man within the mask becomes the god yet remains himself. And we realize that the god he now seems to be was what he had essentially been all the time. Bird Jaguar is the animating force within the mask of the divine at the same time that the essence of the divine spirit is the life force within him. The X-ray convention by which this image on the stela is designed and constructed *in itself* makes this truth apparent. In the timeless moment of ritual, a moment captured in this stunning work of mythic art, the identities of Bird Jaguar and the god thus merge to reveal a truth more fundamental than those that are found in the natural world.

THE MAYA HERO JOURNEY

The Hero Journey of the Hero Twins, from the *Popol Vuh*

In this lengthy section of the *Popol Vuh,*[69] which occurs after the unsuccessful attempts by the gods to create humanity and before their
final, successful attempt, we are given the exploits of the hero twins,
Hunahpu and Xbalanque. These exploits take place both on the surface
of the earth and in Xibalba, the underworld, and the twins, in their
apotheosis, eventually rise to the heavens. Thus they unite all the levels of the cosmos, metaphorically bringing the spiritual dimension of
the upper and lower worlds to the surface of the earth. By so doing they
prefigure and provide a model for the earthly ruler through whom the
boon of the world of the spirit can come to his people.

The narration of the adventures of Hunahpu and Xbalanque is
long and complex, but the progression is clear; it is the progression of
the hero from birth to his eventual apotheosis. This tale begins *in medias res* with the confrontation between the false sun, Seven Macaw by
name, and the twins. They destroy the impostor, going on to their
other adventures, after which one of them will become the true sun.
Following that beginning, the *Popol Vuh* returns to the real beginning,
the adventures of the father and uncle of the hero twins, adventures
that will set the stage for those of their sons and nephews. The failure
of this first set of heroes to defeat the lords of death in Xibalba leads to
their own death. But their death leads in turn to the miraculous conception and birth of Hunahpu and Xbalanque.

After a childhood that demonstrates their special nature, the
hero twins find the ball game gear of their father and uncle, i.e., their
destiny, and, like those earlier heroes, descend to Xibalba to battle the
lords of death. After a number of tests and trials, they eventually master death itself, rising to the sky as the sun and moon. The sense of this
apotheosis is clear: their victory in Xibalba assures the cyclic renewal
of life in this world. Just as the sun and the moon can be counted on to
be reborn each day, month, and year, so life can be counted on not to
end. Death is but the prelude to rebirth. It is thus significant that the
creation of the present humanity comes *after* this descent into the
realm of death, after the defeat of death by the hero twins and their
apotheosis, which brings the boon of cyclic renewal to humanity. Like
the hero twins, the Maya ruler will serve as a conduit through whom
the renewal of the world of the spirit can be channeled to mankind.

There are two recent translations of the *Popol Vuh,* and they are
quite different from one another. We present here the translation by

Dennis Tedlock, the more recent of the two, but we would encourage the interested reader to see also the readily available translation of Munro Edmonson.[70]

THE HERO JOURNEY OF THE HERO TWINS

Translated from the Quiché Maya by Dennis Tedlock. Originally published in Dennis Tedlock, trans., *Popol Vuh: The Mayan Book of the Dawn of Life,* 86–94, 105, 109–17, 119–20, 128–31, 133–37, 143–60. Copyright 1985 by Dennis Tedlock. Reprinted by permission of Simon & Schuster, Inc. The division into sections is that of the editors.

I

There was just a trace of early dawn on the face of the earth, there was no sun. But there was one who magnified himself; Seven Macaw is his name. The sky-earth was already there, but the face of the sun-moon was clouded over. Even so, it is said that his light provided a sign for the people who were flooded. He was like a person of genius in his being.

"I am great. My place is now higher than that of the human work, the human design. I am their sun and I am their light, and I am also their months.

"So be it: my light is great. I am the walkway and I am the foothold of the people, because my eyes are of metal. My teeth just glitter with jewels, and turquoise as well; they stand out blue with stones like the face of the sky.

"And this nose of mine shines white into the distance like the moon. Since my nest is metal, it lights up the face of the earth. When I come forth before my nest, I am like the sun and moon for those who are born in the light, begotten in the light. It must be so, because my face reaches into the distance," says Seven Macaw.

It is not true that he is the sun, this Seven Macaw, yet he magnifies himself, his wings, his metal. But the scope of his face lies right around his own perch; his face does not reach everywhere beneath the sky. The faces of the sun, moon, and stars are not yet visible, it has not yet dawned.

And so Seven Macaw puffs himself up as the days and the months, though the light of the sun and moon has not yet clarified. He only wished for surpassing greatness. This was when the flood was worked upon the manikins, woodcarvings.

And now we shall explain how Seven Macaw died, when the people were vanquished, done in by the mason and sculptor.

Here is the beginning of the defeat and destruction of the day of Seven Macaw by the two boys, the first named Hunahpu and the second named Xbalanque. Being gods, the two of them saw evil in his attempt at self-magnification before the Heart of Sky. So the boys talked:

"It's no good without life, without people here on the face of the earth."

"Well then, let's try a shot. We could shoot him while he's at his meal. We could make him ill, then put an end to his riches, his jade, his metal, his jewels, his gems, the source of his brilliance. Everyone might do as he does, but it should not come to be that fiery splendor is merely a matter of metal. So be it," said the boys, each one with a blowgun on his shoulder, the two of them together.

And this Seven Macaw has two sons: the first of these is Zipacna, and the second is the Earthquake. And Chimalmat is the name of their mother, the wife of Seven Macaw.

And this is Zipacna, this is the one to build up the great mountains: Fire Mouth, Hunahpu, Cave by the Water, Xcanul, Macamob, Huliznab, as the names of the mountains that were there at the dawn are spoken. They were brought forth by Zipacna in a single night.

And now this is the Earthquake. The mountains are moved by him; the mountains, small and great, are softened by him. The sons of Seven Macaw did this just as a means of self-magnification.

"Here am I: I am the sun," said Seven Macaw.

"Here am I: I am the maker of the earth," said Zipacna.

"As for me, I bring down the sky, I make an avalanche of all the earth," said Earthquake. The sons of Seven Macaw are alike, and like him: they got their greatness from their father.

And the two boys saw evil in this, since our first mother and father could not yet be made. Therefore deaths and disappearances were planned by the two boys.

And here is the shooting of Seven Macaw by the two boys. We shall explain the defeat of each one of those who engaged in self-magnification.

This is the great tree of Seven Macaw, a nance, and this is the food of Seven Macaw. In order to eat the fruit of the nance he goes up the tree every day. Since Hunahpu and Xbalanque have seen where he feeds, they are now hiding beneath the tree of Seven Macaw, they are keeping quiet here, the two boys are in the leaves of the tree.

And when Seven Macaw arrived, perching over his meal, the nance, it was then that he was shot by Hunahpu. The blowgun shot went right to his jaw, breaking his mouth. Then he went up over the tree and fell flat on the ground. Suddenly Hunahpu appeared, running. He set out to grab him, but actually it was the arm of Hunahpu that was seized by Seven Macaw. He yanked it straight back, he bent it back at the shoulder. Then Seven Macaw tore it right out of Hunahpu. Even so, the boys did well: the first round was not their defeat by Seven Macaw.

And when Seven Macaw had taken the arm of Hunahpu, he went home. Holding his jaw very carefully, he arrived:

"What have you got there?" said Chimalmat, the wife of Seven Macaw.

"What is it but those two tricksters? They've shot me, they've dislocated my jaw. All my teeth are just loose, now they ache. But once what I've got is over the fire—hanging there, dangling over the fire—then they can just come and get it. They're real tricksters!" said Seven Macaw, then he hung up the arm of Hunahpu.

Meanwhile Hunahpu and Xbalanque were thinking. And then they invoked a grandfather, a truly white-haired grandfather, and a grandmother, a truly humble grandmother—just bent-over, elderly people. Great White Peccary is the name of the grandfather, and Great White Tapir is the name of the grandmother. The boys said to the grandmother and grandfather:

"Please travel with us when we go to get our arm from Seven Macaw; we'll just follow right behind you. You'll tell him:

'Do forgive us our grandchildren, who travel with us. Their mother and father are dead, and so they follow along there, behind us. Perhaps we should give them away, since all we do is pull worms out of teeth.' So we'll seem like children to Seven Macaw, even though *we're* giving *you* the instructions," the two boys told them.

"Very well," they replied.

After that they approached the place where Seven Macaw was in front of his home. When the grandmother and grandfather passed by, the two boys were romping along behind them. When they passed below the lord's house, Seven Macaw was yelling his mouth off because of his teeth. And when Seven Macaw saw the grandfather and grandmother traveling with them:

"Where are you headed, our grandfather?" said the lord.

"We're just making our living, your lordship," they replied.

"Why are you working for a living? Aren't those your children traveling with you?"

"No, they're not, your lordship. They're our grandchildren, our descendants, but it is nevertheless *we* who take pity on *them*. The bit of food they get is the portion we give them, your lordship," replied the grandmother and grandfather. Since the lord is getting done in by the pain in his teeth, it is only with great effort that he speaks again:

"I implore you, please take pity on me! What sweets can you make, what poisons can you cure?" said the lord.

"We just pull the worms out of teeth, and we just cure eyes. We just set bones, your lordship," they replied.

"Very well, please cure my teeth. They really ache, every day. It's insufferable! I get no sleep because of them—and my eyes. They just shot me, those two tricksters! Ever since it started I haven't eaten because of it. Therefore take pity on me! Perhaps it's because my teeth are loose now."

"Very well, your lordship. It's a worm, gnawing at the bone. It's merely a matter of putting in a replacement and taking the teeth out, sir."

"But perhaps it's not good for my teeth to come out—since I am, after all, a lord. My finery is in my teeth—and my eyes."

"But then we'll put in a replacement. Ground bone will be put back in." And this is the "ground bone": it's only white corn.

"Very well. Yank them out! Give me some help here!" he replied.

And when the teeth of Seven Macaw came out, it was only white corn that went in as a replacement for his teeth—just a coating shining white, that corn in his mouth. His face fell at once, he no longer looked like a lord. The last of his teeth came out, the jewels that had stood out blue from his mouth.

And then the eyes of Seven Macaw were cured. When his eyes were trimmed back the last of his metal came out. Still he felt no pain; he just looked on while the last of his greatness left him. It was just as Hunahpu and Xbalanque had intended.

And when Seven Macaw died, Hunahpu got back his arm. And Chimalmat, the wife of Seven Macaw, also died.

Such was the loss of the riches of Seven Macaw: only the doctors got the jewels and gems that had made him arrogant, here on the face of the earth. The genius of the grandmother, the genius of the grandfather did its work when they took back their arm: it was implanted and the break got well again. Just as they had wished the death of Seven Macaw, so they brought it about. They had seen evil in his self-magnification.

[There follow three episodes in the earthly lives of Hunahpu and Xbalanque, including the story of the killing of the first son of Seven Macaw, Zipacna, the maker of mountains. Asking him to help them, the Four Hundred Boys trick him, burying him in a hole he was helping to dig, but he turns the tables on them and kills them all, only to be outwitted in his turn by Hunahpu and Xbalanque and turned to stone when he is buried under a mountain. The twins then defeat the second son of Seven Macaw, named Earthquake, by casting a spell on the bird they give him to eat, causing him to end up covered by earth.]

II

And now we shall name the name of the father of Hunahpu and Xbalanque. Let's drink to him, and let's just drink to the telling and accounting of the begetting of Hunahpu and Xbalanque. We shall tell just half of it, just a part of the account of their father. Here follows the account.

These are the names: One Hunahpu and Seven Hunahpu, as they are called.

And these are their parents: Xpiyacoc, Xmucane. In the blackness, in the night, One Hunahpu and Seven Hunahpu were born to Xpiyacoc and Xmucane.

[Here the myth describes the beginning of the struggle that One Hunahpu, the father of Hunahpu and Xbalanque, and Seven Hunahpu, their uncle, wage with the Lords of Xibalba.]

And now for the messengers of One and Seven Death:

"You're going, you Military Keepers of the Mat, to summon One and Seven Hunahpu. You'll tell them, when you arrive:

' "They must come," the lords say to you. "Would that they might come to play ball with us here. Then we could have some excitement with them. We are truly amazed at them. Therefore they should come," say the lords, "and they should bring their playthings, their yokes and arm guards should come, along with their rubber ball," say the lords,' you will say when you arrive," the messengers were told.

And these messengers of theirs are owls: Shooting Owl, One-legged Owl, Macaw Owl, Skull Owl, as the messengers of Xibalba are called.

There is Shooting Owl, like a point, just piercing.

And there is One-legged Owl, with just one leg; he has wings.

And there is Macaw Owl, with a red back; he has wings.

And there is also Skull Owl, with only a head alone; he has no legs, but he does have wings.

There are four messengers, Military Keepers of the Mat in rank.

And when they came out of Xibalba they arrived quickly, alighting above the ball court where One and Seven Hunahpu were playing, at the ball court called Great Abyss at Carchah. The owls, arriving in a flurry over the ball court, now repeated their words, reciting the exact words of One Death, Seven Death, Pus Master, Jaundice Master, Bone Scepter, Skull Scepter, House Corner, Blood Gatherer, Trash Master, Stab Master, Wing, Packstrap, as all the lords are named. Their words were repeated by the owls.

"Don't the lords One and Seven Death speak truly?"

"Truly indeed," the owls replied. "We'll accompany you.

'They're to bring along all their gaming equipment,' say the lords."

"Very well, but wait for us while we notify our mother," they replied.

And when they went to their house, they spoke to their mother; their father had died:

"We're going, our dear mother, even though we've just arrived. The messengers of the lord have come to get us:

' "They should come," he says,' they say, giving us orders. We'll leave our rubber ball behind here," they said, then they went to tie it up under the roof of the house. "Until we return—then we'll put it in play again."

They told One Monkey and One Artisan:

"As for you, just play and just sing, write and carve to warm our house and to warm the heart of your grandmother." When they had been given their instructions, their grandmother Xmucane sobbed, she had to weep.

"We're going, we're not dying. Don't be sad," said One and Seven Hunahpu, then they left.

After that One and Seven Hunahpu left, guided down the road by the messengers.

And then they descended the road to Xibalba, going down a steep cliff, and they descended until they came out where the rapids cut through, the roaring canyon narrows named Neck Canyon. They passed through there, then they passed on into the River of Churning Spikes. They passed through countless spikes but they were not stabbed.

And then they came to water again, to blood: Blood River. They crossed but did not drink. They came to a river, but a river filled with pus. Still they were not defeated, but passed through again.

And then they came to the Crossroads, but here they were defeated, at the Crossroads:

Red Road was one and Black Road another.

White Road was one and Yellow Road another.

There were four roads, and Black Road spoke:

"I am the one you are taking. I am the lord's road," said the road. And they were defeated there: this was the Road of Xibalba.

And then they came to the council place of the lords of Xibalba, and they were defeated again there. The ones seated first there are just manikins, just woodcarvings dressed up by Xibalba. And they greeted the first ones:

"Morning, One Death," they said to the manikin. "Morning, Seven Death," they said to the woodcarving in turn.

So they did not win out, and the lords of Xibalba shouted out with laughter over this. All the lords just shouted with laughter because they had triumphed; in their hearts they had beaten One and Seven Hunahpu. They laughed on until One and Seven Death spoke:

"It's good that you've come. Tomorrow you must put your yokes and arm guards into action," they were told.

"Sit here on our bench," they were told, but the only bench they were offered was a burning-hot rock.

So now they were burned on the bench; they really jumped around on the bench now, but they got no relief. They really got up fast, having burned their butts. At this the Xibalbans laughed again, they began to shriek with laughter, the laughter rose up like a serpent in their very cores, all the lords of Xibalba laughed themselves down to their blood and bones.

"Just go in the house. Your torch and cigars will be brought to your sleeping quarters," the boys were told.

After that they came to the Dark House, a house with darkness alone inside. Meanwhile the Xibalbans shared their thoughts:

"Let's just sacrifice them tomorrow. It can only turn out to be quick; they'll die quickly because of our playing equipment, our gaming things," the Xibalbans are saying among themselves.

This ball of theirs is just a spherical knife. White Dagger is the name of the ball, the ball of Xibalba. Their ball is just ground down to make it smooth; the ball of Xibalba is just surfaced with crushed bone to make it firm.

And One and Seven Hunahpu went inside Dark House.

And then their torch was brought, only one torch, already lit, sent by One and Seven Death, along with a cigar for each of them, also already lit, sent by the lords. When these were brought to One and Seven Hunahpu they were cowering, here in the dark. When the bearer of their torch and cigars arrived, the torch was bright as it entered; their torch and both of their cigars were burning. The bearer spoke:

" 'They must be sure to return them in the morning—not finished, but just as they look now. They must return them intact,' the lords say to you," they were told, and they were defeated. They finished the torch and they finished the cigars that had been brought to them.

And Xibalba is packed with tests, heaps and piles of tests.

This is the first one: the Dark House, with darkness alone inside.

And the second is named Rattling House, heavy with cold inside, whistling with drafts, clattering with hail. A deep chill comes inside here.

And the third is named Jaguar House, with jaguars alone inside, jostling one another, crowding together, with gnashing teeth. They're scratching around; these jaguars are shut inside the house.

Bat House is the name of the fourth test, with bats alone inside the house, squeaking, shrieking, darting through the house. The bats are shut inside; they can't get out.

And the fifth is named Razor House, with blades alone inside. The blades are moving back and forth, ripping, slashing through the house.

These are the first tests of Xibalba, but One and Seven Hunahpu never entered into them, except for the one named earlier, the specified test house.

And when One and Seven Hunahpu went back before One and Seven Death, they were asked:

"Where are my cigars? What of my torch? They were brought to you last night!"

"We finished them, your lordship."

"Very well. This very day, your day is finished, you will die, you will disappear, and we shall break you off. Here you will hide your faces: you are to be sacrificed!" said One and Seven Death.

And then they were sacrificed and buried. They were buried at the Place of Ball Game Sacrifice, as it is called. The head of One Hunahpu was cut off; only his body was buried with his younger brother.

"Put his head in the fork of the tree that stands by the road," said One and Seven Death.

And when his head was put in the fork of the tree, the tree bore fruit. It would not have had any fruit, had not the head of One Hunahpu been put in the fork of the tree.

This is the calabash tree, as we call it today, or "the head of One Hunahpu," as it is said.

And then One and Seven Death were amazed at the fruit of the tree. The fruit grows out everywhere, and it isn't clear where the head of One Hunahpu is; now it looks just the way the calabashes look. All the Xibalbans see this, when they come to look.

The state of the tree loomed large in their thoughts, because it came about at the same time the head of One Hunahpu was put in the fork. The Xibalbans said among themselves:

"No one is to pick the fruit, nor is anyone to go beneath the tree," they said. They restricted themselves; all of Xibalba held back.

It isn't clear which is the head of One Hunahpu; now it's exactly the same as the fruit of the tree. Calabash tree came to be its name, and much was said about it. A maiden heard about it, and here we shall tell of her arrival.

III

And here is the account of a maiden, the daughter of a lord named Blood Gatherer.

And this is when a maiden heard of it, the daughter of a lord. Blood Gatherer is the name of her father, and Blood Woman is the name of the maiden.

And when he heard the account of the fruit of the tree, her father retold it. And she was amazed at the account:

"I'm not acquainted with that tree they talk about. ' "Its fruit is truly sweet!" they say,' I hear," she said.

Next, she went all alone and arrived where the tree stood. It stood at the Place of Ball Game Sacrifice:

"What? Well! What's the fruit of this tree? Shouldn't this tree bear something sweet? They shouldn't die, they shouldn't be wasted. Should I pick one?" said the maiden.

And then the bone spoke; it was here in the fork of the tree:

"Why do you want a mere bone, a round thing in the branches of a tree?" said the head of One Hunahpu when it spoke to the maiden. "You don't want it," she was told.

"I do want it," said the maiden.

"Very well. Stretch out your right hand here, so I can see it," said the bone.

"Yes," said the maiden. She stretched out her right hand, up there in front of the bone.

And then the bone spit out its saliva, which landed squarely in the hand of the maiden.

And then she looked in her hand, she inspected it right away, but the bone's saliva wasn't in her hand.

"It is just a sign I have given you, my saliva, my spittle. This, my head, has nothing on it—just bone, nothing of meat. It's just the same with the head of a great lord: it's just the flesh that makes his face look good. And when he dies, people get frightened by his bones. After that, his son is like his saliva, his spittle, in his being, whether it be the son of a lord or the son of a craftsman, an orator. The father does not disappear, but goes on being fulfilled. Neither dimmed nor destroyed is the face of a lord, a warrior, craftsman, orator. Rather, he will leave his daughters and sons. So it is that I have done likewise through you. Now go up there on the face of the earth; you will not die. Keep the word. So be it," said the head of One and Seven Hunahpu—they were of one mind when they did it.

This was the word Hurricane, Newborn Thunderbolt, Raw Thunderbolt had given them. In the same way, by the time the maiden returned to her home, she had been given many instructions. Right away something was generated in her belly, from the saliva alone, and this was the generation of Hunahpu and Xbalanque.

And when the maiden got home and six months had passed, she was found out by her father. Blood Gatherer is the name of her father.

And after the maiden was noticed by her father, when he saw that she was now with child, all the lords then shared their thoughts— One and Seven Death, along with Blood Gatherer:

"This daughter of mine is with child, lords. It's just a bastard," Blood Gatherer said when he joined the lords.

"Very well. Get her to open her mouth. If she doesn't tell, then sacrifice her. Go far away and sacrifice her."

"Very well, your lordships," he replied. After that, he questioned his daughter:

"Who is responsible for the child in your belly, my daughter?" he said.

"There is no child, my father, sir; there is no man whose face I've known," she replied.

"Very well. It really is a bastard you carry! Take her away for sacrifice, you Military Keepers of the Mat. Bring back her heart in a bowl, so the lords can take it in their hands this very day," the owls were told, the four of them.

Then they left, carrying the bowl. When they left they took the maiden by the hand, bringing along the White Dagger, the instrument of sacrifice.

"It would not turn out well if you sacrificed me, messengers, because it is not a bastard that's in my belly. What's in my belly generated all by itself when I went to marvel at the head of One Hunahpu, which is there at the Place of Ball Game Sacrifice. So please stop: don't do your sacrifice, messengers," said the maiden. Then they talked:

"What are we going to use in place of her heart? We were told by her father:

'Bring back her heart. The lords will take it in their hands, they will satisfy themselves, they will make themselves familiar with its composition. Hurry, bring it back in a bowl, put her heart in the bowl.' Isn't that what we've been told? What shall we deliver in the bowl? What we want above all is that you should not die," said the messengers.

"Very well. My heart must not be theirs, nor will your homes be here. Nor will you simply force people to die, but hereafter, what will be truly yours will be the true bearers of bastards. And hereafter, as for One and Seven Death, only blood, only nodules of sap, will be theirs. So be it that these things are presented before them, and not that hearts are burned before them. So be it: use the fruit of a tree," said the maiden. And it was red tree sap she went out to gather in the bowl.

After it congealed, the substitute for her heart became round. When the sap of the croton tree was tapped, tree sap like blood, it became the substitute for her blood. When she rolled the blood around inside there, the sap of the croton tree, it formed a surface like blood, glistening red now, round inside the bowl. When the tree was cut open by the maiden, the so-called cochineal croton, the sap is what she called blood, and so there is talk of "nodules of blood."

"So you have been blessed with the face of the earth. It shall be yours," she told the owls.

"Very well, maiden. We'll show you the way up there. You just walk on ahead; we have yet to deliver this apparent duplicate of your heart before the lords," said the messengers.

And when they came before the lords, they were all watching closely:

"Hasn't it turned out well?" said One Death.

"It has turned out well, your lordships, and this is her heart. It's in the bowl."

"Very well. So I'll look," said One Death, and when he lifted it up with his fingers, its surface was soaked with gore, its surface glistened red with blood.

"Good. Stir up the fire, put it over the fire," said One Death.

After that they dried it over the fire, and the Xibalbans savored the aroma. They all ended up standing here, they leaned over it intently. They found the smoke of the blood to be truly sweet!

And while they stayed at their cooking, the owls went to show the maiden the way out. They sent her up through a hole onto the earth, and then the guides returned below.

In this way the lords of Xibalba were defeated by a maiden; all of them were blinded.

[Blood Woman comes to the mother of One Monkey and One Artisan while pregnant with Hunahpu and Xbalanque and proves that she is her daughter-in-law.]

And this is their birth; we shall tell of it here.

Then it came to the day of their birth, and the maiden named Blood Woman gave birth. The grandmother was not present when they were born; they were born suddenly. Two of them were born, named Hunahpu and Xbalanque. They were born in the mountains, and then they came into the house. Since they weren't sleeping:

"Throw them out of here! They're really loudmouths!" said the grandmother.

After that, when they put them on an anthill, they slept soundly there. And when they removed them from there, they put them in brambles next.

And this is what One Monkey and One Artisan wanted: that they should die on the anthill and die in the brambles. One Monkey and One Artisan wanted this because they were rowdyish and flushed with jealousy. They didn't allow their younger brothers in the house at first, as if they didn't even know them, but even so they flourished in the mountains.

And One Monkey and One Artisan were great flautists and singers, and as they grew up they went through great suffering and pain. It had cost them suffering to become great knowers. Through it all they became flautists, singers, and writers, carvers. They did everything well. They simply knew it when they were born, they simply had genius. And they were the successors of their fathers who had gone to Xibalba, their dead fathers.

Since One Monkey and One Artisan were great knowers, in their hearts they already realized everything when their younger brothers came into being, but they didn't reveal their insight because of their jealousy.

[That jealousy caused One Monkey and One Artisan to treat their younger half-brothers, Hunahpu and Xbalanque, very cruelly. In retaliation the hero twins used their wits to defeat them. They sent their older half-brothers up a tree to catch some birds, turning them into monkeys while they were in the tree. As monkeys, even their mother laughed at them. Then, deciding to clear a space for a garden plot, the twins discovered that the animals of the forest continually replaced the wild plants that they cleared. They tried to catch the animals but they were unsuccessful until . . .]

IV

And one more came, the last one now, jumping as he came, then they cut him off. In their net they caught the rat.

And then they grabbed him and squeezed him behind the head. They tried to choke him; they burned his tail over a fire. Ever since the rat's tail got caught, there's been no hair on his tail, and his eyes have been the way they are since the boys tried to choke him, Hunahpu and Xbalanque.

"I will not die by your hand! Gardening is not your job, but there is something that is," said the rat.

"Where is what is ours? Go ahead and name it," the boys told the rat.

"Will you let me go then? My word is in my belly, and after I name it for you, you'll give me my morsel of food," said the rat.

"We'll give you your food, so name it," he was told.

"Very well. It's something that belonged to your fathers, named One Hunahpu and Seven Hunahpu, who died in Xibalba. What remains is their gaming equipment. They left it up under the roof of the house: their kilts, their arm guards, their rubber ball. But your grandmother doesn't take these down in front of you, because this is how your fathers died."

"You know the truth, don't you!" the boys told the rat.

There was great joy in their hearts when they got word of the rubber ball. When the rat had named it they gave the rat his food, and this is his food: corn kernels, squash seeds, chili, beans, pataxte, cacao. These are his.

"If anything of yours is stored or gets wasted, then gnaw away," the rat was told by Hunahpu and Xbalanque.

"Very well, boys. But what will your grandmother say if she sees me?" he said.

"Don't be fainthearted. We're here. We know what our grandmother needs to be told. We'll set you up under the corner of the roof right away. When that's taken care of you'll go straight to where the things were left, and we'll look up there under the roof, but it's our stew we'll be looking at," they told the rat when they gave him his instructions.

Hunahpu and Xbalanque made their plans overnight and arrived right at noon, and it wasn't obvious that they had a rat with them when they arrived. One of them went right inside the house when he reached it, while the other went to the corner of the house, quickly setting up the rat. And then they asked their grandmother for their meal:

"Just grind something for our stew, we want chili sauce, our dear grandmother," they said.

After that, she ground chili for their stew. A bowl of broth was set out in front of them, but they were just fooling their grandmother and mother. They had emptied the water jar:

"We're really parched! Bring us a drink," they told their grandmother.

"Yes," she said, then she went, and they kept on eating. They weren't really hungry; they just put on false appearances.

And then they saw the rat reflected in their chili sauce: here was the rat loosening the ball that had been left in the peak of the roof. When they saw him in the chili sauce they sent a mosquito, that creature the mosquito, similar to a gnat. He went to the water, then he punctured the side of the grandmother's jar. The water just gushed out from the side of her jar. She tried, but she could not stop up the side of her jar.

"What has our grandmother done? We're choking for lack of water, our parched throats will do us in," they told their mother, then they sent her there.

After that, the rat cut the ball loose. It dropped from beneath the roof, along with the yokes, arm guards, kilts. These were taken away then; they went to hide them on the road, the road to the ball court.

After that, they went to join their grandmother at the water, and their grandmother and mother were unable to stop up the side of the jar, either one of them.

After that, the boys arrived, each with his blowgun. When they arrived at the water:

"What have you done? We got weary at heart, so we came," they said.

"Look at the side of my jar! It cannot be stopped," said their grandmother, and they quickly stopped it up.

And they came back together, the two of them ahead of their grandmother.

In this way, the matter of the rubber ball was arranged.

Happy now, they went to play ball at the court. So they played ball at a distance, all by themselves. They swept out the court of their fathers.

And then it came into the hearing of the lords of Xibalba:

"Who's begun a game again up there, over our heads? Don't they have any shame, stomping around this way? Didn't One and Seven Hunahpu die trying to magnify themselves in front of us? So, you must deliver another summons," they said as before, One and Seven Death, all the lords.

"They are hereby summoned," they told their messengers. "You are to say, on reaching them:

' "They must come," say the lords. "We would play ball with them here. In seven days we'll have a game," say the lords,' you will say when you arrive," the messengers were told.

And then they came along a wide roadway, the road to the house of the boys, which actually ended at their house, so that the messengers came directly to their grandmother. As for the boys, they were away playing ball when the messengers of Xibalba got there.

" 'Truly, they are to come,' say the lords," said the messengers of Xibalba. So then and there the day was specified by the messengers of Xibalba:

" 'In seven days our game will take place,' " Xmucane was told there.

"Very well. They'll go when the day comes, messengers," said the grandmother, and the messengers left. They went back.

So now the grandmother's heart was broken:

"How can I send for my grandchildren? Isn't it really Xibalba, just as it was when the messengers came long ago, when their fathers went to die?" said the grandmother, sobbing, at home by herself. . . .

"From Xibalba comes the messenger of One and Seven Death:

' "In seven days they are to come here. We'll play ball. Their gaming equipment must come along: rubber ball, yokes, arm guards, kilts. This will make for some excitement here," say the lords, "is the word that came from them,"' says your grandmother. So your grandmother says you must come. Truly your grandmother cries, she calls out to you to come."

"Isn't it the truth!" the boys said in their thoughts. When they heard it they left at once and got to their grandmother, but they went there only to give their grandmother instructions:

"We're on our way, dear grandmother. We're just giving you instructions. So here is the sign of our word. We'll leave it with you. Each of us will plant an ear of corn. We'll plant them in the center of our house. When the corn dries up, this will be a sign of our death:

'Perhaps they died,' you'll say, when it dries up. And when the sprouting comes:

'Perhaps they live,' you'll say, our dear grandmother and mother. From now on, this is the sign of our word. We're leaving it with you," they said, then they left.

Hunahpu planted one and Xbalanque planted another. They were planted right there in the house: neither in the mountains nor where the earth is damp, but where the earth is dry, in the middle of the inside of their house. They left them planted there, then went off, each with his own blowgun.

They went down to Xibalba, quickly going down the face of a cliff, and they crossed over the bottom of a canyon with rapids. They passed right through the birds—the ones called throng birds—and then they crossed Pus River and Blood River, intended as traps by Xibalba. They did not step in, but simply crossed over on their blowguns, and then they went on over to the Crossroads. But they knew about the roads of Xibalba: Black Road, White Road, Red Road, Green Road.

And there they summoned that creature named the mosquito. Having heard that he's a spy, they sent him ahead:

"Bite them one by one. First bite the first one seated there, then bite every last one of them, and it will be yours alone to suck the blood of people in the roads," the mosquito was told.

"Very well," replied the mosquito, then he took Black Road and stopped at the two manikins, the woodcarvings, that were seated first. They were all dressed up, and he bit the first of them. It didn't speak, so he bit again. When he bit the one seated second, again it didn't speak, and then he bit the third one, the one seated third actually being One Death.

"Yeow!" each one said as he was bitten.

"What?" each one replied.

"Ouch!" said One Death.

"What is it, One Death?"

"Something's bitten me."

"It's—ouch! There's something that's bitten me," the one seated fourth said next.

"What is it, Seven Death?"

"Something's bitten me." The one seated fifth spoke next:

"Ow! Ow!" he said.

"What, House Corner?" Seven Death said to him.

"Something's bitten me," he said next. The one seated sixth was bitten:

"Ouch!"

"What is it, Blood Gatherer?" House Corner said to him.

"Something's bitten me," he said next. Then the one seated seventh was bitten:

"Ouch!" he said next.

"What is it, Pus Master?" Blood Gatherer said to him.

"Something's bitten me," he said next. The one seated eighth was bitten next:

"Ouch!" he said next.

"What is it, Jaundice Master?" Pus Master said to him next.

"Something's bitten me," he said next. Then the one seated ninth was bitten next:

"Ouch!" he said.

"What is it, Bone Scepter?" Jaundice Master said to him.

"Something's bitten me," he said next. Then the one seated tenth in order was bitten next:

"Ouch!"

"What is it, Skull Scepter?" said Bone Scepter.

"Something's bitten me," he said next. Then the one seated eleventh was bitten next:

"Ouch!" he said next.

"What is it, Wing?" Skull Scepter said to him next.

"Something's bitten me," he said next. Then the one seated twelfth was bitten next:

"Ouch!" he said next.

"What, Packstrap?" he was asked next.

"Something's bitten me," he said next. Then the one seated thirteenth was bitten next:

"Ouch!"

"What is it, Bloody Teeth?" Packstrap said to him.

"Something's bitten me," he said next. Then the one seated fourteenth was bitten next:

"Ouch! Something's bitten me," he said next.

"Bloody Claws?" Bloody Teeth said to him next.

And such was the naming of their names, they named them all among themselves. They showed their faces and named their names, each one named by the one ranking above him, and naming in turn the name of the one seated next to him. There wasn't a single name they missed, naming every last one of their names when they were bitten by the hair that Hunahpu had plucked from his own shin. It wasn't really a mosquito that bit them. It went to hear all their names for Hunahpu and Xbalanque.

After that Hunahpu and Xbalanque went on, and then they came to where the Xibalbans were:

"Bid the lords good day," said someone who was seated there. It was a deceiver who spoke.

"These aren't lords! These are manikins, woodcarvings!" they said as they came up.

And after that, they bid them good morning:

"Morning, One Death. Morning, Seven Death.
Morning, House Corner. Morning, Blood Gatherer.
Morning, Pus Master. Morning, Jaundice Master.
Morning, Bone Scepter. Morning, Skull Scepter.
Morning, Wing. Morning, Packstrap.
Morning, Bloody Teeth. Morning, Bloody Claws,"

they said when they arrived, and all of their identities were accounted for. They named every one of their names; there wasn't a single name they missed. When this was required of them, no name was omitted by them.

"Sit here," they were told. They were wanted on the bench, but they didn't want it:

"This bench isn't for us! It's just a stone slab for cooking," said Hunahpu and Xbalanque. They were not defeated.

"Very well. Just get in the house," they were told.

And after that, they entered Dark House. They were not defeated there. This was the first test they entered in Xibalba, and as far as the Xibalbans were concerned they were as good as defeated.

First they entered Dark House.

And after that, the messenger of One Death brought their torch, burning when it arrived, along with one cigar apiece.

" 'Here is their torch,' says the lord. 'They must return the torch in the morning, along with the cigars. They must return them intact,' say the lords," the messenger said when he arrived.

"Very well," they said, but they didn't burn the torch—instead, something that looked like fire was substituted. This was the tail of the macaw, which looked like a torch to the sentries. And as for the cigars, they just put fireflies at the tips of those cigars, which they kept lit all night.

"We've defeated them," said the sentries, but the torch was not consumed—it just looked that way. And as for the cigars, there wasn't anything burning there—it just looked that way. When these things were taken back to the lords:

"What's happening? Where did they come from? Who begot them and bore them? Our hearts are really hurting, because what they're doing to us is no good. They're different in looks and different in their very being," they said among themselves.

[Then, playing ball with the Xibalbans, who insist on using their own ball inside of which is hidden White Dagger, the twins allow the Xibalbans to defeat them but manage to survive. As a result of their loss, they must return the next day with four bowls of flowers for the winning Xibalbans. They are sent to Razor House, a place filled with cutting blades, for the night. They survive the cutting blades and send ants to cut flowers from the Xibalbans' own gardens. When the Xibalbans discover that they have been paid with their own flowers, they punish the birds who were assigned to protect the gardens. The twins then manage to survive the ordeal of Cold House, filled with drafts and hail; Jaguar House, full of hungry jaguars; and a house continually filled with flames.]

Now they were put inside Bat House, with bats alone inside the house, a house of snatch-bats, monstrous beasts, their snouts like knives, the instruments of death. To come before these is to be finished off at once.

When they were inside they just slept in their blowgun; they were not bitten by the members of the household. But this is where they gave one of themselves up because of a snatch-bat that came down, he came along just as one of them showed himself. They did it because it was actually what they were asking for, what they had in mind.

And all night the bats are making noise:

"Squeak! Squeak!"

they say, and they say it all night.

Then it let up a little. The bats were no longer moving around. So there, one of the boys crawled to the end of the blowgun, since Xbalanque said:

"Hunahpu? Can you see how long it is till dawn?"

"Well, perhaps I should look to see how long it is," he replied. So he kept trying to look out the muzzle of the blowgun, he tried to see the dawn.

And then his head was taken off by a snatch-bat, leaving Hunahpu's body still stuffed inside.

"What's going on? Hasn't it dawned?" said Xbalanque. No longer is there any movement from Hunahpu. "What's this? Hunahpu hasn't left, has he? What have you done?" He no longer moves; now there is only heavy breathing.

After that, Xbalanque despaired:

"Alas! We've given it all up!" he said. And elsewhere, the head meanwhile went rolling onto the court, in accordance with the word of One and Seven Death, and all the Xibalbans were happy over the head of Hunahpu.

After that, Xbalanque summoned all the animals: coati, peccary, all the animals, small and great. It was at night, still nighttime when he asked them for their food:

"Whatever your foods are, each one of you: that's what I summoned you for, to bring your food here," Xbalanque told them.

"Very well," they replied, then they went to get what's theirs, then indeed they all came back.

There's the one who only brought his rotten wood.

There's the one who only brought leaves.

There's the one who only brought stones.

There's the one who only brought earth, on through the varied foods of the animals, small and great, until the very last one remained: the coati. He brought a squash, bumping it along with his snout as he came.

And this became a simulated head for Hunahpu. His eyes were carved right away, then brains came from the thinker, from the sky. This was the Heart of Sky, Hurricane, who came down, came on down into Bat House. The face wasn't finished any too quickly; it came out well. His strength was just the same, he looked handsome, he spoke just the same.

And this is when it was trying to dawn, reddening along the horizon:

"Now make the streaks, man," the possum was told.

"Yes," said the old man. When he made the streaks he made it dark again; the old man made four streaks.

"Possum is making streaks," people say today, ever since he made the early dawn red and blue, establishing its very being.

"Isn't it good?" Hunahpu was asked.

"Good indeed," he replied. His head was as if it had every bone; it had become like his real head.

After that, they had a talk, they made arrangements with each other:

"How about not playing ball yourself? You should just make lots of threats, while I should be the one to take all the action," Xbalanque told him. After that, he gave instructions to a rabbit:

"Your place is there above the court, on top. Stay there in the oaks," the rabbit was told by Xbalanque, "until the ball comes to you, then take off while I get to work," the rabbit was told. He got his instructions while it was still dark.

After that, when it dawned, both of them were just as well as ever.

And when the ball was dropped in again, it was the head of Hunahpu that rolled over the court:

"We've won! You're done!

Give up! You lost!"

they were told. But even so Hunahpu was shouting:

"Punt the head as a ball!" he told them.

"Well, we're not going to do them any more harm with threats," and with this the lords of Xibalba sent off the ball and Xbalanque received it, the ball was stopped by his yoke, then he hit it hard and it took off, the ball passed straight out of the court, bouncing just once, just twice, and stopping among the oaks. Then the rabbit took off hopping, then they went off in pursuit, then all the Xibalbans went off, shouting, shrieking, they went after the rabbit, off went the whole of Xibalba.

After that, the boys got Hunahpu's head back. Then Xbalanque planted the squash; this is when he went to set the squash above the court.

So the head of Hunahpu was really a head again, and the two of them were happy again. And the others, those Xibalbans, were still going on in search of the ball.

After that, having recovered the ball from among the oaks, the boys cried out to them:

"Come back! Here's the ball! We've found it!" they said, so they stopped. When the Xibalbans got back:

"Have we been seeing things?" they said. Then they began their ball game again, and they made equal plays on both sides again.

After that, the squash was punted by Xbalanque. The squash was wearing out; it fell on the court, bringing to light its light-colored seeds, as plain as day right in front of them.

"How did you get ahold of that? Where did it come from?" said Xibalba.

With this, the masters of Xibalba were defeated by Hunahpu and Xbalanque. There was great danger there, but they did not die from all the things that were done to them.

And here it is: the epitaph, the death of Hunahpu and Xbalanque. Here it is: now we shall name their epitaph, their death. They did whatever they were instructed to do, going through all the dangers, the troubles that were made for them, but they did not die from the tests of Xibalba, nor were they defeated by all the voracious animals that inhabit Xibalba.

After that, they summoned two midmost seers, similar to readers. Here are their names: Xulu, Pacam, both knowers.

"Perhaps there will be questions from the lords of Xibalba about our death. They are thinking about how to overcome us because we haven't died, nor have we been defeated. We've exhausted all their tests. Not even the animals got us. So this is the sign, here in our hearts: their instrument for our death will be a stone oven. All the Xibalbans have gathered together. Isn't our death inevitable? So this is your plan, here we shall name it: if you come to be questioned by them about our death, once we've been burned, what will you say, Xulu and Pacam? If they ask you:

'Wouldn't it be good if we dumped their bones in the canyon?'

'Perhaps it wouldn't be good, since they would only come back to life again,' you will say.

'Perhaps this would be good: we'll just hang them up in a tree,' they'll say to you next:

'Certainly that's no good, since you would see their faces,' you will say, and then they'll speak to you for the third time:

'Well, here's the only good thing: we'll just dump their bones in the river.' If that's what they ask you next:

'This is a good death for them, and it would also be good to grind their bones on a stone, just as corn is refined into flour, and refine each of them separately, and then:

Spill them into the river,
sprinkle them on the water's way,
among the mountains, small and great,'

you will say, and then you will have carried out the instructions we've named for you," said Hunahpu and Xbalanque. When they gave these instructions they already knew they would die.

This is the making of the oven, the great stone oven. The Xibalbans made it like the places where the sweet drink is cooked, they opened it to a great width.

After that, messengers came to get the boys, the messengers of One and Seven Death:

" 'They must come. We'll go with the boys, to see the treat we've cooked up for them,' say the lords, you boys," they were told.

"Very well," they replied. They went running and arrived at the mouth of the oven.

And there they tried to force them into a game:

"Here, let's jump over our drink four times, clear across, one of us after the other, boys," they were told by One Death.

"You'll never put that one over on us. Don't we know what our death is, you lords? Watch!" they said, then they faced each other. They grabbed each other by the arms and went head first into the oven.

And there they died, together, and now all the Xibalbans were happy, raising their shouts, raising their cheers:

"We've really beaten them! They didn't give up easily," they said.

After that they summoned Xulu and Pacam, who kept their word: the bones went just where the boys had wanted them. Once the Xibalbans had done the divination, the bones were ground and spilled in the river, but they didn't go far—they just sank to the bottom of the water.

They became handsome boys; they looked just the same as before when they reappeared.

And on the fifth day they reappeared. They were seen in the water by the people. The two of them looked like channel catfish when their faces were seen by Xibalba. And having germinated in the waters, they appeared the day after that as two vagabonds, with rags before and rags behind, and rags all over too. They seemed unrefined when they were examined by Xibalba; they acted differently now.

It was only the Dance of the Poorwill, the Dance of the Weasel, only Armadillos they danced.

Only swallowing Swords, only Walking on Stilts now they danced.

They performed many miracles now. They would set fire to a house, as if they were really burning it, and suddenly bring it back again. Now Xibalba was full of admiration.

Next they would sacrifice themselves, one of them dying for the other, stretched out as if in death. First they would kill themselves, but then they would suddenly look alive again. The Xibalbans could only admire what they did. Everything they did now was already the groundwork for their defeat of Xibalba.

And after that, news of their dances came to the ears of the lords, One and Seven Death. When they heard it they said:

"Who are these two vagabonds? Are they really such a delight? And is their dancing really that pretty? They do everything!" they said. An account of them had reached the lords. It sounded delightful, so then they entreated their messengers to notify them that they must come:

" ' "If only they'd come make a show for us, we'd wonder at them and marvel at them," say the lords,' you will say," the messengers were told. So they came to the dancers, then spoke the words of the lords to them.

"But we don't want to, because we're really ashamed. Just plain no. Wouldn't we be afraid to go inside there, into a lordly house? Because we'd really look bad. Wouldn't we just be wide-eyed? Take pity on us! Wouldn't we look like mere dancers to them? What would we say to our fellow vagabonds? There are others who also want us to dance today, to liven things up with us, so we can't do likewise for the lords, and likewise is not what we want, messengers," said Hunahpu and Xbalanque.

Even so, they were prevailed upon: through troubles, through torments, they went on their tortuous way. They didn't want to walk fast. Many times they had to be forced; the messengers went ahead of them as guides but had to keep coming back. And so they went to the lord.

And they came to the lords. Feigning great humility, they bowed their heads all the way to the ground when they arrived. They brought themselves low, doubled over, flattened out, down to the rags, to the tatters. They really looked like vagabonds when they arrived.

So then they were asked what their mountain and tribe were, and they were also asked about their mother and father:

"Where do you come from?" they were asked.

"We've never known, lord. We don't know the identity of our mother and father. We must've been small when they died," was all they said. They didn't give any names.

"Very well. Please entertain us, then. What do you want us to give you in payment?" they were asked.

"Well, we don't want anything. To tell the truth, we're afraid," they told the lord.

"Don't be afraid. Don't be ashamed. Just dance this way: first you'll dance to sacrifice yourselves, you'll set fire to my house after that, you'll act out all the things you know. We want to be entertained. This is our heart's desire, the reason you had to be sent for, dear vagabonds. We'll give you payment," they were told.

So then they began their songs and dances, and then all the Xibalbans arrived, the spectators crowded the floor, and they danced everything: they danced the Weasel, they danced the Poorwill, they danced the Armadillo. Then the lord said to them:

"Sacrifice my dog, then bring him back to life again," they were told.

"Yes," they said.

When they sacrificed the dog
he then came back to life.
And that dog was really happy
when he came back to life.
Back and forth he wagged his tail
when he came back to life.

And the lord said to them:

"Well, you have yet to set my home on fire," they were told next, so then they set fire to the home of the lord. The house was packed with all the lords, but they were not burned. They quickly fixed it back again, lest the house of One Death be consumed all at once, and all the lords were amazed, and they went on dancing this way. They were overjoyed.

And then they were asked by the lord:

"You have yet to kill a person! Make a sacrifice without death!" they were told.

"Very well," they said.

And then they took hold of a human sacrifice.

And they held up a human heart on high.

And they showed its roundness to the lords.

And now One and Seven Death admired it, and now that person was brought right back to life. His heart was overjoyed when he came back to life, and the lords were amazed:

"Sacrifice yet again, even do it to yourselves! Let's see it! At heart, that's the dance we really want from you," the lords said now.

"Very well, lord," they replied, and then they sacrificed themselves.

And this is the sacrifice of Hunahpu by Xbalanque. One by one his legs, his arms were spread wide. His head came off, rolled far away outside. His heart, dug out, was smothered in a leaf, and all the Xibalbans went crazy at the sight.

So now, only one of them was dancing there: Xbalanque.

"Get up!" he said, and Hunahpu came back to life. The two of them were overjoyed at this—and likewise the lords rejoiced, as if they were doing it themselves. One and Seven Death were as glad at heart as if they themselves were actually doing the dance.

And then the hearts of the lords were filled with longing, with yearning for the dance of Hunahpu and Xbalanque, so then came these words from One and Seven Death:

"Do it to us! Sacrifice us!" they said. "Sacrifice both of us!" said One and Seven Death to Hunahpu and Xbalanque.

"Very well. You ought to come back to life. After all, aren't you Death? And aren't we making you happy, along with the vassals of your domain?" they told the lords.

And this one was the first to be sacrificed: the lord at the very top, the one whose name is One Death, the ruler of Xibalba.

And with One Death dead, the next to be taken was Seven Death. They did not come back to life.

And then the Xibalbans were getting up to leave, those who had seen the lords die. They underwent heart sacrifice there, and the heart sacrifice was performed on the two lords only for the purpose of destroying them.

As soon as they had killed the one lord without bringing him back to life, the other lord had been meek and tearful before the dancers. He didn't consent, he didn't accept it:

"Take pity on me!" he said when he realized. All their vassals took the road to the great canyon, in one single mass they filled up the deep abyss. So they piled up there and gathered together, countless ants, tumbling down into the canyon, as if they were being herded there. And when they arrived, they all bent low in surrender, they arrived meek and tearful.

Such was the defeat of the rulers of Xibalba. The boys accomplished it only through wonders, only through self-transformation.

And then they named their names, they gave themselves names before all of Xibalba:

"Listen: we shall name our names, and we shall also name the names of our fathers for you. Here we are: we are Hunahpu and Xbalanque by name. And these are our fathers, the ones you killed: One Hunahpu and Seven Hunahpu by name. And we are here to clear the road of the torments and troubles of our fathers. And so we have suffered all the troubles you've caused us. And so we are putting an end to all of you. We're going to kill you. No one can save you now," they were told. And then all the Xibalbans got down on the ground and cried out:

"Take pity on us, Hunahpu and Xbalanque! It is true that we wronged your fathers, the ones you name. Those two are buried at the Place of Ball Game Sacrifice," they replied.

"Very well. Now this is our word, we shall name it for you. All of you listen, you Xibalbans: because of this, your day and your descendants will not be great. Moreover, the gifts you receive will no longer be great, but reduced to scabrous nodules of sap. There will be no cleanly blotted blood for you, just griddles, just gourds, just brittle things broken to pieces. Further, you will only feed on creatures of the meadows and clearings. None of those who are born in the light, begotten in the light will be yours. Only the worthless will yield themselves up before you. These will be the guilty, the violent, the wretched, the afflicted. Wherever the blame is clear, that is where you will come in, rather than just making sudden attacks on people in general. And you will hear petitions over headed-up sap," all the Xibalbans were told.

Such was the beginning of their disappearance and the denial of their worship.

> Their ancient day was not a great one,
> these ancient people only wanted conflict,
> their ancient names are not really divine,
> but fearful is the ancient evil of their faces.
>
> They are makers of enemies, users of owls,
> they are inciters to wrongs and violence,
> they are masters of hidden intentions as well,
> they are black and white,
> masters of stupidity, masters of perplexity,

as it is said. By putting on appearances they cause dismay.

Such was the loss of their greatness and brilliance. Their domain did not return to greatness. This was accomplished by Hunahpu and Xbalanque.

And this is their grandmother, crying and calling out in front of the corn ears they left planted. Corn plants grew, then dried up.

And this was when they were burned in the oven; then the corn plants grew again.

And this was when their grandmother burned something, she burned copal before the corn as a memorial to them. There was happiness in their grandmother's heart the second time the corn plants sprouted. Then the ears were deified by their grandmother, and she gave them names: Middle of the House, Middle of the Harvest, Living Corn, Earthen Floor became their names.

And she named the ears Middle of the House, Middle of the Harvest, because they had planted them right in the middle of the inside of their home.

And she further named them Earthen Floor, Living Corn, since the corn ears had been placed up above an earthen floor.

And she also named them Living Corn, because the corn plants had grown again. So they were named by Xmucane. They had been left behind, planted by Hunahpu and Xbalanque, simply as a way for their grandmother to remember them.

And the first to die, a long time before, had been their fathers, One Hunahpu and Seven Hunahpu. And they saw the face of their father again, there in Xibalba. Their father spoke to them again when they had defeated Xibalba.

And here their father is put back together by them. They put Seven Hunahpu back together; they went to the Place of Ball Game Sacrifice to put him together. He had wanted his face to become just as it was, but when he was asked to name everything, and once he had found the name of the mouth, the nose, the eyes of his face, there was very little else to be said. Although his mouth could not name the names of each of his former parts, he had at least spoken again.

And so it remained that they were respectful of their father's heart, even though they left him at the Place of Ball Game Sacrifice:

"You will be prayed to here," his sons told him, and his heart was comforted. "You will be the first resort, and you will be the first to have your day kept by those who will be born in the light, begotten in the light. Your name will not be lost. So be it," they told their father when they comforted his heart.

"We merely cleared the road of your death, your loss, the pain, the suffering that were inflicted upon you."

And such was the instruction they gave when all the Xibalbans had been finally defeated. And then the two boys ascended this way, here into the middle of the light, and they ascended straight on into the sky, and the sun belongs to one and the moon to the other. When it became light within the sky, on the face of the earth, they were there in the sky.

And this was also the ascent of the Four Hundred Boys killed by Zipacna.

And these came to accompany the two of them. They became the sky's own stars.

THE FLAYED GOD

The Fall into Xibalba: The Palenque Sarcophagus Lid

In a tomb deep within the Temple of Inscriptions at Palenque rests the sarcophagus containing the remains of Pacal, ruler of Palenque from A.D. 615 to 683. The massive lid covering the sarcophagus bears a beautiful and complex image sculpted in low relief depicting the moment of Pacal's falling backward, out of balance, into the maw of the Earth Monster. He is, of course, entering Xibalba just as the hero twins of the *Popol Vuh* entered that dread land, and he will follow their lead in doing battle with and eventually overcoming the lords of death. Michael Coe, in fact, suggests that Pacal is here represented as one of the hero twins of the *Popol Vuh* because "the legend of the resurrection of Hun Hunahpu was infused into the mythological history of this, and other sites, where the rulers themselves were regarded as the living descendents, or incarnates of the Hero Twins, Hunahpu and Xbalanque."[71] Like them, he will achieve an apotheosis, being reborn as a divine ancestor who, in some mysterious sense, will continue to guide the fortunes of the people of Palenque.

Pacal is represented here as falling down the world tree, the vertical axis of the cosmos along which movement into the realm of the spirit is possible. But this is a peculiar world tree, one that bears a remarkable resemblance to a corn stalk. That resemblance suggests in its own way the idea of rebirth, equating the corn and the ruler as participants in the fundamental cycle of life. The central image of the tree thus does more than represent the vertical axis of the cosmos. A stunning example of the multivocality of a single image, it brings together a number of sun-related cycles referring to regeneration on a series of metaphoric levels—the growth of corn, the transfiguration of ancestors, the movement of power from dead ancestors to living rulers—all of them affirmations of the belief that "a king dies, but a god is born."[72] Whether scholars interpret this plant as a world tree or a corn plant, all agree that the common denominator is the theme of the rising, falling, and regenerative pattern of the sun as it applies, in this specific instance, to rulership.

Thus Pacal is identified here with the symbol of the setting sun, the quadripartite monster, with whom he is metaphorically "equivalent" at the time of his death. This equivalency inevitably suggests his rebirth with the rising sun, as does the jade effigy of the sun god buried with him in his tomb. Like the world tree, whose roots grow into the underworld but whose branches reach into the heavens, symbolized here by the quetzal or moan bird sitting atop them, Pacal is shown suspended in time between the heavens and the underworld, "a part of all three worlds, a mortal king who is to be reborn a god."[73]

That view of this scene is corroborated by the presence of what Robertson has called a "psychoduct," or hollow stone tube, a representation of the mother's serpentine umbilical cord, indicative of true lineage rights, that connects Pacal's sarcophagus deep in the inner recesses of the pyramid to the temple that crowns the structure and gives it its name, the Temple of Inscriptions.

Dancing out of Death: A Limestone Panel from Palenque

Having fallen down the world tree into Xibalba, the realm of the dead, as we have seen illustrated on the relief sculpted on the sarcophagus lid of Pacal's tomb at Palenque, the ruler, like all heroes, must end his journey by completing the cycle with an apotheosis, a return to mark his "triumph" over death. On this limestone tablet from Palenque's Classic period Temple 14 (A.D. 705), we find the portrayal of the dead king Chan-Bahlum, son of Pacal. Having defeated the lords of death, he dances triumphantly before us, as did the hero twins of the *Popol Vuh* in the course of their victorious return from Xibalba. Framed on either side by two heavily inscribed columns, the two figures in the scene stand on a platform of shells symbolizing water, the lowest part of which, according to Linda Schele and Mary Ellen Miller, represents the water of the underworld from which the king returns.

"The kin 'sun'sign he wears in his headdress, along with a personified tree, denotes the path he has followed in his journey into and out of Xibalba." As he dances toward her and throws his loincloth aside, he is greeted by his dead mother, identified in the glyphic narration as Lady Ahpo-Hel, who seems to be lifting herself from the ground to welcome him to the realm of his heroic ancestors. "She lifts god K [the image she is holding in her hand] toward her son, making sure to align its head toward her so that when Chan-Bahlum takes it, its staff will be in the proper position for ritual display." The glyphic inscription on the columns provides information about this dance of rebirth and "equates the apotheosis of Chan-Bahlum with mythological events that occurred during a previous creation," suggesting that *in illo tempore* the gods and goddesses also carried out the same ritual.[74] Among other things, this return from Xibalba is one that is equated with the journey of the moon goddess, symbolic of the continual death that brings with it the promise of rebirth.

The complexity of this scene is attested to by the variety of scholarly interpretations it has been given. Karen Bassie-Sweet, for example, analyzing the glyphs with great care, concludes that "the location of the event is a cave" and that "for the Maya, the cave acted as a passage of transition between the real and invisible world. As such, the cave made an ideal setting for these rites of passage."[75] In any case, however, the focus of the scene is surely placed on the triumphant return of the hero, who, like Xbalanque, "was dancing there" before he brought Hunahpu back to life by simply saying "Get up!" after which everyone rejoiced as they looked on, "as if they themselves were actually doing the dance." Surely the artist who carved this magnificent panel expected that all those who were privileged to view it would rejoice "as if they themselves were actually doing the dance," for it gave them assurance from both the mythological and the historical past that they too would return as "the sky's own stars."

THE AZTEC HERO JOURNEY

Quetzalcoatl's Hero Journey, from the *Florentine Codex*

This marvelous account of the glory of the Toltecs and their fall from that glory at the hands of sorcerers[76] is reminiscent of the fall of Dido and with her the great city of Carthage in Virgil's *Aeneid*. In both cases the spirit and the fate of the city are inextricably linked to the ruler. In the Old World myth we see Dido, like Quetzalcoatl in the New World myth, first in her majestic city, where everywhere there is evidence of "the artist's workmanship, the craftsman's labor." Aeneas watches her as she "moved in her company, a queen rejoicing,/Ordering on her kingdom's rising glory." But that glory must fall, and it falls in a way remarkably similar to the manner in which Quetzalcoatl succumbs. Dido gives in to her passion for Aeneas, a passion set up as a trick by the gods, and after her fall, "the towers no longer rise, the youth are slack . . . /[and] Walls halt halfway to heaven."[77] After she builds her own funeral pyre, like Quetzalcoatl's raft of serpents, the goddess Isis comes to her at her dying moment and "from the body releases the soul."

There are, of course, many differences between these similar visions of the Old and New Worlds, but both tragedies of the great fall of the ruler and the people who depend on that ruler are presented by their narrators with a deep sense of pathos, and their essence is remarkably comparable. Neither the mythic dream nor the ideal society can be sustained; life inevitably intrudes, but the universal nature of this mythic pattern suggests that a people must have its dream of the Golden Age as an ideal to guide them, as a vision of the possible rule of spirit in this fallen world of nature.

It is fascinating that the structure of this narrative, a structure presumably fashioned by Sahagún's native informants, abruptly juxtaposes the ideal city of Quetzalcoatl to the "real" city of Uemac, the later ruler. In that jolting structural movement from the ideal to the real, we have the perfect counterpoint to Quetzalcoatl's fall from a life of ideal purity to a state of human weakness. The ideal must give way to the real, but the ideal continues to exist in the myth, in the mind, in the world of the spirit. Quetzalcoatl will "fashion a raft of serpents" and "set off across the sea," but he will return.

QUETZALCOATL'S HERO JOURNEY

Translated from the Nahuatl by Arthur J. O. Anderson and Charles E. Dibble. Originally published in Bernardino de Sahagún, *General History of the Things of New Spain, Book 3: The Origin of the Gods.* Translated by Arthur J. O. Anderson and Charles E. Dibble (Santa Fe, NM: School of American Research, and Salt Lake City: Univ. of Utah, 1952), 13–36. Reprinted by permission of the publisher.

I

WHICH TELLETH—IN WHICH IS RELATED—THE STORY OF QUETZALCOATL, WHO WAS A GREAT WIZARD; AND OF THE PLACE WHERE HE RULED, AND OF WHAT HE DID WHEN HE WENT AWAY.

This Quetzalcoatl they considered a god. They all adored him as a god. He was prayed to in olden times there at Tula.

And there was his temple, which was very tall and high; lofty and towering. Very many were its steps, extending in a multitude, and not wide; but each one, in truth, was very narrow. On each step, the sole of one's foot could not be extended.

There, it is said, he lay; he lay covered; and he lay with only his face covered. And, it is said, he was monstrous.

His face was like a huge, battered stone, a great fallen rock; it was not made like that of men. And his beard was very long—exceedingly long. He was heavily bearded.

And the Toltecs, his vassals, were highly skilled. Nothing that they did was difficult for them. They cut green stone, and they cast gold, and they made other works of the craftsman and the feather worker. Very skilled were they. These started and proceeded from Quetzalcoatl—all craft works and wisdom.

And there stood his green stone house, and his golden house, and his coral house, and his shell house, and his house of beams, his turquoise house, and his house of precious feathers.

And for his vassals the Toltecs, nothing with which they dealt was too distant. Very quickly they could arrive whither they went. And because they were fleet, they were named tlanquacemilhuime.

And there was a hill named Tzatzitepetl. Just so is it named today. It is said that there the crier stationed himself; for that which was required he placed himself there in order to announce it. He was heard clearly in distant places; everywhere was heard that which he said, the laws that were made. Swiftly all would come forth to learn what Quetzalcoatl had commanded the people.

And also they were very rich. Of no value were food and all sustenance. It is said that all the squashes were very large, and some were quite round. And the ears of maize were as large as hand grinding stones, and long. They could hardly be embraced in one's arms. And the amaranth plants—verily, they climbed up them; they could be climbed. And also colored cotton prospered—bright red, yellow, rose colored, violet, green, azure, verdigris color, whitish, brown, shadowy, rose red, and coyote colored. All different colored cottons were this way; so they grew; they did not dye them.

And there dwelt all varieties of birds of precious feather—the blue cotinga, the quetzal, the troupial, the red spoonbill, and all the different birds, which spoke very well; which sang right sweetly. And all the green stones and gold were not costly. Very much of all this was owned. And also chocolate—xochicacauatl—was made. In very many places there was chocolate.

And these Toltecs enjoyed great wealth; they were rich; never were they poor. Nothing did they lack in their homes. Never was there want. And the small ears of maize were of no use to them; they only burned them to heat the sweat baths.

And this Quetzalcoatl also did penances. He bled the calf of his leg to stain thorns with blood. And he bathed at midnight. And he bathed there where his bathing place was, at a placed name Xippacoyan. Him the fire priests imitated, and the other priests. And the priests took their manner of conduct from the life of Quetzalcoatl. By it they ordained the law of Tula. Thus were customs established here in Mexico.

II

WHICH TELLETH HOW THE GLORY OF QUETZALCOATL CAME TO AN END, AND HOW THREE SORCERERS CAME TO HIM, AND WHAT THEY DID.

And at this time, Quetzalcoatl and all the Toltecs became slothful. And there approached and came, as evil sorcerers, three demons— Uitzilopochtli, Titlacauan, and Tlacauepan. All three practised sorcery that they might bring ruin to Tula.

This Titlacauan began casting the spell. It is told that he turned himself into a little old man. He counterfeited and took the form of one who was much bent and whose hair was very white, very silvery. Thereupon he went to the home of Quetzalcoatl.

When he had gone there, he then said to the retainers: "I wish to see the chief, Quetzalcoatl."

Then the others replied to him: "Go hence, old man. The chief is sick. Thou wilt vex him."

Then the old man said: "Nay, verily I will see him; verily I must come to him."

They said to him: "So be it. Wait a little. We shall tell him."

And thereupon they informed Quetzalcoatl. They said to him: "My prince, an old man hath come to speak with thee, one who seemeth like a net, like a trap for thee. We would turn him away, but he wisheth not to go. He saith only: 'I will see the chief for myself.'"

Then said Quetzalcoatl: "Let him come; let him enter. For I have awaited him for some little time."

Then they brought him in to Quetzalcoatl.

Thereupon the old man came and said to him: "My grandson, my chief, how is thy health? Here is a potion which I have brought for thee. Drink it."

And then Quetzalcoatl said: "Come here, O old one. Thou art spent; thou hast tired thyself. For some time I have awaited thee."

And then the old man replied to him: "My grandson, how, in sooth, is thy health?"

Then Quetzalcoatl said to him: "Verily, much do I ail in all parts. Nowhere am I well—my hands, my feet. In truth, my body is tired, as if it were undone."

And then the old one said to him: "Here is the potion, good, soothing, and intoxicating. If thou shalt drink of it, it will relieve and heal thy body. And thou shalt weep; thy heart will become troubled. Thou shalt think upon thy death. And also thou shalt think upon where thou shalt go."

Then Quetzalcoatl said: "Where am I to go, old one?"

Then the old man said to him: "Yea, thou shalt go there to Tollan-Tlapallan. A man there standeth guard, one already aged. Ye shall consult with each other. And when thou shalt return here, thou shalt again have been made a child."

On this, Quetzalcoatl was much moved. And the old man once more said: "Be of good cheer. Drink the potion."

Then Quetzalcoatl said: "Old man, I will not drink of it."

Then the old man said to him: "Drink of it; thou shalt feel a need for it. Nay, only place some of it before thee as thy small portion in case thou feelest thy desire for it. Taste only a little of it."

And Quetzalcoatl then tasted a little, and afterwards drank heartily of it.

Then said Quetzalcoatl: "What is this? It is very good. The sickness is now abated. Where went the pain? No longer am I sick."

Then the old man said: "Drink of it once again; the potion is good. Thus will thy body gain strength."

And as soon as he had once more drunk of it—all,—then he became sotted. Thereupon he wept, and greatly was he moved. Thus, at this time, was Quetzalcoatl aroused; his heart was quickened. No longer could he forget what had happened, but went on reflecting, realizing that indeed the devil had tricked him.

And the potion which the old man had offered him, it is told, was white wine. And it is said that this wine was made of the sap of the maguey called teometl.

III

WHICH TELLETH OF ANOTHER FRAUD WHICH THE SORCERER TITLACAUAN WROUGHT.

And behold another thing which Titlacauan did, thus casting a spell. He took the form and played the part of a stranger. He walked about with his virile member hanging uncovered, and sold green chilis. He went to sit in the market place, before the palace entrance.

And the daughter of Uemac was very fair. Many among the Toltecs desired her and sought her, that they might marry her. But to none would Uemac listen. He gave her to no one.

And this daughter of Uemac looked out into the market place and saw the stranger with virile member hanging uncovered.

And when she had seen him, she went into the house. Thereupon she sickened; she became tense and inflamed because of her desire of the stranger's member.

And Uemac then learned that his daughter was sick. He said to the women who guarded her: "What hath happened? What hath she done? How began that which hath inflamed my daughter?"

Then the women who guarded her said to him: "It is he, the stranger who selleth green chilis. He hath inflamed and vexed her. Thus it began; thus sickness seized her."

And Uemac, the chief, thereupon commanded and said: "O Toltecs, let the green chili vending stranger be sought out; let him appear before me."

Thereupon was he sought everywhere. And when no one came forth, thereupon the herald cried out from Tzatzitepetl. He said: "O Toltecs, if perchance ye see the green chili vending stranger, bring him here. The chief seeketh him."

Thereupon they looked and went everywhere; they went scattered through Tula as they looked. And when they had tired themselves and seen him nowhere, then they came back to tell the chief that verily nowhere could they see him.

And afterwards the stranger appeared of his own will in the same place where he had formerly come to sit when first he was seen.

And when he had been seen, then they went in haste to tell the chief. They said: "The stranger hath appeared."

Then Uemac said: "Let him come at once."

Then the Toltecs quickly went to seize the stranger. They brought him before the chief.

And when they had brought him, thereupon the chief said to him: "Where is thy home?"

Then the other replied to him: "I am a stranger. I sell little chilis."

Then the chief said to him: "Where hast thou been, stranger? Don thy breech clout; cover thyself."

Then the stranger replied to him: "Nay, but to this manner are we accustomed."

And the chief then said to him: "But thou hast afflicted my daughter. Thou art the one who must heal her."

Then the stranger said to him: "My dear stranger, my dear lord, this may not be. Rather slay me, kill me, let me die. What sayest thou to me? I am not the only one who selleth green chilis."

And then the chief said: "Nay, thou shalt heal her. Have no fear."

And thereupon they arranged his hair and they bathed him. Then they anointed him, they gave him a breech clout and girt him with it.

And when they had arrayed him, thereupon the chief said to him: "Look upon my daughter there where she is guarded."

And when he went there, then he lay with her, and then the woman was well. Later the stranger became the chief's son-in-law.

IV

WHICH TELLETH HOW THE TOLTECS WERE ANGERED BECAUSE OF THE MARRIAGE OF THE DAUGHTER OF UEMAC; AND OF ANOTHER WORK OF SORCERY WHICH TITLACAUAN WROUGHT.

And upon this, the Toltecs jested about Uemac; they mocked him and spoke in malice of him. They said: "And so the chief hath taken a stranger as son-in-law!" Thereafter the chief summoned the Toltecs; he said to them: "I have heard that jests are made of me, that already I am laughed at, for I have made the stranger my son-in-law. And this shall ye do—by deceit abandon him while fighting at Cacatepec and Coatepec."

And thereupon the Toltecs announced war; they all set out. Thereupon they went, that they might leave the son-in-law to his fate.

And when they had gone off to war, thereupon they planted apart the stranger and all the dwarfs and cripples.

When they had planted them apart, thereupon the Toltecs departed, to capture men—to take men from their foes, the Coatepeca.

And the stranger said to all the dwarfs and cripples: "Have no fear. Here we shall destroy them; here, by our hands, they will meet their doom."

And after this, thereupon the enemy took after the Toltecs. They thought to themselves that the foe would there slay the stranger, from whom in this manner they went, leaving him tricked, leaving him to die.

And upon this they hurried to inform the chief, Uemac. They said to him: "Lo, we have gone, abandoning the stranger, who was thy beloved son-in-law."

And Uemac rejoiced exceedingly, for he thought that his death was fact. For he was ashamed of the stranger whom he had made his son-in-law.

And this stranger, when they had gone leaving him abandoned in battle, when their foes, the Coatepeca and the Cacatepeca had already come up, thereupon commanded the dwarfs and the hunchbacks, and said to them: "Pay good heed! Have no fear! Be not cowards! Lose not heart! For already I know that ye will take them all captive, that in some manner we shall slay all of them!"

And when their foes came upon them and fell upon them, then they verily attacked and trampled over them. They slew them; they brought ruin on them; they destroyed them. Multitudes without number they slew of their foes.

And when the chief heard of it, he was greatly bemused and saddened. Upon this he summoned the Toltecs and said to them: "Let us go to meet our beloved son-in-law."

And the Toltecs then surged and burst forth. Thereupon they accompanied the chief; they went dispersed about him; they went circling him, to meet the stranger. The Toltecs took their panoply with them—the quetzal feather head device, and the turquoise mosaic shield. When they reached him, thereupon they gave and presented him the quetzal feather head device and the turquoise mosaic shield—all their array which they had with them.

With this they proceeded dancing; they came dancing the captives' dance; they came bearing the array on their backs. They came singing in his honor; the song came forth resounding and reechoing. They came blowing flutes in his honor; the shell trumpets roared and rang out. The shell trumpets approached, growing in sound.

And when they went to reach the palace, then they pasted the stranger's head with feathers, and they anointed him with yellow paint. And his face was spread with a red unguent. And all his friends were thus adorned.

And then Uemac said to his son-in-law: "Lo, now are the hearts of the Toltecs satisfied that thou art my son-in-law. Thou hast done well. Be received on this soil. Rest thy feet."

V

WHERE IS RELATED YET ANOTHER ACT OF MAGIC WHICH THE SORCERER BROUGHT TO PASS SO THAT THE TOLTECS DIED AS THEY PERFORMED PENANCES AND DANCED.

A second work of sorcery this demon wrought: When he had been pasted with yellow feathers, when he had bested his enemies, he then brought it about that they should dance and sing, that they should intone a song.

Thereupon the herald made his cry, from the summit of Tzatzitepetl; he cried out to and informed those in all the world over.

Verily everywhere they heard the cry of the herald. And very swiftly all came to Tula.

And when this was done, then the sorcerer went there to Texcalpan. And everyone, all the vassals, went with him. And when all the youths and maidens had gathered together, they could not be counted; they were very numerous.

Thereupon the demon began to sing. He sounded the drum; he beat his ground drum. Thereupon all danced; they went as if leaping; all grasped hands; or took hold of each other from behind. With much contentment was it sung; the sound of the song resounded, and rose and fell.

And the song which was chanted was only one which he then invented.

And when he intoned the song, right then they answered it. From his lips they took the song.

And the singing and dancing began at dusk. And when it ceased, it was midnight.

And as all danced, as the movement was vibrant and most intense, very many then fell on the crags in the canyon. All died there, and then were turned into rocks.

And as for the others at the craggy canyon, the demon then broke the bridge. And the bridge was of stone. Forthwith all fell there where they crossed the water. All turned into rocks.

And how this was done, not then did the Toltecs understand. It was as if they were besotted.

And many times was there singing and dancing there at Texcalpan. And as many times as there was song and dance, so many times was there slaughter. All were dashed upon the crags.

They fell; verily, the Toltecs destroyed themselves.

VI

WHICH TELLETH OF ANOTHER ACT OF MAGIC WHICH THAT SAME SORCERER WROUGHT, WHEREBY YET MANY MORE TOLTECS DIED.

Behold yet another act of sorcery which the demon brought to pass.

It is said that once upon a time he took the form of a valiant warrior. He commanded the herald, the crier, that he should cry to the whole world that they come hence.

The crier said: "Let all men come! Let all the vassals come here! Ye shall go there to Xochitlan. The floating gardens will be harvested."

Thereupon came all the vassals. They came to the flower garden. (And as for naming it Xochitlan: they say it was the flower field of Quetzalcoatl.)

And when the Toltecs had come, gathered and massed together, thereupon the brave warrior slew them; he smote them; he beat the backs of their heads; in sooth, many of them, without number, died at his hands. For he slew them.

And the rest of them, who indeed fled running, who were in headlong flight, went fleeing from his hands. As they went off, seeking to escape, as they ran, they injured one another and there they died. And still others trampled and crushed one another. All died there.

VII

WHICH TELLETH OF YET ANOTHER WORK OF MAGIC WHICH THIS SAME SORCERER WROUGHT, BY WHICH MANY MORE TOLTECS PERISHED.

Behold still another act of sorcery which the demon did. He came to seat himself in the middle of the market place. He called himself Tlacauepan or Cuexcochtzin. There he caused to dance a figure like a child. (They say it was Uitzilopochtli.) In his hand he held him as he made him dance.

And when the Toltecs saw this, thereupon they crowded toward him; they stumbled toward him in order to see it. Very many men were there trampled and died in the press as the others crushed them to death.

And when thus many times it came to pass that large numbers died in this way, as they looked while he made the figure dance, this same demon said, with shouts, "O Toltecs, what sort of sorcery is this? Is it not an omen of evil that one is made to dance? As for this one, let him die; let him be stoned!"

Then they stoned him. He fell under the stones. And when this was done, his body thereafter stank; it smelt quite frightful; in truth, it wounded the head. And wheresoever the wind carried the stench, there the common folk died.

And when already very many men had thus died of its fumes, thereupon to the Toltecs this same demon said: "Let this dead one be cast away; let him be thrown out. For already his odor destroyeth men. Let him be dragged away."

And the Toltecs thereupon put a rope about the body and then sought to drag it away. And now when they tried to heave it, they could not move it. It was very heavy—this, to which at first they had paid little heed, of which they had thought as of little import.

Then a message went out, and the herald said: "Let all men come here! Bring here your heavy ropes that ye may go and cast away the dead one."

And when the Toltecs came to gather together, thereupon they fastened the dead one with ropes. Then the Toltecs murmured; they said to themselves: "O Toltecs, along with it! Let it be pulled!"

But they could not then raise it; they could not move it. And when one of the ropes broke, then died all. As many as extended along the rope tumbled; they fell all mingled together, and then died.

And when they could in no way drag it, when they could not approach it, thereupon the demon said to the Toltecs: "O Toltecs, he hath need of his song."

Thereupon he chanted the song for the Toltecs. He intoned: "Drag away our log, Tlacauepan the demon."

And as they chanted, forthwith they thus made the dead one move; they came forward with it; they proceeded shouting. When a rope again snapped, then on all of them the log fell, so that it ran over them. And many were indeed crushed. So were they crushed that thus they died.

And when all the rest who had gone to cast away the dead one, Tlacauepan, thereupon turned back, it was as if they paid no heed to all that had been done to them. No longer did they consider it an evil omen; they were as if besotted.

VIII

WHICH TELLETH OF STILL ANOTHER WORK OF MAGIC WHICH THIS SAME SORCERER BROUGHT TO PASS, BY WHICH HE CAST A SPELL ON TULA.

Behold also how the devil brought evil to Tula.

It is said that a white kite, with wounded head pierced by an arrow, flew by, passing to and fro over the Toltecs, not far above them. It kept nearing the earth as it flew back and forth. They saw it clearly as they stood and lingered looking upward.

Behold too yet another act of sorcery which was taken as an evil omen for the Toltecs. It is said that a mountain, called Cacatepetl, burned. By night, it was evident from afar how it burned. The flames rose high. When the Toltecs saw it, they became very restless; they raised their hands to heaven; there was great anxiety. All cried out, all shouted together. No longer was there tranquillity; no longer was there peace. And when they saw this omen of evil, they said: "O Toltecs, now is all in truth going from us; already the power of the Toltecs goeth. Yea, we are forsaken. What shall we do? Whither shall we go? O unhappy we! Let us take heart!"

Behold yet another act of sorcery. It is said that stones rained on the Toltecs. And when the stones rained, then a large sacrificial stone fell from the heavens; there at Chapoltepecuitlapilcol it came falling down. And afterwards a little old woman lived there. She sold paper flags; she walked about saying: "Here are your little flags." And any destined to die said: "Buy me one," and thereupon went where the sacrificial stone was. None asked: "What now dost thou do?" They were as if lost.

IX

IN WHICH IS TOLD YET ANOTHER WORK OF MAGIC WHICH THIS SAME SORCERER WROUGHT, BY WHICH HE MOCKED THEM, BY WHICH TULA WAS UNDONE, AND THROUGH WHICH HE SLEW NOT A FEW TOLTECS.

Behold also the manner in which sorcery was practised against the Toltecs.

It is said that the food soured—very bitter did it become. It could not be placed in one's mouth; none of the Toltecs could eat the food. In truth, so were the Toltecs mocked.

And an old woman (they said and considered that it was the devil who appeared and took the form of an old woman) came to sit there at Xochitlan. There she toasted maize. And the maize which she toasted spread its fragrance over all the region. In truth it expanded and spread among all who dwelt there. All over the land was spread the odor of the toasted maize.

And when they smelled the toasted maize, the Toltecs found the smell good; they found it satisfying and pleasing. And when they smelled it, quickly they came here and swiftly, reaching here in only a very few moments. (For it is said that the Toltecs thought no place distant; they thought nowhere too remote. Even though they might live far away, swiftly they arrived, and also as rapidly returned whence they had come.)

And then, as many as had gathered together she slew and destroyed—all. Not then might they make their return. A great mockery was made of the Toltecs, since the devil had slain very many of them. It is said that in sooth he made sport of the Toltecs.

X

WHICH TELLETH HOW QUETZALCOATL DEPARTED AND LEFT IN FLIGHT WHEN HE WENT TO TLAPALLAN, AND OF THE MANY THINGS WHICH HE DID ON THE WAY.

And still many more acts of sorcery were done to the Toltecs in order to destroy Tula.

And when these things happened, Quetzalcoatl was now troubled and saddened, and thereupon was minded that he should go—that he should abandon his city of Tula.

Thereupon he made ready. It is said that he had everything burned—his house of gold, his house of coral; and still other works of art, the marvelous and costly things, all of these he buried, he hid there in treacherous places: either within the mountains or in the canyons.

And, moreover, the cacao trees he changed into mesquites. And all the birds of precious feather—the quetzal, the blue cotinga, the red spoonbill—all these he sent away beforehand. Taking the road before him, they went toward Anauac.

And when this was done, then he set forth; thereupon he followed the road.

Then he came to arrive at a place called Quauhtitlan. A very thick tree arose there, and very tall. He stood by it. Then he called for his mirror. Thereupon he looked at himself; he saw himself in the glass and said: "Verily, now I am an old man." Then he named the place Ueuequauhtitlan. And then he cast and hurled stones at the tree. And as he stoned it, the stones remained firmly encrusted and affixed to the great tree. Always thus have they been visible. Thus are they seen; beginning at the foot, they rise there to its top.

And as Quetzalcoatl followed the road, they went blowing flutes for him.

Once more he came to rest at another place. Upon a stone Quetzalcoatl rested himself. He supported himself on it with his hands. Thereupon he looked toward Tula, and then wept; as one sobbing he wept. Now he shed two hail stones as tears over his face; they rolled over his face. Thus fell tear drops which verily pierced holes in the stone.

XI

HERE ARE TOLD THE SIGNS WHICH QUETZALCOATL LEFT IN PLACE UPON THE STONE WITH HIS HANDS, WHEN HE RESTED HIMSELF THERE, WHERE HE SAT.

And as he supported himself by his hands on the rock, he left deep imprints, as if it were on mud that he had planted the palms of his hands. Likewise his buttocks remained well marked on the rock where he was. Verily they are now visible. Because of the hollows, this place was named Temacpalco.

And then when he arose he came to reach a place name Tepanoayan, where there was water. A river burst forth which was very wide and long. Quetzalcoatl laid stones and made there a bridge. Then he crossed over on it, and so it is named Tepanoayan.

And once more he set forth and then came to reach another point, a place named Coaapan. And when he was there, devils sought to turn him back. They tried to send him back and stop him.

They said to him: "Where dost thou go? Where art thou bound? Why goest thou now leaving the city? To whom dost thou go leaving it? Who will perform the penances?"

Then Quetzalcoatl said to the demons: "Indeed, in no way can anyone force me; for I must go on."

Then the demons said to Quetzalcoatl: "Whither goest thou?"

Then Quetzalcoatl said to them: "I go there to Tlapallan, for I go to learn my fate."

And then they said to him: "What wilt thou do?"

Then Quetzalcoatl replied: "I am called hence. The sun hath called me."

Then they said to him: "It is well. Go, leaving all the works of craftsmanship."

Then he left all the arts—the casting of gold, the cutting of precious stones, the carving of wood, sculpturing in stone, the knowledge of the scribes, the art of feather working. All these they wrested from him by force; they made him abandon all; they seized all from him.

And when this was done, Quetzalcoatl thereupon cast his jewels into a spring of water, and then they were swallowed up. Therefore he named that place Cozcaapan which now is called Coaapan.

And thereupon he moved on and came to reach another point, a place named Cochtocan. And there a demon then came forth to meet him.

He said to him: "Whither goest thou?"

Then Quetzalcoatl said: "It is there to Tlapallan that I go, to learn my fate."

Then the demon said to him: "It is well. Drink this, the wine which I have brought here."

Quetzalcoatl said: "Nay, it may not be that I drink, even though it might be but little that I taste."

Then once more the devil said to him: "Verily, it may not be that thou shalt not drink nor taste of it. For no one do I give leave, or permit, to depart whom I give no wine and not make drunk and besotted. So do as I bid thee; be of good cheer and drink it."

Quetzalcoatl then drank the wine with a drinking tube.

And when he had drunk, he quickly fell asleep in the road. He lay thundering as he slept, resounding a great distance as he snored. And when he awoke, thereupon he looked to one side and the other. He looked at himself, and arranged his hair. Then he named the place Cochtocan.

XII

WHICH TELLETH HOW THE VASSALS OF QUETZALCOATL FROZE IN THE ICE AND DIED AS THEY PASSED BETWEEN IZTACTEPETL AND POPOCATEPETL; AND OF OTHERS OF HIS EXPLOITS.

Then once again he set forth and came to climb between Popocatepetl and Iztactepetl. He led all the dwarfs and hunchbacks, his servants. It snowed upon them, and there they froze; they died of the cold.

And Quetzalcoatl thereupon was greatly moved and wept to himself. And he sang much to himself as he wept and sighed.

Thereupon he looked at a distance to another white mountain, named Poyauhtecatl. Again he set forth, making the rounds of all places, everywhere passing through the villages. And so, they say, he set down many of his signs, by which he is known.

In another place it is said that he took his pleasure on a mountain. He came sliding down it, to its foot; he came bouncing down it.

And elsewhere he planted in the ground maguey fibers. At another place he built a ball court, all of stone. And in the middle of it, where the line was, the earth lay open, reaching deep; for it was thus pierced. And elsewhere he shot, as an arrow, a bombax ceiba tree, shooting it likewise into the midst of another bombax ceiba so that one rested piercing the other. And elsewhere he built a house all underground at a place named Mictlan.

And elsewhere he set up a huge rock. It is said that one might move it with his little finger; easily it swayed; from side to side it would teeter. And it is said that when many men pushed it, then it would not move, even though many would try hard. If they sought to move it, they could not budge it.

And there were many more things which he did in all the villages. And it is said that he named all the mountains. And in all places he gave all the names here.

And when he had done these things, then he went to reach the sea coast. Thereupon he fashioned a raft of serpents. When he had arranged the raft, there he placed himself, as if it were his boat. Then he set off going across the sea. No one knows how he came to arrive there at Tlapallan.

Quetzalcoatl's Hero Journey, from the *Anales de Cuauhtitlan*

Originally written in Nahuatl around 1570, the *Anales de Cuauhtitlan* is one of the most important and extensive sources of Aztec myth and history. In form it is a chronicle: it lists each year and then narrates the events of that year, if any. In what has been called an "expansion narrative," it includes an account of the adventures of Ce Acatl Topiltzin Quetzalcoatl, an account that shows profound insight into the symbolic implications of the mythic narrative. Although the actual author is not known,[78] much of its mythic insight, offered in the guise of history, is symbolically attributed to Quetzalcoatl, the personification of wisdom, a wisdom associated with Ometeotl, the generative force of the cosmos. Quetzalcoatl "cried out" to the place of "Duality Above Nine Heavens," that is, to Ometeotl, the god of duality. Realizing the greatness of that cosmic force, epitomized by and embodied in the god who gave order to the universe and who was metaphorically the essence of the life force, "the universal cosmic energy from which all life gained sustenance," he entreats Ometeotl to provide insight into the nature of that duality, the nature of all life.[79] As ruler Quetzalcoatl thus acts as a conduit through which that essence of the divine can enter the world of human life.

But immersed in the purity of this life of the spirit, he is unable to recognize the other side, the human side, of his own duality, that which is represented by Tezcatlipoca and his sorcerers, who will bring him the ominous symbolic mirror that will reveal not only his own mortality but also mankind's darker side. By the time he dies he has explored this other side of human nature, and when, at his death, he is "changed to the star that appears at dawn," Venus, the morning star, the "alter ego" of Venus as evening star, his own dual nature has become apparent. As the myth makes clear, the morning star is a destructive force as well as a benevolent one, depending on the particular day of the calendar on which it appears. But "in each of these signs did the elders pay him their homage." His apotheosis as the nature of duality is complete.

Willard Gingerich, the translator of this version of the story of Quetzalcoatl, in an application of the techniques of close literary analysis to a reading of the text, points out that Quetzalcoatl's vital dates, which complete a fifty-two-year cycle from 1 Reed to 1 Reed, "are too symmetrical to be anything but ritualistic and symbolic," and he suggests that "the *Anales* narrator creates . . . an *illo tempore* vignette of a perfect pre-Cortesian (and pre-Aztec) society with a perfectly integrated human psyche at the center. None of it ever existed, of course, except in the nostalgia of the narrator and his sources."[80] That mythic narrative of Quetzalcoatl's "fall," of the flawed ruler and the jealous tempter, creates a sense of tragedy reminiscent of the great Greek drama of the fifth century B.C. The story of Quetzalcoatl's confrontation with his own mortality, narrated with great psychological sensitivity and profound metaphorical overtones, is one of the most moving and universally appealing of the Aztec mythic texts.

QUETZALCOATL'S HERO JOURNEY

This is an original translation from the Nahuatl by Willard Gingerich, prepared for this volume.

I

1 Reed: It is recounted, it is said, in this year was born Quetzalcoatl, the one called Our Honored Prince High Priest One Reed Quetzalcoatl; and it is said his mother's name was Chimalman. And also in this fashion was Quetzalcoatl placed within his mother's womb: she swallowed a precious green stone, it is told.

[Years] 2 Flint, 3 House, 4 Rabbit, 5 Reed, 6 Flint, 7 House, 8 Rabbit, 9 Reed.

In this year 9 Reed Quetzalcoatl searched for his father, when he had come to a little knowledge, being now nine years old. He said, "What is my dear father like? May I see him? May I look on his face?"

And then he was told, "He has died with honor, he is buried there. Go look upon him."

Then Quetzalcoatl went there at once and dug up his bones and buried them again in the temple of the one called Quilaztli.

[Years] 10 Flint, 11 House, 12 Rabbit, 13 Reed, 1 Flint, 2 House, 3 Rabbit, 4 Reed, 5 Flint, 6 House, 7 Rabbit, 8 Reed, 9 Flint, 10 House.

In this year died in honor the Lord Speaker of Cuauhtitlan, Huactli, who had ruled for sixty-two years. He was the Lord Speaker who knew not the sowing of maize, the edible foodstuffs. His people knew not the making of tilmal capes. They wore only skin clothing; their food was only rabbits, snakes, birds, and deer. Nowhere did they keep houses, but only wandered from place to place.

11 Rabbit: The lady Xiuhtlacuiloxochitzin was installed as Speaker. Her grass dwelling stood at the side of the market plaza where Tepextitenco is today. And the city, Cuauhtitlan, passed to her since she was the wife of Huactli, it is said, and because she spoke often to the devil Itzpapalotl.

12 Reed, 13 Flint, 1 House, 2 Rabbit: This year Quetzalcoatl arrived there in Tollantzinco, where during four years he built his House of Fasting, his House of Turquoise-inlaid boards. From there he passed to Cuextlan, from which place he laid a bridge across the water which, it is said, still survives.

3 Reed, 4 Flint, 5 House: In this year the Toltecs took Quetzalcoatl and installed him on the throne there in Tollan and he was their priest; in another part his story has been written.

6 Rabbit, 7 Reed: Lady Xiuhtlacuiloxochitzin died; she had ruled twelve years in Cuauhtitlan.

8 Flint: In this year Ayauhcoyotzin was installed as Lord Speaker of Cuauhtitlan at the place known as Tecpanquauhtla.

9 House, 10 Rabbit, 11 Reed, 12 Flint, 13 House, 1 Rabbit, 2 Reed: (It is the word of Tetzcoco that in this year died Quetzalcoatl, Our Lord of Tollan Colhuacan.) In this year 2 Reed he built his House of Fasting, his place of penance and of prayer. He, Our Lord One Reed Quetzalcoatl, carefully laid out his four houses: his turquoise-plank house, his coral-inlay house, his whiteshell-inlay house, and his quetzal-feather house where he prayed frequently, performed penance and observed his fasts.

And at the exact hour of midnight he went down to the place called Atecpan Amochco, by the water, and there he humbly inserted his penitential spines, which he did as well on the heights of Xicocotl and Huitzco and Tzincoc and Nonohualcatepec. And his penitential spines were made of precious greenstone and he offered them up on a bed of quetzal feathers. And for incense he burned turquoise, greenstone, coral; and his blood offerings were of serpents, birds, butterflies which he sacrificed.

And it is recounted, it is said he prayed often, he sought godhead in the depths of heaven and invoked it by the names

Citlalinicue, Citlallatonac
Tonacacihuatl, Tonacateuctli
Tecolliquenqui, Eztlaquenqui
Tlallamanac, Tlallichcatl.

And the place to which he cried out was known as Omeyocan Chiucnepaniuhcan, "Duality Above Nine Heavens."

And so in this manner he knew those who there kept their dwellings, calling upon and petitioning them insistently in most honorable humility and contrition.

And finally it was he who revealed the grandeur of wealth: jadestone, turquoise, gold—yellow and white, coral, mother-of-pearl, plumage of the quetzal, the cotinga, the roseate spoonbill, the troupial, the trogon and the heron. And he revealed the multicolored cacao as well as multicolored cotton. He was a great Toltec, a grand artisan, in all his earthenware, painted blue green, white, yellow, red and a multitude of colors.

And in the time that he lived he began, he founded his temple and set its serpent columns, but he did not finish and he did not give up hope.

And in the time that he lived he did not show his face before the people; deep within his house he lived where he was protected.

And his heralds kept him, in many places they enclosed him well.

And in every place he stayed, in each and every place were his heralds, and there were the Jadestone Mat, the Quetzal Mat, the Gold Mat of his authority.

And it was recounted, it has been said, his House of Fasting was built in four parts.

And it is recounted, it is said, how many times in vain the Human Owl sorcerers sought to humiliate Quetzalcoatl so that he would make his offerings of humans, that he would sacrifice men.

But he never desired it nor consented. For greatly did he love his common people, his Toltecs, and his offerings, the sacrifices he made continually, were but serpents, birds and butterflies.

And it is recounted, it is said that the owl sorcerers became greatly angered and began tormenting, mocking and humiliating him, saying they wanted in this way to make him miserable. And thus would they drive him out, and truly it was done.

[Years] 3 Flint, 4 House, 5 Rabbit, 6 Reed, 7 Flint, 8 House, 9 Rabbit, 10 Reed, 11 Flint, 12 House, 13 Rabbit, 1 Reed: In this year Quetzalcoatl died. And it is said he went to Tlillan Tlapallan, to die there.

Then was Matlacxochitl installed as Speaker in Tollan.

II

Now, it is recounted how Quetzalcoatl conducted himself when he disregarded the desire of the owl sorcerers that he should make human offerings, that he should sacrifice men.

The owl sorcerers counseled together, those whose names were Tezcatlipoca, Ihuimecatl and Toltecatl. They said, "Certainly it is necessary that he abandon the city, which we will occupy." They said, "Let us brew the pulque which we will give him to drink; so he will be corrupted and so he will no longer perform his sacramental penances."

And then Tezcatlipoca said, "I say we must give him his own body, that he should see it." And so it would be done, that in this way they might punish him with great severity. Then Tezcatlipoca went ahead, carrying a small, double-sided mirror, enwrapped.

And when he had arrived where Quetzalcoatl was, he said to the heralds who protected him, "Please do the honor of saying to the High Priest: 'Truly, Telpochtli, the Young Man, has come to you and wishes most humbly to deliver to you, to humbly show before you your body.' "

And the heralds went in to him and delivered the message. Quetzalcoatl said to them, "What is this thing, grandfather-heralds, what is this body of mine that he has brought here? Examine it; then he will enter."

But he did not wish them to see it. He said, "Truly, I myself must show it to him; tell him this." They went to tell him, "He will not consent. He very much wishes to show you himself." Quetzalcoatl said, "Let him come in, grandfathers."

They went to summon Tezcatlipoca who came in and greeted him saying, "My beloved Prince and High Priest One Reed Quetzalcoatl. I salute your grace, and I arrive to set before you your beloved body." Quetzalcoatl said, "You have wearied yourself in this work, grandfather. From where did you come? What is this thing you call my 'body'? Show it to me."

He said, "My Beloved Prince and High Priest, certainly I am your humble subject. I come from the lower slopes of Mt. Nonohualca. Won't you please look upon your beloved body?"

Then he brought him the mirror and said, "May it please you to know, to look upon yourself, my Beloved Prince, for you will appear there in the mirror."

So then Quetzalcoatl looked upon himself, and he was overcome with horror. He said, "If my subjects see me, perhaps they will flee." For his eyelids were swollen, his eyes sunken deep in their sockets, his face all heavily pockmarked and furrowed; he was a monstrous sight. When he had seen himself in the mirror, he said, "My subjects shall never see me; I will stay here."

Then Tezcatlipoca turned away and withdrew; he called urgently for Ihuimecatl so that they might fully abuse him. Ihuimecatl said, "Let Coyotlinahual 'Shape-shifting Coyote,' the feather-artist, go in to him now." The shape-shifter listened to their suggestion, that he would be the one sent. Coyotlinahual the feather-artist said, "It is good. Let me be the one to go, the one to see Quetzalcoatl."

Then he went, and said to Quetzalcoatl, "My beloved prince, I come to say to your grace in all reverence, come out, show yourself before your subjects. Permit me to array and prepare you so that they might look upon you." Quetzalcoatl said to him, "Prepare them, grandfather, I will see what they are."

And so then Coyotlinahual the feather-artist fashioned them; first he made Quetzalcoatl's plumed headdress, then his turquoise inlay mask. He took red with which to paint his mouth; he took yellow with which to stripe his face. Next he prepared his serpent teeth, then his beard of cotinga and roseate spoonbill feathers across his lower face.

And so he arrayed him in his attire and he was Quetzalcoatl. Then he handed him the mirror, and when he looked on himself he was very pleased with what he saw. Then Quetzalcoatl abandoned forthwith the place where he was guarded.

And so then Coyotlinahual the feather artist went to Ihuimecatl and said, "Certainly I have caused Quetzalcoatl to emerge. Now it's your turn." He replied, "That's fine."

Then he befriended one named Toltecatl and they went off together, and they arrived at a place called Xonacapacoyan where they met with a farmer named Maxtlaton who guarded Toltec Mountain.

And then they also grew herbal greens, tomatoes, chili, green corn and beans, and in only a few days it was done. And there also were magueys in that place which they requested of Maxtlaton. For only four days they fermented the pulque. Next, they collected it; they found wild honeycombs and with these they collected and mixed the pulque.

Then they went to the home of Quetzalcoatl there in Tollan. They took all their herbs, their chili, etc., and the pulque. They arrived and requested entrance, but those who guarded Quetzalcoatl refused them. Twice and three times they returned but were not received. The last time they were asked where was their home? They responded and said, "Why, there on Priest's Mountain, Toltec Mountain." And hearing this, Quetzalcoatl said, "Let them come in." They entered and greeted him and then finally gave him the green herbs, etc.

And when he had eaten, they entreated him once more: they gave him the pulque. But he said, "No, I will not drink it; I am fasting.

Does it not intoxicate? Is it not fatal?" They answered him, "Do taste it with your honorable finger. It is certainly strong and fresh."

Quetzalcoatl tasted it with his finger and found it good. He said, "Allow me to drink, grandfathers; three drinks." "You must drink four," the owl sorcerers said to him, and they gave him the fifth, saying, "This is your ritual libation."

And when he had drunk it, they served it to everyone, to all the heralds they gave five drinks. They made them completely drunk.

Then again the owl sorcerers spoke to Quetzalcoatl and said, "My Beloved Prince, may it please your grace to sing. This is the blessed song it shall honor you to lift up." Then Ihuimecatl raised the song:

> *"My house of quetzal, quetzal*
> *my house of troupial*
> *my house of redshell—*
> *I must already lose them*
> *for my carelessness, An ya!"*

And Quetzalcoatl was now full of joy; he said, "Bring my sister, Quetzalpetlatl. Let us be drunken together!" So his heralds went to Mt. Nonohualca where she practiced her meritorious penances. They said to her, "My beloved princess, noble lady of fasts, Quetzalpetlatl: We have come for you; the High Priest Quetzalcoatl awaits you. Will it not please you to go into his presence?" She answered, "It is good, herald grandfather; let us be off."

And upon arrival she sat herself beside Quetzalcoatl and they served her the pulque, four drinks and then the fifth, her ritual libation. The seducers Ihuimecatl and Toltecatl then also raised another song before the sister of Quetzalcoatl:

> *"My sister, Where now will you live?*
> *O Quetzalpetlatl, let's make ourselves drunk!*
> *Ay, ya, yya, yn, ye, an."*

When they were fully drunken, they no longer said, "If it were not for the merit we earn . . . ," nor did they go down to the water's edge, nor any more plant spines in their bodies. At dawn they performed no sacraments and when the sun appeared they were stricken with anguish, their hearts were orphaned in remorse.

Then Quetzalcoatl spoke and said, "O how unfortunate I am!" And then he composed the lament of his exile; he sang there:

"No longer is even a single day-sign counted in my house;
Let it be here, aya, where he was guarded, let it be here.
Let it already be, let it happen,"

he chanted,

"He who owns the body of earth can be but miserable and
   afflicted.
All that is precious is no more;
Certainly I return to sober virtue."

The second time he chanted his song:

"Aya, she had formed and shaped me,
she who is my mother, an ya,
Coacueye, the goddess;
ah, her son, yyaa,
I weep, yya, ye an."

And when Quetzalcoatl had sung, all his heralds were overcome with sadness and wept also. Then they also sang and raised the chant in that place:

"Aya, He gave us a life of abundant riches;
He who is my Lord, he, Quetzalcoatl.
Lost, your jadestone headdress;
the tree, broken and bleeding.
Let us look already upon him,
Let us weep also."

And when the heralds finished singing, then Quetzalcoatl said to them there, "Grandfather heralds, let it be finished. Let me abandon the city, let me go. Send word that a stone sarcophagus be made." Then they quickly prepared the sarcophagus and when it was prepared and finished, they laid Quetzalcoatl within it.

And he had lain in the sarcophagus only four days when he became ill. Then he said to his heralds, "Let it be finished, grandfather heralds. Let us depart. Conceal and hide all around the felicity and the rich prosperity we have revealed, and all the property of our inheritance."

And the heralds did as he said. They hid them well in the place where Quetzalcoatl's bath was, a place called Atecpan Amochco.

So then Quetzalcoatl left. He rose up, summoned his heralds, and wept deeply for them.

Then they departed in search of Tlillan, Tlapallan, Tlatlayan "The Black, the Red Land, Place of the Burning."

And he looked upon every place and traveled everywhere, but no place was satisfactory to him. And when he found at last the place he sought, then once more he wept in sad contrition.

And it was again on the day 1 Reed, it is recounted, it is said, when he arrived at Teoapan Ilhuicaatenco, "Along the divine water, At the shore of heavenly water." Then he halted and stood; he wept, took up his vestments and adorned himself in his insignia, his turquoise mask, etc.

And when he was fully adorned then with his own hand he set himself on fire, he offered himself up in flame.[81]

So the place where Quetzalcoatl went to immolate himself came to be called Tlatlayan, "Place of the Burning."

And it is said that even as he burned, his ashes emerged and arose: and there appeared, before the sight of everyone, all the birds of great value which emerged and rose into the sky. They saw the roseate spoonbill, the cotinga, the trogon, the heron, the yellow parrot, the scarlet macaw, the white-bellied parrot, and every other bird of precious plumage.

And when the ashes were extinguished, then arose his heart, the quetzal bird itself; they saw it. And so they knew he had entered the sky within the sky.

The old ones used to say he was transformed to the dawn star; thus it is said that when Quetzalcoatl died this star appeared, and so he is named Tlahuizcalpanteuctli, "Lord of the Dawn House."

They used to say that when he died he did not appear for four days; he went to live in Mictlan, the Nether World, they said.

And also in another four days he made for himself arrows. So in eight days appeared the great star which was named Quetzalcoatl, and this, they said, is when he was enthroned as Lord.

And so they knew when he came to appear, each individual tonal or day-sign under which he falls upon men, he fires his arrows, he is provoked. If on 1 Crocodile, he shoots arrows at old men and women all alike; if on 1 Jaguar, if 1 Deer, if 1 Flower, he shoots well-born children; and if on 1 Reed, he strikes all the ruling speakers, as also on 1 Death. And if on 1 Rain, he shoots the rain; rain will cease. And if on 1 Motion, he shoots the young men and women; and if on 1 Water, then drought comes.

Each of these day-signs, therefore, was held in veneration by the elders, both men and women.

So it is recounted how for Quetzalcoatl all was in vain. He was born under a day-sign 1 Reed and he also died under 1 Reed. Thus it is completely read,[82] thus it is exhausted, fifty-two years or one full calendar round. So it all came to an end in this year One Reed.[83]

It was said that Matlacxochitl took his place as Speaker there in Tollan.

Life, Death, and the Ruler: A Huastec Stone Sculpture

In the area known as the Huasteca that lies north of Papantla, Veracruz, on the Gulf coast, we find one of the most intriguing and least studied cultures of pre-Columbian Mesoamerica. Including the important site at Tamuín, it flourished during the early Postclassic period and seems to have been influenced by both the Mixtecs and the Toltecs, producing nonetheless a unique and striking art style of which the piece pictured here is characteristic in its seeming simplicity and its subtle sophistication.

The unforgettable power of this stone sculpture of an anthropomorphic figure—identified by some scholars as a priest and as a ruler by others—derives from the sophisticated play of forms and graphic symbols in its composition—from the juxtaposition of the abstract heart in place of the navel to the skull image in the headdress, an image that is itself juxtaposed to the living face just beneath it, and from the juxtaposition of the strangely columnar legs and heavily carved, angular arms that seem still to be part of the stone from which they are not quite freed to the delicacy of the face, the skull, and the dress of the figure.

Although the totality of the figure, including his carefully decorated headdress, pectoral, and loincloth, must be taken into account in any interpretation of the piece, two symbolic features are clearly meant by the artist to provide the figure's focal points. First, the unusual depiction and place-ment of the heart, the symbolic center of the human life force, at the place of the navel—mythically the center of the world—clearly identifies this figure with the cosmic life force. His heart is the heart of the cosmos, and it is through him that the cosmic life force can enter this world. Second, the repetition of the form of the living head in the skull that surmounts it surely is meant to image forth the cycle of life and death; the living face will soon be the skull, but, as the heart below guarantees, the skull will again live. These graphic and symbolic elements clearly express the most elemental Mesoamerican mythical conception of fertility, of the duality of life and death, of the necessity of sacrifice, indicated by the prominent heart, to assure rebirth, and of the relationship of the ruler to this eternal cycle.

The headdress on which the skull appears is important in itself, for it is the conical hat worn by Quetzalcoatl in his aspect as Ehecatl the wind god. Through this hat, the priest-ruler here depicted is thus identified with both Ce Acatl Topiltzin Quetzalcoatl, the paradigmatic ruler whose hero journey unites life and death, and Ehecatl, the fertility deity who embodies the cyclical unity of life and death in quite another way. Ehecatl's connection with fertility fits well with the conclusions Sil-via Trejo has drawn from an extensive study of the Huastec sculpture of the Rio Tamuín area. She demonstrates that such sophisticated sculptures as this one have simpler, smaller predecessors and that those earlier pieces show clearly their roots in a phallic fertility cult associated with the Huasteca.[84]

Trejo's final assessment of these Huastec sculptures surely describes this work of mythic art: "The sculptures of the Rio Tamuín are a magnificent testimony to their creators. Their style can be summarized in their two most basic characteristics: the perfection of their execution and the rich-ness of their symbolism. What results are splendid works of art with profound symbolic meaning."[85]

THE MIGRATION MYTH IN ITS AZTEC EMBODIMENT

The Birth of Huitzilopochtli, from the *Florentine Codex*

Sahagún's account of the birth of Huitzilopochtli,[86] the tutelary god of the Aztecs, their leader on their long migration from their mythical island homeland of Aztlan to the heights of imperial splendor in their island capitol of Tenochtitlan, emphasizes exactly those qualities that were the Aztec ideal, and the depictions of the god in Aztec art (see Figure 20) reinforce those associations. His blue staff is central to the imagery delineating his symbolic function as war god and leader of the Aztec state, for that staff represents the fire serpent, Xiuhcoatl, with which he "struck Coyolxauhqui, he cut off her head," in the myth of his birth. His shield, darts, and dart thrower, all blue, derived from the same myth and suggested again his association with war. That shield was adorned with a quincunx composed of five tufts of eagle feathers, suggesting the central position of Tenochtitlan and the Aztec people in the world of time and space. Thus the items he carried, like his actions in the myth, suggested his function as deified leader of the Aztec state as well as his connection with warfare. He was, metaphorically, the eagle or "the bird of darts."

While Huitzilopochtli is consistently linked with the eagle, symbolic of both ferocity and closeness to the sun, his name associates him with another, very different bird. That name means literally "hummingbird on the left," and left meant south to a people who determined directions by facing in the direction of the path of the sun. In their southward migration they were thus returning to the birthplace of Huitzilopochtli in something akin to both a seasonal (and thus cyclical) migration and a return to their ancestral lands. In following the sun, they were also following the eagle, however, and the eagle symbolized the warrior aspect of Huitzilopochtli shown in his fearlessly routing his sister and her followers in their assault on Coatlicue (Image 23), their mother.

The myth implicitly relates the "cyclical" nature of the migration to Huitzilopochtli's birth and defense of his mother, Coatlicue, from the assault of Coyolxauhqui and her followers since those events suggest the cyclical nature of the sun's daily rebirth, its creating the "life" of day after the "death" of night symbolized by the destruction of Coyolxauhqui (Image 24), the moon, and her four hundred followers, the stars of the night sky. This emphasis on rebirth, in turn, fits well with the Aztec belief, recorded by Sahagún, that the hummingbird died in the dry season, attaching itself by its bill to the bark of a tree, where it hung until the beginning of the rainy season, when it came to life once more.

Thus for Aztec Mexico, Huitzilopochtli simultaneously symbolized the regenerative power of the world of the spirit and the imperial power of the Aztec state. For that reason he was seen as a manifestation of Ometeotl, and that exalted status, celebrated in myth, was also revealed by the sacrificial ritual performed periodically in the temple of Huitzilopochtli atop the pyramid of the Templo Mayor at the symbolic center of the Aztec capital. The sacrificial victims whose blood would nourish the sun were sacrificed on the stone atop the pyramid in the Temple of Huitzilopochtli, and their lifeless bodies were tumbled down the steps of the pyramid, coming to rest near the recently discovered monumental relief of the dismembered Coyolxauhqui. This reenactment of the myth suggested that the sun's creating life for man must be reciprocated by man's providing life for the sun.

"Human sacrifice was an alchemy by which life was made out of death,"[87] and as the people of the sun, the Aztecs had a divinely imposed responsibility to perform that alchemy. As modern scholars have pointed out, however, that duty coincided nicely with the militaristic nature of the Aztec state; warfare could be seen as providing captives for the divinely required sacrifices, while it also extended the dominions under Aztec sway and reinforced Aztec power. Human sacrifice took on its all-important role in Aztec society precisely because it met both mythic and political needs. That Huitzilopochtli, the divine embodiment of the warrior, as this myth attests, was the primary focus of this sacrificial ritual demonstrates his importance to the Aztecs in the symbolic mediation between the worlds of spirit and matter.

 ## THE BIRTH OF HUITZILOPOCHTLI

Translated from the Nahuatl by Miguel León-Portilla. Reprinted from Miguel León-Portilla, ed., *Native Mesoamerican Spirituality*, 220–25. Copyright 1980 by The Missionary Society of St. Paul the Apostle in the State of New York. Used by permission of Paulist Press.

The Aztecs greatly revered Huitzilopochtli;
they knew his origin, his beginning,
was in this manner:

In Coatepec, on the way to Tula,
there was living,
there dwelt a woman
by the name of Coatlicue.
She was mother of the four hundred gods of the south
and their sister
by name Coyolxauhqui.

And this Coatlicue did penance there,
she swept, it was her task to sweep,
thus she did penance
in Coatepec, the Mountain of the Serpent.
And one day,
when Coatlicue was sweeping,
there fell on her some plumage,
a ball of fine feathers.
Immediately Coatlicue picked them up
and put them in her bosom.
When she finished sweeping,
she looked for the feathers
she had put in her bosom,
but she found nothing there.
At that moment Coatlicue was with child.

The four hundred gods of the south,
seeing their mother was with child,
were very annoyed and said:
"Who has done this to you?
Who has made you with child?
This insults us, dishonors us."
And their sister Coyolxauhqui
said to them:
"My brothers, she has dishonored us,
we must kill our mother,
the wicked woman who is now with child.
Who gave her what she carries in her womb?"

When Coatlicue learned of this,
she was very frightened,
she was very sad.
But her son Huitzilopochtli, in her womb,
comforted her, said to her:
"Do not be afraid,
I know what I must do."
Coatlicue, having heard
the words of her son,
was consoled,
her heart was quiet,
she felt at peace.

But meanwhile the four hundred gods of the south
came together to make a decision,
and together they decided
to kill their mother,
because she had disgraced them.
They were very angry,
they were very agitated,
as if the heart had gone out of them.
Coyolxauhqui incited them,
she inflamed the anger of her brothers,
so that they should kill her mother.
And the four hundred gods
made ready,
they attired themselves as for war.

And those four hundred gods of the south
were like captains;
they twisted and bound up their hair
as warriors arrange their long hair.

But one of them called Cuahuitlicac
broke his word.
What the four hundred said,
he went immediately to tell,
he went and revealed it to Huitzilopochitli.
And Huitzilopochtli replied to him:
"Take care, be watchful,
my uncle, for I know well what I must do."

And when finally they came to an agreement,
the four hundred gods were determined to kill,
   to do away with their mother;
then they began to prepare,
Coyolxauhqui directing them.
They were very robust, well equipped,
adorned as for war,
they distributed among themselves their paper garb,
the girdle, the nettles,
the streamers of colored paper;
they tied little bells on the calves of their legs,
the bells called oyohualli.
Their arrows had barbed points.

Then they began to move,
they went in order, in line,
in orderly squadrons,
Coyolxauhqui led them.
But Cuahuitlicac went immediately up onto the mountain,
so as to speak from there to Huitzilopochtli;
he said to him:
"Now they are coming."
Huitzilopochtli replied to him:
"Look carefully which way they are coming."
Then Cuahuitlicac said:
"Now they are coming through Coaxalpan."
And once more Huitzilopochtli asked Cuahuitlicac:
"Look carefully which way they are coming."
Immediately Cuahuitlicac answered him:
"Now they are coming up the side of the mountain."
And yet again Huitzilopochtli said to him:
"Look carefully which way they are coming."
Then Cuahuitlicac said to him:
"Now they are on the top, they are here,
Coyolxauhqui is leading them."

At the moment Huitzilopochtli was born,
he put on his gear,
his shield of eagle feathers,
his darts, his blue dart-thrower.
He painted his face
with diagonal stripes,
in the color called "child's paint."
On his head he arranged fine plumage,
he put on his earplugs.
And on his left foot, which was withered,
he wore a sandal covered with feathers,
and his legs and his arms
were painted blue.

And the so-called Tochancalqui
set fire to the serpent of candlewood,
the one called Xiuhcoatl
that obeyed Huitzilopochtli.
With the serpent of fire he struck Coyolxauhqui,

he cut off her head,
and left it lying there
on the slope of Coatepetl.
The body of Coyolxauhqui
went rolling down the hill,
it fell to pieces,
in different places fell her hands,
her legs, her body.

Then Huitzilopochtli was proud,
he pursued the four hundred gods of the south,
he chased them, drove them off
the top of Coatepetl, the mountain of the snake.
And when he followed them
down to the foot of the mountain,
he pursued them, he chased them like rabbits,
all around the mountain.
He made them run around it four times.
In vain they tried to rally against him,
in vain they turned to attack him,
rattling their bells
and clashing their shields.
Nothing could they do,
nothing could they gain,
with nothing could they defend themselves.
Huitzilopochtli chased them, he drove them away,
he humbled them, he destroyed them, he annihilated them.

Even then he did not leave them,
but continued to pursue them,
and they begged him repeatedly, they said to him:
"It is enough!"

But Huitzilopochtli was not satisfied,
with force he pushed against them,
he pursued them.
Only a very few were able to escape him,
escape from his reach.
They went toward the south,
and because they went toward the south,
they are called gods of the south.
And when Huitzilopochtli had killed them,

when he had given vent to his wrath,
he stripped off their gear,
their ornaments, their anecuyotl;
he put them on, he took possession of them,
he introduced them into his destiny,
he made them his own insignia.

And this Huitzilopochtli, as they say,
was a prodigy,
because only from fine plumage,
which fell into the womb of his mother, Coatlicue,
was he conceived,
he never had any father.
The Aztecs venerated him,
they made sacrifices to him,
honored and served him.
And Huitzilopochtli rewarded
those who did this.
And his cult came from there,
from Coatepec, the Mountain of the Serpent,
as it was practiced from most ancient times.

The Aztec Migration Myth, from the *Florentine Codex*

Although there are a number of variants of the Aztec migration myth, the tale that recounts the beginnings of the Aztec people and their transformation into their present state, this account from Sahagún is unique. It seems to present a series of episodes taking place before those recounted in the other tales, which this account calls "the Mexican tales." Furthermore, Huitzilopochtli plays no role in this description of the development of the Aztecs, although his role in the other tales is central. Similarly, Coatepec, the highly symbolic hill that plays a number of roles in the other tales, is missing from this one. The reason for the differences between this myth and the others is impossible to know. Perhaps this is an earlier version of the myth, as some scholars believe, or a later one, as other scholars believe, or, as the myth itself suggests, one meant to present another phase of the mythic development of the Aztec people.

THE AZTEC MIGRATION MYTH

Translated from the Nahuatl by Charles E. Dibble and Arthur J. O. Anderson. Originally published in Bernardino de Sahagún, *General History of the Things of New Spain, Book 10: The People.* Translated by Charles E. Dibble and Arthur J. O. Anderson (Santa Fe, NM: School of American Research, and Salt Lake City: Univ. of Utah, 1961), 189–97. Reprinted by permission of the publisher.

I

Behold the story which the old people told. In the distant past, which no one can still reckon, which no one can still remember, those who came here to disperse their descendants—the grandfathers, the grandmothers, those called the ones who arrived first, the ones who came first, those who came sweeping the way, those who came with hair bound, those who came to rule in this land, those of the same name, those who seemed to form their own little world—came over the water in boats; they came in many divisions.

And they drew along the coast, the coast to the north. And where they came to beach their boats is named Panotla, which means "where they crossed over the water." Now it is called Pantla. Then they followed along the coast line; they went looking at the mountains, especially the snow-white mountains and the smoking mountains. Going along the coast line, they went to reach Quauhtemallan.

And these did not go of their own volition, for their priests led them. The priests went counseling with their god. Then they came— they arrived—at a place named Tamoanchan, which is to say, "We seek our home." And there they tarried.

And these were wise men called Amoxoaque. The wise men remained not long; soon they went. Once again they embarked and carried off the writings, the books, the paintings; they carried away all the crafts, the casting of metals. And when they departed, they summoned all those they left behind. They said to them: "Our lord, the protector of all, the wind, the night, saith you shall remain. We go leaving you here. Our lord goeth bequeathing you this land; it is your merit, your lot. Our lord, the master of all, goeth still farther, and we go with him. Whither the lord, the night and the wind, our lord, the master of all, goeth, we go accompanying him. He goeth, he goeth back, but he will come, he will come to do his duty, he will come to acknowledge you. When the world is become oppressed, when it is the end of the world, at the time of its ending, he will come to bring it to an end. But until then you shall dwell here; you shall stand guard here. That which lieth here, that which spreadeth germinating, that which resteth in the earth, is your merit, your gift. He maketh it your birthright. For this you followed him here. But we go with him: we go following him whither he goeth."

Thereupon departed those who carried the god on their backs; they carried him wrapped—wrapped in a bundle. It is said that their god went advising them. And as they went, they traveled to the east. They carried the writings, the books, the paintings. They carried the knowledge; they carried all—the song books, the flutes.

II

But four remained of the old men, the wise men: one named Oxomoco, one named Cipactonal, one named Tlaltetecui, one named Xochicauaca. And when the wise men had gone, then these four old men assembled. They took counsel; they said: "The sun will shine, it will dawn. How will the common people live, how will they dwell? He is gone; they carried away the writings. And how will the common people dwell? How will the lands, the mountains be? How will all live? What will govern? What will rule? What will lead? What will show the way? What will be the model, the standard? What will be the example? From what will the start be made? What will become the torch, the light?"

Then they devised the book of days, the book of years, the count of the years, the book of dreams. They arranged the reckoning just as it has been kept. And thus was time recorded during all the time the Tolteca, the Tepaneca, the Mexica, and all the Chichimeca reign endured. No longer can it be remembered, no longer can it be investigated how long they were left in Tamoanchan, which is to say, "We seek our home."

The history of it was saved, but it was burned when Itzcoatl ruled in Mexico. A council of rulers of Mexico took place. They said: "It is not necessary for all the common people to know of the writings; government will be defamed, and this will only spread sorcery in the land; for it containeth many falsehoods."

And they departed from there, from Tamoanchan. Offerings were made at a place named Teotiuacan. And there all the people raised pyramids for the sun and for the moon; then they made many small pyramids where offerings were made. And there leaders were elected, wherefore it is called Teotiuacan. And when the rulers died, they buried them there. Then they built a pyramid over them. The pyramids now stand like small mountains, though made by hand. There is a hollow where they removed the stone to build the pyramids.

And they built the pyramids of the sun and the moon very large, just like mountains. It is unbelievable when it is said they are made by hands, but giants still lived there then. Also it is very apparent from the artificial mountains at Cholollan; they are of sand, of adobe. It is apparent they are only constructed, only made. And so they named it Teotiuacan, because it was the burial place of the rulers. For so was it said: "When we die, it is not true that we die; for still we live, we are resurrected. We still live; we awaken. Do thou likewise." In this manner they spoke to the dead when one had died; if it were a man they spoke to him—they addressed him—as the god Cuecuextzin. And if it were a woman, her they addressed as Chamotzin: "Awaken! It hath reddened; the dawn hath set in. Already singeth the flame-colored cock, the flame-colored swallow; already flieth the flame-colored butterfly."

Thus, the old men said, he who died became a god. They said, "He hath become a god"; that is, he hath died. And thus the ancients deluded themselves so that those who were rulers would be obeyed. All were worshipped as gods when they died; some became the sun, some the moon, etc.

And when they had lived at Tamoanchan a long time, they departed therefrom; they abandoned the land. There they left behind those named the Olmeca Uixtotin. These were magicians, wise men. The name of their leader, their ruler, a sorcerer, was Olmecatl Uixtotli. They brought along sorcery and still other divinations. So, it is said, they followed those who went to the east. And they went to come upon the sea coast. It is said they were those now called Anauaca Mixteca, because they went there. Their ruler was a wise man who showed them the good land.

And there occurred the boring of the maguey. They discovered the good maguey, from which comes the unfermented maguey juice. The name of the woman, who for the first time discovered the boring of the maguey, was Mayauel; but the name of the one who discovered the stick, the root, with which wine was made, was Patecatl. And as for those who made, who prepared wine when it excelled, the name of one was Tepuztecatl; of one, Quatlapanqui; of one, Tlilhoa; of one, Papaiztac; of one, Tzocaca.

And they prepared the wine there at Mount Chichinauhia, and because the wine foamed up, they named the mountain Poconalte-petl. There they prepared the wine and there they drank it. And when wine had been prepared in abundance, very many were summoned; all the rulers, the leaders, the old men, the experienced men. They went there to Mount Chichinauhia, where they arranged themselves as guests.

And so very god-fearing were the old people in that which they said, in that which they did, that all performed the libation to the god. Thus did they do. Then they gave food to each one; they placed wine before each one—in four bowls or four jars, which each one drank. It was about four each that they drank; this they all drank.

And, it is said, the ruler of a group of Huaxteca people who were of one language, not only drank four, but when he had drunk four, demanded still another. Thus he drank five, with which he became well besotted, quite drunk; he no longer knew how he acted. And there before the people he threw off his breech clout.

And since (they said) he showed no respect for divinity, then a conference was held about him. For he had offended when he had cast away his breech clout, when he had been quite besotted. And with shame the Huaxteca abandoned the land; they took all his people with him. All who understood the language moved together; they moved in a body. They traveled there from whence they came, to Panotla, now called Pantla. And as they went with great misgivings of the water, the sea, they settled there. These are called Toueiome, which means "our neighbors." And the name comes from their ruler, named Cuextecatl. They are called Cuexteca.

These, they say, took entertainment, flutes with them, because they amused themselves in many ways. They practised deceit in many ways; thus they made believe that the hut burned, that they made water appear, that they dismembered themselves. They did many kinds of things. But they abandoned not their shameful conduct, their drunkenness. They were much given to wine. And thus they imitated the father, the leader, of the Huaxteca; for the men always went about naked. They never provided themselves with breech clouts until the true Christian faith came. And because he had become besotted, because he had drunk the fifth wine jar there at Poconaltepec, the Huaxteca always went about as if drunk; they were always as if they had gone eating Datura stramonium.

And of him who is untrained, who goeth about as if drunk, these words are said: "He is the image of a Huaxteca. Hast thou perchance finished the fifth wine jar? He drank the fifth wine jar. He drank not only the four wine jars, he finished the fifth wine jar."

III

And when the reign had endured a long time in the place named Tamoanchan, then the seat of power passed to a place named Xomiltepec. And there at Xomiltepec the rulers, the old men, the priests conferred. They said: "The master of all hath called us; he hath called each one of those who worship him as a god." They said: "We shall not live here, we shall not dwell here, we shall go in search of land. The night and the wind, the master of all, hath traveled beyond."

Then they set themselves in motion; all moved—the boys, the old men, the young women, the old women. They went very slowly, very deliberately; they went to settle together there at Teotiuacan. There law was established, there rulers were installed. The wise, the sorcerers, the nenonotzaleque were installed as rulers. The leading men were installed.

Then they departed; they moved very slowly. Their leaders accompanied them; they went leading each group. The members of each group understood their own language. Each had its leader, its ruler. To them went speaking the one they worshipped. And the Tolteca were the ones who took the very lead.

And the leader of the Otomi left the others at Coatepec. He introduced his people into the forest. It is said that since they lived there, they always made their offerings on the mountain tops. And they sought out only the mountain slopes to build houses there.

And then these different people went on: the Tolteca, the Mexica, the Nahua. All the people, as they sought land, encountered the plains, the deserts. The one they worshipped accompanied them; he went speaking to them. No more could they recall how long they had wandered; for a long time they traveled over the desert. They went to settle at a place in the desert, in a valley among the crags, a very dangerous place. And the people wept; they were saddened, they suffered affliction; there was no more to eat, no more to drink.

And at this place there were, or as one said, there are, seven caves. These different people made them serve as their temples; they went to make their offerings there for a long time. No longer is it remembered how long they resided there.

Then the one whom the Tolteca worshipped spoke to them; he said to them: "Turn back. You shall go from whence you came."

Then they went to make offerings at the cave there at Chicomoztoc. Then they departed. First they came to arrive at a place called Tollantzinco. Then they passed over to Xicocotitlan, called Tollan. And then the Chichlmeca, those called the Teochichimeca followed them. And then the Michoaque followed them. They departed; their ruler, named Amimitl, led them. They traveled there to the west, where they dwell today, toward the setting sun. They also first went to make offerings at the cave, Chicomoztoc.

Then the Nahua, the Tepaneca departed; then those called Acolhuaque, then the Chalca, then the Uexotzinca, the Tlaxcalteca. Each one set forth; they returned here to this place (as was already mentioned), the land of the Mexica.

And the god of the Mexica spoke to them; he said to them: "We go still farther."

Then they went to the east. And as they departed, all of them—all—went to make offerings at Chicomoztoc.

It is for this reason that all the different people glorify themselves; they say that they were created at Chicomoztoc, that from Chicomoztoc they came forth. But there was no emerging from Chicomoztoc; it was merely that offerings were made at Chicomoztoc when they lived in the desert. And thereupon there was departing, there was returning. Here and there the people were granted land; boundaries were established.

But the Mexica traveled farther on; they went seeking land. And according to the traditions of the old people, it is said that the name of the place where they turned back was Colhuacan, Mexico. And how long they lived there at Colhuacan, how long they lived on the desert, no more does one know.

And then the Mexica returned. Their god addressed them; he said to them: "Go. Return whence you came. I will lead you; I will show you the way." Then they set forth; they came here. The places by which the Mexica passed, exist, are painted, are named in the Mexican accounts.

And when the Mexica came (for it is true they wandered a long time), they were the last. As they came, as they followed their course, nowhere were they welcomed; they were cursed everywhere; they were no longer recognized. Everywhere they were told: "Who are the uncouth people? Whence do you come?"

Thus they could settle nowhere; in no other place was repose accorded them; they were pursued everywhere. They went passing Tollan, Ichpuchco, Ecatepec, then Chiquiuhtepetitlan, then Chapultepec, where they went all together to settle. And then there was rule at Azcapotzalco, at Coatlichan, at Colhuacan. There was no Mexico; where Mexico now is, was still patches of reeds, of rushes. And when there at Chapultepec the Mexica were attacked, war was made against them. And the Mexica moved to Colhuacan, where they remained some time.

Then they came to the place which is now called Tenochtitlan. Where they went to settle was within the limits of the cultivated fields of the Tepaneca, where they border the Acolhuaque. They went to settle among the reeds and rushes, because they came to settle in the land of another. Entry was impossible; there was no vacant land. They became the vassals and subjects of those of Azcapotzalco.

These different people all called themselves Chichimeca. All boasted the Chichimeca estate, because all had gone into the Chichimeca land where they went to live; all returned from Chichimeca land. But the name of the place is not Chichimeca land; the name of the place is only the desert lands, the house of darts, the north. It is only named Chichimeca land because there live the Chichimeca who eat and drink from hunting. It is said the Mexica called themselves Chichimeca, but properly it is said they called themselves Atlaca Chichimeca.

The different Nahua peoples also are called Chichimeca, because they returned from the Chichimeca land, they returned from the so-called Chicomoztoc. They are the Tepaneca, the Acolhuaque, the Chalca; the people from the hot lands, the Tlalhuica, the Couixca; those beyond the mountains, the Uexotzinca, the Tlaxcalteca; and still other Nahua peoples. They also go bearing their equipment, the arrow, the spear.

The Tolteca are also called Chichlmeca; they are called Tolteca Chichimeca. The Otomi are also called Chicllimeca—Otonchichimeca. The Michoaque are also called Chichimeca. The people to the east are not called Chichimeca; they are called Olmeca, Uixtotin, Nonoualca.

The Finding and Founding of Tenochtitlan, from the *Crónica Mexicayotl*

The *Crónica Mexicayotl*, one of the most important sources of Aztec mythical-historical information, was written in 1609 by Hernando Alvarado Tezozómoc, who was a grandson of Motecuhzoma on his mother's side and a great grandson of Azayacatl on his father's.[88] He tells in this portion of the chronicle of the emergence in 1064 of the Aztecs from Aztlan-Chicomoztoc, led by their god Huitzilopochtli, and their long journey to the place of their destiny, Tenochtitlan. The chronicle as a whole contains this migration myth as well as myths of Huitzilopochtli, descriptions of the establishment of Tenochtitlan, dynastic history, and detailed genealogical data for the pre-Conquest and colonial Indian rulers of Tenochtitlan and Tlatelolco up to about 1579. This selection focuses on five episodes in the migration of the Aztecs, each repeating in varying form the essential details of the myth of Huitzilopochtli, who, like Athena among the Greeks, appears and disappears in accordance with the needs of his people.

Thelma Sullivan, the present translator of this work, the original of which is now in the Bibliothéque National de Paris, claims that in addition to its being one of the great sources of mythology and history for this period, the *Crónica Mexicayotl* is "a saga of true literary merit and heroic dimensions."[89] She has abridged this translation slightly to emphasize those features.

 ### THE FINDING AND FOUNDING OF MEXICO TENOCHTITLAN

Translated from the Nahuatl by Thelma D. Sullivan. Originally published in "The Finding and Founding of Tenochtitlan," translated by Thelma D. Sullivan, in *Tlalocan* 6, no. 4 (1971): 312–36. The myth was divided into sections and editorial corrections were made by the editors.

I

Here it is told, it is recounted,
how the ancients who were called, who were named,
Teochichimeca, Azteca, Mexitin, Chicomoztoca, came, arrived,
when they came to seek,
when they came to gain possession of their land here,
in the great city of Mexico Tenochtitlan. . . .
In the middle of the water where the cactus stands,
where the eagle raises itself up,
where the eagle screeches,
where the eagle spreads his wings,
where the eagle feeds,
where the serpent is torn apart,

where the fish fly,
where the blue waters and yellow waters join,
where the water blazes up,
where feathers came to be known,
among the rushes, among the reeds where the battle is joined,
where the peoples from the four directions are awaited,
there they arrived, there they settled. . . .
They called themselves Teochichimeca, Azteca, Mexitin.
They brought along the image of their god,
the idol that they worshipped.
The Aztecs heard him speak and they answered him;
they did not see how it was he spoke to them. . . .

II

And after the Azteca, Mexitin sailed here from Aztlan,
they arrived in Culhuacan. . . .
They went everywhere in Culhuacan,
in far-off Culhuacan, in Tona ichuacan or Tonallan.
All of them journeyed far—
the people of Michoacan, kin of the Mexicans,
and the people of Malinalco—for all of them came.
And when the Aztecs abandoned the people of Michoacan,
the men and women were amusing themselves in the water at
    a place called Patzcuaro.
They made off with the men's capes and breechcloths
and they took the women's skirts and huipiles.
The men no longer had breechcloths;
they went about with their bottoms bare,
rather, they go about with their bottoms bare, uncovered.
The women gave up their blouses and the men became wearers
    of huipiles.
In this manner they abandoned the people of Michoacan.

III

And the reason Huitzilopochtli went off and abandoned his
    sister, named Malinalxoch, along the way,
that all his fathers abandoned her while she was sleeping,
was because she was cruel,
she was very evil.

She was an eater of people's hearts,
an eater of people's limbs—it was her work—
a bewitcher of people,
an enchanter of people.
She put people to sleep,
she made people eat snakes,
she made people eat scorpions,
she spoke to all the centipedes and spiders
and transformed herself into a sorceress.
She was a very evil woman;
this was why Huitzilopochtli did not like her,
this was why he did not bring his sister, Malinalxoch, with
      him,
that they abandoned her and all her fathers while they were
      sleeping.
Then the priest, Huitzilopochtli spoke,
he addressed his fathers, called the "idol-bearers," . . . he said
      to them,
"O my fathers, the work that Malinalxoch does is not my work.
When I came forth, when I was sent here,
I was given arrows and a shield,
for battle is my work.
And with my belly, with my head,
I shall confront the cities everywhere.
I shall await the peoples from the four directions,
I shall join battle with them,
I shall provide people with drink,
I shall provide people with food!
Here I shall bring together the diverse peoples,
and not in vain, for I shall conquer them,
that I may see the house of jade, the house of gold, the house of
      quetzal feathers;
the house of emeralds, the house of coral, the house of
      amethysts;
the sundry feathers—the lovely cotinga feathers, the roseate
      spoonbill feathers, the trogon feathers—
all the precious feathers;
and the cacao of variegated colors,
and the cotton of variegated colors!

I shall see all this,
for in truth, it is my work,
it was for this that I was sent here.
And now, O my fathers, ready the provisions. Let us go!
Off there we are going to find it! . . ."
And when the sister of Huitzilopochtli, called Malinalxoch,
whom they had abandoned while sleeping,
whom they had gone off and abandoned,
when Malinalxoch awakened, she wept.
She said to her fathers, "O my fathers, where shall we go?
My brother, Huitzilopochtli, has abandoned us by trickery.
Where has the evil one gone?
Let us seek the land where we are to dwell. . . ."
Then they saw the mountain called Texcaltepetl;
they established themselves upon it. . . .
Along the way Malinalxoch became big with child,
and the child of Malinalxoch, a son named Copil, was born.
His father's name was Chimalquauhtli;
he was king of Malinalco. . . .

IV

The others settled at Coatepec. . . .
The Mexicans erected their temple, the house of
      Huitzilopochtli . . .
and they laid down Huitzilopochtli's ball court
and constructed his skull-rack.
Then they blocked the ravine, the gorge.
and the water collected, it filled up.
This was done at the word of Huitzilopochtli.
Then he said to his fathers, the Mexicans,
"O my fathers, the water has collected.
Plant, sow, willows, bald cypresses, reeds, rushes and water-
      lilies!
And the fish, frogs, ajolotes, crayfish, dragonfly larvae,
      ahuihuitlame, ephydrids, and the salamanders multiplied,
and also the izcahuitli,
and the birds, ducks, American coots, and the "red-shouldered"
      and "yellow-throated" grackles.

And Huitzilopochtli said,
"The izcahuitli are my flesh, my blood, my substance."
Then he sang his song,
They all sang and danced;
the song was called Tlaxotecayotl and also Tecuilhuicuicatl;
he composed it there.
Then his fathers, the Centzonhuitznahua, spoke, they said to
     Huitzilopochtli,
"O priest, the work for which you came shall be done here.
You shall await the people,
you shall meet in battle the people from the four directions,
you shall arouse the cities.
With your belly, with your head,
and your heart, your blood, your substance,
you shall capture them,
that you may see what you promised us—
the many jades, the precious stones, the gold,
the quetzal feathers and sundry precious feathers,
the cacao of variegated colors,
the cotton of variegated colors,
the diverse flowers, the diverse fruits, the diverse riches.
For, in truth, you have founded,
you have become the ruler of your city, here in Coatepec.
Let your fathers, your vassals, the Aztecs, the Mexicans, gather
     here!" the Centzonhuitznahua beseeched him.
Huitzilopochtli became enraged,
"What are you saying?" he said.
"Do you know?
Is it your work?
Are you greater than I? I know what I must do!"
Then, atop the temple, his house, Huitzilopochtli began to array
     himself.
When he had arrayed himself,
when he had arrayed himself for battle,
he painted his face the color of a child's excrement,
he made circles around his eyes,
and he took up his shield. . . .
Then he went off;

he went to destroy, he went to slay his uncles, the
      Centzonhuitznahua.
On the sacred ball court he devoured his uncles;
and his mother, she whom he took as his mother, called
      Coyolxauhcihuatl . . .
he cut off her head there and devoured her heart,
Huitzilopochtli devoured it. . . .
The Mexicans were frightened.
The Centzonhuitznahua had thought that the city was to be
      there in Coatepec,
that Mexico was to be there,
but Huitzilopochtli did not want it so.
He made a hole in the dam where the water had been,
and the water broke the dam.
All the bald cypresses, willows, reeds, rushes and water lilies
      withered.
All the fish, frogs, ajolotes, ephydrids and insects,
and the crayfish and dragonfly larvae that lived in the water
      died . . .
and all the birds perished.

V

Then Huitzilopochtli set out,
he went off with his fathers, his vassals, the Mexicans. . . .
They came, they settled behind Chapultepec in a place called
      Techcatitlan. . . .
Then Huitzilopochtli gave orders to the Mexicans . . .
he said to the idol-bearers,
"O my fathers, wait, for you shall see,
Wait, for I know what is to happen.
Gird yourselves, be courageous.
Gird yourselves, prepare yourselves.
We shall not dwell here,
we shall find the place off there,
there is where we shall possess it.
Let us await those who shall come to destroy us! . . ."
. . . . . [90]

The son of Malinalxoch, sister of Huitzilopochtli, whose name
      was Copil, spoke, he said to her,
"O my mother, well I know that your brother is off there."
"Yes, your uncle, named Huitzilopochtli, is yonder," she said.
"He abandoned me,
he abandoned me while I was sleeping,
he abandoned me by trickery along the way.
Then we settled here in Texcaltepeticpac."
"Very well, O my mother," said Copil.
"I know that I must look for him in the place he has found
      contentment,
in the place he has settled.
I shall destroy him,
I shall devour him,
and I shall destroy, I shall vanquish his fathers
and the vassals that he took with him.
Well I know all the gifts that are marked for him who is to see,
who is to behold the manifold riches.
And it shall be I.
Mine shall be the knowledge of all the sundry jades and gold,
of the quetzal feathers and the other feathers,
of the cacao of variegated colors,
of the cotton of variegated colors,
of the diverse flowers and diverse fruits.
O my mother, be not sad.
I go now to seek out the evil one, my uncle. . . ."
Then he came.
He arrayed himself, he adorned himself, he who was called
      Copil.
He was very evil,
he was a greater sorcerer than his mother, Malinalxoch;
Copil was a very evil man.
He came in the year 1-House, 1285
and in the place called Zoquitzinco he transformed himself.
Once more he came, and in the place called Atlapalco he
      transformed himself.
He came once again and in the place called Itztapaltemoc he
      transformed himself,

and because Copil transformed himself, because he turned
    himself into a flagstone,
it is now called, all of us call it, Itztapaltetitlan.
And after the transformation of Copil,
after Copil had transformed himself into a flagstone,
once again he returned to his home called Texcaltepeticpac;
(they now call it Malinalco because Malinalxoch dwelt
    there . . .)
Once more Copil came . . .
and in the place called Tecpantzinco he transformed himself.
But Huitzilopochtli knew him at once,
he recognized his nephew, now grown, called Copil.
Then he said to his fathers,
"O my fathers, array yourselves, adorn yourselves,
my nephew, the evil one, is coming.
I am off.
I shall destroy him, I shall slay him!"
He encountered him at the place called Tepetzinco,
and when he saw him, he said,
"Who are you? Where are you from?"
"It is I," he replied,
Again he spoke to him.
"Where is your home?"
"In Texcaltepeticpac," he answered.
Then Huitzilopochtli said, "Good. Are you not he whom my
    sister, Malinalxoch, brought into the world?"
"Yes, I am he," Copil said,
"and I shall capture you, I shall destroy you!
Why did you abandon my mother while she was sleeping?
Why did you abandon her by trickery?
I shall slay you!"
"Very well," Huitzilopochtli said, "Come ahead."
They pursued each other with cunning,
and they captured Copil in Tepetzinco.
When he was dead Huitzilopochtli cut off his head and slashed
    open his chest,
and when he had slashed open his chest, he tore out his
    heart.

Then he placed his head on top of Tepetzintli, which is now
        called Acopilco,
and there the head of Copil died.
And after Huitzilopochtli slew him,
he ran off with Copil's heart.
And the idol-bearer, called Quauhtlequetzqui came upon
        Huitzilopochtli.
When he encountered him, he said,
"You have wearied yourself, O priest."
"Come, O Quauhtlequetzqui," he said.
"Here is the heart of the evil one, Copil.
I have slain him.
Run with it into the rushes, into the reeds.
There you shall see the mat of stone
on which Quetzalcoatl rested when he went away,
and his seats, one red and one black.
There you shall halt
and you shall cast away the heart of Copil."
Then Quauhtlequetzqui went off to cast away the heart.
When he came to the place he had described to him,
he saw the Mat of stone,
and he halted there and cast away the heart;
it fell in among the rushes, in among the reeds. . . .
The place where Quauhcoatl stopped and cast away the
        heart,
we now call Tlalcocomoco. . . .

VI

Then the Mexicans went to Acuezcomac,
they passed through Huehuetlan, Atlixocan,
Teoculhuacan, Tepetocan, Huitzilac, Culhuacan,
Huixachtla, Cahualtepec, Tetlacuixomac.
They settled in Tlapitzahuayan in the year 2-Rabbit, 1286. . . .
In the year 11-Reed, 1295 . . . the Mexicans passed through
        Zacatla. . . .
The people of Chalco drove them out,
they stoned them.

Once again they went to Chapultepec. . . .
Behind Chapultepec all the Tepanecas, Azcapotzalcas and
    Culhuacans,
the Xochimilcas, Cuitlahuacas and Chalcas besieged the
    Mexicans. . . .
The Mexicans were besieged in Chapultepec in 2-Reed, 1299.
Then the Mexicans moved to Acuezcomac. . . .
Then they came, they settled in Mazatlan,
and all the Mexicans gathered in Tepetocan.

VII

Then from there they went to Culhuacan.
Coxcoxtli was the king of Culhuacan. . . .
Then Huitzilopochtli said to the Mexicans,
"My fathers, say to Coxcoxtli, 'Where shall we live?'"
They addressed Coxcoxtli, they said to him,
"O lord, O king, we are beseeching you.
Where shall we go?
We have known this to be your city.
Have mercy on us with a small piece of your land on which we
    may live!"
Coxcoxtli replied, he said, "Very well."
He summoned his Culhuacan chiefs, he said to them,
"Where shall they live?"
"O lord, O king, let them go there," his chiefs said.
"Let the Mexicans live beside the mountain, here in
    Tizaapan."
Then they took them, they established them in Tizaapan.
They advised Coxcoxtli, the king, they said,
"O lord, O king, we have taken the Mexicans to Tizaapan."
"Good," Coxcoxtli said, "They are monstrous, they are evil.
Perhaps they will meet their end there,
perhaps they will be devoured by the snakes,
for it is the dwelling place of many snakes."
But the Mexicans were overjoyed when they saw the snakes.
They cooked them,
they roasted them over the fire, and they ate them. . . .

VIII

In the year 13-Reed, 1323,
the Mexicans had passed, had spent twenty-five years in
    Tizaapan Culhuacan.
Then Huitzilopochtli spoke to his fathers, he said to them,
"O my fathers, another person shall appear whose name is
    Yaocihuatl.
She is my grandmother and we shall have her.
And hear this, O my chiefs, we are not to remain here.
We shall find the place off there.
There is where we shall possess it. . . .
And now gird yourselves, make yourselves ready,
for you have heard that Yaocihuatl, my grandmother, will man-
    ifest herself there.
I command that you go,
that you ask Achitometl for his child, his daughter.
You are to ask him for his precious child,
for I know he shall give her to you."
And then the Mexicans went off,
they went to ask Achitometl for his daughter.
The Mexicans spoke to him, they said,
"O my prince, O lord, O king, we your grandfathers, we your
    vassals, and all the Mexicans,
pray that you grant, that you give us, your jewel, your quetzal
    feather,
your daughter, our granddaughter, the princess.
There, beside the mountain in Tizaapan she will keep guard."
Achitometl said, "Very well, O Mexicans, you may take her with
    you."
He gave her to the Mexicans.
They went off with the daughter of Achitometl,
they brought her,
they settled her in Tizaapan.
Then Huitzilopochtli spoke . . . he said to them,
"O my fathers, I order you to slay the daughter of Achitometl
    and to flay her.
When you have flayed her, you are to dress a priest in her skin."
Then they slew the princess and they flayed her,

and after they flayed her, they dressed a priest in her skin.
Huitzilopochtli then said,
"O my chiefs, go and summon Achitometl."
The Mexicans went off, they went to summon him.
They said, "O our lord, O my grandson, O lord, O king . . .
your grandfathers, the Mexicans beseech you, they say,
'May he come to see, may he come to greet the goddess.
We invite him.'"
Achitometl said, "Very well. Let us go."
He said to his lords, "Let us go to Tizaapan,
the Mexicans have invited us. . . ."
They took along rubber, copal, papers, flowers, and tobacco,
and also what is called the "lord's food" to set down in offering
      before the goddess. . . .
And when Achitometl arrived in Tizaapan, the Mexicans said,
      as they received him,
"You have wearied yourself, O my grandson, O lord, O king.
We, your grandfathers, we, your vassals, shall cause you to
      become ill.
May you see, may you greet your goddess."
"Very good, O my grandfathers," he said.
He took the rubber, the copal, the flowers, the tobacco, and the
      food offering,
and he offered them to her,
he set them down before the false goddess whom they had
      flayed.
Then Achitometl tore off the heads of quail before his goddess;
he still did not see the person before whom he was decapitating
      the quail.
Then he made an offering of incense and the incense-burner
      blazed up,
and Achitometl saw a man in his daughter's skin.
He was horror-struck.
He cried out, he shouted to his lords and to his vassals.
He said, "Who are they, eh, O Culhuacans?
Have you not seen?
They have flayed my daughter!
They shall not remain here, the fiends!
We shall slay them, we shall massacre them!

The evil ones shall be annihilated here!"
They began to fight. . . .
The Culhuacans pursued them, they pursued the Mexicans,
they drove them into the water. . . .
The Culhuacans thought that they had perished in the water,
but they crossed the water on their shields,
they crossed on their arrows and shields.
They bound together the arrows, called tlacochtli,
and those called tlatzontectli,
and, sitting upon them, they crossed the water. . . .
and sitting upon the shields they crossed the water
when the Culhuacans pursued them.
And they came into the rushes, into the reeds at
      Mexicatzinco. . . .
There they dried their battle gear which had become wet,
their insignias, their shields—all their gear.
And their women and children began to weep.
They said, "Where shall we go? Let us remain here in the
      reeds. . . ."

IX

And then the old Mexicans, Quauhtlequetzqui, or Quauhcoatl,
      and also the one called Axolohua went off,
they went into the rushes, into the reeds
at the place that is now called Toltzalan, Acatzalan;
the two of them went to look for the place they were to settle.
And when they came upon it,
they saw the many wondrous things there in the reeds.
This was the reason Huitzilopochtli had given his orders to the
      idol-bearers, his fathers,
Quauhtlequetzqui, or Quauhcoatl, and Axolohua, the priest.
For he had sent them off,
he had told them all that there was in the rushes, in the reeds,
and that there he, Huitzilopochtli, was to stand,
that there he was to keep guard.
He told them with his own lips,
thus he sent off the Mexicans.
And then they saw the white bald cypresses, the white willows,

and the white reeds and the white rushes;
and also the white frogs, the white fish, and the white snakes
      that lived there in the water.
And they saw the springs that joined;
the first spring faced east and was called Tleatl and Atlatlayan,
the second spring faced north and was called Matlalatl and
      also Tozpalatl.
And when they saw this the old men wept.
They said, "Perhaps it is to be here.
We have seen what the priest, Huitzilopochtli, described to us
when he sent us off.
He said, 'In the rushes, in the reeds, you shall see many things.'
And now we have seen them, we have beheld them!
It has come true, his words when he sent us off have come
      true!"
Then they said,
"O Mexicans, let us go, for we have beheld them.
Let us await the word of the priest;
he knows how it shall be done."
Then they came, they sojourned in Temazcaltitlan.
And during the night he saw him,
Huitzilopochtli appeared to the idol-bearer, called
      Quauhtlequetzqui, or Quauhcoatl.
He said to him, "O Quauhcoatl, you have seen all there is in
      among the reeds, in among the rushes,
you have beheld it.
But hear this:
There is something you still have not seen.
Go, go and look at the cactus,
and on it, standing on it, you shall see an eagle.
It is eating, it is warming itself in the sun,
and your hearts will rejoice,
for it is the heart of Copil that you cast away
where you halted in Tlalcocomoco.
There it fell, where you looked, at the edge of the spring,
among the rushes, among the reeds.
And from Copil's heart sprouted what is now called tenochtli.
There we shall be, we shall keep guard,
we shall await, we shall meet the diverse peoples in battle.

With our bellies, with our heads,
with our arrows, with our shields,
we shall confront all who surround us
and we shall vanquish them all,
we shall make them captives,
and thus our city shall be established.
Mexico Tenochtitlan:
where the eagle screeches,
where he spreads his wings,
where the eagle feeds,
where the fish fly,
and where the serpent is torn apart.
Mexico Tenochtitlan!
And many things shall come to pass."
Then Quauhcoatl said to him, "Very well, oh priest. Your heart
    has granted it.
Let all the old men, your fathers, hear."
Then Quauhcoatl gathered the Mexicans together,
he had them hear the words of Huitzilopochtli;
the Mexicans listened.
And then, once more, they went in among the rushes, in among
    the reeds, to the edge of the spring.
And when they came out into the reeds,
there at the edge of the spring, was the tenochtli,
and they saw an eagle on the tenochtli, perched on it, standing
    on it.
It was eating something, it was feeding,
it was pecking at what it was eating.
And when the eagle saw the Mexicans, he bowed his head low.
(They had only seen the eagle from afar.)
Its nest, its pallet, was of every kind of precious feather—
of lovely cotinga feathers, roseate spoonbill feathers, quetzal
    feathers.
And they also saw strewn about the heads of sundry birds,
the heads of precious birds strung together,
and some birds' feet and bones.
And the god called out to them, he said to them,
"O Mexicans, it shall be there!"
(But the Mexicans did not see who spoke.)
It is for this reason they call it Tenochtitlan.

And then the Mexicans wept, they said,
"O happy, O blessed are we!
We have beheld the city that shall be ours!
Let us go, now, let us rest. . . ."
This was in the year 2-House, 1325.

The Beginning of the Migration, from the *Codex Boturini*

The *Codex Boturini,* an early pictorial chronicle published in the sixteenth century in Mexico City, is made up of twenty-one and a half leaves in a fifteen-foot-long paper screenfold painted on only one side. Its images are black, but red lines connect the dates. These very simple images illustrate the history of the Aztecs, beginning with their emigration from Aztlan through their arrival at Chapultepec and beyond, but it ends slightly before their arrival at Tenochtitlan. It thus concurs with the narrative migration myths that depict the people of Tenochtitlan as originally nomadic hunters and gatherers whose homeland was somewhere in the northwest, their mythical place of origin considered to be Chicomoztoc, but sometimes called Aztlan or Culhuacan, meaning "place of the ancestors."

According to one version of the myth, Huizilopochtli, the tutelary god of the Aztecs, appeared in a dream to their shaman priest, telling him to lead the people south to a place where the god would manifest himself as an eagle sitting atop a nopal cactus growing on a rocky island in the middle of a lake, and the first leaf of this manuscript, depicted here, illustrates the beginning of that mythic journey from the island or center of the cosmos, shown here surrounded by water, from which the first people came; included in this scene are six dwellings and a temple. A sitting man and a woman named Chimalma live here. The next image depicts a representative figure boating across the water, after which the footprints begin to show movement on land. That movement brings them to a mountain, often referred to as Colhuacatepec (Mountain of One's Ancestors), surrounding a cave in which there is a temple dedicated to Huitzilopochtli, identified here by a head emerging from the hummingbird jaw within a reed enclosure in the cave. Emerging from the cave on the right side of the pictograph, the footsteps continue, leading to eight images, each with slightly different symbols relating to place glyphs, portraying the eight tribes who will divide Tenochtitlan into eight geographic centers.

Van Zantwijk points out that there are an amazing number of variations of this myth told in the various historical accounts and codices, and he concludes that the points of agreement make clear that the "Seven Caves, the Place (or mountain) of One's Ancestors, and the White Land, or Land of Herons, are mythical places, which might be situated anywhere and might belong to different peoples."[91]

THE FLAYED GOD

The Seven Caves of Chicomoztoc, from the *Historia Tolteca Chichimeca*

In the document known as the *Historia Tolteca Chichimeca,* a work written and painted in Quauhtin-chan, Puebla, one finds this fascinating depiction of the seven caves of Chicomoztoc (see also Color Plate 24). The manuscript, originally written in Nahuatl and one of the major sources for the study of the early post-Toltec and subsequent history of the Chichimec migrations from Chicomoztoc to the central Puebla region, covers the history of the period from 1116 through 1544 A.D. and includes many full-page drawings, six double-page maps, and about forty pages of text.

As we said above in reference to the pictograph from the *Codex Boturini,* the mythical place of the origin of the Aztec people was often considered to be Chicomoztoc, a Nahuatl word meaning "in the seven caves." Chicomoztoc is clearly suggestive not only of the cave itself but also of the cave as the womb of the earth, and since the focus on the emergence of tribes from a cave serves to em-phasize the essentially female character of the earth, the metaphor extends to include the maternal womb as well. Portrayed in this image is the cave, the place of emergence, where the first people came out of the earth, all of whom, according to one version of the myth, were descended from a single primordial couple who lived in Chicomoztoc. These original parents were called Iztacmixcoatl and Ilancueitl, the latter being the mother of the gods as well as the mother of all humanity.

Throughout Mesoamerica the cave has been considered a sacred place, the symbol of creation, of life itself. And because Chicomoztoc is a term generally used to signify a place of emergence and return, as indicated by the many scenes of emergence scattered through the codices, often caves with men and women emerging from them, it is likely that Chicomoztoc is symbolic of the many "places of emergence" in Mesoamerica rather than the name of an actual place.

In this image from the *Historia Tolteca Chichimeca* we recognize the outline of the mountain with its curved peak from the *Codex Boturini.* The cave concealed within the mountain takes the form of a tree with seven small caves composing its rounded branches. We also recognize here the footsteps that in this case are sketched both going into and coming out of the seven caves, suggest-ing perhaps the direction of our reading as well as both the emergence from and the return to the beginning, the place of the ancestors. It is interesting to note that in the construction of artificial sacred spaces throughout Mesoamerica the natural mountain became the man-made pyramid, and the cave became the temple. Doris Heyden has suggested that various pictures illustrating the emergence from Chicomoztoc look remarkably similar to the modifications made by the Teotihua-canos to the inner sanctum of the cave under the Pyramid of the Sun, thereby suggesting the antiquity of the sacredness of the cave[92] and suggesting as well that the Pyramid of the Sun may well be a representation of the mountain that harbors the place of origin.

The Return to Chicomoztoc, the Place of Origin, from the *Historia de las Indias de Nueva España e Islas de Tierra Firme*

This curious story of a return to Chicomoztoc, the place of origin of the Aztec people, occurs in the midst of Fray Diego Durán's account of Aztec dynastic history. While his lengthy history does begin with a mythic account of the Aztec migration, an account drawn from the same original source and thus essentially similar to that of Tezozómoc, which we have included in this section, the bulk of Durán's chronicle is historical. Strangely, this brief myth appears in the middle of that historical material, and while it alludes to the history of the Aztecs, its primary concern seems to be emphasizing the differences between the place of origin in the realm of the spirit and the Aztec capital in the natural world.

Diego Durán was born in Spain but came to Mexico as a young boy, settling with his parents in Texcoco. In 1556, more than thirty years after the Conquest, he became a friar, entering a Dominican monastery in Mexico City. There he found himself in the midst of the still-unresolved conflict between the indigenous and European ways of life, in "an unstable and motley [society, poised between] two religions, two political systems, two races, two languages—in sum, two conflicting societies struggling to adapt to one another in a painful cultural, social, religious, and racial accommodation."[93] He was to spend his life in that struggle and in his darker moments came to doubt that he and his fellow priests were making much progress toward ending the conflict through the meaningful conversion of the indigenous population to the new religion, the new myth.

In 1579 he wrote, "These wretched Indians remain confused. . . . On one hand they believe in God, and on the other they worship idols. They practice their ancient superstitions and rites and mix one with the other." As he realized, they were fitting Christian concepts into the structure of their own spiritual vision: "How ignorant we are of their ancient rites, while how well informed [the natives] are! They show off the god they are adoring right in front of us in the ancient manner. They chant the songs which the elders bequeathed to them especially for that purpose. . . . They sing these things when there is no one around who understands, but, as soon as a person appears who might understand, they change their tune and sing the song made up for Saint Francis with a hallelujah at the end, all to cover up their unrighteousness, interchanging religious themes with pagan gods." His research and writing were a conscious attempt to combat this problem by providing missionaries with information about pagan history, myth, and ritual so that they might recognize pagan practices and extirpate them.

HOW KING MOTECUHZOMA THE FIRST, NOW REIGNING IN GLORY AND MAJESTY, SOUGHT THE PLACE OF ORIGIN OF HIS ANCESTORS, THE SEVEN CAVES IN WHICH THEY HAD DWELT. WITH A DESCRIPTION OF THE SPLENDID PRESENTS WHICH HE SENT TO BE GIVEN TO THOSE WHO MIGHT BE FOUND THERE.

Translated from the Spanish by Doris Heyden. From the forthcoming revised edition of *The Aztecs: The History of the Indies of New Spain,* by Fray Diego Durán, translated with notes by Doris Heyden and Fernando Horcasitas, to be published in 1992 by the University of Oklahoma Press. Reprinted by permission of Doris Heyden and the publisher.

At this point our chronicle tells us that Motecuhzoma, who had become a great monarch possessing glory and wealth, decided to seek out the place where his ancestors had dwelt. He wished to know about the Seven Caves, Chicomoztoc, which his own traditions had so often mentioned. Therefore, he summoned Tlacaelel and said to him, "I have decided to call together some of my valiant warriors and send them, very well armed and provided with a generous part of the wealth we have received through the auspices of the God of All Created Things, of the Day and the Night, the lord for whom we live, so these riches be offered there at the Seven Caves and be given to those who might be found in that place. We also have been told that the mother of our god Huitzilopochtli is still alive, it is possible that she still lives. Let her be given the presents that are taken there, let her be told that she may enjoy that which her son has won with the strength of his arms and chest and his head."

"O powerful lord," Tlacaelel answered, "your royal chest is not moved, is not governed, by your own reasons, nor is your heart moved by human motives; without doubt this has been proposed to you by some eternal deity, the cause of all that is found in nature and by whose providence, O wise lord, you desire to undertake such an enormous enterprise. Now please forgive me, for it would seem that I always try to impose my arguments upon you, but I wish to tell you this:

"You must know, O great lord, that what you have determined to do is not for strong or valiant men, nor does it depend upon skill in the use of arms in warfare, for which you would send men of war, captains bearing ostentatious fighting equipment. Your envoys will not go as conquerors but as explorers. They will seek out the place where our ancestors lived, they will try to find the place where our god Huitzilopochtli was born. No, you must look for wizards, sorcerers, magicians, who with their enchantments and spells can discover that place. Our historians tell us that it is covered thickly with thorny bushes and with great brambles. It is in the midst of marshes, of lagoons which are filled with reeds and rushes, and it will be difficult to find except by great fortune. Therefore, O lord, follow my advice and look for those wizards I have described to you, who will go to that place, who will discover it, and who will then bring you news of it.

"When our people lived there it was a delightful land, a pleasant place. There they lived in leisure, they lived long, they never became weary, they never grew old. They never lacked for anything. But after they departed from their home everything turned into thorns and thistles. The stones became sharp in order to wound, the bushes became prickly and the trees thorny, in order to sting. Everything there turned against them, so they would not be able to remember the place, so they could not return there."

Motecuhzoma agreed to accept the advice of Tlacaelel and called the royal historian, an aged man called Cuauhcoatl, "Eagle Serpent," and addressed him, "O ancient father, I desire to know the true story, the knowledge that is hidden in your books about the Seven Caves where our ancestors, our fathers and grandfathers, lived, and whence they came forth. I wish to know about the place wherein dwelt our god Huitzilopochtli and out of which he led our forefathers."

"O mighty lord," answered Cuauhcoatl, "what I, your unworthy servant, can answer you is that our forebears dwelt in that blissful, happy place called Aztlan, which means 'Whiteness.' In that place there is a great hill in the midst of the waters, and it is called Colhuacan because its summit is twisted, thus it is Colhuacan, meaning 'Twisted Hill.' In this hill were caves or grottoes where our fathers and grandfathers lived for many years. There they lived in leisure, when they were called Mexitin and Aztecs. There they had at their disposal great flocks of ducks of different kinds, herons, cormorants, cranes, and other water fowl. Our ancestors enjoyed the song and melody of the little birds with red and yellow heads. They also possessed many kinds of large beautiful fish. They had the freshness of groves of trees along the edge of the waters. They had springs surrounded by willows, evergreens, and alders, all of them tall and comely. Our ancestors went about in canoes and made plots on which they sowed maize, chile, tomatoes, amaranth, beans, and all kinds of seeds which we now eat and which were brought here from that place.

"However, after they abandoned that delightful place and came to the mainland, everything turned against them. The weeds began to bite, the stones became sharp and cut, the fields were filled with thistles and spines. They encountered brambles and thorns that were difficult to pass through. There was no place to rest, there was no place where they could settle. Everything became filled with vipers, snakes, poisonous little creatures, jaguars and wildcats and other ferocious beasts. And this is the story told by our ancestors, it is what I have found painted in our ancient books. And this, O powerful king, is the answer I can give you to what you ask of me."

The king replied that this account must be a true one, since it was the same as that related by Tlacaelel. He ordered that all the wizards and magicians who could be found in all the provinces be brought before him. Sixty sorcerers were then brought to Motecuhzoma; they were old men, wise in the arts of magic. The king instructed them thus, "O elders, my fathers, I am determined to seek the land that has given birth to the Aztec people, to discover from whence they came, what land it is, and if it is still inhabited, and if the mother of our god Huitzilopochtli still lives. Therefore, prepare to go seek this place in the best way you can and as soon as possible." He had the sorcerers provided with a large number of mantles of all types, with women's clothing, precious stones, gold, fine jewels, quantities of cacao and *teonacaztli,* cotton, black vanilla flowers in large numbers, and beautiful feathers, the finest that could be found. All these riches, the most valuable things available, were given to those sorcerers. And so they would carry out this assignment with all possible care, they were also given mantles for themselves and other compensations, as well as sufficient food for their journey.

Laden with rich gifts, the sixty sorcerers departed and some time later reached a hill called Coatepec in the province of Tula. There they traced magic symbols upon the ground, invoked the demon, and smeared themselves with certain ointments they used and which wizards still use nowadays. . . .

So it is that upon that hill they invoked the Evil Spirit and begged him to show them the home of their ancestors. The Devil, conjured by these spells and pleas, turned some of them into birds and others into wild beasts such as ocelots, jaguars, jackals, wildcats, and took them, together with their gifts, to the land of their forebears.

On reaching the shores of a large lake, from the midst of which emerged the hill called Colhuacan, they resumed their human forms. The chronicle tells us that as they stood on the shore of the lake they saw people going about in canoes, fishing and attending their little farm plots. The natives, seeing the strangers and hearing them speak the same language as they, rowed to the shore and asked them what they wanted and where they came from. The Aztecs answered, "Sirs, we have come from Mexico and we are the envoys of the authorities there. We have come to seek the homeland of our ancestors."

The people of the place asked them, "What god do you adore?" to which they answered, "The great Huitzilopochtli." They added that powerful King Motecuhzoma and his Prime Minister Tlacaelel, had sent them to find Coatlicue, mother of Huitzilopochtli, and Chicomoztoc, the Seven Caves, from which their ancestors had set forth. They also wished to deliver a gift to Coatlicue if she were still alive or to her guardians if she were dead. The people of that place told them to wait while they went to call the custodian of the mother of Huitzilopochtli. They said to him, "O venerable lord, some men have come to these shores who say they are Aztecs and that they were sent here by a great lord called Motecuhzoma and by another named Tlacaelel. They have brought gifts and offerings to the mother of their god Huitzilopochtli and they were ordered to give them to her in person."

"Let them be welcome," the old man replied, "have them brought here."

So the fishermen returned with their canoes and took the sorcerers across the lake to the hill of Colhuacan. The top half of this hill is said to consist of very fine sand, so spongy and deep that it is impossible to climb up it. The Aztecs went into a house at the foot of the hill where the old man lived. They greeted him respectfully and told him, "O venerable sir, O elder, we your servants have come to this place where your word is obeyed and the breath from your mouth is revered."

The old man said to them, "Welcome, my children. Who sent you here?"

"Lord," they answered, "Motecuhzoma and his Prime Minister Tlacaelel, also called Cihuacoatl, sent us."

"Who are Motecuhzoma and Tlacaelel?" asked the custodian. "They were not among those who departed from here. Those who went from this place were Tezacatetl, Acacitli, Ocelopan, Ahuatl, Xomimitl, Ahuexotl, Huicton, and Tenoch. These eight men were the leaders of the barrios. In addition to these, there were four custodians of Huitzilopochtli, all great men, two of them being Cuauhtloquezqui and Axolohua, and two more god-bearers."

"Sir," answered the Aztecs, "we confess to you that these men are no longer known to us, nor have we ever met them. The men you mentioned are gone from this earth, all of them are dead. We have heard them mentioned; that is all."

The old man was amazed at this and asked, "Lord of All Created Things, who killed them? Why is it that all of us are still alive here in the place they abandoned? Why is it that none of us have died? Who are your leaders now?" The wizards answered that the leaders were grandsons of the men he had named. The old man wanted to know who was the father now, the custodian, of the god Huitzilopochtli and he was told that it was a great priest called Cuauhcoatl, who could speak to the god and then relay messages from him. "Did you see the god before coming here?" asked the old man, "did he send a message?" The Aztec sorcerers responded that they had not seen him nor had he sent them; they had been sent by the king and his prime minister.

The old man then asked, "Why does Huitzilopochtli not let us know when he is to return? Before departing he told his mother that he would come back and the unfortunate woman is still waiting, sad and tearful, with no one to console her. Why do you not go see her and speak to her?"

"Sir," they answered, "we have done what our masters commanded and have brought a gift for the great lady. We have been ordered to see her, greet her, and make a present to her from the riches, the spoils, that are enjoyed by her son."

The old man said, "Then pick up what you have brought and follow me."

They put the gifts on their backs and followed the old man who began to climb the hill with ease, without tiring. The Aztec envoys went behind him, their feet sinking into the soft sand, climbing with great difficulty and heaviness. The elder turned his head and when he saw that the sand had almost reached their knees, making it impossible to go on, he said to them, "What is the matter? Are you not coming? Make haste!"

When the Aztecs tried to do this they sank up to their waists in the sand and could not move. They called to the old man who was walking with such lightness that his feet did not seem to touch the ground. "What is wrong with you, O Aztecs?" he asked. "What has made you so heavy? What do you eat in your land?"

"We eat the foods that grow there and we drink chocolate."

The elder responded, "Such food and drink, my children, have made you heavy and they make it difficult for you to reach the place of your ancestors. Those foods will bring you death. The wealth you have we know nothing about; we live poorly and simply. So give me your loads and wait here. I will go call the mistress of this land, the mother of Huitzilopochtli, so that you may see her." He picked up one of the bundles and carried it up the hill as if it were straw. Then he returned for the others and carried them up with great ease.

When all the presents brought by the Aztecs had been taken up the hill, a woman of great age appeared, the ugliest and dirtiest that one could possibly imagine. Her face was so black, so covered with filth, that she looked like something out of Hell. Weeping bitterly she said to the visitors, "Welcome, my sons! Know that since your god, my son Huitzilopochtli, departed from this place, I have been awaiting his return, weeping and mourning. Since that day I have not washed my face, combed my hair or changed my clothes. My sadness and mourning will last until he returns. Is it true, my children, that you have been sent here by the leaders of the seven barrios my son took away with him?"

The envoys raised their eyes and, seeing the hideous and abominable woman, they were filled with fear. They humbled themselves before her. "O great and powerful lady," they said, "we neither saw nor spoke to the heads of the seven groups. We were sent here by your servant Motecuhzoma and his prime minister, Tlacaelel Cihuacoatl, to visit you and to seek out the place where their ancestors lived. They commanded us to kiss your hands in their name. We wish you to know that Motecuhzoma now rules over the great city of Mexico. He is not the first king but the fifth. The first who reigned was Acamapichtli, the second Huitzilihuitl, the third Chimalpopoca, the fourth Itzcoatl, and the fifth sends this message: 'I am your unworthy servant, my name is Huehue Motecuhzoma and I am at your service.'

"And you must know that the first four kings lived with great hunger, poverty, and suffering and had to pay tribute to other provinces, but now the city is free, is prosperous. Roads have been opened to the coast, to the sea, to all the land, and these are safe. Mexico is now the mistress, the princess, the leader and queen of all the cities, all of which pay obedience to her. For now the Aztecs have found the mines of gold and silver and precious stones; they have discovered the home of rich feathers. And as proof of all this Motecuhzoma sends you these gifts which are part of the wealth of your magnificent son Huitzilopochtli, and which the king, with Huitzilopochtli's help, has won with the strength of his arms and chest, his head and his heart, and by the grace of the Lord of All Created Things, of the Day and the Night. And this is all we have to say."

Her weeping calmed by these words, the old woman said, "Welcome then, my sons, I am grateful to my children. Tell me, do the elders who took my son away from here still live?" They answered, "O our lady, they are no longer in this world. They are dead, we never knew them; all that remains is their shadow, the memory of those men." She began to weep again, saying, "But what killed them? All their friends here are still alive."

She continued, "Tell me, children, what is it you bring? Is it something to eat?"

"Great lady, it is food and it is drink; chocolate is drunk, sometimes it is eaten, and at times other foods are mixed with it."

"This heavy food is what has burdened you, my sons," she told them, "this is why you have not been able to climb the hill. But tell me, the clothing worn by my son is like these mantles you have brought, with feathers and rich adornment?"

"Yes, O lady, this is the way he dresses and is adorned, is attired, with these riches, with this splendor, for he is the lord of all this wealth," was their answer.

Coatlicue then spoke, "This is all very well, my children, my heart is now at peace. But when you return you must tell my son to have pity on me, to observe the loneliness in which I live without him. Look at me; life has become fasting and penance because of him. Let him remember what he said to me when he departed:

'O my mother, I will not tarry, I will soon return
After I have led these seven barrios to find a dwelling place,
Where they can settle and populate the land that has been
    promised them.
Once I have led them there, once they are settled and I have
    given them happiness,
I will return. But this will not be until the years of my
    pilgrimage have been completed.
During this time I will wage war against provinces and cities,

Towns and villages. All of these will become my subjects.
But in the same way that I conquered them they will be torn
    from me,
Strangers will take them from me.
And I will be expelled from that land.
Then I will return, then I will return here
Because those whom I subjected with my sword and shield
Will rise against me. They will pick me up by the feet
And cast me down head first.
My weapons and I will roll upon the floor.
It will be then, O mother, when my time has come,
That I will return for you to shelter me.
Until then do not grieve.
But I beg you to give me two pairs of sandals,
One pair to go on this journey and the other for my return.
No! Give me four pairs of sandals,
Two pairs to go on this journey and two for my return!'"

Then the old woman addressed the Aztec envoys, saying, "I told my son to go with good fortune, to not delay, and as soon as he had complied with his obligation to return here. But it seems to me, my children, that he must be content where he is for he has stayed there, and he does not remember his sad mother, nor does he seek her nor heed her words. Therefore I command you to tell him that his time is up, that he must return now. And so that he remember that I wish to see him and that I am his mother, I send him this mantle and this breechcloth of maguey fiber so that he may wear them."

The men took the rough fiber mantle and breechcloth and began to go down the hill. When they were part of the way down the old woman called after them, "Stop! Wait there and you will see how men never grow old in this country! Do you see my old servant? By the time he reaches you he will be a young man!"

The old, very old man began to descend and the lower he went the younger he became. When he reached the Aztecs he appeared to be about twenty years old. Said he, "Do you see that I am now a youth? Well look, this is what happens: I will climb up again and when I am halfway up the hill I will be older." He ascended again and about halfway up he was like a man forty years of age. Then he went up a little more, about twenty steps, and then ascended more. The farther he went up the older he became—much, much older.

"Behold, my sons, the virtue of this hill: the old person who seeks youth can climb to the point on the hill that he wishes and there he will acquire the age he seeks. If he wants to become a boy again, he climbs up to the top; if he wishes to become a young man, he goes up more than halfway; if he desires a good middle age, he goes halfway up. In this way we who live here live a long time, and that is why none of the companions of your ancestors have died, for we become rejuvenated whenever we so desire. You have grown old, you have been harmed, by the chocolate you drink and the rich foods you eat. They have weakened you, they have debilitated you, they have upset your natural system. You have been spoiled by those mantles, feathers and riches that you wear and that you have brought here. All of that has ruined you. But so you will not return without gifts, take these things to your lords."

He ordered that they be given all kinds of ducks and geese and herons and other waterfowl found in that lagoon, and every type of fish that bred there. They also were presented with many kinds of plants that grew in that land, and flowers, many of them made into garlands. Also given were fiber mantles and breechcloths, one for Motecuhzoma and one for Tlacaelel. The old man asked to be pardoned for sending those humble gifts but they were all he had. And with this he said farewell.

The Aztec sorcerers accepted the gifts and then, making the magic symbols and incantations they had made before, and anointing themselves with pitch as they had when they began the journey, they were transformed into the same animals whose forms they had taken earlier and, in this disguise, they traveled to Coatepec Hill. There they turned into their normal human forms, looking at each other, recognizing each other. They arrived one by one, some earlier or later than the others, and after counting their numbers they discovered that some were missing, that there were twenty fewer than when they had set out, so a third had disappeared. Some said that the savage beasts and birds of prey they had encountered had eaten them. . . .

When they returned to Mexico the magicians, the sorcerers, took the gifts to Motecuhzoma and told him, "Lord, we have carried out your order, your word, and have witnessed that which you wished to know: we have seen that land called Aztlan and Colhuacan, where our fathers and grandfathers lived and from where they left on their migration. And we have brought the things that grow and are bred there." They then placed before the king many ears of corn, seeds, and different kinds of flowers, tomatoes and chile—foods and plants grown in that land—and the rough fiber mantles and breechcloths, all things that had been sent by the people of Aztlan-Colhuacan-Chicomoztoc. They told Motecuhzoma everything that had occurred with the mother of Huitzilopochtli and with her old servant, and how they had seen this man change his age, from young to middle aged to very old. They added that in that place all the ancestors who had stayed there were still alive. And that Coatlicue had complained bitterly about her son Huitzilopochtli, for whom she had waited so long. She prophesied that after a certain time he would be expelled from the city of Mexico-Tenochtitlan and would have to return to his original home because in the same way he had subjected other nations, his dominion and control over them would be wrested from him.

The king summoned Tlacaelel and had the sorcerers repeat in his presence everything that had happened on their journey. He had them show Tlacaelel the gifts those people had sent and describe, especially, the great fertility of that land, the freshness of their vegetation, and the manner in which the people obtained all they needed for their sustenance: how they went about in canoes and made plots of land on top of the water where they sowed and harvested the plants they ate; the abundance and variety of fish, some of which were included in the gift they brought; the multitude of water fowl, the melodious song of the small and large birds; the difference in the maize fields, some with ripe corn ready for picking, others nearly ripe, still others with corn just sprouting, and some with grains just planted. In this way there could never be hunger in that land.

The sorcerers then related that it had been impossible for them to climb the hill because they had sunk into the sand up to their waists, while the old man had climbed up easily. This old servant had then taken all the gifts they had brought up the hill and had given them to the mistress of that place, the mother of Huitzilopochtli. The sorcerers had been told that the reason they failed to reach the summit of the hill was that they ate heavy over-rich foods, such as chocolate and certain plants cultivated here in the Valley of Mexico. Coatlicue and the old man had been shocked and saddened to hear that the people who had left Aztlan-Colhuacan-Chicomoztoc long ago were now dead.

Motecuhzoma and Tlacaelel wept and were moved, remembering their ancestors, wistful at not being able to see the land of their origin. After having thanked the magician envoys, and ordering fine presents given them for their work, they requested that these same sorcerers take the maguey fiber mantle and breechcloth to the temple where they would be placed upon Huitzilopochtli, since his own mother had sent them to him.

NOTES

PART I: INTRODUCTION

1. Bernal Díaz del Castillo, *The Discovery and Conquest of Mexico, 1517–1521,* ed. Genaro García, trans. A. P. Maudslay (n.p.: Farrar, Strauss & Cudahy, 1956), 223.
2. Mircea Eliade, *Shamanism: Archaic Techniques of Ecstasy,* trans. Willard R. Trask (Princeton, NJ: Princeton Univ. Press, 1964), 333.
3. Joseph Campbell, *The Way of the Animal Powers,* vol. 1 of *Historical Atlas of World Mythology* (New York: Alfred van der Marck Editions, 1983), 9.
4. Campbell, *Animal Powers,* 49.
5. See Kent V. Flannery and Ronald Spores, "Excavated Sites of the Oaxaca Preceramic," *The Cloud People: Divergent Evolution of the Zapotec and Mixtec Civilizations,* ed. Kent V. Flannery and Joyce Marcus (New York: Academic Press, 1983), 23–25, for a fascinating discussion of such a Preceramic (ca. 5000–4000 B.C.) ritual site located at Geo-Shih in Oaxaca.
6. Marija Gimbutas, *The Language of the Goddess* (San Francisco: Harper & Row, 1989), xix.
7. With the first discoveries of Olmec civilization in the 1930s came a great deal of disagreement as to the location of the Olmec heartland since artifacts in the Olmec art style were found throughout Mesoamerica. Finally agreement seemed to have been reached that the Gulf coast was that heartland, but in a recent article John Graham argues that "one must consider the probability that Olmec style first appeared in Pacific Guatemala" and was transmitted from there to the Gulf coast ("Olmec Diffusion: A Sculptural View from Pacific Guatemala," *Regional Perspectives on the Olmec,* ed. Robert J. Sharer and David C. Grove [Cambridge: Cambridge Univ. Press, 1989], 238–39). Almost all scholars, however, continue to believe that the Gulf coast was the Olmec heartland.
8. Miguel Covarrubias, *Indian Art of Mexico and Central America* (New York: Alfred A. Knopf, 1957), 24.
9. Jacques Soustelle, *The Olmecs: The Oldest Civilization in Mexico,* trans. Helen R. Lane (Garden City, NY: Doubleday, 1984), 81. This has become, again, a somewhat controversial view. In a current treatment of the controversy, *Regional Perspectives on the Olmec,* a series of papers presented in 1983 but published in 1989, Paul Tolstoy argues the now-accepted view that a developmental "gap may have existed" between the various village cultures and the Gulf coast Olmec and that the Olmec-style artifacts found in village culture environments may represent "the visible and rather inadequate expression of a large body of beliefs, ritual practices and attitudes toward the world and society which became unifying characteristics of Mesoamerica from that time onward. It is also possible, though even more difficult to demonstrate, that interaction with the Gulf coast . . . accelerated or even triggered some of the evolutionary processes at that time in other regions of Mesoamerica" ("Western Mesoamerica and the Olmec," *Regional Perspectives on the Olmec,* ed. Robert J. Sharer and David C. Grove [Cambridge: Cambridge Univ. Press, 1989], 300). Arthur Demarest disagrees: "The real answers to these evolutionary questions lie in the elucidation of the complex mosaic of distinctive Formative regional developments, interregional diffusion and stimulus, and the sources and effects of the exchanged innovations. While struggling to segregate and decipher these overlapping processes and interactions, we should not succumb to the temptation to simply elevate our operational term ('Olmec') for this stage and its shared features to a kind of pseudo-explanation—ignoring the evidence that it lacks the uniformity of features and timing to be legitimately considered a single civilization or culture" ("The Olmec and the Rise of Civilization in Eastern Mesoamerica," *Regional Perspectives on the Olmec,* 344).
10. John Paddock, "Yagul during Monte Alban I," *The Cloud People: Divergent Evolution of the Zapotec and Mixtec Civilizations,* ed. Kent V. Flannery and Joyce Marcus (New York: Academic Press, 1983), 98.
11. René Millon, "Teotihuacán," *Archaeology: Myth and Reality: Readings from Scientific American* (San Francisco: W. H. Freeman, 1982), 85.
12. René Millon "The Last Years of Teotihuacan Dominance," *The Collapse of Ancient States and Civilizations,* ed. Norman Yoffee and George L. Cowgill (Tucson: Univ. of Arizona Press, 1988), 110.
13. See, for example, Kathleen Berrin, ed., *Feathered Serpents and Flowering Trees: Reconstructing the Murals of Teotihuacan* (San Francisco: The Fine Arts Museums of San Francisco, 1988), for a discussion by leading scholars of the iconography of a series of newly discovered murals as well as a reevaluation of the iconography of a number of the previously known murals.
14. This is a controversial subject since it has been argued that Chichen influenced Tula rather than vice versa and that the remarkable similarities in the architecture of the two sites result from the restoration efforts of archaeologists who have distorted the original architectural realities.

15. Díaz del Castillo, *Conquest of Mexico,* 190–91.
16. See V. Garth Norman, *Izapa Sculpture,* 2 vols. (Provo, UT: New World Archaeological Foundation, 1973–76), for a fascinating visual survey of the stelae and a somewhat controversial series of very detailed interpretations of their imagery.
17. Linda Schele and David Freidel, *A Forest of Kings: The Untold Story of the Ancient Maya* (New York: William Morrow, 1990), 57.
18. See in this regard the following works by Michael Coe: "Death and the Ancient Maya," *Death and the Afterlife in Pre-Columbian America,* ed. Elizabeth P. Benson (Washington, DC: Dumbarton Oaks, 1975), 87–105; *Lords of the Underworld: Masterpieces of Classic Maya Ceramics* (Princeton, NJ: Princeton Univ. Press, 1978); *Old Gods and Young Heroes: The Pearlman Collection of Maya Ceramics* (n.p.: American Friends of the Israel Museum, 1982); "Ideology of the Maya Tomb," *Maya Iconography,* ed. Elizabeth P. Benson and Gillett C. Griffin (Princeton, NJ: Princeton Univ. Press, 1988), 222–35. See also the following works by Francis Robicsek and Donald M. Hales: *The Maya Book of the Dead: The Ceramic Codex* (Charlottesville: Univ. of Virginia Art Museum, 1981); *Maya Ceramic Vases from the Classic Period* (Charlottesville: Univ. Museum of Virginia, 1982); and "A Ceramic Codex Fragment: The Sacrifice of Xbalanque," *Maya Iconography,* ed. Elizabeth P. Benson and Gillett C. Griffin (Princeton, NJ: Princeton Univ. Press, 1988), 260–76.
19. There are other fragments of undoubtedly pre-Columbian material such as that presented here from the *Codex Vindobonensis* and, perhaps, the *Book of Chilam Balam of Chumayel,* but these are not books devoted in their entirety to myth. Similarly, there are a few sources, these same two, for example, that do not come from the Basin of Mexico.

PART II: THE FIGURE OF THE GODDESS

1. Elinor W. Gadon, *The Once and Future Goddess: A Symbol for Our Time* (San Francisco: Harper & Row, 1989), xii. She quotes Gloria Orenstein, "Creation and Healing: An Empowering Relationship for Women Artists," *Women's Studies International* 8, no. 5, (1985), 456.
2. Christine Niederberger, "Early Sedentary Economy in the Basin of Mexico," *Science* 203 (1979): 138.
3. Niederberger, "Early Sedentary Economy," 138–39.
4. Campbell, *Animal Powers,* 70.
5. Gimbutas, *Language,* 185.
6. Joseph Campbell, *The Sacrifice,* part 1 of *The Way of the Seeded Earth,* vol. 2 of *Historical Atlas of World Mythology* (New York: Harper & Row, 1989), 10.
7. Mircea Eliade, "Mystery and Spiritual Regeneration in Extra-European Religions," trans. Ralph Manheim, *Man and Transformation: Papers from the Eranos Yearbooks,* ed. Joseph Campbell (Princeton, NJ: Princeton Univ. Press, 1964), 35.

8. Robert Bruce, *Lacandon Dream Symbolism* (México: Ediciones Euroamericanas, 1975), 1:101.
9. Bruce, *Lacandon Dream Symbolism,* 1:102–3.
10. Gimbutas, *Language,* 316.
11. Michael Coe, *The Jaguar's Children: Pre-Classic Central Mexico* (New York: The Museum of Primitive Art, 1965), 26.
12. Covarrubias, *Indian Art of Mexico,* 27.
13. Hasso von Winning, "Two-headed Figurines from Mexico," *The Masterkey* 44 (1970): 46.
14. Joseph Campbell, *Mythologies of the Primitive Planters: The Middle and Southern Americas,* part 3 of *The Way of the Seeded Earth,* vol. 2 of *Historical Atlas of World Mythology* (New York: Harper & Row, 1989), 255.
15. Michael Coe, *The Maya,* 4th ed. (New York: Thames & Hudson, 1987), 36.
16. Wigberto Jiménez Moreno, "Mesoamerica before the Toltecs," trans. Maudie Bullington and Charles R. Wicke, *Ancient Oaxaca,* ed. John Paddock (Stanford, CA: Stanford Univ. Press, 1966), 6.
17. Miguel León-Portilla, ed., *Native Mesoamerican Spirituality* (New York: Paulist Press, 1980), 182.
18. Miguel León-Portilla, *Pre-Columbian Literatures of Mexico,* trans. Grace Lobanov and Miguel León-Portilla (Norman: Univ. of Oklahoma Press, 1969), 86.
19. Jill Leslie Furst, "Skeletonization in Mixtec Art: A Re-evaluation," *The Art and Iconography of Late Post-Classic Central Mexico,* ed. Elizabeth Hill Boone (Washington, DC: Dumbarton Oaks, 1982), 207–25.
20. León-Portilla, *Native Mesoamerican Spirituality,* 182.
21. Joseph Campbell, *The Mythic Image* (Princeton, NJ: Princeton Univ. Press, 1974), 160.
22. León-Portilla, *Native Mesoamerican Spirituality,* 267.
23. Carmen María Pijoan A., *Evidencias Rituales en Restos Oseos* (México: Instituto Nacional de Antropología e Historia, 1981), 5–10.
24. Kent Flannery, ed., *The Early Mesoamerican Village* (New York: Academic Press, 1976), 329.
25. For a fuller treatment of the symbolic depth of Xipe Totec, see Peter T. Markman and Roberta H. Markman, *Masks of the Spirit: Image and Metaphor in Mesoamerica* (Berkeley: Univ. of California Press, 1989), 80–82, 116–17.
26. Victor Turner, *Dramas, Fields, and Metaphors: Symbolic Action in Human Society* (Ithaca, NY: Cornell Univ. Press, 1974), 25.
27. Niederberger, 1979. This and all other quotes are from pages 138–39 of this article.
28. Alexander Marshack, *The Roots of Civilization: The Cognitive Beginnings of Man's First Art, Symbol and Notation* (New York: McGraw-Hill, 1972), 260–61.
29. Marshack, *Roots of Civilization,* 283.
30. Coe, *Jaguar's Children,* 26.
31. Marshack, *Roots of Civilization,* 283.

32. Albert V. Kidder, "Preclassic Pottery Figurines of the Guatemalan Highlands," *Archaeology of Southern Mesoamerica,* Part 1, ed. Gordon R. Willey, vol. 2 of *Handbook of Middle American Indians,* ed. Robert Wauchope (Austin: Univ. of Texas Press, 1965), 150.

PART III: OF TIME, SPACE, AND EARTH

1. David Carrasco, *Quetzalcoatl and the Irony of Empire: Myths and Prophecies in the Aztec Tradition* (Chicago: Univ. of Chicago Press, 1982), 27.
2. Thomas Mann, *Joseph and His Brothers,* trans. H. T. Lowe-Porter (New York: Alfred A. Knopf, 1948), 3, 33.
3. Jamake Highwater, *Myth and Sexuality* (New York: New American Library, 1990), 206.
4. Richard F. Townsend, *State and Cosmos in the Art of Tenochtitlan* (Washington, DC: Dumbarton Oaks, 1979), 28–30.
5. Joseph Campbell, *Where the Two Came to Their Father* (Princeton, NJ: Princeton Univ. Press, 1969), 42, n. 17.
6. Eva Hunt, *The Transformation of the Hummingbird: Cultural Roots of a Zinacantecan Mythical Poem* (Ithaca, NY: Cornell Univ. Press, 1977), 55.
7. See Markman and Markman, *Masks of the Spirit,* 135–40, for a more detailed discussion of the "gods" as manifestations of the essence of divinity being called into "existence" for specific ritual and symbolic functions before they disappeared again into the world of the spirit and for a detailed discussion of the specific example of Tezcatlipoca's "unfolding."

PART IV: THE FOURFOLD UNFOLDING

1. Mircea Eliade, *The Quest: History and Meaning in Religion* (Chicago: Univ. of Chicago Press, 1969), 77.
2. León-Portilla, *Native Mesoamerican Spirituality,* 28.
3. Bernardino de Sahagún, *General History of the Things of New Spain,* trans. Charles E. Dibble and Arthur J. O. Anderson (Santa Fe, NM: School of American Research, and Salt Lake City: Univ. of Utah, 1950–78), bk. 6: 167–68.
4. Miguel León-Portilla, *Aztec Thought and Culture: A Study of the Ancient Nahuatl Mind,* trans. Jack Emory Davis (Norman: Univ. of Oklahoma Press, 1963), 87.
5. In his "human" manifestation as Ce Acatl or Topiltzin Quetzalcoatl he was the paradigmatic ruler or the patron of rulership. The myths delineating this manifestation of Quetzalcoatl will be presented in Part VI in our discussion of the mythic structure of rulership.
6. John Eric Sidney Thompson, *Maya History and Religion* (Norman: Univ. of Oklahoma Press, 1970), 203.
7. Maya scholarship has designated the gods with letters since the glyphs representing the names by which they were originally known were indecipherable by scholars. That situation is changing, and we are gradually learning the names the Maya used for their gods.
8. Martin Pickands, "The 'First Father' Legend in Maya Mythology and Iconography," *Third Palenque Round Table, 1978,* Part 2, ed. Merle Greene Robertson (Austin: Univ. of Texas Press, 1978), 124–26.
9. Eduard Seler, "Deities and Religious Conceptions of the Zapotecs," trans. C. P. Bowditch, *Mexican and Central American Antiquities, Calendar Systems, and History* (Washington, DC: Bureau of American Ethnology, 1904), 284, quoted from the dictionary of Father Juan de Córdova. The spelling of the gods' names is given as used in Joseph Whitecotton, *The Zapotecs: Princes, Priests, and Peasants* (Norman: Univ. of Oklahoma Press, 1977), 169, who categorizes both of these gods as Gods of Infinity.
10. As if to add to the confusion, the codex is read from "back" to "front." The opening page is thus numbered 52; the last, 1.
11. This scene has been exceedingly difficult for commentators to explain in detail, but there is general agreement that 9 Wind is somehow making the earth habitable.
12. While these names cannot be read in their present form as calendric names, scholars agree that García probably garbled the original information. They no doubt refer to a 9 Wind pair and are thus comparable to the codex version.
13. Bruce, *Lacandon Dream Symbolism,* 1:103.
14. See Gordon Brotherston, *A Key to the Mesoamerican Reckoning of Time: The Chronology Recorded in Native Texts* (London: British Museum, 1982), 55–58, for an attempt to work out a very complex chronology for the length of each sun.
15. Brotherston, *Mesoamerican Reckoning of Time,* 55.
16. See Wayne Elzey, "The Nahua Myth of the Suns: History and Cosmology in Pre-Hispanic Mexican Religions," *Numen* 23 (1976): 121, for a discussion of the various positions on this issue. Alfonso Caso, *The Aztecs: People of the Sun* (Norman: Univ. of Oklahoma Press, 1958), 16, for example, contends that "the worlds that were continually being created were gradually nearing perfection."
17. Mircea Eliade, *Images and Symbols: Studies in Religious Symbolism,* trans. Philip Mairet (Kansas City, KS: Sheed Andrews and McMeel, 1961), 39, 75.
18. Alfredo López Austin, *The Human Body and Ideology: Concepts of the Ancient Nahuas,* trans. Thelma Ortiz de Montellano and Bernard Ortiz (Provo, UT: Brigham Young Univ., 1988), 1:255.
19. Elzey, "Nahua Myth of the Suns," 130.
20. For the Maya these destructions would occur at the end of their 13 baktun cycle, a period somewhat longer than 5,000 years.
21. Whereas the Aztec accounts speak of four previous ages, John Eric Sidney Thompson suggests that "it is probable that the Maya believed the world had been created four or five times." *The Rise and Fall of*

Maya Civilization, 2nd ed. (Norman: Univ. of Oklahoma Press, 1966), 240–41.

22. The figure of the quincunx carries various specific meanings at different times, but the ultimate referent is always the same. The Maya glyph for *kin,* for example, which means "sun-day-time" and thereby indicates the "primary reality, divine and limitless," (Miguel León-Portilla, *Time and Reality in the Thought of the Maya,* trans. Charles L. Boiles and Fernando Horcasitas [Boston: Beacon Press, 1973], 54), is such a figure, as is the *Kan* cross found at Monte Alban and seen by Caso as representing the solar year. (See Clemency C. Coggins, "The Shape of Time: Some Political Implications of a Four-Part Figure," *American Antiquity* 45 [1980]: 728). *Lamat,* the Maya glyph for Venus, is also a quincunx due, no doubt, to the Maya fascination with the sun-related cycles of that planet. The crossed band element that appears in Maya celestial bands has the same shape as well; along with the *kin* sign and *lamat* glyph it was in use by the Olmecs as early as 900 B.C. (Michael Coe, "Early Steps in the Evolution of Maya Writing," *Origins of Religious Art and Iconography in Preclassic Mesoamerica,* ed. H. B. Nicholson [Los Angeles: UCLA Latin American Center Publications; Ethnic Arts Council of Los Angeles, 1976], 111), suggesting the great antiquity of the symbolic association of the quincunx with time.

23. And, as we have seen and will see again below, most other gods are parts of such quadripartite natures and associated thereby with the color-direction principle fundamental to Mesoamerican thought.

24. In the version in the *Leyenda* the gift of fire was related to a man and woman who survived the deluge at the end of the Fourth Sun.

25. Claude Lévi-Strauss, *The View from Afar,* trans. Joachim Neugroschel and Phoebe Hoss (New York: Basic Books, 1985), 219.

26. Munro Edmonson, trans., *Heaven Born Merida and Its Destiny: The Chilam Balam of Chumayel* (Austin: Univ. of Texas Press, 1986), 30.

27. León-Portilla, *Time and Reality,* 96, 54.

28. Bruce, *Lacandon Dream Symbolism,* 1:99–101.

29. Paul Westheim, *The Art of Ancient Mexico,* trans. Mariana Frenk and Ursula Bernard (Garden City, NY: Anchor Books, 1965), 73.

30. John Eric Sidney Thompson, *A Commentary on the Dresden Codex* (Philadelphia: American Philosophical Society, 1972), 112.

31. Munro Edmonson, trans., *The Book of Counsel: The Popol Vuh of the Quiche Maya of Guatemala* (New Orleans: Tulane Univ., 1971), xv.

32. Barbara Tedlock, *Time and the Highland Maya* (Albuquerque: Univ. of New Mexico Press, 1982), 93.

33. Anthony F. Aveni, *Skywatchers of Ancient Mexico* (Austin: Univ. of Texas Press, 1980), 203.

34. Linda Schele and Mary Ellen Miller, *The Blood of Kings: Dynasty and Ritual in Maya Art* (New York:

George Braziller in association with The Kimbell Art Museum, Fort Worth, TX, 1986), 320.

35. Giorgio de Santillana and Hertha von Dechend, *Hamlet's Mill: An Essay on Myth and the Frame of Time* (Boston: David R. Godine, 1977), 332–33.

36. Aveni, *Skywatchers,* 203.

37. Hermann Hesse, *Magister Ludi (The Glass Bead Game),* trans. Richard Winston and Clara Winston (New York: Bantam, 1970), 104–5.

38. The sources differ as to the specific associations with each direction; these are perhaps the most commonly used. See H. B. Nicholson, "Religion in Pre-Hispanic Central Mexico," *Archaeology of Northern Mesoamerica,* Part 1, ed. Gordon Ekholm and Ignacio Bernal, vol. 10 of *Handbook of Middle American Indians,* ed. Robert Wauchope (Austin: Univ. of Texas Press, 1971), 403, for a detailed delineation of the associations.

39. Thompson, *Maya History,* 233.

40. León-Portilla, *Aztec Thought,* 124.

41. Edmonson, *Chumayel,* 35.

42. It is Chapter 13 in Roys's earlier, very different translation (Ralph L. Roys, *The Book of Chilam Balam of Chumayel* [Norman: Univ. of Oklahoma Press, 1967]).

43. See our earlier discussion of the spatialization of time.

44. Edmonson, *Chumayel,* 30.

45. The events of the day 4 Manik are missing from the original.

46. Edmonson, *Popol Vuh,* xiv.

47. León-Portilla, *Aztec Thought,* 33.

48. León-Portilla, *Aztec Thought,* 37.

49. León-Portilla, *Pre-Columbian Literatures,* 58, 55.

50. The following discussion is based on Jill Leslie Furst, *Codex Vindobonensis Mexicanus I: A Commentary* (Albany: State Univ. of New York at Albany, 1978), 56–67.

51. Furst, *Codex Vindobonensis,* 132–38.

52. See García's telling of the myth and the discussion of it in "The Myths of Creation."

53. Michael Coe, "The Olmec Style and Its Distributions," *Archaeology of Southern Mesoamerica,* Part 2, ed. Gordon R. Willey, vol. 3 of *Handbook of Middle American Indians,* ed. Robert Wauchope (Austin: Univ. of Texas Press, 1965), 774.

54. Norman, *Izapa Sculpture,* 2:11.

55. Gareth W. Lowe, Thomas A. Lee, and Eduardo Martinez Espinosa, *Izapa: An Introduction to the Ruins and Monuments* (Provo, UT: Brigham Young Univ., 1982), 305.

56. Norman, *Izapa Sculpture,* 2:166.

57. Norman, *Izapa Sculpture,* 2:329.

58. Translations from Nicholson, "Religion," 408, and López Austin, *Human Body,* 1988, 1:55.

59. For a detailed discussion of the importance of time to the Maya and the close relationship of time and space, see Part IV, "The Fourfold Unfolding."

60. León-Portilla, *Time and Reality,* 96.

61. Schele and Miller, *Blood of Kings,* 45.
62. León-Portilla, *Time and Reality,* 98.
63. Scholars vary in their interpretation of this figure. Gordon Brotherston, *Image of the New World: The American Continent Portrayed in Native Texts* (London: Thames and Hudson, 1979), 232–33, places the emphasis on the warrior implications while Hunt, *Transformation of the Hummingbird,* 112–13, has a more humorous interpretation.
64. See Hunt, *Transformation of the Hummingbird,* 178–79. She points out that in several Mesoamerican languages, "twenty" is a homonym of "man." It is also, of course, the number of human fingers and toes.
65. Three in the *Codex Borgia,* one in the *Codex Fejérváry-Mayer,* one in the *Codex Laud,* all pre-Hispanic; and one in the colonial *Códice del Museo de America.*
66. See discussion of the fire god in Part II, "The Figure of the Goddess," and in Part IV, "The Fourfold Unfolding."
67. See detailed discussion of the quincunx in Part IV, "The Fourfold Unfolding."
68. For a more detailed discussion of time and space see Part IV "The Fourfold Unfolding."
69. Townsend, *State and Cosmos,* 70.
70. Wayne Elzey, "Some Remarks on the Space and Time of the 'Center' in Aztec Religion," *Estudios de Cultura Nahuatl* 12 (1976): 316.
71. Caso, *The Aztecs,* 32; Elzey, "Nahua Myth," 125; and Fernando Díaz Infante, *La Estela de los Soles o Calendario Azteca* (México: Panorama Editorial, 1986), 28, are among those who have recently argued for this interpretation. But there are alternative interpretations. Townsend, *State and Cosmos,* 67, and Esther Pasztory, *Aztec Art* (New York: Harry N. Abrams, 1983), 170, see the face as a representation of the earth monster, Tlaltecuhtli; Cecilia Klein, "The Identity of the Central Deity on the Aztec Calendar Stone," *Art Bulletin* 58 (1976), sees it as Yohualtecuhtli, the night sun; Rudolph van Zantwijk, *The Aztec Arrangement: The Social History of Pre-Spanish Mexico* (Norman: Univ. of Oklahoma Press, 1985), 229, sees it as Huitzilopochtli, perhaps in the earthbound form of Mexitli. He makes the interesting point that the stone represents the ceremonial center of Tenochtitlan in particular (241) as well as the Aztec cosmos in general. Andrzej Wiercínski, "The Dark and Light Side of the Aztec Stone Calendar and Their Symbolic Significance," *Actas del XLI Congreso Internacional des Americanistas* 2 (1976): 278, shows that in its left-right division as well as in its center the stone is "strongly penetrated by the principle of polarization into the opposites."
72. For a complete explanation of the creation story involving the five suns see Part IV, "The Fourfold Unfolding."
73. For a description of the 260-day calendar see Part IV, "The Fourfold Unfolding."
74. Townsend, *State and Cosmos,* 70.
75. Hunt, *Transformation of the Hummingbird,* 181.
76. Anthony Aveni, *Empires of Time: Calendars, Clocks, and Cultures* (New York: Basic Books, 1989), 261.
77. See van Zantwijk, *The Aztec Arrangement,* 61–62.
78. John B. Glass, "A Census of Native Middle American Pictorial Manuscripts," *Guide to Ethnohistorical Sources,* Part 3, ed. Howard F. Cline, vol. 14 of *Handbook of Middle American Indians,* ed. Robert Wauchope (Austin: Univ. of Texas Press, 1975), 98.
79. See detailed discussions of the sacred calendar and the fifty-two-year cycle in Part IV, "The Fourfold Unfolding."
80. Eduard Seler, *Comentarios al Códice Borgia,* trans. Mariana Frenk (México: Fondo de Cultura Economica, 1963), 1:258.
81. See detailed discussion of the space-time continuum in Part IV, "The Fourfold Unfolding."
82. See detailed discussion of the quincunx in Part IV, "The Fourfold Unfolding."
83. See discussion of the quincunx in Part IV, "The Fourfold Unfolding."
84. See discussion of the spatialization of time in Part IV, "The Fourfold Unfolding."
85. H. B. Nicholson, "Major Sculpture in Pre-Hispanic Central Mexico," *Archaeology of Northern Mesoamerica,* Part 1, ed. Gordon F. Ekholm and Ignacio Bernal, vol. 10 of *Handbook of Middle American Indians,* ed. Robert Wauchope (Austin: Univ. of Texas Press, 1971), 97.
86. See Markman and Markman, *Masks of the Spirit,* 43–47. In contrast, Michael D. Coe, *Mexico,* 3d ed. (New York: Thames and Hudson, 1984, 94), identifies these masks as those of the Fire Serpent, adding that "we have here another version of the first moment of creation."
87. Nicholson, "Major Sculpture," 100.
88. See Markman and Markman, *Masks of the Spirit,* 43–47, for an extensive discussion of the various themes related to this structure such as fertility, sacrifice, etc.

PART V: FLAYED GODS, SNAKE WOMEN, AND WERE-JAGUARS

1. Johanna Broda, "Templo Mayor as Ritual Space," *The Great Temple of Tenochtitlan: Center and Periphery in the Aztec World* (Berkeley: Univ. of California Press, 1987), 69–70.
2. Full descriptions of the ritual may be found in Fray Diego Durán, *Book of the Gods and Rites and The Ancient Calendar,* trans. and ed. Fernando Horcasitas and Doris Heyden (Norman: Univ. of Oklahoma Press, 1971), 175–84, and Sahagún, *General History,* vol. 2, 46–54. These detailed descriptions provide a great deal of evidence to support the agricultural interpretation of Xipe Totec and to suggest the complexity of the metaphoric play of inner and outer.

3. Seler, *Comentarios*, 1:127–35.

4. H. B. Nicholson, "The Cult of Xipe Totec in Mesoamerica," *Religion en Mesoamerica: XII Mesa Redonda, Sociedad Mexicana de Antropología,* ed. Jaime Litvak King and Noemi Castillo Tejero (México: Sociedad Mexicana de Antropología, 1972), 217.

5. Laurette Séjourné, *Burning Water: Thought and Religion in Ancient Mexico* (Berkeley, CA: Shambhala, 1976), 148–55.

6. Sahagún, *General History,* vol. 2, 48.

7. See Eliade, "Mystery," 32.

8. Schele and Miller, *Blood of Kings,* 179.

9. Nicholson, "Religion," 402.

10. Schele and Miller, *Blood of Kings,* 144.

11. Jacques Soustelle, *The Four Suns,* trans. E. Ross (New York: Grossman, 1971), 179.

12. Durán, *Book,* 263.

13. Patricia R. Anawalt, "Analysis of the Aztec Quechquemitl: An Exercise in Inference," *The Art and Iconography of Late Post-Classic Central Mexico,* ed. Elizabeth Hill Boone (Washington, DC: Dumbarton Oaks, 1982), 52.

14. Patricia R. Anawalt, "Understanding Aztec Human Sacrifice," *Archaeology* (Sept./Oct. 1982): 44.

15. Peter T. Furst, "Shamanistic Survivals in Mesoamerican Religion," *Actas del XLI Congreso Internacional des Americanistas* 6 (1976): 152.

16. Furst, "Skeletonization," 207, 221.

17. Robicsek and Hales, *Maya Ceramic Vases,* 149.

18. León-Portilla, *Native Mesoamerican Spirituality,* 187.

19. Quoted in Macduff Everton, *The Modern Maya: A Culture in Transition,* ed. Ulrich Keller and Charles Demangate (Albuquerque: Univ. of New Mexico Press, 1991), 49.

20. Thompson, *Rise and Fall,* 235–37.

21. Miguel León-Portilla, "El Maiz: Nuestro Susteno, Su Realidad Divina y Humana en Mesoamerica," *América Indigena* 48 (1988): 477.

22. Thelma D. Sullivan, "Tlazolteotl-Ixcuina: The Great Spinner and Weaver," *The Art and Iconography of Late Post-Classic Central Mexico* (Washington, DC: Dumbarton Oaks, 1982), 24.

23. The moon had both feminine and masculine aspects in Mesoamerica.

24. Furst, *Codex Vindobonensis,* 168.

25. H. B. Nicholson, "An Aztec Stone Image of a Fertility Goddess," *Baessler-Archiv.* Neue Folge 11 (1964): 145.

26. This is the fundamental position argued, quite convincingly, by Alexander Marshack in *The Roots of Civilization* (1972) and elsewhere. Although he does not apply his theory to Mesoamerica, the early figurines, as we have suggested above, fit his concept beautifully.

27. The figure formed by this crossing of warp and woof is, of course, the quincunx, which, as we have explained above, was central to the Mesoamerican conception of the essential nature of reality.

28. Sullivan, "Tlazolteotl-Ixcuina," 14.

29. Joseph Campbell, *The Masks of God: Occidental Mythology* (New York: Viking Press, 1964), 9.

30. Willard Gingerich, "Three Nahuatl Hymns on the Mother Archetype," *Mexican Studies/Estudios Mexicanos* 4 (1988): 203–5.

31. Susan Gillespie, *The Aztec Kings: The Construction of Rulership in Mexica History* (Tucson: Univ. of Arizona Press, 1989), 60.

32. This summary is drawn from Durán, *Book,* 229–37; this account can be profitably compared with the more detailed and complex account in Sahagún, *General History,* vol. 2, 110–16.

33. Sullivan, "Tlazolteotl-Ixcuina," 7. Sullivan discusses in detail the various names by which she was called and the implications of their meanings.

34. Other sources attribute this myth to the goddess Tlazolteotl, suggesting once again the interchangeability of the attributes of the fertility goddesses. See Salvador Díaz Cíntora, *Xochiquétzal: Estudio de Mitología Náhuatl* (México: Universidad Nacional Autónoma de México, 1990), 34.

35. Nicholson, "Religion," 431. After a discussion of the myth involving the birth of Huitzilopochtli from one aspect of the Earth Mother, Coatlicue, Nicholson retells several myth fragments that survive saying that "the greatest number of these mythic fragments involve Xochiquetzal and may be remnants of a fairly extensive cycle revolving around the young goddess of flowers and lust."

36. Gillespie, *Aztec Kings,* 63, 67. She points out that in the Crónica X accounts Toci is said to be his mother and in other accounts Coatlicue is replaced by Coyolxauhqui.

37. The myth is presented in Part VI, "Feathered Serpents and Hero Twins."

38. Gingerich, "Three Nahuatl Hymns," 193.

39. Gillespie, *Aztec Kings,* 94.

40. John Eric Sidney Thompson, "The Moon Goddess in Middle America, with Notes on Related Deities," *Contributions to American Anthropology and History,* vol. 5, no. 29 (Washington, DC: Carnegie Institution of Washington, 1939), 134.

41. Thompson, *Commentary,* 48.

42. Schele and Miller, *Blood of Kings,* 143–44.

43. Norman Hammond, "The Sun Is Hid: Classic Depictions of a Maya Myth," *Fourth Palenque Round Table, 1980,* ed. Elizabeth P. Benson (San Francisco: The Pre-Columbian Research Institute, 1980), 172.

44. Thompson, *Maya History,* 366–67.

45. Arthur Miller, *On the Edge of the Sea: Mural Painting at Tancah-Tulum, Quintana Roo, Mexico* (Washington, DC: Dumbarton Oaks, 1982), 86–87.

46. Cecilia F. Klein, "Post Classic Mexican Death Imagery as a Sign of Cyclic Completion," *Death*

and the Afterlife in Pre-Columbian America, ed. Elizabeth P. Benson (Washington, DC: Dumbarton Oaks, 1975), 71.

47. Alana Cordy-Collins, "Earth Mother/Earth Monster Symbolism in Ecuadorian Manteño Art," *Pre-Columbian Art History: Selected Readings,* ed. Alana Cordy-Collins (Palo Alto, CA: Peek Publications, 1982), 206.

48. See Thompson, *Maya History,* 220–23, for detailed descriptions of the various depictions of the Maya earth monsters.

49. Townsend, *State and Cosmos,* 29–30.

50. Erich Neumann, *The Great Mother: An Analysis of the Archetype,* 2nd ed., trans. Ralph Manheim (Princeton, NJ: Princeton Univ. Press, 1963), 185.

51. Gillespie, *Aztec Kings,* 93; she credits Sullivan, "Tlazolteotl-Ixcuina," 30.

52. Sahagún, *General History,* vol. 1, 9.

53. Sahagún, *General History,* vol. 1, 7.

54. Thelma D. Sullivan, trans., "A Prayer to Tlaloc," *Estudios de Cultura Nahuatl* 5 (1965): 41.

55. Séjourné, *Burning Water,* 99. As Séjourné acknowledges, it is generally felt that water and fire together, *atl-tlachinolli,* was the Mexican symbolical expression for war. Her argument (pp. 99–111), central to the thesis of her book, that the symbol must be interpreted in a far more fundamental manner is persuasive in this case, at least, in the light of the subordination of war to fertility in the Hymn.

56. Willard Gingerich, "Tlaloc, His Song," *Latin American Literatures* 1 (1977): 80. The following discussion is based on this article from which the quotations were taken.

57. Durán, *Book,* 165.

58. R. H. Barlow, "Remarks on a Nahuatl Hymn," *Tlalocan* 4, no. 2 (1963): 187.

59. Barlow, "Nahuatl Hymn," 185.

60. See Stephan F. de Borhegyi, *The Pre-Columbian Ballgames: A Pan-Mesoamerican Tradition* (Milwaukee, WI: Milwaukee Public Museum, 1980), for a survey of the ball game as it is depicted in pre-Columbian art.

61. Schele and Miller, *Blood of Kings,* 243–45, provide an extensive account of the details of the game included in the *Popol Vuh.*

62. Michael Edwin Kampen, *The Sculptures of El Tajin, Veracruz, Mexico* (Gainesville: Univ. of Florida Press, 1972), n.p.

63. Campbell, *The Sacrifice,* 37.

64. Gingerich, "Three Nahuatl Hymns," 204–5.

65. Sahagún, *General History,* vol. 2, 110ff.

66. This quotation is from Gingerich, "Three Nahuatl Hymns," as are all of the quotations that follow.

67. Gingerich, "Three Nahuatl Hymns," 226.

68. Gingerich, "Three Nahuatl Hymns." Cecilia Klein, "Rethinking Cihuacoatl: Aztec Political Imagery of the Conquered Woman," *Smoke and Mist: Mesoamerican Studies in Memory of Thelma D. Sullivan,* ed. J. Kathryn Josserand and Karen Dakin (Oxford:

B.A.R., 1988), 237, concurs, discussing her appetite for human hearts and blood in order to maintain her colossal strength and to guarantee her ongoing benevolence.

69. Gingerich, "Three Nahuatl Hymns," 231–32.

70. Gertrude P. Kurath and Samuel Martí, *Dances of Anáhuac: The Choreography and Music of Precortesian Dances* (New York: Wenner-Gren Foundation for Anthropological Research, 1964), 12.

71. Justino Fernández, *A Guide to Mexican Art: From Its Beginnings to the Present,* trans. Joshua C. Taylor (Chicago: Univ. of Chicago Press, 1969), 43.

72. Justino Fernández, *Coatlicue: Estetica del Arte Indigena Antigua,* 2nd ed. (México: Instituto de Investigaciones Esteticas, Universidad Nacional Autonoma de México, 1959), 210–11.

73. Townsend, *State and Cosmos,* 30.

74. Fernández, *Guide,* 42.

75. Caso, *The Aztecs,* 54.

76. Fernández, *Guide,* 44–45.

77. Pedro Armillas, "Volume and Form in Native Art," *Prehispanic Mexican Art,* trans. Lancelot C. Sheppard (New York: G. P. Putnam's Sons, 1972), 209.

78. Rubén Bonifaz Nuño, *The Art in the Great Temple, México-Tenochtitlan,* trans. W. Yeomans (México: Instituto Nacional de Antropología e Historia, 1981), 23.

79. Klein, "Death Imagery," 72.

80. H. B. Nicholson, *Art of Aztec Mexico: Treasures of Tenochtitlan* (Washington, DC: National Gallery of Art, 1983), 61.

81. Nicholson, *Art of Aztec Mexico,* 79.

82. Nicholson, *Art of Aztec Mexico,* 79.

83. Gingerich, "Tlaloc," 80.

84. For a full account of this development, see Markman and Markman, *Masks of the Spirit,* 8–62.

85. This has become a very controversial subject among Mesoamericanists. Ours is the traditional view, but others see the features of serpents, toads, and even ducks where we, and most Mesoamericanists, see jaguar features. See Markman and Markman, *Masks of the Spirit,* 15, for a summary of these views, and Rubén Bonifaz Nuño, *Hombres y Serpientes: Iconografía Olmeca* (México: Universidad Nacional Autónoma de Mexico, 1989) for the latest serpent theory.

86. In two articles, "Rethinking the Zapotec Urn" and "Zapotec Religion," both in Kent V. Flannery and Joyce Marcus, eds., *The Cloud People: Divergent Evolution of the Zapotec and Mixtec Civilizations* (New York: Academic Press, 1983), Joyce Marcus has argued that Cocijo is actually a god of lightning, but she agrees that his function relates to the provision of water.

87. John Paddock, *Lord 5 Flower's Family: Rulers of Zaachila and Cuilapan* (Nashville, TN: Vanderbilt Univ., 1983), 93.

88. The classic formulation of this position is in Alfonso Caso and Ignacio Bernal, *Urnas de Oaxaca*

(México: Instituto Nacional de Antropología e Historia, 1952).

89. Paddock, "Yagul," 98.

90. Covarrubias, *Indian Art of Mexico,* 151.

91. Eduard Seler, "The Antiquities of Castillo de Teayo," *Collected Works of Eduard Seler,* trans. and ed. Charles P. Bowditch (n.p.: n.p., n.d.), 3:3:52.

92. Doris Heyden, "Symbolism of Ceramics from the Templo Mayor," *The Aztec Templo Mayor,* ed. Elizabeth Hill Boone (Washington, DC: Dumbarton Oaks, 1987), 110.

93. Eduardo Matos Moctezuma, "The Templo Mayor of Tenochtitlan: History and Interpretation," trans. John G. Copeland (Berkeley: Univ. of California Press, 1987), 38.

94. Norman, *Izapa Sculpture,* 2:87.

95. Norman, *Izapa Sculpture,* 2:89.

96. Thompson, *Maya History,* 252.

97. Thompson, *Commentary,* 94.

98. For full discussions of this extremely complex image see Schele and Miller, *Blood of Kings,* 304–5, 310–12; Robicsek and Hales, *Maya Book of the Dead,* 95–96, 154; Markman and Markman, *Masks of the Spirit,* 60.

99. Miller, *On the Edge,* 85.

100. Carasco, *Quetzalcoatl,* 70.

PART VI: FEATHERED SERPENTS AND HERO TWINS

1. Joseph Campbell, *The Hero with a Thousand Faces* (Princeton, NJ: Princeton Univ. Press, 1949), 315.

2. Campbell, *Hero,* 315–16.

3. Schele and Miller, *Blood of Kings,* 321.

4. See, for example, Willard Gingerich, "Quetzalcoatl and the Agon of Time: A Literary Reading of the Anales de Cuauhtitlan," *Voices of the First America: Text and Context in the New World,* ed. Gordon Brotherston, *New Scholar* 10 (1986): 41–60, and Gillespie regarding Topiltzin Quetzalcoatl; in addition, the cyclicity of rulership has in recent years been discussed in great detail in Munro S. Edmonson, *The Ancient Future of the Itza: The Book of Chilam Balam of Tizimin* (Austin: Univ. of Texas Press, 1982); Arthur G. Miller, *Maya Rulers of Time: A Study of Architectural Sculpture at Tikal, Guatemala* (Philadelphia: The University Museum, 1986); and Richard N. Luxton, "Balam Dz'ib: The Arrival of Christianity among the Yucatec Maya," *Voices of the First America: Text and Context in the New World,* ed. Gordon Brotherston, *New Scholar* 10 (1986): 159–80 for the Maya and tangentially by Alfredo López Austin, *Hombre Dios: Religión y Política en el Mundo Náhuatl* (México: Instituto de Investigaciones Históricas, Universidad Nacional Autonóma de México, 1973), and Serge Gruzinski, *Man-Gods in the Mexican Highlands: Indian Power and Colonial Society, 1520-1800,* trans. Eileen Corrigan (Stanford, CA: Stanford Univ. Press, 1989), for the peoples of the Basin of Mexico.

5. Miller, *Maya Rulers,* 17.

6. See Edmonson, *Ancient Future* and *Heaven Born,* for a detailed discussion of this cyclical rotation and of the books of *Chilam Balam* as "prophetic history—as the ancient past and the ineluctable future of the Mayan people" (*Ancient Future,* xi), and see Rosemary Sharp, *Chacs and Chiefs: The Iconology of Mosaic Stone Sculpture in Pre-Conquest Yucatan, Mexico* (Washington, DC: Dumbarton Oaks, 1981), for another suggestion of such a rotational system in the Yucatan.

7. Gruzinski, *Man-Gods,* 24.

8. Sahagún, *General History,* vol. 12, 42. See Gillespie, *Aztec Kings,* 192–95, for a discussion of the historical accuracy of Sahagún's account.

9. Peter Mathews, "Maya Early Classic Monuments and Inscriptions," *A Consideration of the Early Classic Period in the Maya Lowlands* (Albany: State Univ. of New York at Albany, 1985), 52–53.

10. Gordon Brotherston, "Tula: Touchstone of the Mesoamerican Era," *Voices of the First America: Text and Context in the New World,* ed. Gordon Brotherston, *New Scholar* 10 (1986): 29–30.

11. Gruzinski, *Man-Gods,* 19–20.

12. Schele and Miller, *Blood of Kings,* 183.

13. Theodore H. Gaster, "Myth and Story," *Sacred Narrative: Readings in the Theory of Myth,* ed. Alan Dundes (Berkeley: Univ. of California Press, 1984), 123. For a statement of this view in specifically Mesoamerican terms see Gruzinski, *Man-Gods,* 22.

14. A number of scholars have suggested links between shamanism and rulership in Mesoamerica. Charles E. Lincoln, for example, says "Maya rulership has its origins in shamanism" ("Ceramics and Ceramic Chronology," *A Consideration of the Early Classic Period in the Maya Lowlands* [Albany: State Univ. of New York at Albany, 1985], 79); and see David A. Freidel and Linda Schele, "Kingship in the Late Preclassic Maya Lowlands: The Instruments and Places of Ritual Power," *American Anthropologist* 90 (1988). For a fuller consideration of the shamanistic underpinnings of Mesoamerican spiritual thought see Markman and Markman, *Masks of the Spirit,* 101–7.

15. Nicholson, "Religion," 412.

16. Carolyn Tate, "The Maya Cauac Monster's Formal Development and Dynastic Contexts," *Pre-Columbian Art History: Selected Readings,* ed. Alana Cordy-Collins (Palo Alto, CA: Peek Publications, 1982), 52.

17. Karen Bassie-Sweet, *From the Mouth of the Dark Cave: Commemorative Sculpture of the Late Classic Maya* (Norman: Univ. of Oklahoma Press, 1991), 29.

18. Schele and Freidel, *Forest of Kings,* 71, but see Bassie-Sweet, *Mouth of the Dark Cave,* 122–24, for a different interpretation of that Maya term.

19. Gruzinski, *Man-Gods,* 24.

20. And in our earlier, fuller treatment of the subject in Markman and Markman, *Masks of the Spirit.*
21. Gaster, "Myth and Story," 115.
22. As we have seen above in our consideration of the myths of creation in Part IV, The Fourfold Unfolding.
23. Schele and Freidel, *Forest of Kings,* 68.
24. And continuous as the sky in the jungle realm of the Maya.
25. These dates are given in Schele and Freidel, *Forest of Kings,* 219, but there is some controversy regarding them. Epigraphers such as Schele and Freidel read the dates engraved on the stone, but archaeologists, who determine dates in other ways, are not so sure. This controversy, of course, may be but another problem caused by our very different view of "historical accuracy" from that of the Maya.
26. Schele and Freidel, *Forest of Kings,* 226.
27. Campbell, *Hero,* 77.
28. Schele and Miller, *Blood of Kings,* 301.
29. Campbell, *Hero,* 30.
30. Linda Schele, "The Xibalba Shuffle: A Dance after Death," *Maya Iconography,* ed. Elizabeth P. Benson and Gillet C. Griffin (Princeton, NJ: Princeton Univ. Press, 1988), 294.
31. See Campbell, *Hero,* 97.
32. Joseph Campbell, *The Power of Myth,* ed. Betty Sue Flowers (New York: Doubleday, 1988), 66.
33. Schele and Freidel, *Forest of Kings,* 488, n. 34.
34. Miller, *Maya Rulers,* 35.
35. López Austin, *Hombre-Dios,* 157.
36. Gruzinski, *Man-Gods,* 23.
37. H. B. Nicholson, in his 1957 Harvard doctoral dissertation, still the definitive work on Quetzalcoatl, counts 57 variants. The most accessible discussion of the major variants is Carrasco, *Quetzalcoatl.*
38. For an insightful discussion of this controversy see Gillespie, *Aztec Kings,* 173–75.
39. Gillespie, *Aztec Kings,* 198.
40. Gingerich, "Quetzalcoatl," 53.
41. Campbell, *Power,* 66.
42. Michael D. Coe and Gordon Whittaker, *Aztec Sorcerers in Seventeenth Century Mexico: The Treatise on Superstitions by Hernando Ruiz de Alarcón* (Albany: State Univ. of New York at Albany, 1982), 30.
43. Richard B. Sewall, *The Vision of Tragedy* (New Haven, CT: Yale Univ. Press, 1959), 6.
44. Willard Gingerich, "*Chipahuacanemiliztli,* 'The Purified Life,' in the Discourses of Book VI, *Florentine Codex,*" *Smoke and Mist: Mesoamerican Studies in Memory of Thelma D. Sullivan,* ed. J. Kathryn Josserand and Karen Dakin (Oxford: B.A.R., 1988), 2:531.
45. The numbering of the sections is our own and refers to the text as reprinted here; we are not following Sahagún's chapter numbers.
46. As a number of scholars have pointed out, we must recognize that those who retold and heard the versions that are now extant were Aztecs living *after* the Conquest and striving to encompass that very Conquest in their key myth. According to Gillespie, for example, "An analysis of the stories of Topiltzin Quetzalcoatl of Tollan . . . provides an example of how quickly and profoundly the Spanish conquest influenced colonial period Aztec conceptions of their past accomplishments, their present situation, and their hopes for the future. . . . The saga of Topiltzin Quetzalcoatl, the Toltec king who was both first and last, accommodated the fundamental notion of the cyclical recurrence of phenomena by grounding the events of the conquest in a past era. With this story of an earlier empire that had risen and fallen, the Aztecs created for themselves a more specific destiny of conquest and destruction after the conquest had already taken place" (*Aztec Kings,* pp. 172–73); and see Gingerich, "Quetzalcoatl."
47. Campbell, *Hero,* 288.
48. See Sahagún, *General History,* vol. 3, 36n, for a concise summary.
49. For a discussion of the cycle of Venus and the significance of its periods in Mesoamerican spiritual thought see Markman and Markman, *Masks of the Spirit,* 115.
50. Translated by Willard Gingerich from the Nahuatl in Sahagún, *General History,* vol. 6, 101, in Gingerich, "*Chipahuacanemiliztli,*" 522. It should be noted that Gingerich indicates uncertainty regarding the correct translation of the Nahuatl he renders as "sharp as a harpoon blade."
51. Eliade, *Images and Symbols,* 51.
52. Carrasco, *Quetzalcoatl,* 64.
53. Dennis Tedlock, trans., *Popol Vuh: The Mayan Book of the Dawn of Life* (New York: Simon & Schuster, 1985), 55.
54. López Austin, *Hombre-Dios,* 60.
55. Gaster, "Myth and Story," 115.
56. Nicholson, "Religion," 426.
57. Gillespie, *Aztec Kings,* 115.
58. Gillespie, *Aztec Kings,* 86–92.
59. Elizabeth H. Boone, *Incarnations of the Aztec Supernatural: The Image of Huitzilopochtli in Mexico and Europe* (Philadelphia: The American Philosophical Society, 1989), 2.
60. This mythic episode is chillingly reenacted in the annual festival of Ochpaniztli devoted to Toci, whom Durán describes as "our Grandmother, Mother of the Gods and Heart of the Earth"; see Durán, *Book,* 229–37, and Sahagún, *General History,* vol. 2, 110–16.
61. Gillespie, *Aztec Kings,* 94.
62. Gillespie, *Aztec Kings,* 215.
63. For details regarding Fray Bernardino de Sahagún and the *Florentine Codex* see the introductory remarks to "The Creation of the Sun and the Moon," (add pg. x-ref, see ms. 212-14).
64. Nicholson, "Religion," 413.
65. David C. Grove and Susan D. Gillespie, "Chalcatzingo's Portrait Figurines and the Cult of the Ruler," *Archaeology* (July/Aug. 1984): 29–33.

66. See, for example, David C. Grove, "Olmec Monuments: Mutilation as a Clue to Meaning," *The Olmec
and Their Neighbors: Essays in Honor of Matthew
W. Stirling,* ed. Elizabeth P. Benson (Washington,
DC: Dumbarton Oaks, 1981), 66.

67. David C. Grove, *The Olmec Paintings of Oxtotitlan
Cave, Guerrero, Mexico* (Washington, DC:
Dumbarton Oaks, 1970), 8, 31.

68. Scholars seem to agree that the mask depicts a god
here, but they do not agree on the identity of the god.
However, each of the various identifications relates
the mask to rulership. Schele and Miller, *Blood of
Kings,* 215, agree that this image is Chac-Xib-Chac.

69. For information regarding the *Popol Vuh,* see the
introductory remarks to "The Birth of All of Heaven
and Earth," (add x-ref, see ms. p. 188-90).

70. Edmonson, *Popol Vuh,* 1971.

71. Robiscek and Hales, *Maya Book of the Dead,* 153.
See also Coe, "Ideology," 234, and Preface to Schele
and Miller, *Blood of Kings,* 4.

72. Merle Greene Robertson, *The Temple of
Inscriptions,* vol. 1 of *The Sculpture of Palenque*
(Princeton, NJ: Princeton Univ. Press, 1983), 56.

73. Robertson, *Temple of Inscriptions,* 62.

74. Schele and Miller, *Blood of Kings,* 272–74.

75. Bassie-Sweet, *Mouth of the Dark Cave,* 240.

76. For details regarding Fray Bernardino de Sahagún
and the *Florentine Codex* see the introductory
remarks to "The Creation of the Sun and the Moon,"
(add x-ref, see ms. p. 212-14).

77. Virgil, *The Aeneid,* trans. Rolfe Humphries (New York:
Charles Scribner's Sons, 1951), 18, 21, 90, and 112.

78. There are, however, a number of theories, as one
would expect, but none of them can be
substantiated.

79. León-Portilla, *Aztec Thought,* 29–31.

80. Gingerich, "Quetzalcoatl," 52.

81. Translator note: The Nahuatl word here puns on
tlecauia—to set something afire—and *tlehcauia*—to

82. Translator note: Does he mean reading the codex is
done, reading Quetzalcoatl's life is done, reading all
Chichimec history is done—or all three at once?

83. Translator note: He seems to see the end prophesied
here, the arrival of Cortés in another year 1 Reed
and the end to come. Truly this 1 Reed is a powerful
tonal and still a testimony to the power of Tlahuiz-
calpantecutli in the later events following the coming
of the Spaniards. Cortés is an arrow of destiny,
hurled at the whole civilization by Lord Quetzalcoatl.

84. *Arte Precolombino de Mexico* (Milano: Olivetti/Electa,
1990), pl. 81.

85. Silvia Trejo, *Escultura Huaxteca de Río Tamuín
(Figuras Masculinas)* (México: Universidad
Nacional Autonoma de México, 1989), 84–85 (our
translation).

86. For details regarding Fray Bernardino de Sahagún
and the *Florentine Codex* see the introductory
remarks for "The Creation of the Sun and the
Moon," (add x-ref, see ms. p. 212-14).

87. Jacques Soustelle, *Daily Life of the Aztecs on the Eve
of Spanish Conquest,* trans. Patrick O'Brian (New
York: Macmillan, 1961), 97.

88. Part of the text has been attributed to Chimalpahin,
whom some authorities claim is the "main author."

89. Thelma D. Sullivan, trans., "The Finding and Founding of Tenochtitlan," *Tlalocan* 6, no. 4 (1971): 312.

90. A portion of the original text is missing here.

91. Van Zantwijk, *The Aztec Arrangement,* 28–33.

92. Doris Heyden, "An Interpretation of the Cave Underneath the Pyramid of the Sun in Teotihuacan,
Mexico," *American Antiquity* 40 (1975): 137.

93. Fray Diego Durán, *Book of the Gods and Rites and
The Ancient Calendar,* trans. Fernando Horcasitas
and Doris Heyden (Norman: Univ. of Oklahoma
Press, 1971), 11.

raise something aloft. Both meanings are intended
simultaneously.

BIBLIOGRAPHY

PRIMARY SOURCES

The primary textual sources from which the mythology of Mesoamerica must be gleaned consist of two basic types: the pictographic texts (now called codices), which were "written" before the Conquest, and the pictographic and alphabetic texts written after the Conquest in an attempt to record pre-Conquest beliefs. We present here a compilation of the most accessible and reliable facsimiles and editions of the most important such texts for the study of mythology. Where editions in English are not available, we list those in Spanish and other languages. The facsimiles published by Akademische Druck- u. Verlagsanstalt are the most accurate photographic reproductions yet made.

THE PRE-CONQUEST CODICES

Codex Borgia (Basin of Mexico)

    Códice Borgia. México: Fondo de Cultura Economica, 1963. This facsimile is accompanied by Mariana Frenk's Spanish translation of Eduard Seler's diagrammatic explication of the drawings and his two-volume commentary, both from 1904.
    Codex Borgia. Graz: Akademische Druck- u. Verlagsanstalt, 1976.

Codex Cospi (Basin of Mexico)

    Codex Cospi. Graz: Akademische Druck- u. Verlagsanstalt, 1968. Foreword by Karl A. Nowotny.
    Códice Cospi. Puebla: Centro Regional de Puebla, 1988. This facsimile is accompanied by a study by Carmen Aguilera.

Codex Fejérváry-Mayer (Basin of Mexico)

    Codex Fejérváry-Mayer. Graz: Akademische Druck- u. Verlagsanstalt, 1971. Foreword by C. A. Burland.

Codex Laud (Basin of Mexico)

    Codex Laud. Graz: Akademische Druck- u. Verlagsanstalt, 1966. Foreword by C. A. Burland.

Codex Vindobonensis (Mixtec)

    Codex Vindobonensis Mexicanus 1. Graz: Akademische Druck- u. Verlagsanstalt, 1963. Foreword by Otto Adelhofer.

Dresden Codex (Maya)

    John Eric Sidney Thompson. *A Commentary on the Dresden Codex.* Philadelphia: American Philosophical Society, 1972. Pp. 121–47 of this volume contain a facsimile of the codex.

THE POST-CONQUEST SOURCES

Anales de Cuauhtitlan (Basin of Mexico)

    In *Códice Chimalpopoca.* Translated by Primo Feliciano Velázquez. México: Universidad Nacional Autonoma de México, 1975. 3–118.

Book of Chilam Balam of Chumayel (Maya)

    Munro S. Edmonson, trans. and annotator. *Heaven Born Merida and Its Destiny: The Book of Chilam Balam of Chumayel.* Austin: Univ. of Texas Press, 1986.
    Ralph L. Roys. *The Book of Chilam Balam of Chumayel.* Norman: Univ. of Oklahoma Press, 1967.

Codex Borbonicus (Basin of Mexico)

    Codex Borbonicus. Graz: Akademische Druck- u. Verlagsanstalt, 1974. Commentary by Karl A. Nowotny and Jacqueline de Durand-Forest.
    Códice Borbónico. México: Siglo Veintiuno, 1979. This facsimile is accompanied by a reprinting of Francisco del Paso y Troncoso. *Descripción, Historia y Exposición del Códice Pictórico de los Antiguos Náuas* (1898), a detailed description of the *Codex Borbonicus.*

Codex Boturini (Basin of Mexico)

    Coleccion de Documentos Conmemorativos del DCL Aniversario de la Fundacion de Tenochtitlan. Documento Num. 1: Códice Botturini (Tira de la Peregrinación). México: Secretaria de Educación Publica, 1975.

Codex Magliabechiano (Basin of Mexico)

    The Book of the Life of the Ancient Mexicans. Berkeley: Univ. of California Press, 1983. Reprint of 1903. This facsimile, introduced by Zelia Nuttall, is accompanied by Elizabeth H. Boone. *The Codex Magliabechiano.* A commentary.

Codex Vaticanus A (Basin of Mexico)

Códice Vaticano Latino 3738. In Vol. 3 of *Antigüe-dades de México, Basadas en la Recopilación de Lord Kingsborough*. México: Secretaría de Hacienda y Crédito Público, 1964. This facsimile contains modern Spanish transcriptions of the original hand-written glosses.
Codex Vaticanus 3738 ("Codex Vat. A," "Codex Ríos"). Graz: Akademische Druck- u. Verlagsanstalt, 1979.

Durán, Fray Diego (Basin of Mexico)

The Aztecs: The History of the Indies of New Spain. Translated by Doris Heyden and Fernando Horcasitas. New York: Orion Press, 1964.
The Aztecs: The History of the Indies of New Spain. Rev. ed. Translated by Doris Heyden and Fernando Horcasitas. Norman: Univ. of Oklahoma Press, in press.
Book of the Gods and Rites and The Ancient Calendar. Translated and edited by Fernando Horcasitas and Doris Heyden. Norman: Univ. of Oklahoma Press, 1971.

García, Fray Gregorio (Mixtec)

Origen de los Indios de el Nuevo Mundo e Indias Occidentales. 2nd printing. Madrid, 1729.

Historia de los Mexicanos por sus Pinturas (Basin of Mexico)

In *Teogonia e Historia de los Mexicanos: Tres Opusculos del Siglo XVI*. Edited by Angel Maria Garibay K. México: Editorial Porrua, 1965, 23–90.

Historia Tolteca-Chichimeca (Basin of Mexico)

Historia Tolteca-Chichimeca. Edited and with com-mentary by Paul Kirchhoff, Lina Odeña Güemes, and Luis Reyes García. 2nd ed. México: Fondo de Cultura Economica, 1989.

Histoyre du Mechique (Basin of Mexico)

Histoyre du Mechique. Edited by Edouard de Jonghe. *Journal de la Société des Américanistes de Paris* 2 (1905): 1–41 (in French).
In *Teogonia e Historia de los Mexicanos: Tres Opus-culos del Siglo XVI*. Translated by Ramón Rosales Munguía, edited by Angel Maria Garibay K. México: Editorial Porrua, 1965, 23–90 (in Spanish).

Ixtlilxochitl, Fernando de Alva (Basin of Mexico)

Obras Históricas. 2 vols. México: Universidad Nacional Autonoma de México, 1975–77.

Landa, Fray Diego de (Maya)

Yucatan before and after the Conquest. Translated by William Gates. New York: Dover, 1978.

Leyenda de los Soles (Basin of Mexico)

In *Códice Chimalpopoca*. Translated by Primo Feliciano Velázquez. México: Universidad Nacional Autonoma de México, 1975, 119–42.

Mendieta, Fray Gerónimo de (Basin of Mexico)

Historia Eclesiástica Indiana. México: Editorial Porrua, 1980.

Popol Vuh (Maya)

Munro S. Edmonson, trans. and annotator. *The Book of Counsel: The Popol Vuh of the Quiche Maya of Guatemala*. Publications of the Middle American Research Institute, no. 35. New Orleans: Tulane Univ., 1971.
Dennis Tedlock, trans. *Popol Vuh: The Mayan Book of the Dawn of Life*. New York: Simon & Schuster, 1985.

Sahagún, Bernardino de (Basin of Mexico)

General History of the Things of New Spain (Florentine Codex). Translated by Charles E. Dibble and Arthur J. O. Anderson. 13 vols. Santa Fe, NM: School of American Research, and Salt Lake City: Univ. of Utah, 1950–78.

Tezozómoc, Hernando Alvarado (Basin of Mexico)

Crónica Mexicayotl. Translated by Adrián León. México: Universidad Nacional Autonoma de México, 1975.
Crónica Mexicana. 3rd ed. Edited by Manuel Orozco y Berra. México: Editorial Porrua, 1980.

SECONDARY SOURCES

We present here the most valuable scholarly works dealing with Mesoamerican mythology, concentrating on those in English, as well as other works to which we have referred.

Anawalt, Patricia R. "Analysis of the Aztec Quech-quemitl: An Exercise in Inference." *The Art and Iconography of Late Post-Classic Central Mexico*. Edited by Elizabeth Hill Boone. Washington, DC: Dumbarton Oaks, 1982, 37–72.
———. "Understanding Aztec Human Sacrifice." *Archae-ology* (Sept./Oct. 1982): 38–45.
Armillas, Pedro. "Volume and Form in Native Art." *Pre-hispanic Mexican Art*. Translated by Lancelot C. Sheppard. New York: G. P. Putnam's Sons, 1972, 187–262.
Arte Precolombino de Mexico. Milano: Olivetti/Electa, 1990.
Aveni, Anthony F. *Skywatchers of Ancient Mexico*. Austin: Univ. of Texas Press, 1980.

———. *Empires of Time: Calendars, Clocks, and Cultures.* New York: Basic Books, 1989.

Barlow, R. H. "Remarks on a Nahuatl Hymn." *Tlalocan* 4, no. 2 (1963): 185–92.

Bassie-Sweet, Karen. *From the Mouth of the Dark Cave: Commemorative Sculpture of the Late Classic Maya.* Norman: Univ. of Oklahoma Press, 1991.

Bernal, Ignacio. *The Olmec World.* Translated by Doris Heyden and Fernando Horcasitas. Berkeley: Univ. of California Press, 1969.

Berrin, Kathleen, ed. *Feathered Serpents and Flowering Trees: Reconstructing the Murals of Teotihuacan.* San Francisco: The Fine Arts Museums of San Francisco, 1988.

Bonifaz Nuño, Rubén. *The Art in the Great Temple, México-Tenochtitlan.* Translated by W. Yeomans. México: Instituto Nacional de Antropología e Historia, 1981.

———. *Imagen de Tláloc: Hipótesis Iconográfica y Textual.* México: Universidad Nacional Autónoma de México, 1986.

———. *Hombres y Serpientes: Iconografía Olmeca.* México: Universidad Nacional Autónoma de México, 1989.

Boone, Elizabeth H. *Incarnations of the Aztec Supernatural: The Image of Huitzilopochtli in Mexico and Europe.* Transactions of the American Philosophical Society, vol. 79, no. 2. Philadelphia: The American Philosophical Society, 1989.

Borhegyi, Stephan F. de. *The Pre-Columbian Ballgames: A Pan-Mesoamerican Tradition.* Contributions in Anthropology and History, no. 1. Milwaukee, WI: Milwaukee Public Museum, 1980.

Bricker, Victoria Reifler. *The Indian Christ, the Indian King: The Historical Substrate of Maya Myth and Ritual.* Austin: Univ. of Texas Press, 1981.

Broda, Johanna. "The Provenience of the Offerings: Tribute and Cosmovisión." *The Aztec Templo Mayor.* Edited by Elizabeth Hill Boone. Washington, DC: Dumbarton Oaks, 1987, 211–56.

———. "Templo Mayor As Ritual Space." *The Great Temple of Tenochtitlan: Center and Periphery in the Aztec World.* Berkeley: Univ. of California Press, 1987, 61–123.

Brotherston, Gordon. "Huitzilopochtli and What Was Made of Him." *Mesoamerican Archaeology: New Approaches.* Edited by Norman Hammond. Austin: Univ. of Texas Press, 1974, 155–66.

———. *Image of the New World: The American Continent Portrayed in Native Texts.* London: Thames and Hudson, 1979.

———. *A Key to the Mesoamerican Reckoning of Time: The Chronology Recorded in Native Texts.* British Museum Occasional Papers, no. 38. London: British Museum, 1982.

———. "Tula: Touchstone of the Mesoamerican Era." *Voices of the First America: Text and Context in the New World.* Edited by Gordon Brotherston. *New Scholar* 10 (1986): 19–40 .

Bruce, Robert D. *Lacandon Dream Symbolism.* 2 vols. México: Ediciones Euroamericanas Klaus Thiele, 1975.

Burland, Cottie A. *The Gods of Mexico.* New York: Capricorn Books, 1968.

Burland, Cottie A., and Werner Forman. *Feathered Serpent and Smoking Mirror.* New York: G. P. Putnam's Sons, 1975.

Campbell, Joseph. *The Hero with a Thousand Faces.* The Bollingen Series, no. 17. Princeton, NJ: Princeton Univ. Press, 1949.

———. *The Masks of God: Primitive Mythology.* New York: The Viking Press, 1959.

———. *The Masks of God: Occidental Mythology.* New York: The Viking Press, 1964.

———. "The Historical Development of Mythology." *Myth and Mythmaking.* Edited by Henry A. Murray. Boston: Beacon Press, 1968, 19–45.

———. *The Masks of God: Creative Mythology.* New York: The Viking Press, 1968.

———. *Where the Two Came to Their Father.* 1943. Reprint. The Bollingen Series, no. 1. Princeton, NJ: Princeton Univ. Press, 1969.

———. *The Mythic Image.* The Bollingen Series, no. 100. Princeton, NJ: Princeton Univ. Press, 1974.

———. *The Way of the Animal Powers.* Vol. 1 of *Historical Atlas of World Mythology.* New York: Alfred van der Marck Editions, 1983.

———. *The Inner Reaches of Outer Space: Metaphor as Myth and as Religion.* New York: Alfred van der Marck Editions, 1986.

———. *The Power of Myth,* with Bill Moyers. Edited by Betty Sue Flowers. New York: Doubleday, 1988.

———. *Mythologies of the Primitive Planters: The Middle and Southern Americas.* Part 3 of *The Way of the Seeded Earth.* Vol. 2 of *Historical Atlas of World Mythology.* New York: Harper & Row, 1989.

———. *The Sacrifice.* Part 1 of *The Way of the Seeded Earth.* Vol. 2 of *Historical Atlas of World Mythology.* New York: Harper & Row, 1989.

Carrasco, David. *Quetzalcoatl and the Irony of Empire: Myths and Prophecies in the Aztec Tradition.* Chicago: Univ. of Chicago Press, 1982.

———. "Myth, Cosmic Terror, and the Templo Mayor." *The Great Temple of Tenochtitlan: Center and Periphery in the Aztec World.* Berkeley: Univ. of California Press, 1987, 124–62.

———. *Religions of Mesoamerica: Cosmovision and Ceremonial Centers.* San Francisco: Harper & Row, 1990.

Caso, Alfonso. *The Aztecs: People of the Sun.* Translated by Lowell Dunham. Norman: Univ. of Oklahoma Press, 1958.

Caso, Alfonso, and Ignacio Bernal. *Urnas de Oaxaca.* Memorias del Instituto Nacional de Antropología e Historia, no. 2. México: Instituto Nacional de Antropología e Historia, 1952.

Castellón Huerta, Blas Román. "Mitos Cosmogónicos de los Nahuas Antiguos." *Mitos Cosmogónicos del México Indígena.* Edited by Jesús Monjarás-Ruiz. México: Instituto Nacional de Antropología e Historia, 1987, 125–76.

Coe, Michael D. *The Jaguar's Children: Pre-Classic Central Mexico.* New York: The Museum of Primitive Art, 1965.

———. "The Olmec Style and Its Distributions." *Archaeology of Southern Mesoamerica, Part 2.* Edited by Gordon R. Willey. Vol. 3 of *Handbook of Middle American Indians.* Edited by Robert Wauchope. Austin: Univ. of Texas Press, 1965, 739–75.

———. "The Iconology of Olmec Art." *The Iconography of Middle American Sculpture.* New York: The Metropolitan Museum of Art, 1973, 1–12.

———. "Death and The Ancient Maya." *Death and the Afterlife in Pre-Columbian America.* Edited by Elizabeth P. Benson. Washington, DC: Dumbarton Oaks, 1975, 87–105.

———. "Early Steps in the Evolution of Maya Writing." *Origins of Religious Art and Iconography in Preclassic Mesoamerica.* Edited by H. B. Nicholson. Los Angeles: UCLA Latin American Center Publications, Ethnic Arts Council of Los Angeles, 1976, 107–21.

———. *Lords of the Underworld: Masterpieces of Classic Maya Ceramics.* Princeton, NJ: Princeton Univ. Press, 1978.

———. "Religion and the Rise of Mesoamerican States." *The Transition to Statehood in the New World.* Edited by Grant D. Jones and Robert R. Kautz. Cambridge: Cambridge Univ. Press, 1981, 157–71.

———. *Old Gods and Young Heroes: The Pearlman Collection of Maya Ceramics.* N.p.: American Friends of the Israel Museum, 1982.

———. *Mexico.* 3d ed. New York: Thames and Hudson, 1984.

———. Preface to *The Blood of Kings: Dynasty and Ritual in Maya Art,* by Linda Schele and Mary Ellen Miller. New York: George Braziller, Inc., in association with the Kimbell Art Museum, Fort Worth, TX, 1986.

———. *The Maya.* 4th ed. New York: Thames and Hudson, 1987.

———. "Ideology of the Maya Tomb." *Maya Iconography.* Edited by Elizabeth P. Benson and Gillett C. Griffin. Princeton, NJ: Princeton Univ. Press, 1988, 222–35.

Coe, Michael D., and Gordon Whittaker. *Aztec Sorcerers in Seventeenth Century Mexico: The Treatise on Superstitions by Hernando Ruiz de Alarcón.*

Albany: Institute for Mesoamerican Studies, State Univ. of New York at Albany, 1982.

Coggins, Clemency C. "The Shape of Time: Some Political Implications of a Four-Part Figure." *American Antiquity* 45 (1980): 727–39.

Cordy-Collins, Alana. "Earth Mother/Earth Monster Symbolism in Ecuadorian Manteño Art." *Pre-Columbian Art History: Selected Readings.* Edited by Alana Cordy-Collins. Palo Alto, CA: Peek Publications, 1982, 205–30.

Covarrubias, Miguel. *Indian Art of Mexico and Central America.* New York: Alfred A. Knopf, 1957.

de la Garza, Mercedes. "Analysis Comparativo de la *Historia de los Mexicanos por Sus Pinturas* y la *Leyenda de los Soles." Estudios de Cultura Náhuatl* 16 (1983): 123–34.

———. "Los Mayas: Antiguas y Nuevas Palabras sobre el Origen." *Mitos Cosmogónicos del México Indígena.* Edited by Jesús Monjarás-Ruiz. México: Instituto Nacional de Antropología e Historia, 1987, 15–86.

Demarest, Arthur. "The Olmec and the Rise of Civilization in Eastern Mesoamerica." *Regional Perspectives on the Olmec.* Edited by Robert J. Sharer and David C. Grove. Cambridge: Cambridge Univ. Press, 1989, 303–44.

Díaz Cíntora, Salvador. *Xochiquétzal: Estudio de Mitología Náhuatl.* México: Universidad Nacional Autónoma de México, 1990.

Díaz del Castillo, Bernal. *The Discovery and Conquest of Mexico, 1517–1521.* Edited by Genaro Garcia, translated by A. P. Maudslay. N.p.: Farrar, Strauss and Cudahy, 1956.

Díaz Infante, Fernando. *La Estela de los Soles o Calendario Azteca.* México: Panorama Editorial, 1986.

Dieterlin, Germaine. Introduction to *Conversations with Ogotemmêli: An Introduction to Dogon Religious Ideas,* by Marcel Griaule. London: Oxford Univ. Press, 1965.

Durán, Fray Diego. *Book of the Gods and Rites and the Ancient Calendar.* Edited and translated by Fernando Horcasitas and Doris Heyden. Norman: Univ. of Oklahoma Press, 1971.

Edmonson, Munro S., translator and annotator. *The Book of Counsel: The Popol Vuh of the Quiche Maya of Guatemala.* Publications of the Middle American Research Institute, no. 35. New Orleans: Middle American Research Institute, Tulane Univ., 1971.

———, trans. and annotator. *The Ancient Future of the Itza: The Book of Chilam Balam of Tizimin.* Austin: Univ. of Texas Press, 1982.

———, trans. and annotator. *Heaven Born Merida and Its Destiny: The Book of Chilam Balam of Chumayel.* Austin: Univ. of Texas Press, 1986.

———. *The Book of the Year: Middle American Calendrical Systems.* Salt Lake City: Univ. of Utah Press, 1988.

Eliade, Mircea. *Images and Symbols: Studies in Religious Symbolism.* Translated by Philip Mairet. Kansas City, KS: Sheed Andrews and McMeel, 1961.

———. "Mystery and Spiritual Regeneration in Extra-European Religions." Translated by Ralph Manheim. *Man and Transformation: Papers from the Eranos Yearbooks.* Edited by Joseph Campbell. The Bollingen Series, no. 30.5. Princeton, NJ: Princeton Univ. Press, 1964, 3–36.

———. *The Quest: History and Meaning in Religion.* Chicago: Univ. of Chicago Press, 1969.

———. *Shamanism: Archaic Techniques of Ecstasy.* Translated by Willard R. Trask. The Bollingen Series, no. 76. Princeton, NJ: Princeton Univ. Press, 1964.

Elzey, Wayne. "The Nahua Myth of the Suns: History and Cosmology in Pre-Hispanic Mexican Religions." *Numen* 23 (1976): 114–35.

———. "Some Remarks on the Space and Time of the 'Center' in Aztec Religion." *Estudios de Cultura Nahuatl* 12 (1976): 315–34.

Everton, Macduff. *The Modern Maya: A Culture in Transition.* Edited by Ulrich Keller and Charles Demangate. Albuquerque: Univ. of New Mexico Press, 1991.

Fernández, Justino. *Coatlicue: Estetica del Arte Indigena Antigua.* 2nd ed. México: Instituto de Investigaciones Esteticas, Universidad Nacional Autonoma de México, 1959.

———. *A Guide to Mexican Art: From Its Beginnings to the Present.* Translated by Joshua C. Taylor. Chicago: Univ. of Chicago Press, 1969.

Fingarette, Herbert. *The Self in Transformation: Psychoanalysis, Philosophy, and the Life of the Spirit.* New York: Harper & Row/Harper Torchbooks, 1963.

Flannery, Kent V., ed. *The Early Mesoamerican Village.* New York: Academic Press, 1976.

Flannery, Kent V., and Ronald Spores. "Excavated Sites of the Oaxaca Preceramic." *The Cloud People: Divergent Evolution of the Zapotec and Mixtec Civilizations.* Edited by Kent V. Flannery and Joyce Marcus. New York: Academic Press, 1983, 20–26.

Frankfort, Henri, and H. A. Frankfort. "Myth and Reality." *The Intellectual Adventure of Ancient Man: An Essay on Speculative Thought in the Ancient Near East.* Orig. pub. 1946. Chicago: Univ. of Chicago Press, 1977, 3–30.

Freidel, David A., and Linda Schele. "Kingship in the Late Preclassic Maya Lowlands: The Instruments and Places of Ritual Power." *American Anthropologist* 90 (1988): 547–67.

Furst, Jill Leslie. *Codex Vindobonensis Mexicanus I: A Commentary.* Publications of the Institute For Mesoamerican Studies, no. 4. Albany: State Univ. of New York at Albany, 1978.

———. "Skeletonization in Mixtec Art: A Re-evaluation." *The Art and Iconography of Late Post-Classic Central Mexico.* Edited by Elizabeth Hill Boone. Washington, DC: Dumbarton Oaks, 1982, 207–25.

Furst, Peter T. "Shamanistic Survivals in Mesoamerican Religion." *Actas del XLI Congreso Internacional des Americanistas* 6 (1976): 149–57.

Gadon, Elinor W. *The Once and Future Goddess: A Symbol for Our Time.* San Francisco: Harper & Row, 1989.

Gardner, Brant. "Reconstructing the Ethnohistory of Myth: A Structural Study of the Aztec 'Legend of the Suns.'" *Symbol and Meaning beyond the Closed Community: Essays in Mesoamerican Ideas.* Edited by Gary H. Gossen. Studies in Culture and Society, no. 1. Albany: Institute for Mesoamerican Studies, the Univ. at Albany, State Univ. of New York, 1986, 19–34.

Garibay K., Angel Maria. *Historia de la Literatura Náhuatl.* 2 vols. 2nd ed. Orig. pub. 1953. México: Editorial Porrua, 1986.

Gaster, Theodore H. "Myth and Story." Orig. pub. 1954. *Sacred Narrative: Readings in the Theory of Myth.* Edited by Alan Dundes. Berkeley: Univ. of California Press, 1984.

Gillespie, Susan D. *The Aztec Kings: The Construction of Rulership in Mexica History.* Tucson: Univ. of Arizona Press, 1989.

Gimbutas, Marija. *The Goddesses and Gods of Old Europe, 6500–3500 BC: Myths and Cult Images.* Berkeley: Univ. of California Press, 1982.

———. *The Language of the Goddess: Unearthing the Hidden Symbols of Western Civilization.* San Francisco: Harper & Row, 1989.

———. *The Civilization of the Goddess: The World of Old Europe.* Edited by Joan Marler. San Francisco: HarperSanFrancisco, 1991.

Gingerich, Willard. "Tlaloc, His Song." *Latin American Literatures* 1 (1977): 79–88.

———. "Quetzalcoatl and the Agon of Time: A Literary Reading of the *Anales de Cuauhtitlan.*" *Voices of the First America: Text and Context in the New World.* Edited by Gordon Brotherston. *New Scholar* 10 (1986): 41–60.

———. "*Chipahuacanemiliztli,* 'The Purified Life,' in the Discourses of Book VI, *Florentine Codex.*" *Smoke and Mist: Mesoamerican Studies in Memory of Thelma D. Sullivan.* Vol. 2. Edited by J. Kathryn Josserand and Karen Dakin. BAR International Series, vol. 402. Oxford: B.A.R., 1988, 517–44.

———. "Three Nahuatl Hymns on the Mother Archetype: An Interpretive Commentary." *Mexican Studies/ Estudios Mexicanos* 4 (1988): 191–244.

Glass, John B. "A Census of Native Middle American Pictorial Manuscripts." *Guide to Ethnohistorical Sources, Part 3.* Edited by Howard F. Cline. Vol. 14 of *Handbook of Middle American Indians.* Edited by Robert Wauchope. Austin: Univ. of Texas Press, 1975, 81–252.

Graham, John. "Olmec Diffusion: A Sculptural View from Pacific Guatemala." *Regional Perspectives on the Olmec.* Edited by Robert J. Sharer and David C. Grove. Cambridge: Cambridge Univ. Press, 1989, 227–46.

Graulich, Michel. "The Metaphor of the Day in Ancient Mexican Myth and Ritual." *Current Anthropology* 22 (1981): 45–60.

———. "Myths of Paradise Lost in Pre-Hispanic Central Mexico." *Current Anthropology* 24 (1983): 575–88.

———. "Aspects Mythiques des Peregrinations Mexicas." *The Native Sources and the History of the Valley of Mexico.* Edited by Jacqueline de Durand-Forest. BAR International Series, vol. 204. Oxford: B.A.R., 1984, 24–75.

Grove, David C. *The Olmec Paintings of Oxtotitlan Cave, Guerrero, Mexico.* Studies in Precolumbian Art and Archaeology, no. 16. Washington, DC: Dumbarton Oaks, 1970.

———. "Olmec Monuments: Mutilation as a Clue to Meaning." *The Olmec and Their Neighbors: Essays in Honor of Matthew W. Stirling.* Edited by Elizabeth P. Benson. Washington, DC: Dumbarton Oaks, 1981, 49–68.

Grove, David C., and Susan D. Gillespie. "Chalcatzingo's Portrait Figurines and the Cult of the Ruler." *Archaeology* (July/Aug. 1984): 27–33.

Gruzinski, Serge. *Man-Gods in the Mexican Highlands: Indian Power and Colonial Society, 1520–1800.* Translated by Eileen Corrigan. Stanford, CA: Stanford Univ. Press, 1989.

Hammond, Norman. "The Sun Is Hid: Classic Depictions of a Maya Myth." *Fourth Palenque Round Table, 1980.* Edited by Elizabeth P. Benson. San Francisco: The Pre-Columbian Research Institute, 1980, 167–74.

Hesse, Hermann. *Magister Ludi (The Glass Bead Game).* Translated by Richard Winston and Clara Winston. New York: Bantam, 1970.

Heyden, Doris. "An Interpretation of the Cave underneath the Pyramid of the Sun in Teotihuacan, Mexico." *American Antiquity* 40 (1975): 131–47.

———. "Symbolism of Ceramics from the Templo Mayor." *The Aztec Templo Mayor.* Edited by Elizabeth Hill Boone. Washington, DC: Dumbarton Oaks, 1987, 109–30.

———. "'Uno Venado' y la Creación del Cosmos en la Crónica y los Códices de Oaxaca." *Mitos Cosmogónicos del México Indígena.* Edited by Jesús Monjarás-Ruiz. México: Instituto Nacional de Antropología e Historia, 1987, 87–124.

Highwater, Jamake. *The Primal Mind: Vision and Reality in Indian America.* New York: Harper & Row, 1981.

———. *Myth and Sexuality.* New York: New American Library, 1990.

Hunt, Eva. *The Transformation of the Hummingbird: Cultural Roots of a Zinacantecan Mythical Poem.* Ithaca, NY: Cornell Univ. Press, 1977.

Hvidtfeldt, Arild. *Teotl and Ixiptlatli: Some Central Conceptions in Ancient Mexican Religion.* Translated by Niels Haislund. Copenhagen: Munksgaard, 1958.

Jiménez Moreno, Wigberto. "Mesoamerica before the Toltecs." Translated by Maudie Bullington and Charles R. Wicke. *Ancient Oaxaca.* Edited by John Paddock. Stanford, CA: Stanford Univ. Press, 1966, 3–82.

Kampen, Michael Edwin. *The Sculptures of El Tajín, Veracruz, Mexico.* Gainesville: Univ. of Florida Press, 1972.

Kidder, Albert V. "Preclassic Pottery Figurines of the Guatemalan Highlands." *Archaeology of Southern Mesoamerica, Part 1.* Edited by Gordon R. Willey. Vol. 2 of *Handbook of Middle American Indians.* Edited by Robert Wauchope. Austin: Univ. of Texas Press, 1965, 146–55.

Kinzhalov, R. V. "Toward a Reconstruction of the Olmec Mythological System." *Cultural Continuity in Mesoamerica.* Edited by David L. Browman. The Hague: Mouton Publishers, 1978, 278–288.

Klein, Cecilia F. "Post Classic Mexican Death Imagery as a Sign of Cyclic Completion." *Death and the Afterlife in Pre-Columbian America.* Edited by Elizabeth P. Benson. Washington, DC: Dumbarton Oaks, 1975, 69–86.

———. "The Identity of the Central Deity on the Aztec Calendar Stone." *Art Bulletin* 58 (1976): 1–12.

———. "Rethinking Cihuacoatl: Aztec Political Imagery of the Conquered Woman." *Smoke and Mist: Mesoamerican Studies in Memory of Thelma D. Sullivan.* Vol. 1. Edited by J. Kathryn Josserand and Karen Dakin. BAR International Series, vol. 402. Oxford: B.A.R., 1988, 237–77.

Kurath, Gertrude P., and Samuel Martí. *Dances of Anáhuac: The Choreography and Music of Precortesian Dances.* Viking Fund Publications in Anthropology, no. 38. New York: Wenner-Gren Foundation for Anthropological Research, 1964.

León-Portilla, Miguel. *Aztec Thought and Culture: A Study of the Ancient Nahuatl Mind.* Translated by Jack Emory Davis. Norman: Univ. of Oklahoma Press, 1963.

———. *Pre-Columbian Literatures of Mexico.* Translated by Grace Lobanov and Miguel León-Portilla. Norman: Univ. of Oklahoma Press, 1969.

———. *Time and Reality in the Thought of the Maya.* Translated by Charles L. Boiles and Fernando Horcasitas. Boston: Beacon Press, 1973.

———, ed. *Native Mesoamerican Spirituality.* New York: Paulist Press, 1980.

———. "El Maiz: Nuestro Sustento, Su Realidad Divina y Humana en Mesoamerica." *América Indigena* 48, no. 3 (1988): 477–502.

Lévi-Strauss, Claude. *The View from Afar.* Translated by Joachim Neugroschel and Phoebe Hoss. New York: Basic Books, 1985.

Limón Olvera, Silvia. *Las Cuevas y el Mito de Origen: Los Casos Inca y Mexica.* México: Consejo Nacional para la Cultura y las Artes, 1990.

Lincoln, Charles E. "Ceramics and Ceramic Chronology." *A Consideration of the Early Classic Period in the Maya Lowlands.* Publications of the Institute for Mesoamerican Studies, no. 10. Albany: State Univ. of New York at Albany, 1985, 55–94.

López Austin, Alfredo. *Hombre-Dios: Religión y Política en el Mundo Náhuatl.* México: Instituto de Investigaciones Históricas, Universidad Nacional Autónoma de México, 1973.

———. *The Human Body and Ideology: Concepts of the Ancient Nahuas.* Translated by Thelma Ortiz de Montellano and Bernard Ortiz. 2 vols. Salt Lake City: Univ. of Utah Press, 1988.

Lowe, Gareth W., Thomas A. Lee, and Eduardo Martinez Espinosa. *Izapa: An Introduction to the Ruins and Monuments.* Papers of the New World Archaeological Foundation, no. 31. Provo, UT: Brigham Young Univ., 1982.

Luxton, Richard N. "Balam Dz'ib: The Arrival of Christianity Among the Yucatec Maya." *Voices of the First America: Text and Context in the New World.* Edited by Gordon Brotherston. *New Scholar* 10 (1986): 159–80.

Mann, Thomas. *Joseph and His Brothers.* Translated by H. T. Lowe-Porter. New York: Alfred A. Knopf, 1948.

Marcus, Joyce. "Rethinking the Zapotec Urn." *The Cloud People: Divergent Evolution of the Zapotec and Mixtec Civilizations.* Edited by Kent V. Flannery and Joyce Marcus. New York: Academic Press, 1983, 144–48.

———. "Zapotec Religion." *The Cloud People: Divergent Evolution of the Zapotec and Mixtec Civilizations.* Edited by Kent V. Flannery and Joyce Marcus. New York: Academic Press, 1983, 345–51.

Markman, Peter T., and Roberta H. Markman. *Masks of the Spirit: Image and Metaphor in Mesoamerica.* Berkeley: Univ. of California Press, 1989.

———. "In the Beginning: Origins of Man and Myth." *Joseph Campbell: Transformations of Myth through Time.* San Diego, CA: Harcourt Brace Jovanovich, 1990, 15–26.

———. "Where People Lived Legends: American Indian Myths." *Joseph Campbell: Transformations of Myth through Time.* San Diego, CA: Harcourt Brace Jovanovich, 1990, 27–40.

Marshack, Alexander. *The Roots of Civilization: The Cognitive Beginnings of Man's First Art, Symbol and Notation.* New York: McGraw-Hill, 1972.

Mathews, Peter. "Maya Early Classic Monuments and Inscriptions." *A Consideration of the Early Classic*

Period in the Maya Lowlands. Publications of the Institute For Mesoamerican Studies, no. 10. Albany: State Univ. of New York at Albany, 1985, 5–54.

Matos Moctezuma, Eduardo. "Symbolism of the Templo Mayor." *The Aztec Templo Mayor.* Edited by Elizabeth Hill Boone. Washington, DC: Dumbarton Oaks, 1987, 185–210.

———. "The Templo Mayor of Tenochtitlan: History and Interpretation." Translated by John G. Copeland. *The Great Temple of Tenochtitlan: Center and Periphery in the Aztec World.* Berkeley: Univ. of California Press, 1987, 15–60.

Milbrath, Susan. *A Study of Olmec Sculptural Chronology.* Studies in Pre-Columbian Art and Archaeology, no. 23. Washington, DC: Dumbarton Oaks, 1985.

Miller, Arthur G. *On the Edge of the Sea: Mural Painting at Tancah-Tulum, Quintana Roo, Mexico.* Washington, DC: Dumbarton Oaks, 1982.

———. *Maya Rulers of Time: A Study of Architectural Sculpture at Tikal, Guatemala.* Philadelphia: The Univ. Museum, Univ. of Pennsylvania, 1986.

Millon, René. "Teotihuacán." Orig. pub. 1967. *Archaeology: Myth and Reality: Readings from Scientific American.* San Francisco: W. H. Freeman, 1982.

———. "The Last Years of Teotihuacan Dominance." *The Collapse of Ancient States and Civilizations.* Edited by Norman Yoffee and George L. Cowgill. Tucson: Univ. of Arizona Press, 1988, 102–64.

Moreno de los Arcos, Roberto. "Los Cinco Soles Cosmogónicos." *Estudios de Cultura Náhuatl* 7 (1967): 183–210.

Neumann, Erich. *The Great Mother: An Analysis of the Archetype.* 2nd ed. Translated by Ralph Manheim. The Bollingen Series, no. 47. Princeton, NJ: Princeton Univ. Press, 1963.

Nicholson, H. B. "An Aztec Stone Image of a Fertility Goddess." *Baessler-Archiv. Neue Folge* 11 (1964): 145–65.

———. "Major Sculpture in Pre-Hispanic Central Mexico." *Archaeology of Northern Mesoamerica, Part 1.* Edited by Gordon F. Ekholm and Ignacio Bernal. Vol. 10 of *Handbook of Middle American Indians.* Edited by Robert Wauchope. Austin: Univ. of Texas Press, 1971, 92–134.

———. "Religion in Pre-Hispanic Central Mexico." *Archaeology of Northern Mesoamerica, Part 1.* Edited by Gordon F. Ekholm and Ignacio Bernal. Vol. 10 of *Handbook of Middle American Indians.* Edited by Robert Wauchope. Austin: Univ. of Texas Press, 1971, 395–446.

———. "The Cult of Xipe Totec in Mesoamerica." *Religion en Mesoamerica: XII Mesa Redonda, Sociedad Mexicana de Antropología.* Edited by Jaime Litvak King and Noemi Castillo Tejero.

México: Sociedad Mexicana de Antropología, 1972, 213–218c.

———. "Ehecatl Quetzalcoatl vs. Topiltzin Quetzalcoatl of Tollan: A Problem in Mesoamerican Religion and History." *Actes du XLIIe Congrès International des Américanistes* 6 (1976): 35–47.

———. "The Deity 9 Wind 'Ehecatl-Quetzalcoatl' in the Mixteca Pictorials." *Journal of Latin American Lore* 4 (1978): 61–92.

———. *Art of Aztec Mexico: Treasures of Tenochtitlan.* Washington, DC: National Gallery of Art, Washington, 1983.

Niederberger, Christine. "Early Sedentary Economy in the Basin of Mexico." *Science* 203 (1979): 131–42.

Norman, V. Garth. *Izapa Sculpture.* 2 vols. Papers of the New World Archaeological Foundation, no. 30. Provo, UT: New World Archaeological Foundation, Brigham Young Univ., 1973–76.

Orenstein, Gloria. "Creation and Healing: An Empowering Relationship for Women Artists." *Women's Studies International* 8 (1985).

Paddock, John. "Oaxaca in Ancient Mesoamerica." *Ancient Oaxaca.* Edited by John Paddock. Stanford, CA: Stanford Univ. Press, 1966, 87–240.

———. *Lord 5 Flower's Family: Rulers of Zaachila and Cuilapan.* Publications in Anthropology, no. 29. Nashville, TN: Vanderbilt Univ., 1983.

———. "Yagul during Monte Alban I." *The Cloud People: Divergent Evolution of the Zapotec and Mixtec Civilizations.* Edited by Kent V. Flannery and Joyce Marcus. New York: Academic Press, 1983, 98–99.

Pasztory, Esther. *The Iconography of the Teotihuacan Tlaloc.* Studies in Pre-Columbian Art and Archaeology, no. 15. Washington, DC: Dumbarton Oaks, 1974.

———. *Aztec Art.* New York: Harry N. Abrams, 1983.

Paz, Octavio. "Will for Form." *Mexico: Splendor of Thirty Centuries.* New York: Bulfinch Press/The Metropolitan Museum of Art, 1990, 3–38.

Pickands, Martin. "The 'First Father' Legend in Maya Mythology and Iconography." *Third Palenque Round Table, 1978, Part 2.* Edited by Merle Greene Robertson. Austin: Univ. of Texas Press, 1978, 124–37.

———. "The Hero Myth in Maya Folklore." *Symbol and Meaning Beyond the Closed Community: Essays in Mesoamerican Ideas.* Edited by Gary H. Gossen. Studies in Culture and Society, no. 1. Albany: Institute for Mesoamerican Studies, The University at Albany, State Univ. of New York, 1986, 101–23.

Pijoan A., Carmen María. *Evidencias Rituales en Restos Oseos.* Cuadernos del Museo Nacional de Antropología. México: Instituto Nacional de Antropología e Historia, 1981.

Piña Chan, Román. *Quetzalcóatl: Serpiente Emplumada.* México: Fondo de Cultura Económica, 1977.

Robertson, Merle Greene. *The Temple of Inscriptions.* Vol. 1 of *The Sculpture of Palenque.* Princeton, NJ: Princeton Univ. Press, 1983.

Robicsek, Francis. *The Smoking Gods: Tobacco in Maya Art, History, and Religion.* Norman: Univ. of Oklahoma Press, 1978.

Robicsek, Francis, and Donald M. Hales. *The Maya Book of the Dead: The Ceramic Codex.* Charlottesville: Univ. of Virginia Art Museum, 1981.

———. *Maya Ceramic Vases from the Classic Period.* Charlottesville: Univ. Museum of Virginia, 1982.

———. "A Ceramic Codex Fragment: The Sacrifice of Xbalanque." *Maya Iconography.* Edited by Elizabeth P. Benson and Gillett G. Griffin. Princeton, NJ: Princeton Univ. Press, 1988, 260–76.

Roys, Ralph L. *The Book of Chilam Balam of Chumayel.* Norman: Univ. of Oklahoma Press, 1967.

Sahagún, Bernardino de. *General History of the Things of New Spain.* Translated by Charles E. Dibble and Arthur J. O. Anderson. 13 vols. Santa Fe, NM: School of American Research, and Salt Lake City: Univ. of Utah, 1950–78.

Santillana, Giorgio de, and Hertha von Dechend. *Hamlet's Mill: An Essay on Myth and the Frame of Time.* Boston: David R. Godine, 1977.

Schele, Linda. "The Xibalba Shuffle: A Dance after Death." *Maya Iconography.* Edited by Elizabeth P. Benson and Gillett C. Griffin. Princeton, NJ: Princeton Univ. Press, 1988, 294–317.

Schele, Linda, and David Freidel. *A Forest of Kings: The Untold Story of the Ancient Maya.* New York: William Morrow, 1990.

Schele, Linda, and Mary Ellen Miller. *The Blood of Kings: Dynasty and Ritual in Maya Art.* New York: George Braziller, Inc., in association with the Kimbell Art Museum, Fort Worth, TX, 1986.

Séjourné, Laurette. *Burning Water: Thought and Religion in Ancient Mexico.* Berkeley, CA: Shambhala, 1976. Orig. pub. 1956.

Seler, Eduard. "Venus Period in the Picture Writings of the Borgian Codex Group." Translated by C. P. Bowditch. *Mexican and Central American Antiquities, Calendar Systems, and History.* Bulletin no. 28. Washington, DC: Bureau of American Ethnology, 1904, 352–91.

———. *Comentarios al Códice Borgia.* 2 vols. Translated by Mariana Frenk. México: Fondo de Cultura Económica, 1963. Orig. pub. 1904, in German.

———. "The Antiquities of Castillo de Teayo." *Collected Works of Eduard Seler.* Translated and edited by Charles P. Bowditch. N.p.: n.p., n.d. Vol. 3, 3:38–57.

Sewall, Richard B. *The Vision of Tragedy.* New Haven, CT: Yale Univ. Press, 1959.

Sharp, Rosemary. *Chacs and Chiefs: The Iconology of Mosaic Stone Sculpture in Pre-conquest Yucatan,*

Mexico. Studies in Precolumbian Art and Archaeology, no. 24. Washington, DC: Dumbarton Oaks, 1981.

Soustelle, Jacques. *Daily Life of the Aztecs on the Eve of the Spanish Conquest.* Translated by Patrick O'Brian. New York: Macmillan, 1961.

———. *The Four Suns.* Translated by E. Ross. New York: Grossman, 1971.

———. *The Olmecs: The Oldest Civilization in Mexico.* Translated by Helen R. Lane. Garden City, NY: Doubleday, 1984.

Spores, Ronald. "Mixtec Religion." *The Cloud People: Divergent Evolution of the Zapotec and Mixtec Civilizations.* Edited by Kent V. Flannery and Joyce Marcus. New York: Academic Press, 1983, 342–45.

Sullivan, Thelma D., translator. "A Prayer to Tlaloc." *Estudios de Cultura Náhuatl* 5 (1965): 41–55.

———, trans. "The Finding and Founding of Mexico Tenochtitlan." *Tlalocan* 6, no. 4 (1971): 312–36.

———. "Tlazolteotl-Ixcuina: The Great Spinner and Weaver." *The Art and Iconography of Late Postclassic Central Mexico.* Edited by Elizabeth Hill Boone. Washington, DC: Dumbarton Oaks, 1982, 7–36.

Tate, Carolyn. "The Maya Cauac Monster's Formal Development and Dynastic Contexts." *Pre-Columbian Art History: Selected Readings.* Edited by Alana Cordy-Collins. Palo Alto, CA: Peek Publications, 1982.

Tedlock, Barbara. *Time and the Highland Maya.* Albuquerque: Univ. of New Mexico Press, 1982.

Tedlock, Dennis, trans. *Popol Vuh: The Mayan Book of the Dawn of Life.* New York: Simon & Schuster, 1985.

Thompson, John Eric Sidney. "The Moon Goddess in Middle America, with Notes on Related Deities." *Contributions to American Anthropology and History.* Vol. 5, no. 29. Washington, DC: Carnegie Institution of Washington, 1939, 127–73.

———. *The Rise and Fall of Maya Civilization.* 2nd ed. Norman: Univ. of Oklahoma Press, 1966.

———. *Maya History and Religion.* Norman: Univ. of Oklahoma Press, 1970.

———. *A Commentary on the Dresden Codex.* Memoirs of the American Philosophical Society, vol. 93. Philadelphia: American Philosophical Society, 1972.

Tolstoy, Paul. "Western Mesoamerica and the Olmec." *Regional Perspectives on the Olmec.* Edited by Robert J. Sharer and David C. Grove. Cambridge: Cambridge Univ. Press, 1989, 275–302.

Townsend, Richard F. *State and Cosmos in the Art of Tenochtitlan.* Studies in Pre-Columbian Art and Archaeology, no. 20. Washington, DC: Dumbarton Oaks, 1979.

Trejo, Silvia. *Escultura Huaxteca de Río Tamuín (Figuras Masculinas).* México: Universidad Nacional Autonoma de México, 1989.

Turner, Victor. *The Ritual Process: Structure and Anti-Structure.* Ithaca, NY: Cornell Univ. Press, 1969.

———. *Dramas, Fields, and Metaphors: Symbolic Action in Human Society.* Ithaca, NY: Cornell Univ. Press, 1974.

van Zantwijk, Rudolph. *The Aztec Arrangement: The Social History of Pre-Spanish Mexico.* Norman: Univ. of Oklahoma Press, 1985.

Virgil. *The Aeneid.* Translated by Rolfe Humphries. New York: Charles Scribner's Sons, 1951.

von Winning, Hasso. "Two-Headed Figurines from Mexico." *The Masterkey* 44 (1970): 45–53.

Westheim, Paul. *The Art of Ancient Mexico.* Translated by Mariana Frenk and Ursula Bernard. Garden City, NY: Anchor Books, 1965.

Whitecotton, Joseph W. *The Zapotecs: Princes, Priests, and Peasants.* Norman: Univ. of Oklahoma Press, 1977.

Wiercinski, Andrzej. "The Dark and Light Side of the Aztec Stone Calendar and Their Symbolic Significance." *Actas del XLI Congreso Internacional des Americanistas* 2 (1976): 275–78.

Wilkerson, S. Jeffrey K. "The Ethnographic Works of Andrés de Olmos, Precursor and Contemporary of Sahagún." *Sixteenth-Century Mexico: The Work of Sahagún.* Edited by Munro S. Edmonson. Albuquerque: Univ. of New Mexico Press, 1974, 27–78.

———. *El Tajín.* Xalapa: Universidad Veracruzana, 1987.

ILLUSTRATION SOURCES AND CREDITS

Unless otherwise noted, all photographs were taken, with permission, by Peter and Roberta Markman. The following abbreviations are used:

MAX: Museo de Antropología de Xalapa

MNA: Museo Nacional de Antropología, Mexico City

PMLV: Parque Museo de La Venta, Villahermosa

FIGURES

1. American Museum of Natural History, New York
2. MNA
3. Anahuacalli Museum, Mexico City
4. Reproduced by permission of Fondo de Cultura Económica from *Códice Borgia,* edicion facsimilar, 1980, p. 5
5. Reproduced by permission of Fondo de Cultura Económica from *Códice Borgia,* edicion facsimilar, 1980, p. 42
6. MNA
7. MNA
8. MNA
9. Reproduced by permission of Akademische Druck- u. Verlaganstalt from *Codex Vindobonensis Mexicanus 1,* 1963, p. 48
10. Reproduced by permission of Akademische Druck- u. Verlaganstalt from *Codex Vindobonensis Mexicanus 1,* 1963, p. 47
11. From the *Codex Fejérváry-Mayer*
12. MNA
13. Zaachila archaeological zone
14. Reproduced by permission of Salvat Mexicana de Ediciones, S. A. de C. V., *The Mayas* by Alberto Ruz, 1983, p. 133
15. MNA
16. Drawing by Linda Schele, reproduced by permission
17. Reproduced by permission of the American Philosophical Society from the facsimile in *A Commentary on the Dresden Codex* by John Eric Sidney Thompson, 1972, p. 21C
18. MNA
19. Museo Missionario Etnologico, Musei Vaticani, the Vatican

20. Reproduced by permission of Siglo Veintiuno editores, S.A. from *Códice Borbónico,* edicion facsimilar, 1981, p. 34

COLOR PLATES

1. MNA
2. MNA
3. MNA
4. MAX
5. Reproduced by permission of Akademische Druck- u. Verlaganstalt from *Codex Vindobonensis Mexicanus 1,* 1963, p. 37
6. Reproduced by permission of Akademische Druck- u. Verlaganstalt from *Altmexikos Heilige Bücher* by Hans Biedermann, 1971, p. 83
7. Reproduced by permission of Akademische Druck- u. Verlaganstalt from *Codex Borgia,* 1976, p. 27
8. MNA
9. MNA
10. MNA
11. Museo del Templo Mayor, Mexico City
12. MNA
13. Reproduced by permission of Akademische Druck- u. Verlaganstalt from *Altmexikos Heilige Bücher* by Hans Biedermann, 1971, p. 98
14. MNA
15. Reproduced by permission of Siglo Veintiuno editores, S.A., from *Códice Borbónico,* edicion facsimilar, 1981, p. 30
16. MNA
17. MAX
18. Reproduced by permission of Siglo Veintiuno editores, S.A., from *Códice Borbónico,* edicion facsimilar, 1981, p. 13
19. MNA
20. Tepantitla, Teotihuacan archaeological zone
21. Private collection, photograph © Justin Kerr 1981, reproduced by permission
22. Reproduced by permission of Siglo Veintiuno editores, S.A., from *Códice Borbónico,* edicion facsimilar, 1981, p. 22

23. Reproduced by permission of Akademische Druck u. Verlaganstalt from *Codex Borgia,* 1976, p. 56

24. Reproduced by permission of Fondo de Cultura Económica from *Historia Tolteca-Chichimeca,* edited by Paul Kirchoff, Lina Odeña Güemes and Luis Reyes García, 1989, p. 28

IMAGES

1. Reproduced by permission of Salvat Mexicana de Ediciones, S. A. de C. V.
2. MNA
3. Private collection
4. MNA
5. MNA
6. Reproduced by permission of Akademische Druck- u. Verlaganstalt from *Codex Vindobonensis Mexicanus 1,* 1963, p. 37
7. Reproduced by permission of the New World Archaeological Foundation from *Izapa Sculpture, Part I: Album* by V. Garth Norman, 1973, Plate 10
8. Reproduced by permission of Akademische Druck- u. Verlaganstalt from *Codex Vaticanus 3738,* 1979, pp. 1-2
9. After Spinden
10. After Spinden
11. Reproduced by permission of Akademische Druck- u. Verlaganstalt from *Codex Borgia,* 1976, p. 17
12. Reproduced by permission of Akademische Druck- u. Verlaganstalt from *Codex Vaticanus 3738,* 1979, p. 54r
13. MNA
14. Photograph and drawing, MNA
15. Reproduced by permission of Akademische Druck- u. Verlaganstalt from *Altmexikos Heilige Bücher* by Hans Biedermann, 1971, p. 83
16. Reproduced by permission of Akademische Druck- u. Verlaganstalt from *Codex Borgia,* 1976, p. 27
17. El Tajin archaeological zone
18. Teotihuacan archaeological zone
19. MNA
20. El Tajin archaeological zone
21. Chichen Itza archaeological zone
22. MNA
23. MNA
24. Museo del Templo Mayor, Mexico City

25. MNA
26. MNA
27. MNA
28. MNA
29. MNA
30. American Museum of Natural History, New York
31. Drawing by Hasso von Winning, reproduced by permission of UCLA Latin American Center Publications from "Late and Terminal Preclassic: The Emergence of Teotihuacan," by Hasso von Winning, in *Origins of Religious Art and Iconography in Preclassic Mesoamerica,"* edited by H. B. Nicholson, 1976, p. 151
32. MNA
33. MNA
34. MNA
35. Cacaxtla archaeological zone
36. MAX
37. Castillo de Teayo archaeological zone
38. Museo del Templo Mayor, Mexico City
39. Reproduced by permission of the New World Archaeological Foundation from *Izapa Sculpture, Part I: Album* by V. Garth Norman, 1973, Plate 2
40. Reproduced by permission of the American Philosophical Society from the facsimile in *A Commentary on the Dresden Codex* by John Eric Sidney Thompson, 1972, pp. 29–30
41. Private collection, photograph © Justin Kerr 1981, reproduced by permission
42. Labna archaeological zone
43. MNA
44. Drawing by Frances Pratt. Reproduced by permission of Akademische Druck- u. Verlaganstalt from *Chalcacingo* by Carlo T. E. Gay, 1971, p. 41
45. PMLV
46. Drawing by David Grove, reproduced by permission
47. MNA
48. Drawing by Linda Schele, reproduced by permission
49. Photograph courtesy of Merle Greene Robertson, reproduced by permission
50. Drawing by Linda Schele, reproduced by permission
51. MNA
52. Reproduced by permission of Secretaría de Educación Pública from *Códice Botturini*
53. Reproduced by permission of Fondo de Cultura Económica from *Historia Tolteca-Chichimeca,* edited by Paul Kirchoff, Lina Odeña Güemes, and Luis Reyes García, 1989, p. 28

INDEX